White Saris and Sweet Mangoes

The publisher gratefully acknowledges the generous contribution to this book provided by the General Endowment Fund of the Associates of the University of California Press.

White Saris and Sweet Mangoes

Aging, Gender, and Body in North India

SARAH LAMB

University of California Press

BERKELEY LOS ANGELES LONDON

University of California Press
Berkeley and Los Angeles, California

University of California Press, Ltd.
London, England

All photographs taken by author

Grateful acknowledgment is made for permission to reprint portions of the author's earlier articles: "Aging, Gender and Widowhood: Perspectives from Rural West Bengal," from *Contributions to Indian Sociology* 33, no. 3 (1999), and "The Making and Unmaking of Persons: Notes on Aging and Gender in North India," reprinted by permission of the American Anthropological Association from *Ethos* 25, no. 3 (September 1997), not for futher reproduction.

Library of Congress Cataloging-in-Publication Data

Lamb, Sarah
White saris and sweet mangoes : aging, gender, and body in North India / Sarah Lamb.
p. cm.
Includes bibliographical references and index.
ISBN 978-0-520-22001-0 (pbk. : alk. paper)

1. Aged—India—Bengal—Social conditions. 2. Aging—India—Bengal—Family relations. 3. Aged—India—Bengal—Psychological aspects.

HQ1064.14 L36 2000
305.26'0954'14—dc21 99-088195

Manufactured in the United States of America

10 09 08

10 9 8 7 6

The paper used in this publication meets the minimum requirements of ANSI/NISO Z39.48-1992 (R 1997) (*Permanence of Paper*). ♾

Contents

Illustrations

MAP

FIGURES

PHOTOGRAPHS

Tables

Preface

This book is about aging, gender, and the making and unmaking of persons. Early on in my days in Mangaldihi (the village in West Bengal where I did most of the research for this book), I came across a white-clothed widow in her seventies called Mejo Ma (Middle Mother), sitting in the dusty lane in front of her home. She could not stop complaining about clinging. Her attachments to her family, to things, to good food, and to her own body were so tight, she said, that she was afraid of lingering for years in a decrepit state, unable to die. "How will I leave all these kids and things and go?" she lamented. She feared that after her body died her soul would not ascend but would remain emotionally shackled nearby as a ghost.

Ethnographic knowledge is always influenced by the life experiences of the anthropologist. What anthropologists perceive in the field and what they choose to write primarily about is whatever matters most to them. What struck me, while living and doing research in Mangaldihi, was not so much old age per se, but the ways people thought about and managed one of the fundamental dilemmas of the life course—its compelling intensity, on the one hand, and its irrevocable transience, on the other—a dilemma highlighted for Bengalis (and for us all, perhaps, in some ways) in late life. As a child living in northern California, I had observed a grandmother and great-grandmother each widowed and living alone in a big, separate house. These older adults, like my divorced parents and adults in general, struck me as very independent beings whose dwindling relations with others left them too isolated for their own or anyone else's comfort.

Mejo Ma's predicament was a little different, though. She felt that her connections to others were not too loose but too *tight*. Another ancient villager, a spry ninety-seven-year-old Brahman widow named Khudi Thakrun, pursued many attachments that she did not consider worrisome, even though others did. She lived in a house with three generations of descendants and daily roamed the village to gossip with friends, arrange marriages, seek out the sweetest mangoes and bananas, and transact her prosperous business of moneylending. Other residents spoke of her disapprovingly, saying that her outgoing behavior would cause her soul after death to become an insatiable ghost troubling the village.

People in Mangaldihi spoke of their connections to the people, places, and things of their worlds as *māyā,* a multivalent term often translated as "illusion" but to Bengalis having the more immediate meaning of attachment, affection, compassion, love. People described maya to me as something wonderful and compelling, yet nonetheless problematic and painful—because the more maya people feel for other persons, places, and things, the more difficult become the separations that inevitably ensue. This is a dilemma faced especially in late life, people said, for the longer one lives, the stronger and more numerous the ties of maya become. Yet it is in late life also when relations are the most ephemeral, as people face the myriad leave-takings of death. Gurusaday Mukherjee, a middle-aged Brahman man, explained to me one day with tears in his eyes: "[In old age, a person] realizes that he will have to leave everything in this earth and go away. When I die, then I will have to leave everyone and everything—my children and everything. Then all of the love and all of the affection that I will have—that is all maya. It will make tears come."

These sentiments of the older women and men I came to know in Mangaldihi reminded me of what I had felt when getting to know my now husband, then college companion, ten years before going to Mangaldihi. I would tell him that it is painful to fall in love, because it will be all the more painful when it ends. (He was perplexed, saying that we never had to separate if we did not wish to.) Their statements about maya also reminded me of a passage I had first read a few years earlier in Wendy Doniger O'Flaherty's *Dreams, Illusion, and Other Realities.* She describes the way some Indian textual traditions present *saṃsāra,* or the nature of existence in the fluctuating world: "[M]any people distrusted *saṃsāra* not because the world was full of pain but rather that it was so wonderful that one could not bear to be parted from it over and over again at the end of each life, to be torn away from all the people one had come to love" (1984:299).

Anthropology invites us to expand our sense of human possibilities through the study of particular forms of life. Clifford Geertz (1973:30) has suggested that "The essential vocation of . . . anthropology is not to answer our deepest questions but to make available to us answers that others, guarding other sheep in other valleys, have given, and thus to include them in the consultable record of what [human beings have] said." In today's world, one cannot really claim that India or the people of Mangaldihi are "other"— culturally or geographically—for I now know almost as many Bengalis here in the United States as I did in Mangaldihi. It is not the "otherness" of "other sheep in other valleys" that is important to an anthropological quest. But the discipline's enduring value does lie, as Geertz suggests, in its venture to explore in depth particular people's answers—within any cultural and historical setting—to abiding human questions.

Over the following pages, I explore the ways the Bengalis I knew in Mangaldihi thought about and practiced aging, and how their visions of aging were tied to their understandings of the making and taking apart of social relations—including those of gender—over the life course. These questions form crucial components of Bengali understandings of the human condition, and of what it is to be a person.

Many people and institutions have contributed to this project, in ways more profound than I can express here, over the years that it has been in the making. My fieldwork in India was funded by the Fulbright-Hays Program, the American Institute of Indian Studies, and the Wenner-Gren Foundation for Anthropological Research. I received additional support for periods of research and writing from the American Association of University Women, the Committee on Southern Asian Studies at the University of Chicago, the National Institute of Aging (grant #T3200045 in Sociocultural Gerontology, Linda Mitteness, director), and a Marver and Sheva Bernstein Faculty Fellowship at Brandeis University. In India, the Fulbright Foundation and the American Institute of Indian Studies provided far more than simply funding. They offered indispensable assistance, nurturance, and intellectual guidance from my first arrival in Calcutta to my departure from Delhi. I am indebted especially to Uma Das Gupta of the Fulbright Foundation and to Tarun Mitra of AIIS.

This book has grown out of the knowledge and erudition gained from my teachers at the University of Chicago, where this project first took shape. My most profound debt is to McKim Marriott. His wisdom, penetrating marginalia, and generous discussions have challenged, inspired, and sustained me and this work in innumerable ways. I am also indebted to the invigorating intellectual insights I have gained from the mentoring of Jean Comaroff, Ralph Nicholas, Nancy Munn, Bernard Cohn, and Terence Turner. Edward Dimock, Clinton Seely, and Aditinath Sarkar at the University of Chicago, and Sipra Chatterjee at AIIS in Calcutta, imparted to me not only knowledge of the Bengali language but also a great admiration for Bengali literature, culture, and people.

Other colleagues, professionals, and friends have offered time, conversations, and critical readings that have been of great value. They include Shelley Adler, Meg Armstrong, Deb Kumar Banerjee, Kumkum and Ranjit Bhattacharya, P. K. Bhowmick, Amy Borovoy, Marty Chen, Lawrence Cohen, Jody Shapiro Davie, Bob Desjarlais, Ann Gold, Kathleen Hall, Linda Hess, Lee Horne, Eugene Irschick, Pauline Kolenda, Frank Korom, Stanley Kurtz, Sajal Majumdar, Rachel and Scott McDermott, Ernestine McHugh, Chas McKhann, Linda Mitteness, Aloka Mitra, Michael Nunley, Gloria Raheja, P. N. (Baccu) Roy, Nancy Scheper-Hughes, Richard Shweder, Stefan Timmermans, Becky Tolen, Sylvia Vatuk, Donna Wulff, and especially Diane Mines. My colleagues in anthropology and women's studies at Brandeis University over the past several years have provided a supportive and stimulating abode. I am grateful to the editors at the University of California Press—in particular Laura Driussi, Alice Falk, Sue Heinemann, and Lynne Withey—for their support of this work and for their editorial sagacity. Several anonymous reviewers also provided very useful suggestions.

Two research assistants in Mangaldihi, Rabindranath Mukherjee and Dipendra Narayan Thakur, assiduously gave of their time in conducting a village census, drawing maps, and transcribing tapes. At Brandeis, Hagar Doitel and Michelle Risley provided welcome assistance uncovering sources and sketching diagrams.

It is impossible to thank individually all the many people in Mangaldihi, Santiniketan, and Calcutta who have provided me with hospitality, friendship, and knowledge during the two and a half years I have thus far spent there. I am grateful to them all but wish to mention a few in particular. Indira Dey ("Masima"), Mita Basu, Mangal, Jamphul, Buri, and Bhudan all helped provide me with a beautiful and sustaining refuge in Santiniketan to which I could periodically retreat. The people of nearby Goyalpara village—especially Chabi, Ranga, Savitri, Bandana, and Latika—extended a warm and open friendship that never failed to rejuvenate and surprise me. During my long early stints of language training and later research in Calcutta, Satyabrata Bhattacharyya and his family, N. N. Chakraborty and "Boudi," Subal and Chotu Halder, Mithu and Chunam Mitra and their parents, Bula and Monu Saha, and Ajit Kumar Sinha all provided me with sustaining hospitality and friendship.

Most important, it was the people of the village of Mangaldihi who very literally made this research possible, by taking me into their homes and lives as a "sister" and "daughter" for eighteen months. Dulal Mukherjee and his family generously welcomed me as part of their family compound when others were still wondering about my presence. My primary companion, Hena Mukherjee, gave me unwavering support, advice, and friendship during what were sometimes trying times for us both. Her family and that of Mamata and Jiban Krishna Mukherjee were like second families to me in the village. Gurusaday Mukherjee devoted long hours to teaching me patiently about the ways of village society and Hindu religion. And the many elder or "grown" (*bṛiddha*) women and men of Mangaldihi—Choto Ma, Mejo Ma, Khudi Thakrun, and Bhogi Bagdi notably among them—gave me hours of their time, revealing their life stories and confiding their aspirations and fears. It is their experiences and reflections about daily life that make up the heart of this study.

Finally, I could not be the person or scholar I am today without the loving support, knowledge, and inspiration gained from members of my family. My father, Sydney Lamb, was the one who first incited me at a very young age to question and explore how we and others make sense of the worlds we live in. My mother, Sharon Rowell, has always encouraged me to pursue my dreams and to do what I wished (even if that would mean *not* to complete a dissertation or write a book). Susan Lamb and Doris Black have also, in distinct and important ways, encouraged me and my work. My two daughters, Rachel and Lauren, were born during the period of the writing of this book. They have brought so much joy and perspective into my life. They have also helped me come to understand what many of the older women in Mangaldihi meant when they spoke of the intensity of a mother's maya for her child, as always greater than a child's maya for her mother. Although the exigencies of children and diverse jobs have meant that my husband Ed and I do not read as many of each other's written words as we once did, I can still attest that without Ed's love, patience, shrewd discussions, and selfless support, this book would not have emerged as it has.

Note on Translation and Transliteration

Unless otherwise noted, all statements and conversations reported over the following pages came from interviews and conversations that I either tape-recorded or jotted down in fieldnotes during or several hours after the discussions. All translations of conversations, stories, songs, and printed Bengali materials are my own, unless otherwise noted.

Italicized terms in Bengali have been transliterated using standard diacritics, with certain alterations made to preserve some faithfulness to pronunciation in Bengali. In Bengali, the medial *a* is usually pronounced closer to an "o" than an "a," so I have occasionally chosen to transliterate it as an "o," especially when this change is commonly made (such as *boṛo* for "big," instead of *baṛa*). The final *a* in Bengali is usually not pronounced, so it has been omitted from most words (e.g., *saṃsār,* rather than *saṃsāra*). I employ a tilde where a *candrabindu* symbol would have occurred in the original. There are a few terms, such as *māyā,* that I use repeatedly throughout the book; they appear in italics and diacritics on the first usage only. All frequently used Bengali terms can be found in the glossary. Names and other proper nouns have been given their common English spellings (e.g., Calcutta, Krishna).

Introduction

Perspectives through Age

My sons all grew up, and I "gave" all their weddings. All of them have their own families, and now to whose do I belong? Now whose am I? I am no longer anyone. Now one son is saying, "I came from a hole in the ground." Another is saying, "I fell from the sky." Another is saying, "I came from God." And yet another is saying, "My hands and feet came on their own; I grew up on my own." Who am I now? I'm speaking the truth. What kind of thing is a mother?

Billo's Ma, elderly widow

A mother, a grandmother is like a deity.

Hena, unmarried young woman

I'm still embarrassed to say that I live in a "home." But what can I do? . . . Affection and compassion no longer exist as they did.

Masima, old age home resident

We place so much importance on the body; we think of it as a very valuable thing. But this is an erroneous, deluded belief. When age happens, the body gets worn out like old, worn clothes; and when we die it is discarded. All things of this world are perishable, transitory. It is only God and the soul that are lasting.

Gurusaday Mukherjee, middle-aged man

This book explores aging as a means of gaining perspective on notions of gender, the body, kinship, and the forces of culture. It does so in West Bengal, India, because of the rich understandings of aging found there, as suggested by the passages quoted above.

One common image of older women in India is that of powerful matriarchs who have finally come into their own as elderly mothers, mothers-in-law, and grandmothers, revered in some ways, as Hena reports, as deities. But when older women, like Billo's Ma, describe their own lives, they more often speak not of power and reverence but of losses and waning powers, of being forgotten by sons and their wives, of having poured out love, breast milk, and effort to raise their children and serve their families all of their lives—and in the end never receiving as much as they have given.

Another common image is voiced by Gurusaday: that old age highlights the perishability of the body and all earthly matters, signaling a time to focus on God, the soul (*ātmā*), and the heavenly sojourns or rebirths that will take place after this evanescent life. But for Masima, old age is a time when she is forced to break her family ties and seek an institutional refuge in a "modern," secular city. The multifaceted lens of aging is used in this book for viewing the varied ways social ties may be formed and taken apart, and bodies and genders transformed.

Several theoretical concerns emerge out of this ethnography, having to do with recent initiatives within anthropology and gender theory to rethink notions of culture, gender, and the body. When I first began to study the experiences of aging among those I knew in West Bengal, what struck me immediately was how different the shape and feeling of social relations and gender constructions looked to me through the eyes of the elderly women and men I sought out. The accounts I had read of South Asian social life had been based predominantly on the perspectives of younger and middle-aged adults.[1] For instance, South Asian women are commonly depicted as requiring veiling and modesty; but I saw white-haired women who left their homes to roam village lanes, not only with their heads and faces uncovered but bared to the waist on hot days, without regard for showing their long-dry breasts. I had read younger adults' views of older women as having the power to limit a daughter-in-law's movements, to interfere with a son's marital intimacies, and the like; yet the older women I knew spoke of feeling that *they* were losing in the contest for a son's affection, loyalty, and favor. Studies of Indian widowhood rarely distinguished between the consequences of widowhood for a woman in her youth and for a woman past menopause, although I found striking differences. And what of all the people who told me that older women were, in important ways, "like men," implying that what differentiates a "man" from a "woman" is not constant over the life course?

In attempting to find ways to think and write about these competing discourses on social practices, I found some legitimation and guidance in recent shifts in both anthropology and feminist studies toward viewing "culture" and "women" as multivocal, contradictory, and inconsistent. I also came to realize that perspectives surrounding aging in Bengal could be used to push these theoretical innovations even further and could address ongoing problems in our thinking, especially about gender and the body.

CULTURE, GENDER, AND MULTIVOCALITY

The concept of "culture" has had many identities. Current anthropological discussions reflect significant change over recent years, from a concept that stressed coherence and systematicity to one emphasizing heterogeneity and open-endedness.[2] In the mid–twentieth century, during what many now label as the "modernist" period, culture was generally understood as a more or less publicly shared, internally homogeneous and distinctive system of patterns, symbols, or meanings.[3] Such a perspective, critics now argue, assumes that all members of a culture more or less agree with each other, just as people of one culture are also set off, uniquely different, from people of other cultures.[4] An ethnographer taking such a viewpoint need not attend to the particular voices, experiences, and perspectives of specific members of a culture or society, since all (presumably) share in its values, visions, and ways of thinking. As Renato Rosaldo (1989:32) comments, "In this [earlier anthropological] tradition, culture and society determined individual personalities and consciousness; they enjoyed the objective status of systems. Not unlike a grammar, they stood on their own, independent from the individuals who followed their rules."

Such critiques themselves are often exaggerated and oversimplified. Robert Brightman (1995:541) points out with justice, "Neither in earlier disciplinary history nor as deployed in recent anthropological writing does the culture concept consistently exhibit the attributes of ahistoricism, totalization, holism, legalism, and coherence with which its critics selectively reconstitute it." Indeed, some passages from leading "modernist" anthropologists such as Bronislaw Malinowski or Edward Sapir sound as if they might have been written today. Malinowski asserted in 1926 (p. 121) that "human cultural reality is not a consistent logical scheme, but rather a seething mixture of conflicting principles." In 1938 Sapir concluded that anthropology is concerned "not with a society nor with a specimen of primitive man nor with a cross-section of the history of primitive culture, but with a *finite,* though indefinite, *number of human beings,* who gave themselves the privilege of *differing from each other* not only in matters generally considered 'one's own business' but even on questions which clearly transcended the private individual's concern" (Sapir 1949:569–70, qtd. in Brightman 1995:533; my italics). By the mid-1960s Victor Turner was arguing that "[a symbol] is alive only in so far as it is 'pregnant with meaning' for men and women, who interact by observing, *transgressing,* and *manipulating for private ends* the norms and values that the symbol expresses" (1967:44, my italics). We are witnessing, then, not a total transformation or revolution but a change in emphasis, a shifting of discursive paradigms, in how we think and talk about anthropological analysis. Nonetheless, it is fair to say that coherence, totality, and systematicity did largely characterize the view of culture and society I received in my early years of graduate training at the University of Chicago in the mid-1980s.

I remember going into anthropology to study *people* (having completed an undergraduate major in religious studies that focused more on texts, abstractions, and generalities than on real people's everyday lives). Several months into the required graduate theory course appropriately labeled "Systems," however, I wrote a perplexed letter home; although I was learning fascinating things about "social wholes," "total social wholes," "social facts," "total social facts," "social structures," "social systems," "cultures," and so on, I had yet to encounter any recognizable persons (with unique, divergent experiences and perspectives), or any of the ambiguities, contests, or messy edges that I thought sociocultural—*human*—life was filled with.

I was to discover that many of my generation shared these concerns. By the late 1980s, when I was embarking on my dissertation research in West Bengal, India, works began to appear that argued for the importance of heeding particular voices, lived experiences, and contests. Actually, these paradigm shifts began to emerge even earlier, rooted in many of the theoretical innovations and endeavors of the 1970s and early 1980s. The interpretive anthropology of Clifford Geertz (1973) and Paul Rabinow (1977), for instance, began to emphasize that a culture is not a fixed and complete (and entirely systematic, integrated) whole, but rather something emergent and co-created in dialogue, both among members of a culture and between informants and anthropologists. The practice theory of the late 1970s and 1980s (e.g., Bourdieu 1977, 1990; Ortner 1984) was also influential in bringing the individual actor or person to center stage and emphasizing individual agency (cf. Knauft 1996:105–40). The highly influential political philosophers Michel Foucault (e.g., 1979, 1980b, 1980c) and Antonio Gramsci (1971) scrutinized the inescapable technologies of power that shape social relations and forms of knowledge. Feminisms, gay and lesbian liberation, and civil rights movements also questioned the apolitical nature of culture and representation, along with anthropology's previous universalizing tendencies—making us heed the "differences" of class, race, ethnicity, gender, age, and sexuality. By the late 1980s, one could say that postmodernism (incorporating a mélange of these perspectives) had burst into anthropology, bringing with it a profound wariness of generalizations and totalizing theories, and emphasizing divergent perspectives, particularities, difference, and power.

Theories of culture also had to accommodate the changing demographics of a contemporary transnational world. People, ideas, and goods flow now with increasing profusion and speed across borders, making any idea of a neatly bounded, separate, and unique "culture" implausible.[5] This is true in rural West Bengal (where BBC programs play on the radio, *Oprah* is a favorite on television, and people, including social scientists, tourists, and kin, come and go across national borders), just as it is true in New York City. As Bruce Knauft (1996:44) puts it: "Culture is now best seen not as an integrated entity, tied to a fixed group of people, but as a shifting and contested process of constructing collective identity."

This view of the fluid, multivocal, and contested nature of culture has in fact become so widely accepted that, as E. Valentine Daniel (1996:361–62) notes, "Contestation itself has become a cliché, . . . an obliging mannerism, part of a higher-order consensus [among anthropologists]." Yet such a view does not imply that we can no longer say that anything is shared or distinctive about a culture. In fact, some shared ground must exist even to make disagreement, contest, and resistance meaningful (see chapter 2 and afterword, and E. V. Daniel 1996:361). Nonetheless, it is no longer tenable to think of culture as a *neatly* shared, stable, and bounded system. Rather, most see it now—if they continue to accept the idea of culture at all (see, e.g., Abu-Lughod 1991)—as an ongoing process of creating collectivity out of the divergent and shifting perspectives and voices of those who make its conversations.

Around the same time that social theorists were refashioning the concept of culture to include the disparate voices and contests of its members, feminist theorists were endeavoring to rethink, de-essentialize, and fragment the concept of "woman."[6] This was not true, however, when the anthropology of women, or feminist anthropology, first emerged in the early 1970s. Consistent with the modernist tendencies of the times, early feminist anthropologists had sought grand theories that could answer vexing questions—in particular, the basis for the "universality" of female subordination. Two highly influential theories were those of Michelle Rosaldo (1974) and Sherry Ortner (1974). Each argued that the meaning, shape, and value of being a "woman" is profoundly variable (and thus not the result of a simple, universal biology); nonetheless, certain universally found cultural phenomena, such as women's association with "domesticity" (Rosaldo) or "nature" (Ortner), result in the subordination or devaluation of women in all societies. Thus, although ostensibly arguing for variety, Rosaldo and Ortner both posit a universal core or base defining women, tied especially to notions of female physiology, sexuality, and reproductivity. Because women everywhere menstruate and bear and raise children (and are in other ways associated with their bodies, sexuality, reproductivity, and domesticity), we can find a commonality to the notion of "woman" cross-culturally and we can discern an underlying logic as to why women are everywhere, in crucial ways, subordinate to men.

Such universalizing theories were not long-lived. They came under fire from Rosaldo (1980) and Ortner (1996) themselves, as well as from others who critically reinterpreted the notion of a universal category of women by incorporating issues of race, nation, class, and sexual orientation, as well as cyborg imagery.[7] Women, Chandra Mohanty (1991:55) argues, cannot be assumed to be "an already constituted, coherent group with identical interests and desires, regardless of class, ethnic or racial location." Ortner (1996:137) similarly warns against the tendency to slip into an "assumption that 'women' in some global and sociologically unqualified sense really exist out there in the world, as a natural class of objects with their own distinctive attributes."

Gender theorists have now come to recognize that what it means to be a woman (*and* man—though to date this category has been less discussed) takes such distinct shape in specific times and places, and along crucial axes of difference (most commonly listed as the multiple racial, ethnic, class, and sexual identities of women), that it is not possible to hold up a universal category of women with a presumed common, essential significance. Furthermore, even within a particular time, place, social group, or individual, gender identity is likely to be fluid, partial, and fragmentary. As a result, *methods* of gender analysis in anthropology, like those of cultural analysis, have come to focus more and more on particularity, specificity of contexts, flux, and contradiction (see Abu-Lughod 1993; Moore 1994:11–12), while moving away from universalizing theories and generalizations.

Anthropology's new emphasis on multivocality, fluidity, and heterogeneity has certainly informed recent work on gender in South Asia. Gloria Raheja and Ann Gold (1994), for instance, explore compellingly the multiple perspectives evident in women's songs, stories, personal narratives, and everyday talk in rural north India. Against scholarly representations that have portrayed the "submission [of women] to a monolithic 'tradition,'" Raheja and Gold (1994:xviii–xix) argue that, in fact, women's speech reveals great heterogeneity and resistance: "When Indian women represent themselves in their own words, no single unitary voice is heard; we have only begun to listen to a few of these voices" (p. 9). In their study of Hindu and Muslim women's lives in north India, Patricia and Roger Jeffery (1996:19–20) similarly argue that women in rural Bijnor "did not speak with a single voice." They stress: "[W]e have . . . tried to avoid inventing a single reality out of the complex and ambiguous realities of women's daily lives."

Yet when I turned to this literature to try to understand older women's (and men's) lives in Mangaldihi, I did not find all that I needed. Although the past two decades have seen a surge of work on South Asian women, very little has concerned the later years of women's lives.[8] Raheja and Gold's important study (1994) does include an engrossing narrative of "a widow in her sixties" (pp. 164–81), but the work as a whole focuses on the stories and songs of younger sisters, wives, and daughters-in-law. Although Jeffery and Jeffery make the crucial point that women's positions and interests change throughout the life cycle (1996:2), their data are also concentrated on women in their childbearing years, as their original research focused on pregnancy and reproductive histories. Stanley Kurtz's engaging study (1992) likewise centers on images of young women as mothers raising their children. The many works concerned with issues such as purdah, veiling, modesty, marriage, and sexuality also pertain chiefly to younger women, although researchers rarely feel it necessary to acknowledge and examine the significance of their focus.[9]

When an older woman does figure in studies of gender in South Asia, she appears most often as a villain (such as a domineering mother-in-law) in the story of a younger woman who is the writer's primary concern; or she is more generally a repository and enforcer of patrilineal kinship ideologies, dominant social norms, and "traditions" (cf. S. Vatuk 1995:290; Lamb 1997a).[10] Of course, we should attend to the voices of younger women who do present older women (and men) in such a way, voices that scholars have only recently begun seriously to listen to. For instance, Raheja and Gold provide a rich collection of songs from a young bride's or daughter-in-law's perspective that show how young wives can resist ideals of wifely obedience to a husband's older kin (1994:121–48). One of many gems is a dancing song sung by women gathered at home while the groom's party is congregating at the bride's natal village (p. 127):

> [Bride speaking]
> How can I come, how can I come near you?
> Husband, your grandmother is very cunning.
> She fights with me and then puts her own cot down next to our bed.
>
> [Husband speaking]
> Beautiful one, take the sword from my hand.
> Come waving it, come brandishing it, come near me.
> The drum will sound, the cymbals will sound, they'll sound the whole night through.

Are younger women alone in resisting, rebelling, complaining, offering alternative visions of family and social life? Raheja and Gold make the important observation that older women *join* their younger daughters and daughters-in-law in singing these rebellious songs, suggesting perhaps women's "ironic apprehension of the oppressiveness of a kinship ideology that splits their identities and pits one woman against another" (1994:148). But what would older women's (or men's) songs and stories look like if *they* were the central characters and tellers of the tales? How do *they* view the coming of a young bride? the marriage of a daughter or a son? their own changing sexuality? approaching mortality?

THE ANTHROPOLOGY OF AGING

One place to turn for insight into these matters is writings on the anthropology of aging. Over the past two decades, interest in this new field has burgeoned forth in a series of edited volumes as well as numerous book-length explorations of old age in this and other societies.[11] Yet even though this area of inquiry has developed contemporaneously with investigations into the heterogeneous and fluid nature of cultures and genders, the two have proceeded on parallel tracks. Just as old people are often separated socially in the United States (in old age homes and age-segregated retirement communities), aging is also often separated theoretically in anthropological discourse and treated as a closed domain of inquiry, isolated from broader questions about how sociocultural worlds are constituted more generally. This tendency extends back to classic ethnographies (before old age had become a popular object of study in its own right), where chapters on the "life cycle" often included subheadings such as "childhood," "adulthood," "old age," and so on but seldom used these descriptions as integral parts of the analysis of other aspects of social life (cf. Keith and Kertzer 1984:23–24).[12]

Likewise, anthropologists concerned with the fluid and contestatory nature of cultures and genders tend to overlook processes of aging. Contemporary studies of gender, as well as other features of social life, commonly list (in a now almost obligatory practice) race, class, gender, ethnicity, sexual orientation, and (in India) caste as crucial distinctions that cut across all groups; but age is mentioned only rarely. Thus many of the potential advantages that attention to age can bring—by training our gaze on flux, multivocality, change, and process—have been ignored. Marilyn Strathern, in her study of women and society in Melanesia, builds on the feminist insight that "in dealing with relations between the sexes, one is dealing with social relations at large" (1988:35). I would extend this notion to our dealings with age. Social relations are "aged" just as they are gendered, though of course the meanings and politics of age alter according to cultural and historical context. Processes of aging (however defined) cut across all of our bodies and lives; they play a central role in how we construct gender identities, power relations, and the wider social and material worlds we inhabit—indeed, what it is to be a person.

By overlooking age, those in women's studies and gender theory have increased the difficulty of their task of theorizing about the ways women and men are constituted as gendered beings. In her 1985 plenary session speech to the National Women's Studies Association in Seattle, Barbara MacDonald charged that women's studies has made invisible the lives of women over sixty, having failed in the classroom to provide any feminist analysis of women's aging: "Has it never occurred to those of you in Women's Studies, as you ignore the meaning and the politics of the lives of women beyond our reproductive years, that this is male thinking? Has it never occurred to you as you build feminist theory that ageism is a central feminist issue?" (1986:21). The brief references to studies in South Asia have already shown how focusing exclusively on younger women tends to limit our understanding of the fluctuating and nuanced character of women's lives. Freezing women's lives in one stage—as wives, daughters-in-law, or young mothers—is even more limiting when we consider the place of "the body" in recent anthropological and feminist theory.

THE BODY IN POSTMODERN AND FEMINIST ANTHROPOLOGY

> When you get old, everything becomes closed or stopped. That which happens between husband and wife stops. Menstruation stops. And then when your husband dies, eating all hot food stops as well. This is so that the body will dry out and not be hot.
>
> Mejo Ma, older Brahman widow, Mangaldihi

Over recent years anthropology and feminist theory (like the wider academy) have focused intensely on the body, with new works pouring forth at a rapid pace: *The Woman in the Body* (E. Martin 1987), *The Body in the Mind* (Johnson 1987), *Fragments for a History of the Human Body* (Feher 1989), *Gender/Body/Knowledge* (Jaggar and Bordo 1989), *Body and Emotion* (Desjarlais 1992), *Bodies That Matter* (Butler 1993), *Bodies and Persons* (Lambek and Strathern 1998), *Body Talk* (Zita 1998), *Body Image* (Grogan 1999), and many more. I introduce briefly here some of the major trends in our current theorizing about the body, for I believe that Bengali ethno-theories of the body—the ways many Bengalis use bodily images and processes to define old age and gender relations—can help us address some of the problems in the current anthropological and feminist literature, which has tended to present "the body" as a reified, decontextualized, somehow transhistorical and transcultural object.

Emily Martin (1992) explains this current surge of attention by pointing out that the body as we have known it (during a Fordist era of mass production) is being replaced by a new kind of body suitable for late capitalism, the postmodern era of flexible accumulation; it is precisely during such times of transition, when phenomena are coming to an end, that they draw academic and public attention. I would suggest instead that the body has become popular in the humanities and social sciences because it is tangible, particular, and located—a stone we can touch, so to speak—amid the shifting sands of postmodernism (cf. John and Jean Comaroff 1992:39–40). While the postmodern cultural theory of the past two decades has discouraged efforts to speak of general, all-encompassing (modernist) systems or principles, the body seems to provide a unique vehicle for situating perspectives and giving a particular locatedness. Focusing on the body becomes a way both to move away from overarching totalizations and *at the same time* to provide something apparently tangible, experienced, and "real" to hang on to and study. Susan Bordo observes that in a Cartesian worldview there is no place for the body, since the body, by situating and thereby relativizing any perspective, prevents the possibility of an all-encompassing, transcendent ("*object*-ive") perspective. For postmodern thinkers, in contrast, there is no escape from human perspective: "The body, accordingly, is reconceived. . . . No longer an obstacle to knowledge[,] . . . the body is seen instead as the vehicle of the human making and remaking of the world, constantly shifting location, capable of revealing endlessly new 'points of view' on things" (1990:143–44; the quotation refers to Suleiman 1986).

Foucault's extremely influential analyses of the workings of power in modern society also focus on the body (1973, 1975, 1979, 1980b, 1980c). Rather than treating power as an abstract force, he examines how forms of power are localized, inscribed on, and inflicted on individual bodies and populations (the social body) as these bodies are controlled, regulated, and disciplined within particular prisons, asylums, hospitals, psychiatrists' offices, and universities. Michael Jackson, influenced by the earlier works of Maurice Merleau-Ponty (1962) and Pierre Bourdieu (1977), similarly focuses on embodied practice and knowledge in social analysis. Jackson (1989:119–55) explains his focus on bodily movement and praxis as a means of pushing away from "disembodied" and abstract theories of culture, which he, like

Bordo, sees as grounded in the Cartesian split between knowing subject and unknowing inert body. He critiques his earlier "bourgeois" conception of culture—that is, "as something 'superorganic,' something separable from the quotidian world of bodily movements and practical tasks" (p. 126)—and he argues that in order to make anthropological discourse more consonant with the practices and interests of the people we study, we must focus our ethnographic analyses on particular body movements and practices, on the embodied character of lived experience as *habitus* (pp. 119–55; cf. Bourdieu 1977, 1990).

In gender and feminist theory as well, the body has played a leading but much more ambivalent role. When social theorists developed the term "gender" in the late 1960s, they set it against "sex," depicting that which is socially or culturally constructed as opposed to that which is biologically given (cf. Nicholson 1994:79–80). Here, the body fell into the domain of sex and nature, while gender was a matter of culture. Today, feminist theorists continue to see gender (i.e., beliefs and practices surrounding male/female distinctions) as culturally constructed, but their positions diverge regarding the place of the *body* and *sex* in relation to gender.

For some, the body functions crucially (as in postmodern anthropology in general) in providing a locatedness to abstract social theory and analysis (e.g., Bordo 1990:145; Marshall 1996). Many feminist theorists take the significance of the body even further, claiming (often subtly or by implication only) that we need to recognize the specifically *female* body in order to theorize about what it is to be a woman.[13] This position can appear under different guises—biological determinism, biological essentialism, biological foundationalism, or feminism of difference (cf. Nicholson 1994)—but in each case it is assumed that real bodily, or biological, phenomena differentiating women and men are used in all societies (though perhaps in varying ways) to shape a male/female distinction. Here, the body and biology are taken as the *basis* on which cultural meanings of gender are constructed. Linda Nicholson (1994) calls this a "coatrack" view of the body, as the body is viewed as the common base or coatrack on which different cultural artifacts of gender are hung.

One crucial advantage of such a position is that it enables feminists to postulate both commonalities *and* differences among women. As Nicholson (1994:81) puts it: "[The coatrack view] enabled many feminists to maintain the claim often associated with biological determinism—that the constancies of nature are responsible for certain social constancies—without having to accept one of the crucial disadvantages of such a position from a feminist perspective—that such social constancies cannot be transformed."

Claiming the female body as a common ground broadly uniting the category of woman across histories and cultures is also thought to support feminism's political program. Many argue that unless we provide a clear basis defining what it is to be a woman (transhistorically and transculturally), then we cannot generate a politics around this term (e.g., Downs 1993; cf. Nicholson 1994:99–100). The body seems to provide just that necessary common ground. In these arguments—not surprisingly, perhaps—the qualities thought to distinguish women's bodies surround reproduction, motherhood, and sexuality, qualities generally associated with femininity in the West.

An equally strong counterview of the relationship between the body and gender in contemporary feminist discourse, however, is very wary of any theory that depends on a precultural or pancultural notion of the body to define women and gender. Thus Ortner (1996:137) remarks: "Personally, I thought the whole point of feminism was to bring about a situation in which women were *not* seen as a natural class of being, defined primarily by their bodies." Many are justifiably resistant to ideas that seem to assert an unalterable, essential female nature; critics often challenge the original formulation of the sex/gender distinction, arguing that the body, or sex, itself is *part* of the social construction of gender. Even when a social group recognizes distinctions between male and female bodies, these are always interpreted through a cultural lens. A society not only shapes beliefs and practices around what we have become accustomed to label "gender," it also shapes the way the *body* appears and is interpreted—meaning that the body (and sex) can be best understood to be *part* of gender.[14] As Foucault (1980a, 1980b) has demonstrated, bodies have no "sex" outside of discourses that define them as sexed.

These theorists believe not that the body necessarily becomes irrelevant to feminist analysis but simply that it cannot be held up as a pre- or transcultural given. Instead it becomes, as Nicholson (1994:101) puts it, "a historically specific variable whose meaning and import are recognized as potentially different in different historical contexts." She persuasively argues:

> Most societies known to Western scholarship do appear to have some kind of a male/female distinction. Moreover, most appear to relate this distinction to some kind of bodily distinction between women and men. . . . [But] "some kind of male/female distinction" and "some kind of bodily distinction" include a wide range of possible subtle differences in the meaning of the male/female distinction and of how the bodily distinction works in relationship to it. . . . In short, while all of these societies certainly possess some kind of a male/female distinction

> and also relate this distinction in some important way or another to the body, subtle differences in how the body itself is viewed may contain some very basic implications for what it means to be male or female. (p. 96)

This brings me to what I want to say about the body in relation to my work on aging and gender in West Bengal. Those I knew in Bengal used rich imagery of the body to define, practice, manage, and control processes of aging and of gendered identity. They were highly body- and material-oriented in their constructions of social identity. Aging was defined in Mangaldihi, for instance, largely in terms of "cooling" and "drying," processes that were at once somatic and social, emotional, and spiritual (see chapters 2, 4, and 6). Dominant discourses defined gender identities, too, in terms of bodily natures: women were often spoken of as more "open" and "hot" than men (somatically and socially)—at least until their postmenopausal and postmarital years, when their bodies became cooler and more self-contained, and their practices and social identities in some ways more "like men's" (chapters 6, 7).

However, in striving to think and write about this material, I found that much contemporary theorizing about "the body" in anthropology and feminist discourse could not work in Bengal, because many of the "body" theorists have failed to recognize the historicity and cultural particularity of their own insights. Taking very specific Euro-American notions of the body and assuming these to be universally valid, they have tended to reify the body as an individual, material place—an isolable thing. This tendency, I should note, is one that extends back to the pioneering work of Mary Douglas (1966, 1970), who assumed the body to be "a model that can stand for any *bounded* system" (1966:115, my italics). Of course, from a phenomenological point of view, we *can* reasonably assume that all people more or less experience some sense of a unique body-self (Mauss 1985 [1938]). But there are also many societies (and some contexts within our own society) where other perceptions, experiences, and constructions of the body are highlighted—ones that do not (wholly or even predominantly) assume the body to be local, tangible, bounded, stable, or individually experienced, as current theoretical discourses on the body presuppose.

For instance, as the following pages will show, much of what the Bengalis in Mangaldihi perceived and discussed as their "bodies" included wider processes and substances than those directly tangible or limited to their own bodily boundaries. Properties of one person's body existed in others' bodies, in the places they lived, and in the objects they owned and handled (chapter 1). It may make more sense, then, to assume bodies to be (like persons) open, composite, and "dividual" (Marriott 1976). Bengalis spoke of a body or person as materially and emotionally *part* of other bodies, persons, places, and things; a body was said to belong to a "family" (*saṃsār*) rather than to a single person (chapter 2).[15] Moreover, when they described the bodily changes that are part of aging—such as cooling and drying—they were speaking just as much about social-relational processes as somatic ones: for to become cool and dry in the body means to become increasingly (substantially *and* socially) self-contained and noninteractive (chapters 4, 6). So, although I believe that a focus on some form of locatedness and positioned subjectivity is itself a salutary move in contemporary sociocultural theory, it may not be appropriate to assume that "the body" (as a kind of precultural materiality) can provide us this subjectivity (cf. T. Turner 1995; Pollack 1996).

Furthermore, the body is not "male" or "female" in any constant, transhistorical, or transcultural way, as presumed in so much feminist theory grounded on a notion of female bodiliness. *We* certainly think about gender in terms of essential bodily differences between the two sexes, in this particular historical moment,[16] and thus we (many Americans) have great difficulty looking past such an assumption. I find that the idea of the cultural construction of *gender* (as roles, beliefs, practices, etc.) is easy for my students to accept, but the notion that the *body* itself (the ways it is used to signify maleness and femaleness) is also a cultural construction runs into much more resistance.

The ways the Bengalis in Mangaldihi used the body in their constructions of gendered social identities particularly illuminate this problem of the relationship between body and gender, partly because gendered and bodily identities shifted for them in specific ways during their lives. Gender was not a constant determined by dichotomous physical differences between women and men. The Bengalis I knew definitely used the body to define gender differences, but not in terms of a fixed, binary male/female distinction; instead, they often explained the biologies of the two sexes in terms of differences in the relative amounts of qualities, such as "heat" and "openness," that all bodies and persons possess. All bodies (male and female, young and old) possess relative amounts of heat (or coolness), fluidity (or dryness), and openness (or boundedness). Women, in general, were commonly described as being more open and hot than men (features that distinguished their female gender). But these qualities fluctuated significantly over the life course, with important somatic as well as social, political, and spiritual implications. Women after puberty, particularly during their married and reproductive years, were taken to be the most "hot" (*garam*) and "open" (*kholā*), especially because of their involvement in menstruation, marriage, sexuality, and childbirth—all processes thought to entail, for women, substances going into and out of the (open) body, as well as the "heating" properties of sexual desire (chapter 6). However, as women went through the social and somatic processes of aging (including menopause, the cessation of childbearing, and widowhood), they were seen as becoming increasingly "cool" and "dry," and thus, in important ways, "like men"—which brought them increasing freedom of movement beyond the home and the options to participate in inner temple life, wear men's white clothing (dhotis), and expose the body (chapters 6, 7). It is not that older women ever precisely *become* men. But it would be nonetheless highly misleading to think here of women and men, femaleness and maleness, as binary, opposing categories, grounded in unchanging physical differences.

By paying attention to age anywhere, we could train our gaze on this kind of flux in the ways the body is used to create gendered identities. The relatively few cross-cultural studies to date on gender identities over the life course have often found that what it is to be a woman shifts significantly in late life.[17] For instance, Fitz John Porter Poole describes how old, no longer married, and postmenopausal women among the Bimin-Kuskusmin of Papua New Guinea are thought to be asexual and of ambiguous gender, neither exactly male or female but "betwixt and between" (1981:117). This androgynous status gives older women ritual and leadership opportunities that younger women and men do not have. Judith Brown (1982, 1992) and Karen Brodkin Sacks (1992) observe through surveys of cross-cultural data that later life is often a time in which a woman has her greatest power, status, and autonomy, enjoying prerogatives that are often characterized as "male." Such freedoms can come about because of a presumed asexuality (as in India), but in some societies—for example, among the Lusi of Papua New Guinea (Counts 1992), the Garifuna of the Black Carib (Kerns 1992), and the !Kung of southern Africa (Lee 1992; Shostak 1981)—middle age brings expanded freedom for women to joke about sexuality and to display sexual interest, activities that are also often seen as "male" privileges. Women's aging bodies can sometimes evoke more negative associations—for instance, a sense of waning femininity, sexuality, beauty, or social usefulness.[18] Such views are especially common in reflections on aging and women in the United States (see Chapkis 1986:5–35; J. Alexander et al. 1986).

The diversity and richness of such data on changing images of bodies and genders reveal the profound limitations in focusing on only one life stage (namely, the reproductive phase) in our theorizing about what it is to be a "woman" (*or* a "man"), as if gendered identity were essential and fixed. Yet this relatively large, interesting set of ethnographic data on aging still has not been widely incorporated into the level of gender *theory.*[19] It is striking that so much gender and feminist theory persists in focusing on sexual reproduction, motherhood, and the household. As Micaela di Leonardo (1991:26) reports, even in the postmodern era "Both feminist essentialists and conservative anti-feminists have continued to draw on the nineteenth-century storehouse of moral motherhood symbolism, stressing women's innate identity with and nurturance of children and nature." She adds, "[Feminists] have fallen victim to the vision of an innately nurturant, maternal womankind" (p. 27). Ortner (1996:137) similarly blames "certain problematic directions in feminist theory, which concentrate heavily on female physiology, sexuality, and reproductivity," for the ongoing tendency to assume that "'women' in some global and sociologically unqualified sense really exist out there in the world, as a natural class of objects with their own distinctive attributes."

It has been easy for many feminist theorists to think of women (transculturally and transhistorically) in relation to reproduction and motherhood, largely overlooking postreproductive life phases, because that is how we tend to define women within our own dominant popular cultural and medical discourses in the United States. Margaret Lock (1993) has done particularly illuminating work in this area. She examines assumptions made in the basic scientific and medical literature, and in popular writings, over the latter part of the twentieth century on aging women in the United States. Aging women are generally represented as "anomalies" (pp. xxiv–xxvii). For example, two leading physicians write in an article addressed to specialists in geriatrics, "The unpalatable truth must be faced that all postmenopausal women are castrates" (R. Wilson and Wilson 1963:347, qtd. in Lock 1993:xvi, 346). Helene Deutsch, in her *Psychology of Women* (1945), professes: "Women's capacity for reproduction normally lasts as long as menstruation is regular. With the cessation of the function, she ends her service to the species" (qtd. in Lock 1993:xiv). By the 1960s, menopause had been designated as an estrogen "deficiency disease," characterized by the failure of the ovaries to secrete the hormone taken to be the "essence" of the female. The barely concealed assumption underlying such medical views is that reproduction of the species is what female life is all about (p. xxvii). In medical research on menopause, the chemistry of women of reproductive age is taken as the standard measure for what is "normal" and "healthy," thereby marking the aging female body as abnormal (pp. xxxii–xxxiii). These are presumably some of the reasons why menopause management and its spin-off, hormone replacement therapy, are currently such big business in the United States—the only country in the world (industrialized or not) in which hormone replacement therapy is so widespread. Many American physicians recommend it to almost all their patients, in a seeming attempt to keep women, in some way, "young," "normal," and "female."[20] Wendy Chapkis (1986), who also incisively examines popular American culture, finds that although all people—men and women—fight against the changes of age, it is women's bodies especially that we feel compelled to control and preserve, resisting the "changing landscapes" of time.

Such popular and scientific assumptions surrounding aging women have permeated our theorizing about gender and the body as well; it becomes "natural" for gender/feminist theory to center on female reproductivity, as if this were the most significant, singular dimension of women's bodies and biologies, and thus, by extension, the crux of their sociocultural identities, in all times and places. Such theories are illuminating if we use them to examine our own values. (In this way, one can use social theory as a window into the belief systems and assumptions of those who produce it.) But these same theories can lead us far astray if we import them unquestioningly to the analysis of other times and places. In addition, they perpetuate within our own society hegemonic norms, negating the identities and experiences of those women who have chosen *not* to center their lives around reproduction.

A focus on the body, or bodies, *can* be provocative and enlightening, then, if we explore the specific and multiple ways the body (and female and male bodies) is furnished meaning and significance within particular cultural-historical contexts. In this project, it is valuable to examine how variable cultural notions of the body serve specific interests within societies: how relations of power may be experienced, implemented, contested, and negotiated by alternate ways of speaking about and representing the body (cf. Lock and Scheper-Hughes 1987, Scheper-Hughes 1992). Heeding local meanings of the body may also necessitate moving beyond our current preoccupation with the body altogether. Thus, I explore in the following pages the ways specific representations of the body are used to define persons, aging, and gender, but I am not assuming the body to be already present in some sense as a starting point. Here I find Henrietta Moore's counsel to be valuable: "In fact," she writes, "I would suggest for the time being that we might be better working back towards sex, gender, sexual difference and the body, rather than taking them as a set of starting points" (1994:27).

LIVING IN MANGALDIHI

Most of what I report here describes people of modest means and middle or higher Hindu caste residing in the center of the village of Mangaldihi, where

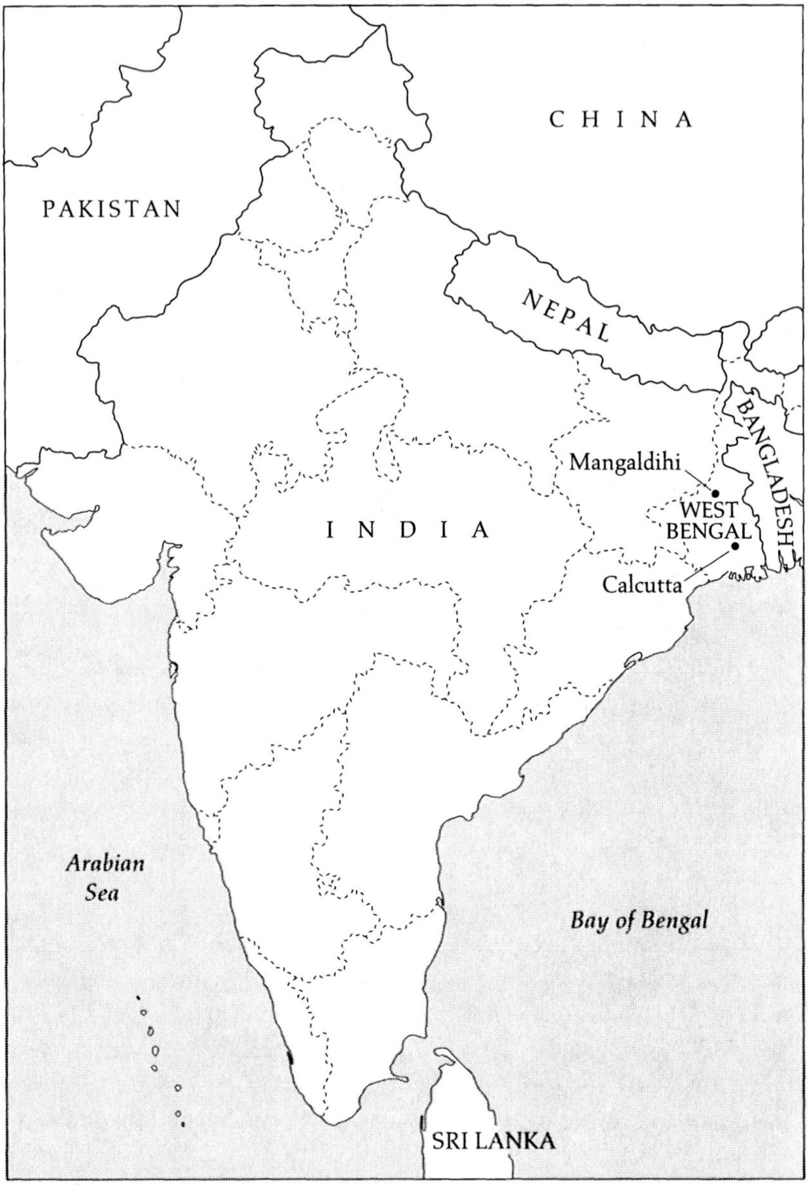
CHINA
PAKISTAN
NEPAL
BANGLADESH
Mangaldihi
WEST BENGAL
Calcutta
INDIA
Arabian Sea
Bay of Bengal
SRI LANKA

India

I lived for a year and a half from 1989 to 1990. Mangaldihi is located in West Bengal, India, about 150 kilometers from Calcutta, where I had previously lived and studied language in 1985 and 1986 (see map). The village of some 1,700 residents and 335 households comprised seventeen different Hindu caste (or *jāti*) groups, one neighborhood of Muslims, and one neighborhood of tribal Santals.[21]

Brahmans were recognized as being the village's "dominant" caste, as measured by landholdings, political clout, social mores, and the history of the village. Oral traditions told that Mangaldihi had been founded about 250 years earlier by Brahmans carrying figures of the deities Syamcand and Madan Gapal—forms of Krishna—from Brindaban far to the east, to protect them from Muslim invaders. Brahmans still lived in the village's central neighborhoods, and the village's major religious festivals still revolved around their ancient Vaishnavite deities. Brahmans also owned the majority of the village's land (60 percent), although their landholdings had significantly decreased over the past several decades under a series of government land reforms.[22] Most of the village's Brahman families still supported themselves by farming (rice was the staple crop), but only a handful of families owned more than ten acres of land. Most supplemented their agricultural income by finding salaried jobs in nearby cities and towns, working as priests, or opening small village grocery, tea, and video shops.

Numerically, the Brahmans in Mangaldihi were just about matched by the Bagdis, a lower or Scheduled Caste group occupying several village neighborhoods.[23] The Bagdis were much poorer than the Brahmans, owning an average of just a bit more than half an acre of land per household. They supported themselves mainly by working in Brahman households, tilling Brahman land, fishing, and cultivating small plots of their own. Bagdi representatives always secured several seats on the local *panchāyat* (government representative system), though, and they had a strong cultural and political presence in the village. Tables 1 to 3 list the other *jāti* groups of Mangaldihi, their traditional and current occupations, and size of their landholdings. Although most in the village did have enough to eat, very few were wealthy, and many families had to struggle to get by. There was a general feeling of scarcity and want in the village, which clearly seeped into the ways people structured and experienced their family relationships, their processes of aging, and the kinds of jealousy and bonds of maya, affection, and love that I describe in the following pages.

It was in a Brahman neighborhood that I settled, in the mud hut—nearly abandoned—of a wealthy Brahman family who had since moved to an adjacent three-story brick house. They later invited me to move into an up-

Table 1. *Jātis* of Mangaldihi by Number and Occupation

Jāti Name	*Number of Households*	*Traditional Occupation*	*Occupation in Mangaldihi*
Bagdi*	95	Agricultural laborer, fisher	Agricultural laborer, fisher, servant, cow tender
Brahman	84	Priest	Landowner, priest, salaried job, shopkeeper
Santal	34	Tribal	Agricultural laborer
Musalman (Muslim)	23	Cultivator	Owner cultivator, agricultural laborer, shopkeeper
Muci* (or Bayen)	22	Leatherworker, musician, drummer	Agricultural laborer musician, drummer
Kulu	15	Oil presser	Owner cultivator, shopkeeper, salaried job
Bauri*	14	Agricultural laborer	Agricultural laborer
Kora	14	Tribal	Agricultural laborer
Baisnab (or Bairagya)	10	Religious mendicant	Owner cultivator, shopkeeper, salaried job
Barui	6	Betel nut cultivator	Owner cultivator, shopkeeper, salaried job
Dhoba*	3	Washerman	Washerman, owner cultivator
Hari*	3	Midwife, drummer	Agricultural laborer
Napit	3	Barber	Barber, owner cultivator
Bene	2	Merchant	Shopkeeper, salaried job, landowner
Suri*	2	Liquor maker	Shopkeeper, liquor maker, owner cultivator
Dhatri*	1	Midwife	Agricultural laborer
Karmakar*	1	Blacksmith	Blacksmith, owner cultivator
Sadgop	1	Cultivator	Owner cultivator
Sutradhar	1	Carpenter	Carpenter, owner cultivator

Table 1—*Continued*

KEY: * *Jātis* classified by the government as Scheduled Caste.

Agricultural laborer	Those who cultivate the land of others but own no (or very little) land of their own (see also table 3).
Owner cultivator	Those who own and cultivate their own land.
Landowner	Those who own land but do not cultivate it themselves.

stairs room of that house. So it was almost inevitable that I became closest to the village's Brahman community, and it is their voices that figure in the following pages most saliently. I also spent a good deal of time in Bagdi neighborhoods, and I strove to interact with and gather data from members of each of Mangaldihi's other caste and ethnic groups. I often found a high degree of variation in the ways the different castes or *jātis* of Mangaldihi practiced and perceived matters of gender and aging, distinctions that I highlight when especially relevant.

My research focused on older women and men. I often found them hanging out at temples, on roadsides, and in the courtyards of their homes, relatively free from the work that so engrossed most of their younger adult kin. We spent hours together talking about life, family relations and struggles, fears and hopes surrounding death, memories of childhood and romance, current television dramas, the problems of poverty, the sufferings of women, and the changing nature of modern society. I sought out men as much as I did women, for "gender" (one of the problems I was most interested in) must, I believe, include women *and men.* Indeed, gender studies done in South Asia have generally been weakened by the relative dearth of attention paid to men. In the field of gender studies, "gender" has been used largely as a code for "women."[24] Women and men are equally gendered beings, however, and neither can be understood in isolation from the other and from the broader social worlds in which gender identities are constituted.

One of my main aims in hanging out with these older women and men in Mangaldihi was to gain a sense of their voices, lived worlds, and everyday experiences. Lawrence Cohen (1998) has written a fascinating, masterful account of constructions of old age and senility among families and institutions in the Indian city of Varanasi, and more generally in India's gerontological and popular cultural texts. Perhaps partly because he is focusing on *senility,* Cohen largely omits old people's *own* voices and experiences. (Senile, or in Varanasi parlance "weak-brained" or "hot-minded," old people are presumably elusive informants.) I have taken Mangaldihi's older people themselves as key subjects, as I have scrutinized how they envisioned, prac-

Table 2. Distribution of Landholdings in Mangaldihi, 1990

Size of Holding (acres)	*Number of Households*
Landless	115
< 1	83
1–5	87
5–10	39
10–15	7
15–20	4
> 20	0

Table 3. Distribution of Landholdings in Mangaldihi by *Jāti*

Jāti Name	*Number of Households*	*Total Land Held (in acres)*	*Average Landholding (acres per household)*	*Percent of Total Village Land*
Brahman	84	406	4.8	58.4
Kulu	15	69	4.6	9.9
Musalman	23	56	2.4	8.1
Bagdi	95	53	0.6	7.6
Barui	6	36	6.0	5.2
Baisnab	10	13	1.3	1.9
Bene	2	12	6.0	1.7
Suri	2	12	6.0	1.7
Muci	22	11	0.5	1.6
Sadgop	1	7	7.0	1.0
Napit	3	6	2.0	0.9
Dhoba	3	4	1.3	0.6
Santal	34	4	0.1	0.6
Kora	14	3	0.2	0.4
Bauri	14	1	0.1	0.1
Karmakar	1	1	1.0	0.1
Sutradhar	1	1	1.0	0.1
Dhatri	1	0	0	0.0
Hari	1	0	0	0.0

ticed, and experienced their own aging, embodiment, family relationships, grapplings with love and maya, and everyday lives in the world.

But since I myself was a younger woman, recently married, in my late twenties and early thirties, I also spent a good deal of time with my "peers," younger unmarried and recently married women. My closest daily companion was Hena, a young woman in her mid-twenties who married during my time in Mangaldihi. She shared a room and single pillow with me every night until her marriage, telling me of village gossip, her concerns and dreams, and her own visions of older people. Neighborhood girls and boys also crowded into my room daily, sharing tea and snacks with me; and the younger wives in the neighborhood, when they could free themselves from work, would also make some time for me—as we perhaps bathed together, or took a trip to town to buy a sari, or stopped to make a cup of tea in the still afternoon while others were taking their naps.

I also learned a great deal from these younger people, which highlighted for me the ambiguities, multiple perspectives, and shifting meanings inherent in what it is to be a woman, a man, and a person in this community of West Bengal. I concentrate here on these competing, ambiguous perspectives, and especially on the ways in which the women and men I knew made and remade their social worlds and gendered identities as they moved through the latter phases of their lives.

Although I went to India and Mangaldihi to seek out their stories in the pursuit of writing a dissertation and then a book, many of these older people also sought *me* out as a listener. They called to me as I passed, climbed the three flights of stairs to my home, or tapped me on my arm, saying "You haven't taped my life story yet," "You must write this down," "Did you get that in your notebook?" I hope that the following pages are true to their trust in me to articulate my sense of their experiences, and understandings, of their own lives and the lives of their neighbors.

Part One

PERSONS AND FAMILIES

1 Personhoods

ENTERING A NET OF MAYA IN MANGALDIHI

I arrived in Mangaldihi quite by chance. I had landed in India at the end of December 1988, anxious to begin research. I had thought I would focus on a rural community or village, where it might be easier for me to get to know a wider variety of people, since villagers would tend to be less enclosed than city dwellers within the walls of their own homes and workplaces. Several restless weeks slipped by in Calcutta and then in the sophisticated university town of Santiniketan while I sought suggestions about a specific location. To most of the Bengali city and town people I met, villages (*grām*) were distant, almost foreign places that elicited nostalgia.[1] Ancestral connections might lie there or the roots of one's identity (Calcutta schoolchildren reportedly had to compose an annual essay on "My Village"). But many times I was told that I could not possibly *live* in one. I could perhaps visit a village on a bicycle, but if I were to live there—I would certainly get sick, perhaps even die, and definitely suffer. I finally met a few people who still had family or ancestral homes in villages that they visited regularly. One of these was Manik Banerji, who worked as a schoolteacher near Santiniketan and whose mother's brother lived in a large village called Mangaldihi about thirty kilometers away.

The relationship with a mother's brother (*māmā*) is a very special one for Bengalis, full of pampering and sweetness. One can ask one's mother's brother for almost anything, and he is expected to indulge the request. So when Manik Banerji wrote a letter of introduction for me to his mother's brother in Mangaldihi asking this man to help me out in any way he could, Manik Banerji assured me (with a glint in his eye) that his *māmā* would surely oblige. He gave me directions to the village and house: a crowded bus ride to the town of Parui and then a long cycle rickshaw ride past rice fields and small villages to the sizable village of Mangaldihi, where I could not miss his uncle's three-story brick home, the largest house in the village. And sure enough, the mother's brother, Dulal Mukherjee, generously agreed to let me live in his compound, on the second floor of his family's old and little-used mud house, above a dark and little-used doctor's office, where my landlord kept a store of various medicines.

And so I was introduced to Mangaldihi, where I was to become caught up in what I would later learn to call the "net of maya," or web of attachments, affections, jealousies, and love that in Bengalis' eyes make up social relations. It began on my first night in Mangaldihi when a young woman from the neighborhood, Hena, came to sleep with me and be my companion. Or perhaps it began earlier that day, when I visited Mangaldihi briefly, accepted a glass of sugar water (*śarbat*) in Dulal Mukherjee's home, and agreed to live in his neighborhood. Bengalis regard maya as being formed through the everyday activities of sharing food, touching, sleeping in the same bed, having sexual relations, exchanging words, and living in the same home, in the same neighborhood, or on the same village soil. These attachments link people (family, friends, neighbors), as well as people and the places, animals, and objects that make up their worlds. And once bonds of maya are formed, Bengalis often say, they are very difficult to loosen.

I learned this first through my relationship with Hena, the person with whom I developed the most intimate ties. My landlord and neighbors decided that I should have a companion to sleep with at night and to show me around, so they sent me an unmarried young woman in her early twenties from a poor Brahman family in the neighborhood. At once a younger sister and companion, she soon became a research assistant, a confidante, and a dear friend. After a few weeks went by, however, I decided that I needed to have at least a little time and space to myself (separation being valued by Americans), and I suggested to Hena that she let me sleep alone at night, that I needed the time to study and was not afraid of the village ghosts. Hena burst out weeping, "You're trying to 'cut' (*kāṭā*) the maya! How will I live without you? I won't be able to bear it." So she remained my daily and nightly companion, as we cooked together and shared food, my single pillow, and confidences.

The people in the Mukherjee household and neighborhood also protested vehemently when, after about six months, I attempted to move into a larger, more comfortable home to prepare for my husband's arrival. My neighbors and my landlord's family would not have me moving into what was technically a different neighborhood, although the house was literally only a stone's throw away: "How can you just cut the maya like that and move?

You'll become an 'other person' (*parer lok*)." And I was deluged with milk, fish, sweets, visits, and pleas to persuade me and strengthen our bonds, so that I could not leave.

From the very beginning of my stay in Mangaldihi up until the end, I heard a continual refrain—even after just one shared cup of tea, or a brief conversation on the roadside—"Oh, it is so sad that you have come, for you will have to leave again. How will we cut this maya when you leave? Maya cannot be cut." And one day Sankar, a well-educated young Brahman man from Mangaldihi, sat down next to me on the bus as I was on my way to shop at the market in a nearby town and said: "There is one 'tragedy' [he used the English word] about your coming here. That is that you will have to leave. You must be hearing a lot about this. Bengalis hate separations. They feel so much maya for everything. You know maya? Once there is a relationship (*samparka*), they want to keep it strong (*śakta*). They want everyone to be together always." People would also chide me, "You've just come here to cause maya to grow and then go away."

Human relationships for Mangaldihians involved not only bonds of maya, attachment or affection, but also *hiṃsā*, jealousy. On one of my first expeditions to Mangaldihi I sat behind a Muslim rickshaw driver pedaling along the narrow paved road past fallow winter rice fields. As he gazed at the landscape he said to me, "Birbhum [the district Mangaldihi lies in] is the best place in the world. Everyone here knows each other and everyone loves each other." His words made me feel exceedingly lucky to have happened on such a place: I looked around, with the winter sun warm on my face and arms, and admired the gentle hills undulating into the distance. Now his statement seems even more striking, because it was the only one of its kind that I heard. Much more frequently, I heard about and experienced the pervasive *hiṃsā* in the region's villages. People would tell me, "Bengalis are a very jealous people (*bāṅgālīrā khub hiṃsute jāt*)." And the people of Mangaldihi thought that they were even more jealous than other Bengalis.

I certainly experienced jealousy in Mangaldihi, which seeped into almost everything I and other people did—as people (especially women) bickered and argued about who gave more tea, rice, sugar, snacks, money, fish, land, photos, saris (on loan), attention, and so on to whom; who was favored, who was not; who was loved most, who was not. I often wondered to myself, near despair, if they could be right about the general disposition of Mangaldihians; and if so, *why* had I chosen this village? But it takes a certain amount of intimacy to be involved in such struggles, and so I finally realized that the intense jealousies I often encountered were due in part to my privileged position. Being in some ways one of their own people (*nijer lok*), I was inevitably embroiled in the tangles (*jaṭ*) of jealousy and wants and givings and receivings and affection and love that Bengali relationships entail.

By the end of my stay in Mangaldihi, the people of the village had indeed finally begun to view me as one of them—for they worried less about their pain and tugs of maya than about mine. People would say with compassion, again and again over the weeks before my departure, "We have maya for only one person—you—who will leave and cause us pain. But how much more pain will you suffer! For you have maya for all of us, and will have to leave all of us." They viewed me as in the center of a "net" (*jāl*) of maya, holding multiple strands that I had gathered during my eighteen months there—bonds of affection and attachment for all of the people of the village, and also for all of my things: the household items I had collected and lived with over a year and a half, my saris, my conch shell bangles (a sign of a married woman), my taste for Bengali food (how was I going to get by without eating *ālu posta*, potatoes with poppy seed paste, a regional favorite?), the village deities, the village land. How would I be able to cut the maya for all of these people, places, and objects and leave?

I came to view the ways people reacted to and interpreted my relatively brief and inconsequential stay in Mangaldihi as an avenue toward understanding how Bengalis think about and experience the forming and loosening of social-substantial relations in their own daily lives. Indeed, I found my coming and going to be particularly relevant for understanding practices and attitudes that surround aging and dying. For if the people I knew felt that it would be so exceedingly difficult for a person like me to leave Mangaldihi after residing there for only a number of months, what happens when a person who has lived for years and years with a family, in a village, on a piece of land, with all of his or her possessions, has to take leave of them all and die? Over and over again, this was a worry I heard expressed by older people, and by younger people contemplating their own future.

OPEN PERSONS AND SUBSTANTIAL EXCHANGES

Such concerns about maya and aging—the forming and loosening of emotional relations over a lifetime—speak also to Bengali notions of what it is to be a person. A principal theme in sociocultural studies of South Asia over the past several decades has been the investigation of South Asian notions of what a "person" or "self" is.[2]

Several of these studies have focused on the fluid and open nature of persons in India. This insight was first voiced by McKim Marriott (1976), who with Ronald Inden (Marriott and Inden 1977) pointed to everyday Indian practices reflecting the assumption that persons have more or less open boundaries and may therefore affect one another's natures through transactions of food, services, words, bodily substances, and the like. Marriott and Inden, who described the Indian social and cultural world as one of particulate "flowing substances," suggested that Indians view persons in such a world as "composite" and hence "dividual" or divisible in nature. By contrast, Europeans and Americans view persons as relatively closed, contained and solid "*in*dividuals" (see also Marriott 1990).

E. Valentine Daniel (1984) similarly emphasized that among Tamils, all things are constituted of fluid substances. In perpetual flux, these substances have an inherent capacity to separate and mix with other substances. Thus it is possible—indeed, inevitable—for persons to establish intersubstantial relationships with other people (sexual partners, household and village members) and with the places (land, village, houses) in and with which they live. Such substantial mixings point to what Daniel has called "the cultural reality of the *nonindividual* person." They reveal the "fluidity of enclosures" in Tamil conceptual thought, whether those be the boundaries of a village, the walls of a house, or the skin of a person (1984:9, his italics).

Ronald Inden and Ralph Nicholas (1977) described similar personally transformative transactions among Bengalis, who to form kinship relations partly share and exchange their bodies by means of acts such as birth, marriage, sharing food, and living together (e.g., pp. 13, 17–18). Francis Zimmermann (1979, 1980) and Sudhir Kakar (1982:233–34), too, found notions of the fluid and substantially interpenetrative nature of persons, gods, places, and things in Ayurvedic texts and practices. Zimmermann in particular emphasized that the body in Ayurveda exists in a state of fluidity or *snehatvā*. The body is composed of a network of channels and fluids, which flow not only within the body but also among persons and their environments (Zimmermann 1979).

In Mangaldihi, I first encountered a notion of persons as relatively open and unbounded as manifest in what is called "mutual touching" (*chõy-āchũyi*). The people I knew were concerned about whom and what they touched because touching involves a mutual transfer of substantial qualities from one person or thing to the next. Initially, I saw their concern most clearly in the management of "impurity" (*aśuddhatā*) in daily life.[3] High-caste Hindus avoided touching low-caste Hindus; Hindus avoided touching Muslims or tribal Santals; people of all castes frequently avoided touching those who were in states of "impurity" because of recent activities (e.g., defecating, visiting a hospital, or handling a dead body); persons about to make a ritual offering to a deity avoided touching any other person at all. To be sure, people often touched one another in the course of their daily affairs. But when they did, each considered that substantial properties from the other had permeated his or her own body, and the person who was in the "higher" or more "pure" position would often feel it necessary to bathe to rid him- or herself from the effects of the contact.

There are many forms of *chõyāchũyi.* Touching can take the form of simple bodily contact, as when a person touches another's arm with her hand or brushes into another on a crowded bus. It also occurs when two people touch an object at the same time, such as when a person hands a pen or a photo or a cup of tea to someone else, or when two people sit on the same bench or mat at the same time. The objects in such cases conduct substantial qualities between the two people. Mangaldihi villagers told me that the only material that does not act as a conductor in this way is the earth (*māṭi*), including, as a kind of extension of the earth, the mud or cement floors of houses and courtyards. Thus, to avoid touching and the exchanges of substance that touching entails, people often refrained from handing objects to each other directly; instead, one placed an object on the ground for the other to pick up, or dropped an object into another's outstretched hands. People themselves, like objects, act as conveyors or conductors of contact—so that two people who touch another person at the same time also touch each other. Furthermore, unlike objects, people generally retain the effects of touch: if someone touches one person and then (without bathing) another, this second person is considered to have been touched as well by the first.

It took many confused days and awkward experiences for me to learn about how touching was conceived as part of social interaction in Mangaldihi. People were constantly telling me that I had touched someone "low" (*nicu*) or "impure" (*aśuddha*) and therefore needed to bathe when I, with my definition of what constitutes touching, failed to see how I had touched anyone at all (and felt no need to bathe in any case). I have a particularly vivid memory of visiting Mangaldihi's Muslim neighborhood for the first time, accompanied by my companion, Hena. On our way back to the Brahman neighborhood where we lived, Hena told me that we would both have to bathe. "Why?" I asked. "Because we touched Muslims." "No we didn't," I protested, "We didn't touch anyone while we were there." "Yes we did," she insisted, "We were sitting on the same mat with them, weren't we." "*That's* not touching!" I exclaimed. "Yes it is; of course it is!" "Well, we don't consider that touching in my country," I retorted. A little fed up after a long, hot day, and particularly disturbed by the implied prejudice that the act of bathing entailed, I let slip my usual anthropological stance of attempting to soak in information without challenge. "Well, here," she said as she reached out and touched my upper arm, "*I* touched them and now I touched you, so now you have touched them too, and you have to bathe."

I also experienced, especially during my first few months in Mangaldihi, many people who avoided touching *me*—a non-Hindu and therefore in their eyes potentially very polluting indeed. I visited the home of an elderly Brahman widow several weeks after I had moved into the village in order to give her a photo that I had taken of her grandson. She stretched out her palms to receive it, in a gesture whose meaning would have been obvious to any villager: she did not want to be touched by me. She was requesting that I drop the photo into her open palms without making contact with her. But I only later understood the gesture; at the time, I naively placed the photo directly into her hands, thereby unwittingly contaminating the woman by my touch and making it necessary for her to go again to the pond to bathe.

Some forms of interpersonal exchanges have much more lasting and extensive effects than the relatively brief forms of bodily contact or touching described above, effects that cannot be removed simply by bathing. According to rural Bengalis, when a person cooks, for instance, his or her qualities and bodily substance permeate the cooked food and are therefore absorbed by those who eat it. People who eat the same food together at the same time and in the same location (as in persons served in the same row at a feast) also share substantial qualities with each other. It becomes obvious why people in most parts of India, including Mangaldihi, are so concerned about whose food and with whom they eat: in sharing food, they also share the substance, nature, and qualities of those who prepare, serve, and partake in it.

The people I knew viewed food leavings—food that had been touched with the saliva (*lālā*) of the eater—as also highly permeated with the eater's substance. Leftovers, along with boiled rice, are considered to be *ẽṭo*, a term that refers specifically to food items that have become very highly permeated with the substances of those who have cooked, handled, and eaten them. People were very careful and selective about whose *ẽṭo* they would touch or ingest. Wives would eat their husbands' *ẽṭo* (but often not vice versa), servants would eat their employers' *ẽṭo* foods and wash their *ẽṭo* dishes (but definitely not vice versa), and close sisters or mothers and daughters would often share and trade *ẽṭo* food with each other.

The condition of being *ẽṭo* also spreads easily from a hand that has touched the mouth (either directly or via an object, such as a cup or eating utensil) to other persons and objects. When I drink a cup of tea, for instance, my mouth touches the tea cup, which touches my hand; and thus my hand becomes *ẽṭo*. If I wish to prevent the *ẽṭo* from spreading to other objects and persons, I must quickly wash it. I tried hard to regulate such practices, washing my hand after any eating or drinking, but in the eyes of my neighbors I was clearly not fastidious enough. They would tease me that my whole house and everything in it had become *ẽṭo*, that people concerned with purity and maintaining separateness from others (such as Brahman widows) should not even set foot into my home.

But a more serious breach in my conduct, a more reckless spreading of bodily substances, came much earlier, before people were comfortable enough with me to tease and criticize me about my ways—on my second visit to Mangaldihi, before I had moved to the village. Hena had taken me to her home, where she and her younger sister were eating their noon meal alone; their parents were away. Hena offered me a little bit of their rice and egg curry, and I accepted. When she stood up to clear away the dishes, I thought I would be helpful (in the American style) and I picked up my dish and placed it on the stack that she was holding. Without saying anything at the time, she went down to the pond to wash them. But when I returned to Mangaldihi the next day, she burst into tears and told me that several neighbors had seen her handle my *ẽṭo* dish and told her that they would not be able to touch her. I felt horrible for her. It was of course entirely my fault, for I had carelessly placed my dirty, saliva-covered dish in her hands without going to wash it myself (or at least leaving it on the ground, where she could have inconspicuously later called for a low-caste person to take it away). And her generosity and open-heartedness toward me had caused her to be slandered and ostracized by her neighbors. At the same time, I was also surprised by how uncomfortable, embarrassing, and even stingingly painful it felt to learn that other people found me literally untouchable.

After I left Mangaldihi that day I went to speak with Jamphul, an older Santal tribal woman who worked in my landlady's home in the town of Santiniketan. She was at first indignant when I told her about the incident, saying "Why? Why didn't you just ask them—'Am I poor like you?'"—an interesting response, revealing how she (like many in Mangaldihi) perceived real status and power to come from possession of money, which can in some ways even transform *jāti* or caste hierarchies. Then she added compassionately, "It makes you feel bad (*khārāp*), doesn't it? It makes you feel ill at ease (*aśānti*)." She herself experienced untouchability all the time as a Santal, and like many lower-caste and Santal people in the region she found upper-caste concerns with rank ordering and impurity unjust and hurtful.

Marriott (1976), Daniel (1984), and others who have looked at such interactions have termed the properties that are felt to be transferred among people "substance," translating an inclusive Sanskrit term (*dravya*) for something that is treated as material, though it is not necessarily visible. For want of a better word, I too sometimes use this broad term. But the Bengalis I knew did not use any specific equivalent word or phrase. When they discussed the effects of touching, it was simply clear that something was transferred between persons—that persons, after touching, shared something (parts of themselves, their qualities, their bodily substance) with each other. This transfer formed part of their taken-for-granted, commonsense world, and in our conversations about how touching works, what constitutes touching, and the effects of touching, they could not believe that I did not view touching in the same way. "Touching" (or *chõyā*) simply *means* a mutual contact that has a lasting effect on persons involved, so that the substance of each is changed by the other. Only the most insignificant kinds of touching (i.e., brief external bodily contacts) have effects that can be ended with bathing. Others, such as eating together, handling another's *ẽṭo*, living in the same house, sexual intercourse, and marriage, have more permanent effects. They forge real bonds of relation—*samparka*, "relation," "bodily connections"; or *māyā*, "attachment," "affection"—among persons, who come to share something fundamental.

Ranking in general, particularly the ranking of *jātis*, or castes, has long been taken (particularly by European observers, as summarized by Dumont 1980a) as the most distinctive dimension of Indian society. Thus ethnographies such as those by Adrian Mayer (1960) and Marriott (1968), as well as analyses such as Marriott and Inden's (1974, 1977), focused on asymmetrical transfers of food, water, and bodily substances (hair, saliva in food leavings, feces, menstrual blood, etc.) among castes. Louis Dumont (1980a) treated such transfers as reflecting an otherwise fixed vertical hierarchy of "pure" and "impure" castes, while Marriott (1968) and Marriott and Inden (1974) viewed transactions as continually creative of caste ranks. Marriott (1976) later analyzed intercaste transactions as also creating a second, horizontal dimension of "mixing" or alliance, and Gloria Raheja (1988) a third one of "auspiciousness" or centrality; but all earlier views of transactions had stressed only the differentiation of caste ranks.

I, too, initially found that the most striking and obvious dimension of the exchanges practiced by people in Mangaldihi pertained to *jāti* or caste hierarchy and particularly the managing of "impurity" (*aśuddhatā*) through avoidance. But as the days and months went by, I came to realize that an even more important and pervasive dimension of the open and unbound nature of persons in Mangaldihi had to do with seeking, cultivating, and intensifying mixings with kin, loved ones, friends, neighbors, things, and places. Hena was the first to seek such mixings with me. After I had been in

Mangaldihi for several weeks, she began regularly to come over to my home to trade and mix some of her food with some of mine. Hena's mother would often make *ruṭi* (flat bread) for me and I would cook rice for Hena. Then we would trade vegetables with each other and eat side by side. My landlord's young daughter, Chaitali, would frequently do the same, rushing over after their family's meal was prepared with a plate of rice and cooked vegetables to trade and mix with some of mine. And after two young sisters from the neighborhood became my cooks, they would eat all their meals with me and often rush to clear away my *ẽṭo* dish or wipe the place where I had been eating. I saw also how in their own homes, women in particular would trade rice and food, eat off others' plates, finish one another's *ẽṭo* leftovers, and eagerly call children to them to feed them food from their own plates with their own hands.

Parents, too, would clean away their children's urine, excrement, and mucus without worrying about suffering any kind of bodily impurity. And as I will discuss in chapter 2, Bengalis defined the relations of children with their aged parents in important part by describing how children clean up parents' urine and excrement lovingly and without complaint when they have become incontinent in old age and again after death.

Family and kinship ties in Mangaldihi (as throughout Bengal) were perceived as created and sustained through various kinds of bodily and other mixings, sharings, and exchanges (see also Inden and Nicholas 1977). People of the same "family" were said to "share the same body," as *sapiṇḍas*: a word formed from *piṇḍa*, "body particle" or "ball of rice," and *sa*, "shared" or "same." *Sapiṇḍas* are people who share the same *piṇḍas*, or body particles, passed down from common ancestors, as well as people who offer together the same rice balls to the same ancestors. Families were also constituted by exchanging, sharing, and mixing via all sorts of other media, such as food (especially rice), houses, and blood (*rakta*). Mangaldihi villagers often referred to their families as those who "eat rice from the same pot" (*eki hā̃ṛite khāi*). They also called the members of their families *gharer lok* or "house's people." They spoke of the "pull of blood" (*raktar ṭān*) that they share with parents and siblings, and of the "pull" (*ṭān*) they have for their mother because they drank her breast milk (*buker dudh*) and were carried in her womb (*nāṛī*).

Thus social relations of kinship and friendship, as well as of *jāti*, relied on daily givings and receivings. I found that people in Mangaldihi built boundaries and avoided contact less often than they sought to become parts of each other—through sharing and exchanging their bodily substances, food, possessions, words, affections, and places of residence. This resonates with what Margaret Trawick writes of Tamil households, where mixing (*kalattal, mayakkam*) was viewed as a goal and pleasure in and of itself—one to be celebrated and renewed daily, and taught and learned as a value (1990b, esp. pp. 83–87). These kinds of exchanges result in what rural Bengalis often refer to as maya, the "net" (*jāl*) of bodily-emotional "ties" (*bandhan*), "pulls" (*ṭān*), or "connections" (*samparka*) that make up people and their lived-in worlds.

Such a vision of persons as open and partly constituted by what comes and goes also informed people's conceptions of gender differences over the life course. Many spoke of women as being even more "open" (*kholā*) than men, especially during their married and reproductive years. This not only made women vulnerable to impurities or unwanted substances from outside (as were also the lower castes, several explained, comparing women to Sudras); it also gave women the highly valued capacities to receive a husband's seed and produce a child; to mix with, nurture, and sustain a family (see chapter 6).

People in Mangaldihi likewise expressed the ambivalences and transitions of aging by referring to changes in the fluid and open nature of their bodies and personhoods. Aging was thought to involve simultaneous, contrary pulls in the kinds of ties that make up persons. On the one hand, these ties were felt to grow more numerous and intense as life goes on. On the other hand, aging was thought to involve the difficult work of taking apart the self or unraveling ties, in preparation for the many leave-takings of death (see chapter 4).

STUDYING PERSONS CROSS-CULTURALLY

Melford E. Spiro (1993) takes exception to the findings of several anthropologists, including notable South Asianists (Shweder, Bourne, Dumont, and Marriott),[4] who have suggested that while many non-Westerners deemphasize individuality, Westerners view persons largely as bounded or autonomous individuals. Spiro's article was stimulated by another article on the self by two social psychologists, expert on Japan (Markus and Kitayama 1991), who approvingly cite Clifford Geertz's celebrated characterization of this Western conception as "a rather peculiar idea within the context of the world cultures" (Geertz 1983:59, qtd. in Spiro 1993:107).

According to Geertz, Westerners see the person as a "bounded, unique, more or less integrated motivational and cognitive universe, a dynamic center of awareness, emotion, judgment and action organized into a distinctive whole and set contrastively against other such wholes and against its social and natural background" (1983:59). If such a conception of the person as bounded is cross-culturally "peculiar," then other ("non-Western") people must view persons to be relatively *not* bounded. This premise—which is precisely what Geertz, and after him Hazel Markus and Shinobu Kitayama, does imply—is challenged by Spiro.

I will briefly take up Spiro's key arguments here, because I believe that Bengali ethno-theories of persons can effectively resolve some of Spiro's conundrums. Focusing his argument on the supposed bounded-unbounded (Western–non-Western) dichotomy, he begins by wondering what it could mean to be relatively unbounded as a person. Markus and Kitayama (1991:245) observe that in the case of many "non-Western" selves, "others are included *within* the boundaries of the self" (qtd. in Spiro 1993:108). Spiro responds, "This proposition . . . struck me as strange, because it seemed incomprehensible—what could it mean to say that *others* are included within the boundaries of *my*self?" (pp. 108–9).

The answer to this question rests in large part on what Spiro, Markus and Kitayama, and other scholars mean by the terms "self" or "person." Spiro entertains briefly the notion that Markus and Kitayama could be referring to the self as the psychobiological organism, bounded by the skin. Such a self *could* be permeable to "others"—for example, microorganisms or germs that penetrate the body to cause disease, or spirits that possess an individual. However, such boundary crossings entail only impermanent and abnormal conditions, and Spiro therefore concludes that ethnographers who describe notions of unbounded selves could not be using the term "self" (or "person") to denote the psychobiological organism. The more likely referent, he believes, is some psychological entity: an ego, a soul, or an "I." But we still have a problem, Spiro insists, because all those who believe that others are included within the boundaries of their psychological self would have little, if any, "self-other differentiation." That is, they would lack "the sense that one's self, or one's own person, is bounded, or separate from all other persons" (1993:110). Since all people must be able to differentiate themselves from others, they must think of themselves as bounded and separate from all other persons. This, he argues, is a "distinguishing feature of the very notion of human nature" (p. 110).[5]

These arguments give rise to several interesting questions. First, consider the self as a psychobiological organism. Clearly an unbounded psychobiological self might entail a broader range of possibilities than invading germs or possessing spirits. Even in the scant material from rural West Bengal that

I have presented so far, it is evident that the Bengalis I knew viewed the sharing and exchanging of bodily and other substances—not only with other people but also with the places in which they live and the things that they own and use—as vital to the ways they think about and define themselves and social relations. Parts of other people, places, and things become part of one's own body and person, just as parts of oneself enter into the bodies and thus the persons of others. Bengalis viewed such exchanges as neither abnormal nor temporary (though some are more or less desired, more or less lasting), but rather as an elemental part of everyday life and practice.

This does not mean that the Bengalis I knew could not differentiate themselves psychologically from others—they, like all people, perceptually perform self-other differentiation. But I see no reason for Spiro's assumption that the ability to differentiate one's consciousness from others is dependent on a notion of the self as "bounded, or separate from all other persons." He conflates a sense of personal identity with that of personal boundaries: either people view themselves as perfectly bounded and separate, *or* they lose all capacity to differentiate themselves from others. One can, like the Bengalis I knew, have a clear sense of a differentiable self that *includes* bodily and emotional ties with others. Indeed, these ties make up the very stuff of who and what a (distinct and differentiable) person is.

Furthermore, Spiro's added argument that Hindu and Buddhist theories of karma prove that there can be no "unbounded" Hindu or Buddhist selves seems equally misguided. As Spiro describes it, the Hindu and Buddhist theory of karma holds that every living person is the reincarnation of myriad past selves and that any person's current and future incarnations are the karmic consequences of the actions of "his or her, and only his or her, own person" (1993:112–13, 1982). In short, he argues, "even if it were the case that other selves are included within the boundary of the Burmese [or any Buddhist or Hindu] conception of the self, . . . how then would we explain the fact that the Burmese explicitly affirm that no actor bears any responsibility for the action of others, even though the latter are allegedly included within the boundary of the actor's own self?" (1993:113).

Here Spiro provides only one of the multiple theories of karma held by Hindu Indians, if not Burmese Buddhists. Several anthropological studies of different regions in India, as well as my Bengali informants, recount how karma may be shared among members of a family or community, making it not always simply an individual affair.[6] Susan Wadley and Bruce Derr (1990), for instance, tell of how a devastating fire in the north Indian village of Karimpur spurred a debate among villagers over the extent that karma is shared—the extent that the deeds of one person affect the lives of others. It became clear that "Karimpur residents viewed the fire as a community punishment, not merely an individual one" (p. 142).

The people I knew in West Bengal also offered theories of shared karma to explain a person's or group's misfortune. One respected Brahman priest and his wife were entering into old age with no children; the priest's brother also had none. The family line (*baṃśa*) would be extinguished, and there would be no one to care for the two brothers and their wives in old age. The common village explanation was that they were suffering the karmic fruits of the misdeeds that their dishonest father had performed in his lifetime. As one woman told me, "When a father does sin, his sons have to eat the fruits." Although Hindu South Asians also offer individual theories of karma to explain a single person's own life circumstances, they frequently view karma as something that is shared by whole families or communities.[7]

This brings me to my next point, and here I agree with Spiro: dichotomies between Western and non-Western, individual and nonindividual, bounded and nonbounded conceptions of self or person should not be overdrawn (Spiro 1993:116). Thus, though the ethnographic literature on South Asia shows a long tradition of research holding that Indians (in various ways) de-emphasize individuality,[8] anthropologists have also examined ways in which South Asians view persons in terms that we might consider "individual."[9]

Americans, too, may not always consider themselves to be as neatly bound, closed, and individual as many scholars have presumed. A study by Carol Nemeroff and Paul Rozin (1994), for instance, examines the so-called contagion concept among adult Philadelphians, the majority of whom, it turns out, believe that some kinds of essences ("vibes," "cooties," germs, moral qualities, etc.) are transferred from person to person through everyday exchanges such as sharing a sweater. Some feminist theorists have suggested further that models of the self emphasizing individual autonomy do not adequately describe the self-conceptions of American women, who are more likely than American men to focus more on connectedness to others. Multiple perspectives exist in any society or culture (e.g., Chodorow 1978; Gilligan 1982; Lykes 1985). What are often taken as the mutually exclusive values of "individuality" and "relatedness" may in fact interpenetrate within the same culture. And obviously persons steeped in South Asian culture live in the West and vice versa, making it even more difficult to draw any meaningful boundaries between "Western" and "non-Western" conceptions.

While I believe that it is possible to explore what people believe a "person" or "self" to be, I do not intend to investigate Bengali notions of personhood as a means of contrasting them to a putative generalized "Western" conception of the person. Rather, I use the rural Bengali material to examine views about personhood in a particular society, and then bring these views or ethno-theories into the arena of Western theoretical discussion about persons, selves, and genders.[10] More specifically, I explore how Bengali notions of persons as relatively open and composed of relationships (a notion I will continue to elaborate on) are tied to their perceptions about aging, dying, gender, and the forming and taking apart of social relations over the life course.

2 Family Moral Systems

The most common Bengali term used to refer to what we in English might call a "family" is *saṃsār.* It literally means "that which flows together," from the roots *saṃ,* "together, with," and *sṛ,* "to flow, move." In its most comprehensive sense, *saṃsār* refers to the whole material world (*pṛthibī* or *jagat*) and to the flux of births and deaths that all living beings and things go through together. More commonly, the term designates one's own family or household (which is in some ways viewed as a microcosm of the wider world's processes). Thus *saṃsār* not only refers to the people of a family or household, but also includes any household animals, such as cows, goats, or ducks; any family deities; the space of the house itself; and the material goods of a household—cooking utensils, bedding, wall hangings, and the like. All of this collectively makes up what Bengalis call their *saṃsār,* the assembly of people and things that "flow with" persons as they move through their lives. The *Samsad Bengali-English Dictionary,* like some of my human informants, also lists "the bindings of maya" (*māyābandhan*) as one of the overlapping meanings of *saṃsār*—that is, the bodily and emotional attachments or "bindings" that connect people with the persons and things that make up their households and wider inhabited worlds. It was within *saṃsārs,* or families, in Mangaldihi that much of what constituted age and gender relations was played out. In this and the following chapter, I focus on people's visions of the workings of families.

These visions entailed both consensus—what were often presented to me as shared "Bengali" values—and *dis*sension or conflicting perspectives (for instance, between generations or genders). In today's theoretical climate, it is often dissension or contestation that is highlighted (as I discussed in the introduction). Indeed, contestation—or the absolute heterogeneity of culture—has somehow become an overpowering trope, almost silencing what it was meant to allow for: that is, a heeding of the full range of diverse perspectives, visions, and experiences of those we are seeking to understand.[1] For it is not only anthropologists who have often (perhaps more often in the past) sought generalized or essentialized features of "cultures"; very often people essentialize *themselves*. For instance, those I knew in Mangaldihi commonly spoke to me of "Bengali culture," or "Bengali people"—especially when describing to me (admittedly an outsider, for whom this kind of language might have been thought particularly appropriate) how families work and how aging is constituted within families. Scholars such as Partha Chatterjee (1993) and Pradip Kumar Bose (1995) have examined elite middle-class discourses on the family in nineteenth- and early-twentieth-century Bengal, in which the family was often presented as the inner domain of a national culture, a refuge from external colonial society. Such an awareness of cultural difference also underlay many Mangaldihi villagers' discourses of Bengali family values (a point I discuss further in chapter 3). The workings of intergenerational family relations were presented as key parts of a Bengali local morality, a Bengali world.

The material in this chapter, as the label "family moral *systems*" would suggest, concentrates on such discourses of a shared project. Some readers may be uncomfortable with the level of apparent agreement or systematicity they find. But I have stayed close to the visions and language of many of my informants; and if I had omitted this material, I would not have done justice to the ways they often wished to represent themselves. I will then turn in chapter 3, "Conflicting Generations," to other, equally vital perspectives on age and gender relations within family life. Both chapters explore crucial components of the ways those I knew in Mangaldihi experienced and envisioned processes of aging, gender, and personhood within the arena of family life, an arena informed by specific politics and history.

DEFINING AGE

When I began research in India, I did not decide in advance whom I would consider "old" (although my advisor in Calcutta, troubled by the lack of specificity in my research proposal, advised me to do so: "But whom will you be calling 'old' in your study? Will it be people above age fifty-five? or age sixty-five?"). Instead, I wished to find out how the people I lived with defined aging. Once in Mangaldihi, when I searched for ways to speak about what I would call "old age," I necessarily had to begin by using Bengali words that approximated the topic. I asked what it is to be "grown" or "increased" (*bṛiddha*) or relatively "senior" or "advanced" (*buṛo*) in life and social importance.[2] I soon also heard the term *bayas,* referring to life's "prime stage," or an advanced "age" or "phase" of life.

I was virtually never told directly about age in absolute measures. Most people in Mangaldihi, in fact, did not know their age in years and placed little importance on such information. Although people of course sensed the repetitive cycles of seasons and celestial events as well as the accumulation of changes in their bodies, families, communities, and nation, few counted the particular number of years passed in their lives as markers of identity or of life stage, or kept track of and celebrated their birthdays.

Some of the more elite and literate families, especially among the Brahmans, did keep accounts of birth dates and such in record books, particularly so that they might cast horoscopes when arranging marriages. Some of those in Mangaldihi with salaried jobs also noted their seniority in years for bureaucratic purposes. But such knowledge was generally considered to be elite or technical information, a kind of "symbolic capital" (Bourdieu 1977:171–83) that demonstrated the possession of education, record books, salaried jobs, and the wealth that these goods entailed. One elderly Kora widow answered sharply when I asked her age, "How would I know that kind of thing? That's a matter of paper and pencils. Where would we get things like that? Knowing your age (*bayas*) is for *boṛo* ('big' or 'rich') people like you or Brahmans."

Much as Sylvia Vatuk (1990) had observed in Delhi, in Mangaldihi family criteria, and particularly the marriages of children, were held above all to constitute the beginnings of the senior phase (*buṛo bayas*). The family heads initiated their transition to being "senior" by gradually—often with years of ambivalence, arguing, and competition—handing over their duties of reproduction, cooking, and feeding to "junior" successors, usually sons and sons' wives. When their children married, women would also start to wear white saris, which signified their increasing seniority and asexuality.[3] Since such successions and retirements might occur when members of the ascendant generation were of any age between about thirty-five and sixty, the Bengali senior stage corresponded roughly to the second halves of most villagers' lives and to what today's Americans might call "middle" and "old" age.

People defined aging physically as well, describing the old body as "weak" (*durbal*), "cool" (*ṭhāṇḍā*), "dry" (*śukna*), and sometimes "decrepit" (*jārā*). Lawrence Cohen (1998) scrutinizes the "hot" and "weak" minds of the senile whom he searched out amid the neighborhoods of Varanasi, but in Mangaldihi such changes in the mind—though noted at times—were not commonly stressed as constitutive of old age.

Well-educated Brahmans in Mangaldihi would also sometimes discuss aging in terms of the *āśrama dharma* schema: the idealized four-stage life cycle of the *dharmaśāstras*, the classical Hindu ethical-legal texts.[4] In this schema, men move through a series of four life stages or "shelters" (*āśramas*)—as a student, a married householder, a disengaged forest dweller (*vānaprastha*), and finally a wandering renouncer (*sannyāsī*).[5] When a man sees the sons of his sons and white hair on his head he knows it is time to enter the forest-dweller phase—departing from his home to live as a hermit, or remaining in the household but with a mind focused on God. The final life stage is conceptualized as a time of complete abnegation of the phenomenal world and its pleasures and ties. Some in Mangaldihi compared spiritually minded elders (especially Brahman men) to the forest dwellers or renunciants of the *āśrama dharma* schema, a comparison I scrutinize further in chapter 4.

The people I knew in Mangaldihi often explained the workings, meanings of, and values behind the transitions of aging by referring to transactions—who gives what to whom, and when, and why. In the previous chapter, I described how substantial-emotional connections of maya were created between kin and close companions through sharing and exchanging substances, such as food, material goods, a house's space, breast milk, body particles, words, and the like. But people did more than *share* goods with one another (a relationship I will call "mutuality," following Raheja 1988, esp. p. 243). They also defined and created relatedness in terms of three other distinct modes of transacting, which I will call long-term (deferred) reciprocity (e.g., a parent provides food for a child, expecting the grown child to provide food for the parent years later in return), centrality and peripherality (e.g., an adult is positioned in the donative center of a household, distributing goods and services to peripheral children and elders), and hierarchy (seniors, the "increased" and "grown" folk, give out blessings and guidance to, and receive services and respect from, juniors and little ones).

Gloria Raheja (1988), in her analysis of the prestations or gifts given and received by people in the northern Indian village of Pahansu, has also found it useful to think of configurations of castes and kinsmen in Pahansu in a tripartite set of transactional dimensions—"mutuality," "centrality," and "hierarchy." Her study focuses on the prestations that move *between* households of different castes and kinsmen. In this chapter and the next, I focus on the kinds of givings and receivings that went on *within* households in Mangaldihi. And though an important part of Raheja's study of interhousehold prestations surrounds the dispersal of "inauspiciousness," I encountered no similar transfers within Mangaldihi households. By examining household transactions, I shed light on the internal dynamics of families and on how relations of aging and gender were constituted, thought about, and valued.

LONG-TERM RELATIONS: RECIPROCITY AND INDEBTEDNESS

People in Mangaldihi described Bengali family relations as entailing long-term bonds of reciprocal indebtedness extending throughout life and even after death; focusing on this transactional relationship provided one of their main ways of speaking about the connections binding the generations. Juniors provided care for their elderly parents, reconstructed relations with parents as ancestors after death, and ritually nourished these ancestors as a means of repaying the tremendous debts (*ṛṇ*) owed for producing and caring for them in infancy and childhood. According to my informants, this—the moral obligation to repay the vast debts incurred—was the primary reason adult children cared for their aged parents and nurtured their parents as ancestors after death.[6]

The process of producing and raising children was described by Mangaldihians as a series of givings. Parents give their newborn children a body, made up of their own blood—from the father's seed or semen (*śukra,* a distilled form of blood) and the mother's uterine blood (*rakta, ārtab*), which nourishes the fetus in the womb (*garbha*).[7] Parents then nourish their children with food: a mother's breast milk (*buker dudh*), rice, and treats of sweets and fruit. They also provide their children with material necessities—clothing, bedding, money, and the like. They clean up their infants' urine and feces. They are responsible for their children's having the whole series of life or family cycle rituals (*saṃskārs*), from birth through marriage. And finally, through all of these givings, they endure tremendous suffering (*kaṣṭa*). In the end, after giving to and constructing their children, the parents have largely depleted their own resources and thus they advance to a "senior" (*buṛo*) life phase.

But this series of givings from adult parents to younger children is only one phase of a much longer story. According to Mangaldihians, by giving to and raising their children, parents create in their offspring a tremendous moral debt, or *ṛṇ,* that can never be entirely repaid. Yet children are obligated to *strive* as best they can to pay it off by returning in kind the gifts once given to them, principally by providing for their parents when they become old and by ritually nourishing their parents as ancestors after death. As Gurusaday Mukherjee, Khudi Thakrun's eldest son, explained:

> Looking after parents is the children's (*cheleder*)[8] duty (*kartabya*). Sons pay back (*śodh kare*) the debt (*ṛṇ*) to their parents of childbirth and being raised by them. The mother and father suffer so much (*khubi kaṣṭa kare*) to raise their children. They can't sleep; they wake up in the middle of the night. They clean up their [children's] bowel movements. They worry terribly when the children are sick. And the mother especially suffers (*māyer beśi kaṣṭa hae*). She carries the child in her womb for ten [lunar] months, and she raises him from the blood and milk from her breasts. So if you don't care for your parents, then great sin (*khubi pāp*) and injustice (*anyāe*) happens.

Another Brahman man and family ritual priest serving Mangaldihi, Nimai Bhattcharj, provided a similar explanation:

> Caring for parents is the children's duty (*kartabya*); it is *dharma.* As parents raised their children, children will also care for their parents during their sick years, when they get old (*bṛiddha*). For example, if I am old and I have a bowel movement, my son will clean it and he won't ask, "Why did you do it there?" This is what we did for him when he was young. When I am old and dying, who will take me to go pee and defecate? My children will have to do it.

Women also spoke to me of the long-term relations of reciprocal interdependence and indebtedness they had as daughters-in-law and mothers-in-law. As I will describe below, daughters largely cleared their debts toward their own parents when they married, inheriting at the same time new obligations toward their husbands' parents. These new relations between daughters-in-law and parents-in-law were in part conceived of as reciprocal—for daughters-in-law were often married as young girls. This was especially true of the older women of Mangaldihi, whose marriages took place before child marriage regulations were implemented in India, when brides often were girls as young as eight, five, or even two. Many of these women described how they were cared for, raised, and nurtured by their mothers-in-law as new brides, sleeping with their mothers-in-law at night, and even—one woman told me—nursing from a mother-in-law's breasts. Choto Ma explained the relations of reciprocal interdependence that she, as an older woman, now had with her daughters-in-law: "If our [daughters-in-law] didn't care for us, then who would? At this age? We took these daughters-in-law in. And in our time, our mothers-in-law took us in and cared for us. . . . Now we are dependent on our sons and on our daughters-in-law. It has to be done this way."

The attempt to pay back parents (or parents-in-law) the debts of birth and rearing does not end with care in old age, people said, but continues after death—as children suffer a period of death-separation impurity (*aśauc*) for their parents, perform funeral rites, reconstruct their parents as ancestors, and ritually nourish them. As Subal Gorai put it as he approached the end of the rigorous month of death-separation impurity for his deceased mother: "We must do the observances [of death-separation impurity] for our parents. In doing observances for our mother, we pay her back (*śodh karā hae*) for raising us. She suffered very much for us, so we will now suffer for her also. . . . But our suffering cannot equal hers. We are trying to pay [her] back but we cannot ever do it." When villagers reasoned about such issues with me—about what children give to and owe their aged and deceased parents—I was struck by the near-identity of what parents once gave to their children and what children are later obligated to return. These reciprocated gifts included the gift of a body (after death), food, material necessities, the cleaning of urine and excrement, the final *saṃskār* or funeral rites, and the suffering and toil (*kaṣṭa*) that all of these acts of giving and supporting entailed (table 4).

Some of these forms of reciprocal transaction have already been illustrated by villagers quoted above. For instance, villagers often described their own and others' relations with aged parents by relating how they as adult children clean up the urine and excrement of their parents without complaining, just as their parents once tended to them when they were infants. As we have seen, Nimai Bhattcharj reasoned, "For example, if I am old and I have a bowel movement, my son will clean it and he won't ask, 'Why did you do it there?' This is what we did for him when he was young." Mangaldihi villagers frequently praised the way one Brahman man, Syam Thakur, cared for his very aged father with unfailing devotion until the day he died; Syam Thakur, I was told repeatedly, would himself take the excrement-covered sheets from his father's bed to the pond to be washed, three or four times a day if necessary, never complaining and never (several remarked) tempted to feed his father less so that there would be less waste produced. Although not all old people become incontinent, dealing with a parent's urine and feces was often held up as a paradigmatic component of the relation between an adult child and an elderly parent.

Moreover, people said, just as parents construct their children's bodies by giving birth to them and nourishing them with food, so children (particularly sons) must provide new bodies for their parents after death. I will later explain in detail (chapter 5) the elaborate series of Hindu funeral rituals by which juniors construct new subtle, ancestral bodies for their deceased seniors, and then carefully nourish these bodies through ongoing ritual feedings. In fact, the ten-day (or sometimes longer) period of death-separation

Table 4. Relations of Long-term, Deferred Reciprocity

Phase 1: Initial giving (dāoyā)		*Phase 2: Reciprocated giving, or the deferred repaying of debts (ṛṇ)*	
Medium of Transaction	*Transactors, Senior —> Junior*	*Medium of Transaction*	*Transactors, Junior —> Senior*
Body	Parent —> child	Body	Son (junior —> parent of male line) (*pret, pitṛ*)
Food		Food	
Breast milk	Mother —> child	(Cow's) milk	Junior —> elder, *pret, pitṛ*
Rice	Parent —> child	Rice	Junior —> elder, *pret, pitṛ*
Treats (fruit, sweets, etc.)	Senior —> junior	Treats	Junior —> elder, *pret, pitṛ*
Material goods		Material goods	
Clothing, money, etc.	Parent —> child	Clothing, money, etc.	Junior —> elder, *pret*
Services		Services	
Clean up urine and excrement, daily care, etc.	Parent —> child	Clean up urine and excrement, daily care, etc.	Junior —> Elder
Saṃskārs		*Saṃskārs*	
First feeding of rice, marriage, etc.	Parent —> child	Funeral rites	Juniors —> *pret, pitṛ* (of male line)

KEY:
—> Direction of transaction.
Junior May include a child, child's spouse, grandchild, niece, nephew, etc., and especially sons and daughters-in-law.
Senior May include a parent, parent-in-law, grandparent, aunt, uncle, departed spirit (*pret*), ancestor (*pitṛ*), especially those within one's own family line.
Elder A senior when old.
Pret Departed spirit (see chapter 5).
Pitṛ Ancestor (see chapter 5).

impurity that survivors endure when an elder dies was sometimes compared by villagers to the ten-month period of gestation during which an infant is produced in the womb (cf. Parry 1982:85). And several of my informants stated that by giving birth to their own children, they are also fulfilling a debt (*ṛṇ*) to their parents to produce children to carry on the family line, just as their parents had produced them.[9] By performing the last funeral rites for their parents, children also reciprocate the gift of a *saṃskār* to them. Parents construct their children by giving them the series of *saṃskārs* from birth through marriage, and in turn children give their parents the final *saṃskār*, the "last rites" (*antyeṣṭi*) and "faithful offerings" (*śrāddha*), after death.

Providing parents with food in late life and after death was regarded by villagers as perhaps the most fundamental of all filial obligations. People providing care for their parents in old age often spoke of "giving [them] rice" (*bhāt dāoyā*). They especially stressed the effort mothers expend in nourishing their children, feeding them milk from their own breasts, and the children's obligation to reciprocate this nurturing. Subal Gorai said with emotion as he ministered to his mother during her last days, "[My mother] fed me with milk from her own breasts; how could I not feed her now?" If families could afford it, they often tried to provide their elders, as they do young children, special treats such as fruit and sweets made from milk. Villagers explained that as people grow older, their desire (*lobh*) for special kinds of food increases; if possible this desire should be indulged a bit. After a death occurred, too, junior survivors spent a great deal of effort feeding rice, water, and treats (milk, honey, yogurt, fruit, sweets) to the departed spirit and the ancestors.

Finally, villagers said that adult children have an obligation to provide their aged and deceased parents with the material goods needed to live comfortably. Living parents should receive clothing, a place to sleep, perhaps a little spending money, their medications, and the like; once deceased, in the funeral rites they receive clothing, shoes, a bed, eating utensils, an umbrella, money, and so forth. In this way, just as parents once provided their children with the substance of household life, the children years later reciprocate with these same kinds of goods.

All of these "gifts" to aged and deceased parents—performing the final *saṃskār*, constructing new bodies for them, cleaning them of urine and feces, feeding them, and providing them with material necessities—were spoken of as acts entailing considerable effort (*jatna*) and suffering (*kaṣṭa*). But no matter how much effort the children exert, I was told, they can never equal their parents in suffering and expense.

By engaging in this series of reciprocal transactions, people in Mangaldihi worked to construct long-term bonds of interdependence that connected people across the fluctuations of family life. Crucial to these reciprocations was the dimension of time. Those who engaged in a transaction (of food, a body, material goods) at one particular time (as a gift from parent to child) potentially gained something beyond that time—in future material returns and desired acts provided by their children much later, when they were old. Other anthropologists, such as Marcel Mauss (1967 [1925]) and Nancy Munn (1986), have looked at the kinds of transactions or gift exchanges practiced by people in various parts of the world that similarly aim to create debts in the receiver and thereby possibly win later benefits for the giver. In Mangaldihi, the dynamic applied within intergenerational transactions. The reciprocated transaction was *deferred* to a later family phase, when the parents had become old and the children were adult householders (figure 1). Thus, a major concern here was the *durability* of family relations over time, and not simply the equivalence of reciprocated exchanges.

This kind of thinking—investing now for future family phases and reciprocated returns—was explicit in villagers' reasoning about why they provided care for their elders. At the same time that adult householders were providing for their elders, they were also raising their own children—and looking ahead to the time when *they* would be in the position of the elder receivers, and their own children would (they hoped) be doing the providing. As one woman told me: "If we don't serve and respect our elders, then . . . my own sons and daughters-in-law will not serve me when I get old. If I don't serve my *śāśuṛī* (mother-in-law) now, when I get old, my son will ask me, 'Did you serve your *śāśuṛī?* Why should I serve you?'"

Such long-term reciprocal transactions also served in large part to maintain the "bindings" of a *saṃsār,* or family. A child may cry out in hunger, causing a "pull" (*ṭān*) in his mother—and the mother will give him or her a breast to nurse, or supply a plate of food. So an aging mother can also "pull" in hunger on the bindings that tie her to her child when her breasts are empty of milk in late life—and expect her grown child to provide food in return. These gifts of food, material goods, and bodies back and forth over several family phases and even in death played a major role in sustaining households and family lines, as well as the people who made them up.

Sylvia Vatuk (1990:66 and passim) also writes of relations of "long-term intergenerational reciprocity" within Indian families living near Delhi. She suggests that this conception of parent-child reciprocity as a "life-span relationship" sharply distinguishes Indian from American views of dependence in old age. Studies such as those by Margaret Clark (1972), Margaret Clark and Barbara Anderson (1967), and Maria Vesperi (1985) reveal that many

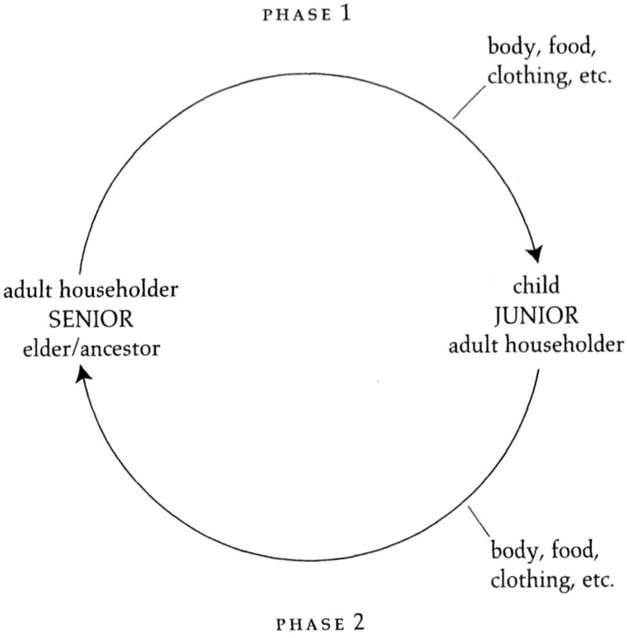

In phase 1	Seniors as adult householders are the givers, juniors as children are the recipients, and a debt *(ṛṇ)* is created in the juniors to reciprocate what is given.
In phase 2	Juniors as adult householders reciprocate gifts to seniors as elders and ancestors; the debts are partially (although never fully) repaid.
In both phases:	The media of transaction are the same; the givers and receivers are simply reversed.

Figure 1. Relations of long-term, deferred reciprocity.

Americans find the need to depend on younger relatives for support in old age destructive to their sense of self-esteem and value as a responsible person. They are distressed primarily because the relationship between an aged parent and younger caregiver is generally *not* perceived by these Americans—either the older person or the caregiver—as reciprocal, but rather as a one-way flow of benefits from the caretaker to the "dependent" (S. Vatuk 1990:65). Furthermore, most Americans expect the benefits in parent-child transactions to flow "down," not "up" from children to parents. It is proper for parents to give to children (even, through gifts of money or inheritances, when their children are adults); but if an adult child gives to an aged parent, then the parent is seen as childlike. Vesperi studied growing old in a Florida city, where these old people "find themselves in life situations where they are defined *a priori* as dependent and child-like. They exist as supplicants, not as partners in reciprocal exchange. The supplicant is a shadowy form, an empty coffer; he or she receives but is not expected to give in return" (1985:71).

Of course, the degree of dependence in old age varies according to class and ethnicity; the problem is particularly acute for poorer people, who late in their lives have no accrued estate to draw from and potentially pass on to children. In *Discipline and Punish* (1979), Michel Foucault raises issues that pertain to this negative construction of dependence in old age. In a modern industrial society, he points out, people have been defined in terms of their ability to produce wealth and the means of their own subsistence; anything less is disciplined or despised.

As I will explore in greater depth in the following chapter, many people in and around Mangaldihi did indeed wonder and worry whether their children would feed them rice in old age; others lived in such poverty that they were unable to support aged family members, however much they might wish to; and still others were left with no children even to hope to depend on. Nonetheless, most continued to think of parent-child relations as long-term reciprocal ones, and those who knew something of the United States reflected on the care, or what they had heard to be the *non*care, of the American elderly with horror. In Mangaldihi, even as many perceived faults and flaws in their relationships, the majority of "senior" people were cared for by sons and their wives in households crowded with cooking fires and descendants (table 5, page 54).

The Marriage of Daughters: Repaying Parental Debts with Mouse's Earth

It was at the marriages of their children that parents instigated the new phase in which the direction of giving would be reversed and begin to flow from children to parents. Specific portions of the marriage rituals performed for both sons and daughters dealt with the issue of repaying debts to parents, though to quite different effect. Women and men in Mangaldihi told me how daughters, like sons, incur vast debts toward their parents by virtue of being produced and raised by them; but unlike a son, a daughter ritually clears away these debts when she marries by performing a ritual of "giving

Table 5. Mangaldihi's Seniors: Sources of Support, 1990

Source of Support	*Number of Seniors*
Lived with sons and *bous*	64
Lived with daughter or other close relatives	5
Supported self through labor (maidservant, cow tender, maker of cow dung patties, etc.)	17
Supported self through independent income (property, savings, etc.)	4
Beggar	3
Total	93

NOTE: "Senior" here was defined as anyone whom my research assistant Dipu (who conducted most of the house-to-house village census) and the household members he spoke with considered to be "senior," "increased," or "old" (*bṛiddha, buṛo*). These were generally those whose children were all married, who had gray or graying hair, who wore mostly white, and so on. All those listed as self-supporting lived adjacent to junior kin.

mouse's earth" (*ĩdurer māṭi dāoyā*) as she leaves her father's home for her father-in-law's home. The morning after the nightlong marriage ceremonies have been performed at the bride's father's home, the bride, groom, and the bride's mother perform a ritual of parting (*bidāe*), one of whose functions is to enable the departing daughter to "pay back" (*śodh karā*) her parents, and especially her mother, for the debts (*ṛṇ*) she has incurred growing up. The mother, daughter, and groom come together next to the vehicle that will carry the daughter and her husband away—usually a rented car ("taxi") if the family is fairly wealthy, a cycle rickshaw or oxcart if poor. Neighbors and relatives crowd around to watch the poignant event, often with tears streaming.

The mother blesses the bride and groom, imbuing them with auspicious substances by first washing their feet with turmeric paste and milk, and then touching their feet with whole rice grains (*dhān*) and sacred grass (*kuśa*). Next she wipes their feet with her unbound hair. Villagers explained that by this act a mother maintains connections with her daughter, even as she sends her away. Hair, especially in its unbound or "open" (*kholā*) condition (i.e., not braided or tied up in a knot), is thought to have properties very conducive to mixing or connecting. A mother also wipes the navel of her newborn child with unbound hair after the umbilical cord has been cut, to mitigate the separative effects of severing this physical bond. So, villagers explained, a mother wipes her departing daughter with her unbound hair to keep the mother and daughter "one" (*ek*). If she were to wipe her daughter's feet (or her newborn child's navel) with her hand, which is colder and more contained, the child would become "other" (*par*).[10] Finally, the mother wipes dry the feet of the bride and groom with a cotton towel, or *gāmchā.*

The critical point of the ritual comes next: the bride's mother stands, opens the blouse under her sari, and has her daughter gesture toward nursing at her breast. Up until now, villagers explained, the mother has nurtured her daughter, and she offers her daughter her breast for the last time, before she turns her over to be fed and supported by her husband and his family. The daughter then takes from a handkerchief a handful of earth dug from a mouse hole (*ĩdurer māṭi,* "the earth of a mouse") and places it into a fold in her mother's sari; she repeats the act three times, as her mother hands the earth back to her. With each offering, the daughter repeats, "Ma, all that I have eaten from you for so many days, I pay back today with this mouse's earth" (*Mā, eto din tomār jā kheyechilām, āj ei ĩdurer māṭi diye tā śodh karlām*). Mother and daughter usually weep as they perform this final act. The mother hands the bride a brass tray or cup filled with rice and sweets that the bride is to give to her mother-in-law when she arrives at her new home. The mother then turns away in tears and usually does not watch her daughter depart.

I heard several theories on the ritual significance of mouse's earth. Some thought that because mice live in the house and eat rice grains, the staple food of a household, they are in some ways like the goddess Laksmi, the goddess of wealth and prosperity who is associated with rice. Mouse's earth can therefore be regarded as a form of wealth, like rice, and can be given to a mother in compensation for her considerable expenditures. Alternatively, Lina Fruzzetti (1982:55–56), who describes a similar ritual among other Bengali women, suggests that the earth of a mouse represents the life of a married woman, who shifts wealth from house to house as the mouse shifts earth. The explanation that seemed most convincing to me, however, derived from the ritual's triviality. Several village women told me emphatically that of course a daughter's debts to her parents can never be truly repaid. That is why the daughter gives such a worthless item to her mother before she leaves, making it plain that she has not matched the value of the debt. One mother of four as yet unmarried daughters said to me, "Can the debt [to one's parents] be paid back with the earth of a mouse? No! That debt will not be repaid."

Nonetheless, because she had gone through the ritual motions of paying back her mother with mouse's earth, a married daughter's debts toward her parents were regarded as formally erased. With the clearing of this debt, the bride also weakened her bonds with her parents, for indebtedness entails a connection between two parties. Not understanding the positive local function of indebtedness, I unwittingly insulted several neighborhood women early on in my stay in Mangaldihi by attempting to pay off debts, returning a borrowed cup of sugar, or paying a few rupees in exchange for having a sari's hem sewn. They would say to me, hurt, "What are you trying to do? Pay back [the debt] and cut off all ties?" For this reason, many mothers told me that they found the ritual of being paid back by their daughters almost impossible to endure. "To hear a daughter say, 'I have paid off my debts to you' (*tomār ṛṇ śodh karlām*)," one woman said, "gives so much pain." Some mused that they would try to find others to perform the ritual in their stead, a husband's brother's wife or the like, but I never saw this happen.

By clearing her parental debts and moving on to her husband's and father-in-law's home, a daughter thus removes herself from the cycle of long-term reciprocal transactions that tie her natal family together. A daughter receives from her parents for years but repays these debts in a ritual instant only, which ends her most vital transactions with them. On rare occasions, especially if there were no sons in the family, a daughter would support her aged parents (see table 5); but doing so was not regarded as her obligation (*dāyitva*). Married daughters also usually continued to visit their natal homes, several times a year and even for weeks at a time, especially over the first few years of marriage. On such visits, they often secretly gave their mothers gifts of money, sari blouses, petticoats, and the like, especially if their husbands' households were better off than their parents'. However, people believed that it did not look good if a married daughter gave too much to her natal parents. Married daughters are transformed from *nijer lok,* "own people," to *kuṭumbs*, relatives by marriage,[11] and thus no longer rightfully had the role of looking after and providing for their parents.

A married daughter does, however, inherit new debts toward her parents-in-law, just as her husband and parents-in-law take on the responsibility of supporting her. The newly married bride brings to her father-in-law's home a brass tray of rice and sweets that she gives to her mother-in-law upon arrival, and this initial gift demonstrates that she has now taken on the obligation to serve and give to them (see also Fruzzetti 1982:55). A daughter-in-law (*bou*) not only provides much of the labor of serving her husband's parents while they are alive, she also must join her husband in observing death-separation impurity, performing funeral rites, and ritually nourishing her parents-in-law as ancestors after their deaths. The daughter-in-law's position as caretaker and server of her husband's parents will become clearer as we examine the marriage rituals of a son.

The Marriage of Sons, the Bringing of Daughters-in-Law, and the Repaying of Parental Debts

Before a son leaves to be married, he performs a ritual that in some respects parallels the daughter's ritual of giving mouse's earth to her mother. As this marriage constitutes the beginning of the parents' "senior" or "increased" age and the end in many ways of the son's childhood dependence on them, the son must mark the shift in direction of the reciprocal relationship with his parents, instigating a new family phase in which he (and his wife) will begin to give to and pay back his parents in exchange for all that they have given to him.

The groom is accompanied on his journey to the bride's home, where the marriage ceremonies will take place, by a group of relatives and friends known as the *bar jātrī*, or "groom's procession," but he leaves his parents behind at home. Immediately before the groom departs, his mother performs a series of ritual acts similar to those for a departing bride-daughter. She washes her son's feet with turmeric paste, milk, and water and wipes them first with her unbound hair and then with a cotton towel. She next stands and is supposed to have her son symbolically nurse at her breast one last time. In practice, many mothers and sons skip this part of the ritual, out of "embarrassment" (*lajjā*). But everyone I spoke with agreed that the offering of the breast or the "feeding of milk" (*dudh khāoyāno*) *should* be done. It signifies, I was told, that the mother's "work" (*kāj*) toward her son is now finished. For his whole life, the mother has fed and cared for her son through offerings of breast milk, food, and love; but from now on his wife will look after him instead.

At this point, the ritual diverges significantly from that performed for a departing daughter-bride. The mother asks her son three times, "Oh, son, where are you going?" And the son responds three times, "Ma, I'm going to bring you a servant" (*Mā, tomār dāsī ānte jābo*). Instead of clearing his debts to his mother by giving her mouse's earth, he announces—with the same number of repetitions as in the bride's ritual—that he will be bringing home a wife, who will be a "servant," or *dāsī*, to her. This daughter-in-law or servant is thus in some ways equivalent to the mouse's earth that a daughter gives her mother—both are offered to a mother in exchange for what she has previously given her child. The son brings home a wife and daughter-in-law to take on with him the obligation of serving his parents and bearing sons to continue the family line. In this way, a son begins the phase of reciprocating his tremendous debts toward his parents, and a daughter-in-law inherits the burden of providing much of the labor that goes into this reciprocation.

CENTRALITY AND PERIPHERALITY

The shift to a new phase in family relations of deferred reciprocity, as sons and their wives begin to give to their aging parents, also brings about a repositioning of family members. The principal married couple of a house whose sons were not yet married were felt to be at the warm, reproductive, and redistributive human "center" (*mājhkhāne*) of life in a Bengali household: they gave food, knowledge, and services to and made decisions for all the others around them, including retirees and the young children who were located on the household's peripheries (figure 2).

Their removal to the outer peripheries of a household brought significant changes for the elders. Although peripherality granted senior men and especially women increased freedoms—to give up burdensome work, wander outside of the household, visit friends or married daughters—it also usually entailed forfeitures of power. Indeed, becoming peripheral within a household was accompanied by losses along many of the same dimensions—of space, transactions, and power—involved in being low caste in Mangaldihi. Much as Brahmans were regarded as being at the "center of the village" (*grāmer mājhkhāne*), with the other, lower castes on "all four sides" (*cārdike*), married adults were viewed as occupying the spatial centers of their households. Brahmans also had more control than any other group over transactions and distributions concerning village resources, such as land, rice, and money, for they owned the largest amount of land, held by far the greatest number of salaried jobs, and hired many of the lower castes as employees and sharecroppers. The lower castes were thus largely supported—albeit often inadequately, many asserted—by the Brahmans, just as the old (and young) were supported by the adults in their families. As a result, Brahmans tended to have the most political and economic power within the village (although the lower *jātis* in Mangaldihi were increasingly gaining local powers, in part because of land reforms and in part because of the *panchāyat* system of local self-government, which now ensured that there would always be a Bagdi representative). Likewise, it was adult householders who tended to have the most domestic power or authority. Although

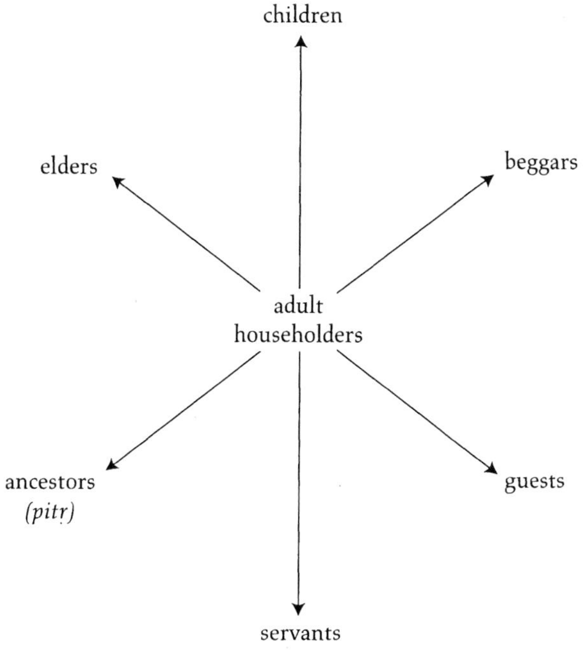

Figure 2. Relations of centrality.

some wealthier, stronger-willed, or more revered seniors, like Khudi Thakrun, often retained quite a lot of domestic authority and centrality until their deaths, their voices were also frequently dismissed by juniors as empty *bak bak* words—just so much hot air and chatter.

HIERARCHIES: SERVING AND BLESSING

At the same time that elders moved out to the relatively powerless peripheries of their households, they also moved "up" on a hierarchical scale of junior-senior relations. Juniors in Mangaldihi gave to and served their elders not only because they were morally obligated to reciprocate their parents' earlier gifts but also because an elder person had a superior position in this hierarchy. Old people were considered to be "big" (*boṛo*), "increased" (*bṛiddha*), "venerable people" (*gurujan*), "over others" (*laker apar*), and even "similar to gods" (*ṭhākurer moto*). Villagers frequently commented that the relationship older parents have with their children is like that of a god and devotee (see also Inden and Nicholas 1977:27).

My landlord's sister Saraswati expounded their society's attitudes toward the aged: "We think of our elders like God (*bhagavān*). . . . We call our grandparents *ṭhākur-mā* (literally, 'god-mother') and *ṭhākur-dādā* (literally, 'god–elder brother') because they are like *ṭhākur*s (visible gods) to us."[12] People in Mangaldihi also often compared Khudi Thakrun to a *ṭhākur* or god. My companion Hena said, "We respect Khudi Thakrun very much, because of her age (*bayas*). Once they get to be that increased (*bṛiddha*), they are *ṭhākur*s (visible gods)." Another young girl exclaimed to me as we roamed through the village lanes past Khudi Thakrun's house: "Khudi Thakrun is the biggest [or 'oldest,' *sab ceye boṛo*] of the whole village. And such a large village as Mangaldihi! That means that she is equal to a god (*ṭhākurer samān*)!" In this hierarchical sense, old persons could be compared to the *higher* castes and classes in Mangaldihi. "Big" (*boṛo*) is a multivalent term with overlapping meanings: a person could be "big" as an elder by having increased his or her seniority, knowledge, and connections over a long life; "big" as a rich person who has accumulated much material wealth; or "big" as a person of a high (*ucca*) caste.

Providing *sevā*, or "service," was one of the major ways that juniors in Mangaldihi brought the hierarchical dimension of their relations with their elders to the fore. This term, like *sevā karā*, "to serve," has implications of rank in Bengali, just as it does in English. In Mangaldihi, *sevā* was something performed for temple deities as well as for elders, and also sometimes for employers.[13] When performed for deities, *sevā* included keeping the temple clean, providing the deity (*ṭhākur*) with daily food and water, offering the deity respectful devotion or *bhaktī*, and often giving the deity daily baths, fanning it in the summer to provide cool relief, and laying it down to sleep for an afternoon rest and at night.

Providing *sevā* for an elder involved similar practices. First, it entailed satisfying the elder's bodily needs and comforts. Aged men and women who praised the service they received from their adult sons and daughters-in-law detailed their ministrations with great specificity: they were fed several times a day, with care and before all others; their legs and feet were massaged; their backs were oiled; their hair was combed and braided; their bodies were fanned in the summer heat; their clothes were washed and their bedrolls were laid out at night. Rendering service to elders also included providing medical care if needed, and the dark-rimmed eyeglasses displayed prominently on the faces of many of Mangaldihi's better-off elders signified the *sevā* of their sons.

Within the first few days of marriage, a daughter-in-law (*bou* or *boumā*) was also expected to begin to perform acts of *sevā* toward her parents-in-law. A new *bou* may shyly and submissively approach her father-in-law to begin massaging his feet as he rests, or she may go to her mother-in-law to pluck out her gray hairs. If a *bou* did not herself initiate such service, a mother-in-law or other senior relative would often gently direct the new *bou* to do so, as serving her in-laws was regarded as one of her most important duties as a wife.

Within the first several weeks following a wedding, it was common for a mother-in-law to travel with her new *bou,* with or without the son, to the homes of relatives to show her off and introduce her to the wider family. One such mother-in-law, my landlord's older sister Saraswati, arrived one day in Mangaldihi with her first daughter-in-law just a week or so after the wedding. Saraswati spent several hours in my home with her *bou,* talking to me about how young people care for their elders in Bengali society. As she spoke, she seemed to gloat with pleasure and pride as she had her gray hairs plucked and her feet massaged by her *bou.* Receiving this service as a mother-in-law was new to her, just as providing it was new to her daughter-in-law, who was about seventeen. This young woman, quiet and submissive, also appeared proud of her novel role of dutifully serving her mother-in-law. Not all *bous* were so eager to serve, but her demeanor was not uncommon. She blushed with pride and embarrassment as the neighbors and relatives praised her service, and as her mother-in-law proclaimed, "Our *bou* is very good. She knows how to work. She rubs oil on our feet. She respects and serves us (*bhaktī-sevā kare*)."

Sevā also included acts of deference. Elders expected their juniors to comply with (*mānā*) their requests, to refrain from talking back and arguing, and to ask their advice (*upadeś*) when making decisions. The young people were also expected to feel "respectful devotion" or *bhaktī* for their elders, a hierarchical form of love also felt for a deity. To display this devotion, as well as inferior status, a junior would often bow down before an elder and would place the dust from the elder's feet on his or her head; this act, called *praṇām,* is performed by devotees for a deity and by servants at times for their employers. To show deference, Bengalis also generally avoid using any senior person's personal name, using instead an appropriate kin term, such as grandmother (*ṭhākurmā, didimā*), father's sister (*pisi*), elder brother (*dādā*), and so forth. Taken together, these acts of deference and respectful devotion manifested *sevā;* if they were not performed, an elder would feel that he or she was not being served well.

Many, however, felt that the obligations of *sevā* could never be satisfied. According to many elders, juniors can never give enough, in the right way, at the right times. According to many juniors, elders make impossible, unjust, unreasonable demands—insisting on a mango months past mango sea-son, demanding a cup of tea after the cooking fire has already been put out, urinating and defecating in bed so many times that no other household work can be done except keep them clean.

Providing *sevā* is ironically also a form of power. At the same time that *sevā* overtly signifies the superiority of the elder being served, more covertly it reveals the elder's declining domestic power and bodily strength. Many of the acts that constitute *sevā* embody this double meaning. As a new, young daughter-in-law submissively plucks the gray hairs from her mother-in-law's head, she displays at the same time the weakening and aging of her mother-in-law's body. The massage also has a double signification: the subservience and inferiority of the junior who provides it, and the worn limbs and weakened body of the senior being massaged. The act of cleaning up an elder's urine and excrement marks a junior's hierarchically inferior position, as someone who will accept even the impure (*aśuddha*) feces of a superior; but it points sharply as well to the elder's incontinence, loss of control over even basic bodily functions, and infantility. Similarly, sons often asked their aged fathers for advice about decisions that both knew the elder really had no control over. As *sevā* demonstrates the aged moving "up" in a hierarchy of older and superior over younger and inferior, it is also part of their movement "out" to the peripheries of household life, where domestic power and bodily strength have diminished.

Blessings, Curses, and Affection: Hierarchical Gifts from Seniors to Juniors

Sevā does not constitute simply a one-way transaction, a flow of services, goods, and benefits from junior to senior. According to Mangaldihi villagers, elders also provided a series of what I call "hierarchical gifts" to their juniors—blessings in exchange for *sevā* and *praṇām*, affection in exchange for respectful devotion, but also curses and complaints to retaliate against neglect. These kinds of gifts were not the same as what parents gave to children as adults and then ceased to give in late life (food, bodies, material goods, etc.); rather parents, as seniors and superiors to their children, provided them *throughout* their lives. These transactions, we will see, were crucial in constituting relations of junior-senior hierarchy within Mangaldihi families (see table 6 and figure 3).

First, it is important to note that although elders may lose much of their previous physical power—for example, control over acquiring and distributing material goods; centrality amid the material exchanges (of food, money, goods, and the like) within households—they were thought to gain

Table 6. Relations of Hierarchy

	Transactors	
Media of Transaction	*Senior* ↓ *Junior*	*Senior* ↑ *Junior*
POSITIVE		
Actions and words	Blessings	*Praṇām*
	Blessings	*Sevā*
	Requests, commands, advice	Compliance, deference, listening
Sentiments (forms of love, *bhālobāsā*)	*Sneha* (affection)	*Bhaktī* (respectful devotion)
NEGATIVE		
Actions and words	Curses	Withholding *prāṇām*
	Complaints	*Sevā*
Sentiments	Dissatisfaction	Disrespect (*asammān*)

other kinds of powers, particularly verbal ones of cursing and blessing, and also of requesting, demanding, and complaining. According to Mangaldihians, old people could use these verbal powers (often subtly) to exert leverage over their juniors—providing a stream of blessings in exchange for acts of *sevā* and *praṇām*, and meting out curses when *sevā* was flagrantly withheld. Mangaldihi villagers said that the blessings (*āśīrbād*) of old people bring great rewards, and that their curses (*abhiśāp*) always "stick" (*lege jāe*). Fear of these curses and anticipation of blessings motivated many villagers, on their own account, to serve their elders well.

One twelve-year-old Mangaldihi girl, Chaitali, told me a story about these powers of old people; she spoke in hushed tones as she hung on my chair while I typed:

> Did you know that old people (*buṛo lok*) can give out curses and blessings, and that they always come to be? My grandfather gave my *jeṭhā* (father's older brother) a curse before he died. He said that my *jeṭhā*'s daughter would die. This was because my *jeṭhā* did not

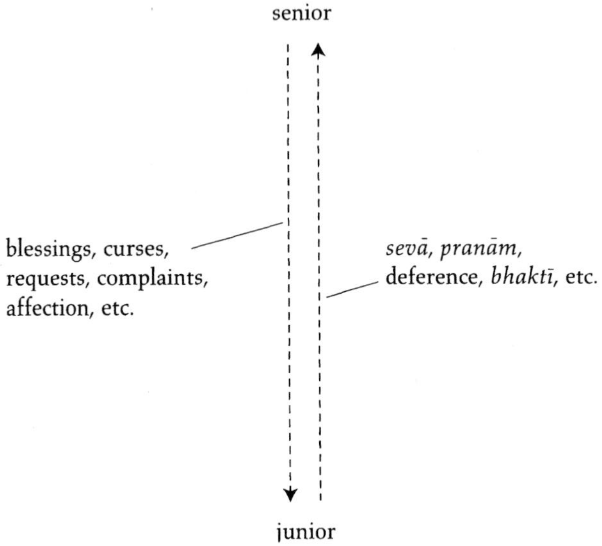

Figure 3. Relations of hierarchy.

> look after him. He didn't clean up his urine and excrement, and he didn't even send him money home from where he worked in Bihar. The curse came to pass [her tone was low and serious]. My *jeṭhā*'s daughter did die a few years ago. She was burned to death in a fire. But my grandfather gave *my* father [the younger son] blessings. My father cared for my grandfather until his death. He fed him and gave him a special chair to sit in, and he cleaned up all of his urine and excrement. So my grandfather gave my father a blessing that he would become rich. And he did.

Indeed, Chaitali's father had become one of the richest men in the village over the past decade or two, thanks to all sorts of profitable business deals involving his land and crops. I heard many other stories like this one in Mangaldihi—stories in which an old person heaps curses on a negligent son, or even in which a whole family line becomes extinct because of the angry curses of a vengeful, neglected elder. The damaging power of old people's curses was often invoked, sometimes after the fact, in explaining the extreme misfortunes befalling a family, such as the early death of a child or the extinction of a lineage.

Even more pervasive were the blessings (*āśīrbād*) that old people bestowed, often in generously flowing streams, in exchange for service, *praṇām,* and loving respect offered to them by their juniors. The most common way that juniors sought blessings and that elders gave them out was through acts of *praṇām*. *Praṇām* does not merely entail a junior's demonstration of respectful devotion to a superior but involves a two-way exchange: the junior or inferior bows down before an elder, and the elder places his or her hands on the junior's bowed head and offers blessings. Especially during ritual gatherings, when relatives assembled from near and far, older people tended to sit and receive endless acts of *praṇām* as they continuously gave gentle blessings: "May you be happy, may you live long, may you have a son, may you get a job, may your health be good, may you have well-being."

It was common to do *praṇām* to household elders each morning on rising, to demonstrate respect and receive blessings; and juniors in Mangaldihi almost always did *praṇām* to their elders before embarking on any sort of journey, to receive blessings to help them on their way. Many families also saved photographs or prints of their deceased elders' feet for the purpose of doing *praṇām* and receiving ancestral blessings. Elders also gave blessings when their juniors offered them acts of *sevā* by massaging their feet, plucking their gray hairs, providing them food or special treats, and the like. If the service or favor was particularly large and appreciated, such as a gift of a sweet ripe mango, then the string of blessings was longer and more enthusiastic.

We might well wonder how old people, who were in many ways thought to be "dry" (*śukna*) and depleted, had the ability to bless and curse. Villagers most frequently explained these verbal powers by pointing out the similarity of old people to gods or *ṭhākurs*, as "above" (*apar*) others, "big" (*boṛo*), "increased" (*bṛiddha*), and "venerable" (*gurujan*). Just as gods have the power to bestow blessings and curses, so do old people with their godlike qualities.

Older people were also thought to be like ascetics in lifestyle and in their largely white clothing; and some noted that both matched the final, *sannyāsa* stage of the *āśrama dharma* schema. Peter van der Veer (1989) states that ascetics gain powers to curse and bless largely through practicing austerities that transform sexual heat into stored creative heat, or *tāpas*, which can in turn be transformed into potent blessings and curses. Like ascetics, senior people in Mangaldihi were largely celibate and removed from many of the heat-producing exchanges at the center of household life. And many told me that as the bodies of old people cooled (as sexual heat cooled), their heads or minds (*māthā*) could remain hot, which often led to anger or excesses of words. Curses and blessings may be a manifestation of such mental or verbal heat, one remaining source of potency that enabled elders to gift their juniors, for good or ill. Some described old people as also having increased quantities of "wind" (*vāta*) in their bodies, a humor that is often associated with troublesome speech. So it may be a combination of factors that gave the verbal emissions of the elderly such destructive or beneficial potency.

In addition to the ability to curse and bless, old people possessed other verbal capacities: they could demand loudly that they be served, and they could complain publicly—causing much embarrassment for their families—that they are not being served well. Through case studies of several older people and their families in chapter 3, I provide illustrations of these kinds of verbal powers, wielded very effectively. As Sylvia Vatuk (1990:73) notes, however, many old people choose not to complain too publicly about the inadequate treatment they receive from juniors, for such complaints make themselves and their entire families, not only the negligent juniors, look bad.

Finally, Bengalis commonly view "affection" (*sneha*) as another gift that flows down from seniors to juniors, moving parallel to the "respectful devotion" (*bhaktī*) that their juniors offer up to them. Affection and respectful devotion are both considered to be forms of "love" (*bhālobāsā*) of the type given and received in hierarchical relationships, as between parents and children and between older and younger siblings (see also Inden and Nicholas 1977:25–29).

Thus, many of the daily transactions practiced by juniors and seniors within Mangaldihi families enforced hierarchical relations of the superior and older over the inferior and younger. What juniors gave to seniors (e.g., *sevā, praṇām, bhaktī*) and what seniors gave to juniors (e.g., blessings, curses, affection) were necessarily different—not equivalent, as in transactions of long-term or deferred reciprocity discussed above—because of each party's different statuses and capacities within the hierarchy. Even as the givers and receivers within relations of deferred reciprocity reversed when elders moved to the peripheries of the household and gave up many of their domestic powers, elders maintained their hierarchical position as superiors. This status would never be reversed and in fact only seemed to increase, as persons grew older and older (and thus more "increased" and godlike), and were then transformed into even more godlike ancestors.

Reciprocity, Centrality, Hierarchy, and Mutuality: Aspects of Family Relations in Mangaldihi

I have been describing the ways in which family relations were ordered and sustained by parents and children, parents-in-law and daughters-in-law, or seniors and juniors in Mangaldihi by means of different transactions—

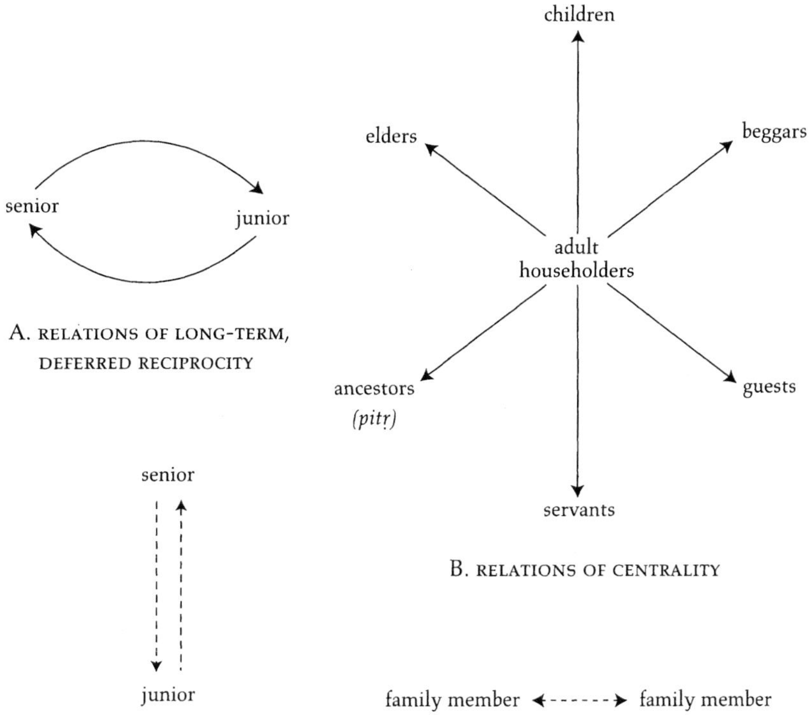

A. RELATIONS OF LONG-TERM, DEFERRED RECIPROCITY

B. RELATIONS OF CENTRALITY

C. RELATIONS OF HIERARCHY

D. RELATIONS OF MUTUALITY

Figure 4. Aspects of family relations in Mangaldihi. *These diagrams were inspired by Raheja's "Ordering of castes and kinsmen in Pahansu" (1988:243, fig. 14).*

of bodies, blood, breast milk, food, material goods, services, blessings, complaints—that in various contexts helped establish reciprocity, centrality, and hierarchy (see diagrams A, B, and C of figure 4). These three forms of ordering intergenerational relations were crucial, I have argued, to how Bengalis in Mangaldihi conceived of the nature of families, family moral systems, gender differences, and what it is to be old.

I began the chapter with another important dimension of family relations, however, which I called "mutuality" (see diagram D of figure 4). Relations of mutuality were also basic to constituting and sustaining families in Mangaldihi. They included acts that were repeated daily, were completed immediately, were nonhierarchical, and involved a mutual exchange of goods and substances—food, a house, love, touching, words—so that members of a household or family came to be mutual parts of each other. Such mutual

Table 7. Relations of Mutuality

Medium of Transaction	*Transactors: Family Member ⟷ Family Member*
Food	Sharing rice: eating rice from the same pot (*eki hā̃ṛite khāoyā*), being part of a "one rice household" (*ekānnabartī paribār*)
House	Living in the same house, being the same "house's people" (*gharer lok, bāṛir lok*)
Love	Giving and receiving *bhālobāsā*, mutual egalitarian love
Touching	Mutual touching, sitting and sleeping side by side, embracing, etc.
Words	Conversation, gossip, storytelling pleasantries, etc.

NOTE: Transactions of mutuality are participated in by all members of a household, not only (or primarily) by juniors and seniors.

transactions included "eating rice from the same pot" (*eki hā̃ṛite khāoyā*); being part of a "one rice household" (*ekannabarti paribār*); living in the same house (*bāṛi* or *ghar*) and mutually partaking in its air, soil, wealth, and spaces; giving and receiving a mutual, egalitarian form of "love" (*bhālobāsā*); touching; and exchanging words (see table 7).

Seniors and juniors within households—even while engaging in any of the other transactions not considered directly mutual—also participated in mutual givings and receivings. Parents, especially mothers, were thought to exchange mutual egalitarian love (*bhālobāsā*) with their children, just as they gave and received forms of hierarchical love, *sneha* (affection) and *bhaktī* (respectful devotion). Likewise, seniors did not merely give their juniors blessings, curses, requests, commands, and complaints but engaged them in verbal exchanges of a mutual nature, such as conversation, gossip and storytelling, pleasantries, and the like. Children's touch of their aged parents was not limited to acts of *praṇām* and the taking of dust from their feet, nor aged parents' touch of their children to placing their hands on their children's heads to bless them; but aged parents and younger children and grandchildren also touched one another as equals, by sitting side by side, embracing, and often (especially grandparents and grandchildren) sleeping together.

Furthermore, the giving and receiving of food and material goods within families was not perceived only in terms of relations of deferred reciprocity and centrality, with adult householders (as those in the "center") the givers and all others (elders, children, guests) the peripheral receivers. The food and wealth of a family or household was also thought to be shared. Even if one set of people acquired, cooked, and served the food and others received it, *both* the givers and receivers were "eating food from the same pot." Such mutual exchanges of love, words, body contact, food, and so on played a significant role in how people in Mangaldihi defined what it was to be a family or *saṃsār.*

But these kinds of relations of mutuality were irrelevant to the positioning of older people within families. All household members, regardless of their phase within a family cycle or degree of centrality or hierarchy, were thought to participate equally in them. To understand how relations between the older and the younger were constructed, perceived, and valued within Mangaldihi families, we must look beyond synchronic relations of mutuality to the kinds of diachronic orderings on which I have focused in this chapter: those of deferred or long-term reciprocity, of centrality, and of hierarchy. These were the orderings that people in Mangaldihi stressed when they spoke of intergenerational relations and when they practiced, in their everyday and ritual lives, transactions that bound together persons across generations within their families.

3 Conflicting Generations

Unreciprocated Houseflows in a Modern Society

At the same time that the people in West Bengal spoke to me of family moral systems that bound persons together across generations, they also worried that the ties connecting persons within families were becoming increasingly loose. I asked one old man, Rabilal, a Mangaldihi beggar of the Muci (leatherworking) caste, what happens when someone gets old, and he replied pessimistically, "When you get old, your sons don't feed you rice." The young girl who cleaned my home, Beli Bagdi, responded when I asked her what would happen to her when she became old: "Either my sons will feed me rice or they won't; there's no certainty." In Bengal's villages and cities, wandering beggars, mostly aged, drift from house to house in search of rice, a cup of hot tea, or a few coins. Old widows dressed in white crowd around the temples in pilgrimage spots waiting for a handful of rice doled out once a day. The opening scenes of the popular Bengali novel and film *Pather Panchali* feature a stooped, toothless old woman who, with no close living relatives, must wander from house to house in her village, constantly moving on after the initial welcome fades (Bandyopadhyay 1968). The powerful 1993 documentary *Moksha* (*Salvation*), directed by Pankaj Butalia, portrays destitute Bengali widows at a Brindaban ashram; they recall poignantly the fights and rejections they experienced in the homes of their sons and daughters-in-law, and their utter loneliness in their separation from kin.

In this chapter, I explore family moral systems from the perspective of the problems and conflicts built into family relations, and in the process I also look at constructions of modernity. For Bengali narratives of modernity center on images of loose, unconnected, uncared-for old persons, who become paradigmatic signs of a wider problem of a disintegrating "modern" (*ādhunik*) society.

CONTRARY PULLS

According to the Bengalis I knew, family conflicts were the most common source of affliction facing people in old age. Four kinds of intergenerational relations seemed to generate the most problems: relations between mothers-in-law (*śāśuṛī*) and daughters-in-law (*bou*), between mothers and married sons, between fathers and sons, and between mothers and married daughters. Mangaldihians viewed these four dyadic bonds as particularly prone to attenuation, partly because of their tendency to conflict with other family bonds. As Margaret Trawick (1990b:157) writes about Tamil families: "At certain times in his or her life, [the] different kinds of bonds [between generations, between siblings, and between spouses] are likely to pull an individual in different directions. As one bond grows closer, another may stretch and break, and someone may be left out in the cold." I was told that bonds between generations were especially vulnerable, as members of each generation moved on to new phases of life and the "pulls" (*ṭān*) of the relationships that these life phases entail. When a son turns toward his wife, he may turn away from his mother. When a daughter-in-law turns toward her own children, she may neglect her parents-in-law. When a daughter moves to her husband's home, she becomes largely "other" to her parents. If a father turns toward God and death, he abandons his mourning sons.

In addition, there are fundamental problems in how relations of intergenerational reciprocity, and family (re)production and exchange systems, are structured in West Bengal. The whole system—as I began to explore in the previous chapter, and as will become more clear below—pivots on a kind of contradiction, as families send their "own" (*nijer*) daughters away to become "other" (*par*) and bring "other" women into their houses to become "own." The women on whom families depend to produce sons and provide much of the labor of caring for elders are thus perceived—by both themselves and others—to be partly "own" and yet at the same time still "other." This ambiguity in the position of women within households, we will see, was the source of many of the conflicts and ruptures within Bengali families.

Mothers-in-Law and Daughters-in-Law
(The problem of bringing in women from "other" houses)

The family relationship perhaps most fraught with tension and contrary pulls, and the one most often blamed by Mangaldihians for the neglect of elders, was that between mother-in-law (*śāśuṛī*) and daughter-in-law (*bou* or *boumā*).[1] Mothers realize when they bring a new wife into the household that they will be largely dependent on her for their well-being in old age. Daughters-in-law cook, serve food, clean clothing, lay out beds for sleeping, massage cramped legs, and comb hair. It is they who will eventually control most of the household affairs, and decide either to provide or not to provide the day-to-day service (*sevā*) to fulfill their mothers-in-law's needs and desires. A daughter-in-law may also have the power to take a son's loyalties away from his parents and even to persuade the son to begin a separate household of his own. Mothers are thus nervous when they arrange their sons' marriages. They search carefully for a *bou* who will be deferential, who will be loyal to her elders, and who knows how to work and to serve well. But they never know for sure. "After all," one woman explained, "my son's wife is not my own belly's daughter (*āmār nijer peṭer meye nae*); she is the daughter of another house (*anya gharer meye*)."

During the first years after a woman's marriage, however, it is the daughter-in-law (*bou*) who lives under the authority of her mother-in-law (*śāśuṛī*). A mother-in-law generally maintains control over domestic affairs for several years after a son's marriage, and she therefore determines which household chores the *bou* performs, whether and where the *bou* can come and go from the household, and when and if she may spend time alone with her husband. During this time, the mother-in-law and daughter-in-law relationship can be very loving and tender. Many women told me stories of how good their *śāśuṛīs* had been to them when they were young and first married, and several compared their *śāśuṛīs* to their own mothers. Some, who had been married before adolescence, spoke of sleeping at night with their *śāśuṛīs* for several years, until they were grown enough to sleep with their husbands; and one, as I noted earlier, told me that she had even nursed at her *śāśuṛī*'s breasts when she had been married years ago at only five.

But the *śāśuṛī-bou* relationship can also be a very difficult and bitter one for a young daughter-in-law. Many complained that their mothers-in-law ordered them around unfairly, treated them like servants (*dāsīs*), and prevented them from getting close to their new husbands. Indeed, a young husband and wife generally will not spend much time at all together during the day, and when they are in the presence of others they may not exchange more than a word or two. Such reticence demonstrates the young couple's modesty, as well as ensuring that the new *bou* will form strong relationships with other household members and not an exclusive one with her husband. Usually the new husband and wife will have a separate room to share at night, but a *śāśuṛī* will often keep her new *bou* up later than anyone else in the household and have her rise the earliest, thereby minimizing the time she can spend alone with her husband. Older women told me stories about how their *śāśuṛīs* used to guard their activities outside of the house as well, following them to the bathing *ghāṭ* (bank of a river or pond) and back with a stick to make sure that they did not loiter or talk to any men along the way.

Several local tales illustrate this vision of the *śāśuṛī* as a dominant near-tyrant ruling over her submissive and fearful *bous*. A group of married and unmarried women of my neighborhood told me one such story one afternoon as we sat casually talking over tea. It was ostensibly about how *musur ḍāl,* a favorite Bengali pulse, came to be red-orange in color and a "non-vegetarian" (*ā̃ṣ*) food, but it also conveys a great deal about *śāśuṛī-bou* relations. The story went like this:

> One day a *śāśuṛī* told her *boumā* to husk some *musur ḍāl.* She told her to bring at least one kilogram to her when she was done. So the *bou* went off to do her task. She soon realized with dismay, though, that the husked *ḍāl* would not come out to be a full kilogram. What would her *śāśuṛī* do? Out of fear of her *śāśuṛī,* the *boumā* took her little son and cut him up into bits to mix with the *ḍāl.* The blood from her son mixed with the *ḍāl,* and this is how it became *ā̃ṣ* [or *āmiṣ,* "nonvegetarian"] and how it got its reddish color.

"You see," one woman interrupted, "how fearful *boumās* used to be of their *śāśuṛīs*? That she would even kill her son out of fear of not complying with her *śāśuṛī*'s request?"

The teller went on:

> The next morning a bird called out, as it still does today, "*Pāye paṛa uṭh putu! Pāye paṛa uṭh putu!*" which means, "Get up, little boy! Get up, little boy!"[2] But how could he get up? He was dead. The *śāśuṛī* then found out what had happened, and she was even more enraged with her *bou.*

"So, you see," she ended, "It's bad if you don't obey your *śāśuṛī,* and it's even worse if you do." Gloria Raheja and Ann Gold (1994) have also compiled many vivid stories of this sort, depicting young daughters-in-law's ambivalent attitudes toward their senior marital kin.

But gradually the tides change. Eventually it is the *bou* who has control over household affairs, who makes decisions about who will do what when and who will eat what when. The years of transition, while the mother-in-law slowly gives up control and the eldest daughter- or daughters-in-law take over, can be full of tumultuous struggle and competition. During this phase, the daughters-in-law are no longer so new and meek that they cannot fight back, and the mothers-in-law are not yet so feeble that their words and wills have no power. The result was some of the fiercest arguments in

Mangaldihi households. I would often hear from nearby houses and courtyards the attendant screaming, pan throwing, and wailing. Women and children from neighboring households would crowd around to watch; but others would shrug their shoulders and say, "Mother-in-law and daughter-in-law are quarreling again" (*śāśuṛī-bou jhagra karche*), as if to imply, "What else is new?"

When a mother-in-law finally ceases to control household affairs, she becomes dependent on her *bou* or *bous* for her well-being, just as her *bous* were once dependent on her. Some mothers-in-law tenderly praise the loving, selfless care their *bous* provide for them. But, more than anyone else, it is the *bou* whom mothers-in-law blame for their unhappy, neglected old age. Two old women of Mangaldihi used to get together almost daily at the bathing ghat to commiserate about their *bous* and argue over whose *bou* was worse. People would tell me to go listen to them to learn about how *bous* mistreat their *śāśuṛīs*, and how *śāśuṛīs* never cease to criticize their *bous*.

Houses thus give each other women from whom they demand the most selfless devotion and exact the most onerous household labor, thereby extracting value from those who are in many ways "other" than their own. It is a little like taking a servant and, as we saw in chapter 2, the process of bringing a wife into the home is ritually referred to as just that: a groom tells his mother three times, "I'm going to bring you a servant" (*tomār dāsī ānte jābo*). Just as Mangaldihi villagers were never quite sure whether they could trust their servants to be honest, hardworking, loyal, and devoted, many felt that they could not *really* trust their daughters-in-law. (As one woman explained, "Daughters don't even look after their own parents; how can we expect a daughter-in-law to look after her parents-in-law?") And just as servants themselves often feel exploited, young wives frequently complain of being forced to labor too hard. It is not until a woman has lived through the period as a young daughter-in-law, has produced and raised sons of her own, and has finally brought her own daughters-in-law into the home that she fully becomes one of the "own people" (*nijer lok*) of a household. It is then that she herself must contend with bringing "other" wives into her house for her sons.

Mothers and Married Sons
(The problem of unreciprocated houseflows)

According to the family moral systems just described, women are expected first to serve others in their households as young wives and daughters-in-law, and then to *be* served as older mothers and mothers-in-law. This shift from serving to being served takes place after the wife produces a son, the hoped-for outcome of the movement of women from house to house. The bond between mother and son, according to many of the village men and women I spoke with, is stronger than all other human bonds. Sons come from deepest within their mother's body, from her womb or *nāṛī*, and thus experience a tremendous "pull of the womb" (*nāṛīr ṭān*) for her. A mother's milk is also a special substance, mixed with the mother's love (*bhālobāsā*) and distilled from her body's blood (*rakta*), which creates a great pull (*ṭān*) of affection and attachment (*māyā*) between her and her children. Moreover, a son often does not move away from his mother at marriage as a daughter does, but lives in the same home with her for the rest of her life.

Nonetheless, older women in Bengal told me many personal and folkloric narratives that pointed not to the durability of the mother-son bond but to its potential to be loosened or broken. This breaking was framed most commonly as a failure of reciprocity: the houseflows—gifts of goods, services, and love that sustain homes and relationships—are blocked before they can flow back up to the mother. Mothers told of how they poured out their breast milk, love, material wealth, and service to their sons and to others for their entire lives, but in the end they received nothing in return. Even village men often spoke to me of the service (*sevā*) women give throughout their lives, a service unequaled by what they receive.

Older women in Mangaldihi usually blamed such failures of reciprocation on their sons' wives. At the center of the complicated relationship between mother-in-law and daughter-in-law is the man who is the mother's son and the wife's husband. A wife is brought into the house in order to serve her mother-in-law and bear children to continue the family line; but she also often replaces her mother-in-law as the primary nurturer and most intimate partner of the son. The mother and wife may compete for years for the son's and husband's attention and loyalty. Sometimes the mother wins: I knew one son who was so devoted to his widowed mother that his wife ended up leaving them, returning to her father's house with their young daughter. Many told me that the bond between husband and wife is much more fragile than that between mother and son.

From a mother's perspective, however, it is more often the daughter-in-law who triumphs in the struggle to gain her son's affections. Thakurma was a Kayastha (high-caste) widow, nearly one hundred years old, who lived in Batikar, a large village near Mangaldihi. She enjoyed talking about the problems of old mothers, their sons, and their daughters-in-law. She herself was proud to live in a large ancestral home with four generations of descendants still eating rice together from the same pot; but she said with sadness that she had seen during her long life the way so many other sons and *bous* forgot their mothers when they grew old: "Mothers raise their children with such effort and pain. But the children don't even recognize their parents when they grow up. Children are created from their father's blood, and they come from their mother's deepest insides within the womb. The mother feeds them her breast milk and cleans up their urine and excrement. But does the son now remember those days? No. The mother uses all of her wealth to raise and educate her son, but at the end he gives nothing back to her." She then began telling a story to illustrate these ways of mothers and sons, and the role *bous* play in tearing sons away from their mothers:[3]

> There was once a mother who raised her only son with much effort and suffering. She used all of her wealth to feed him when he was young and to give him a good education; but in the end he gave nothing back to her. When he grew up and she gave his marriage, he and his wife left her alone and went to spend all of their time traveling around here and there. So what could the mother do? She ended up as a beggar. After a while she made her way to Bakresbar [a local Saivite pilgrimage spot] and there she lined up every day with all of the other old beggars with her begging bowl in front of her.
>
> One day it happened that her son and his wife went on a trip to Bakresbar. There the son's mother was sitting as usual in a line with all of the other beggars along the path to the bathing area. Can a mother ever forget her son? Never. But the son did not recognize his mother. He dropped a coin into her begging dish, and at this moment, his mother called him by his name, the name she had called him when he was a child. He was startled; he knew that no one knew this name but his mother. He was about to stop and say something to her, but his wife would not let him stand there. She pulled on his arm and said, "You don't have to talk with that old woman," and she led him away.

"So, you see," the old widow closed with a sigh, "mothers raise their sons with such tremendous effort and pain, but the sons forget (*mārā cheleder bahut kaṣṭa kare mānuṣ kare, kintu chelerā mane rākhe nā*)."

Another woman—Billo's Ma, a Bagdi widow with four married sons—spoke to me bitterly of how her sons had turned from her now that they had families of their own. She lived in a compound with three of her sons and their wives, but she had a small hut of her own where she slept and cooked separately, supporting herself meagerly by making cow dung patties for fuel for wealthier Brahman households. She told me first, with great emotion and at times breaking into tears, of raising her four sons and two daughters all alone after her husband had died. In order to get food and clothing for her children, she had labored every day in wealthy people's homes and fields, and sold the few ornaments she had brought with her from her parents' house as a bride. But then, she said with chagrin,

> My sons all grew up, and I gave all their weddings. All of them have their own families, and now to whose do I belong? Now whose am I (*ei bār āmi kothākār ke*)? I am no longer anyone (*ār to āmi keu nay*). Now one son is saying, "I came from a hole in the ground." Another is saying, "I fell from the sky." Another is saying, "I came from God." And yet another is saying, "My hands and feet came on their own; I grew up on my own." Who am I now? I'm speaking the truth. What kind of thing is a mother? . . .
>
> Listen. I have four sons. If they had all lived in one place, that would have been good, wouldn't it? If they would all come to eat [together]. If they would take the money they earned, put it into my hand and say, "Ma, will you handle this for me?" Then my heart would have been happy. But now, whatever your brothers [i.e., her sons] bring home—who do they give it to? their mother? or their wives? Huh?

I asked, "You mean your sons give everything to their wives?" Billo's Ma answered, "Yes. They have their own families and their own work. How will I take anything from them?"

In these two stories, a mother yearns for intimacy with her son or sons, but her sons abandon and forget her. They present a sequence of events familiar in others I heard told by and about old mothers: A mother sacrifices everything for her son, but ultimately there is a failure of reciprocity. When the son grows up, he gives nothing back to her. The son turns from his mother to his wife, and in the end he forgets her altogether. Being abandoned and forgotten by her son in this way, the mother is stripped not only of material support but also of her identity as a mother. She is left with no option other than to become one in an indistinguishable line of old beggars, literally or metaphorically. Moreover, the blame in such stories usually falls more on the son's wife than on the son. For although the son abandons and forgets his mother, it is often the son's *wife* who plays the active role in leading him away.

The theme of the immense self-sacrifice of women as mothers, coupled with the failure of reciprocity and betrayal by sons, surfaces powerfully as well in a modern Bengali short story called "Stanadayini" ("Breast-Giver") by Mahasweta Devi (1988). It centers on Jashoda, a poor rural Brahman woman, mother of twenty and nursemaid of thirty more, who spends her life pouring out her body's milk to nourish her own and her master's children. But in the end she is abandoned by them all. When she becomes old and can no longer reproduce or nurse, her almost fifty sons all forget her, and her breasts—the distinguishing organ of the woman as mother—become the site of ugly, festering, cancerous sores. Jashoda cries, "Must I finally sit by the roadside with a tin cup?" (p. 234), and then moans spiritlessly, "If you suckle you're a mother, all lies! Nepal and Gopal [two of her sons] don't look at me, and the Master's boys don't spare a peek to ask how I'm doing." We are told, "The sores on her breast kept mocking her with a hundred mouths, a hundred eyes" (p. 236). In the end, Jashoda dies alone and without identity, save a tag marking her as "Hindu female," and she is cremated by an untouchable.

The author views the narrative as a parable of India—seen as mother-by-hire—after decolonization. If nothing is given back to India as mother, then she like Jashoda will die of a consuming cancer (Spivak 1988:244). But I also hear in this story of the breast-giver the voices of older mothers in Bengal, who lament in their own oral tales: how fickle and short-lived are the joys of motherhood! how women as mothers give of themselves their whole lives and receive nothing in return!

We must remember, however, that most older women in Mangaldihi, even those who told stories of beggared and forgotten mothers, were not forgotten or neglected (at least in any blatant way) by their sons and sons' wives. The image of the mother as beggar works more here as a metaphor conveying a loss of love. Mothers will always love and give to their children more than they are loved and given to in return. Women as wives and mothers give all of their lives, never receiving as much as they have given.

Fathers and Sons
(The problem of a son who is more loyal to his wife than to his father)

The Bengali people I knew did not generally perceive fathers to be widely threatened by neglect in old age. Only a few older men complained to me of inadequate treatment by their children, compared to the countless mothers and mothers-in-law I heard. Furthermore, the two homes for the aged in Calcutta called Navanir (New Nest)—in 1990, the only such homes in Calcutta for non-Christians—were filled with women. Of their 120 residents in 1990, only 7 were men. The residents of the institutions as well as the directors told me that there is no great need for old age homes for men in West Bengal, for most old men are taken care of by their families within their own households.

One of the reasons for this disparity is that most men retain at least nominal control over a household's property and money until they die. By contrast, women in Bengal rarely own or control property in their own right, although some do inherit property from their fathers, especially if their fathers had no sons. Some, too, have influence over their husbands' property while their husbands are alive. But even though Bengal has laws requiring that widows inherit a portion of their husbands' property, virtually no one, in Mangaldihi at least, follows them. Older widows almost uniformly turn over any property (either by verbal agreement or legal transfer) to their sons when their husbands die, if their husbands have not already done so directly. In 1990, out of a total of 335 households in Mangaldihi, only 17 were considered to be headed by women (that is, with women in control of the household property). These included eleven Bagdi, two Santal, two Muslim, one Kulu, and one Muci household (note the total absence of high-caste Hindu households), all of which were headed by widows, most of whom either had no sons or whose sons were not yet grown and married.[4]

Many villagers told me, with some regret and cynicism, that only those who have their own financial resources can expect good treatment in old age;[5] by this logic, more men can be expected to be treated well than women. Possession of property, like the capacity to bless, can be used as a form of leverage; the holder can promise a future inheritance to those who serve him well in old age. Older people with property may also contribute economic resources to the household funds to help defray the cost of caring for them.

Furthermore, men much less often than women are left without a spouse or descendants to perform the actual labor of providing care in old age. Because men are usually several years older than their wives, the majority of Bengali women outlive their husbands to become widows; most men live through their old age still married. Additionally, if a man's first wife dies at a young age or is barren he may easily remarry in the hopes of producing sons, but the majority of Bengali women (especially if upper caste), once married, never again remarry, even if their husbands die or abandon them childless (see chapter 7).

And the village men with whom I spoke seemed to view the father-son bond as uniquely enduring and almost sacred. According to dominant patrilineal discourse in Mangaldihi, father and son are both central, structural parts of the same continuing lineage or *baṃśa* (literally, "bamboo"). Like bamboo, which is a series of continuously linked and growing nodes, the *baṃśa* was regarded as a continuing succession of linked fathers, sons, and wives. A *baṃśa* includes the male line of descendants from a common "seed" ancestor (*bīj-puruṣ*), together with their inmarrying wives and unmarried daughters.[6] Women thus come and go to and from this line, but fathers and sons extend it.

The bond between fathers and sons also lasts after death, as fathers (and then later their sons) are transformed into ancestors and nourished by sons and sons' sons. Women, in contrast, become enduring ancestors not in their own right, but only as parts of their husbands (see chapter 5). Thus by supporting and remembering particularly *fathers,* as old men and then as ancestors (*pitṛ,* literally "father"), sons sustain their own selves, for both fathers and sons make up the same *baṃśa.* All of these factors—a man's greater chances of having control over property, a living wife, sons, and a lasting place in the family line—contributed to local perceptions that older men tend to be served and remembered by their sons, both in old age and after death.

To be sure, there are exceptions: fathers and sons may quarrel and break their ties; sons may cease to feed their fathers rice. Sometimes these ruptures and omitted transactions are caused by poverty. In several households in Mangaldihi, sons may have wished to feed their aged fathers but simply lacked the resources to do so. Rabilal, a beggar of the Muci (leatherworking) caste, was one such neglected father. He himself had become too old and blind to work; his wife struggled in the fields as a day laborer to earn a meager bit of money for both of them, but it was usually not enough. Rabilal would moan, "Even now that I am old, my sons don't feed me rice," and he wandered through the village every day begging for rice and leftovers from cooked meals.

I also witnessed a few serious fights in Mangaldihi households between fathers and sons, though unlike frays between mothers-in-law and *bou*s, these were not regarded as everyday occurrences. Discord most commonly arose over money and sons' wives. The most serious father-son altercation that took place while I was in Mangaldihi turned into a major village event because of its unusual severity. People dropped their work, crowded around to watch, and talked about it for days afterward.

The fight took place in a Brahman household in a neighborhood bordering the one I lived in. One morning the household's only *bou,* a woman I will call Purnima, was cooking in a room with a tin roof. Her father-in-law, Satyabrata Chatterjee, came into the room and complained that the smoke from the cooking fire was ruining the roof. Purnima and her father-in-law began to argue angrily, and Purnima became so enraged that she jumped up and struck her father-in-law on the head with the blunt end of a large iron kitchen knife. Her father-in-law began to beat her. At this point, Purnima's husband, Benu, stepped in to defend his wife; he repeatedly hit his father with a wooden pole, and the old man's head was soon bleeding heavily.

From where I was standing, on a neighbor's roof, I could hear what sounded like the thudding sounds of flesh being beaten, along with terrible shouting. Several other women were watching with me on the roof, but most of the neighborhood's young men and children had rushed up to the household where the fight was taking place. My young work girl, Beli, ran back to report excitedly to us that the son, Benu, had cracked his father's head open, and that the father would most certainly die; but we found out shortly afterward that the man had suffered only a few, relatively minor, cuts on his head. Finally, after the father's youngest son, Bapi, had jumped in to defend his father and beat his older brother's wife, neighbors pulled the family apart, and the eldest son Benu fled with his wife to a neighboring relative's house.

Almost immediately, representative men from all of the neighborhood households (most of whom were from the same *bhāiyat,* or male lineage group) gathered together on the veranda of another house to discuss what should be done with Purnima and her husband. This sort of gathering periodically occurred in Mangaldihi when family or neighborhood problems arose. I listened from the sidelines with several other women, including Purnima herself, who was still distraught and sweating profusely from her exertions. I soon learned that Purnima had never gotten along with her parents-in-law, and particularly her father-in-law, during the ten years of her marriage. Recently things had grown even worse. Her father-in-law had taken out a loan of three thousand rupees (about one hundred dollars) from the bank and he had asked his son Benu to co-sign the loan with him. But the father had not been able to make the loan payments, so recently the bank had been after Benu for the money. Benu himself was without a job and had no income of his own, save the pittance he earned from folding pieces of newspaper into small paper sacks to be used as grocery bags at local stores. This arrangement between Benu and his father thus in itself constituted an inappropriate reversal of father-son relations: even though the father was still the recognized head of the household (*kartā*), he was seeking to secure money from his still unemployed and unpropertied son.

So the burden had fallen on Benu's wife Purnima to get money from her own father to help support them, and to pay back the loan. In this way, daughters-in-law in the region often continued to act as conduits between families, as they drew on wealth from their fathers' homes to bring to their fathers-in-law. But her position angered and embarrassed Purnima, who suffered an unending stream of insults about her in-laws from her father's family. Tensions between the daughter-in-law and the rest of her in-laws (aside from her husband, who was very devoted to her) had therefore heightened considerably.

The men who gathered primarily blamed the "troublemaking" (*badmāiś*) *bou,* Purnima, for the conflict, and several (including her father-in-law) suggested that she no longer be allowed to live in the village. Others proposed a more moderate course of action, which finally prevailed: the young couple, with their one son, would separate completely from the father-in-law's household. Several of the neighborhood men went over to the family's house and removed all of Benu and Purnima's things. They put the couple's possessions in a small, one-room hut adjoining the main house and rummaged up a lock for the new place. They then told the members of the separate households to stay away from each other.

And so the conflict was settled, but not without causing a household to break up and providing days of discussion. Although the village people did insist that the father, Satyabrata, shared in the blame or fault (*doṣ*) for the fight, they mostly condemned Purnima, calling her a "troublemaker" by nature. They would say, "Isn't it horrible that a *bou* could hit her own *śvaśur* (father-in-law)? that she could cause her husband to hit his own father on the head? Chi! Chi! This is a great sin (*mahāpāp*)!" Purnima's husband Benu generally was found to be largely innocent, a naive and simple (*saral*) type caught up in a mess between his wife and father; villagers felt compassion and tenderness (*māyā*) for him. It is very sad to see a father and son become separate (*pṛthak*), they said, over a wife.

Rabindranath Tagore's "Sampatti-Samarpaṇ" ("The Surrendering of Wealth"; 1926:48–54) also deals with the theme of tensions that rupture the ties between fathers and sons. The story, set in late-nineteenth-century rural Bengal, portrays a son who abandons his father over a disagreement about his wife. The father lives with his son, *boumā,* and grandson. The father is old, but he maintains a firm position as head of the household and manages all of the household funds with a miserly strictness. One day his *boumā* becomes very ill, and the son tries to persuade his father to spend the money to take her to an allopathic doctor. But the father insists that such expenses are not necessary, and he instead brings a traditional Ayurvedic doctor, or *kabirāj,* with inexpensive herbal medicines to heal her. After this treatment, the wife dies. The son, deeply pained at the loss, blames his father: he leaves, taking his only son with him.

The villagers who watch these events unfold provide a running commentary. As with similar dramatic family events in Mangaldihi, all the entertaining commotion gives the villagers some pleasure; but after the younger man leaves, they sympathize with the abandoned father about the "sorrow of separating from a son" (*putrabicched dukha*). They cluck their tongues with amazement and disapproval that the son could have valued his relationship with his wife more than that with his father. The villagers exclaim: "A son taking leave of his father over such a trivial thing like a wife! This could only happen in these [i.e., modern] times." They add: "If one wife dies, another wife can be collected before long. But if a father goes, no matter how much one tears out one's hair, another father can never be obtained" (Tagore 1926:49). The story's plot is quite complicated, but in essence things go from bad to worse. The grandfather, who spends a lonely old age worrying about the destruction of his *baṃśa* (family line), becomes quite deranged, and his only grandson is killed. At the end, only the single son is left alive; the *baṃśa* is threatened with extinction.

By his tone, Tagore implies that the grandfather is largely to blame for the disintegration of his family: he is stingy and insists on tightly controlling his money, even when his son is grown and has desires and a family of his own. The story touches also on the effects of global change, here represented by the spread of allopathic medicine, on local intergenerational relations. The son wishes to "modernize" in order to save his wife, while his father clings, perhaps unwisely, to more traditional and less costly ways. But from the villagers' perspective, the son, not the father, is responsible for the rupture. How could a son value his wife more than the bond with his father? A rupture in the father-son bond leads not only to the disintegration of the immediate household but to the end of the whole lineage—and thus denies the enduring meaning of, and reason for, the father-son bond.

Mothers and Married Daughters
(The problem of sending one's own away to become "other")

A daughter has a more fragile relationship with her aging parents than does a son, for a daughter's bonds with her parents are in effect broken when she is given away in marriage. I often heard mothers say of their daughters: "You just keep them with you for a few days and then give them away to an other's house." The bond is precious, but fleeting and ephemeral.

Precisely because married daughters become "other" in this way, most Bengalis state that parents cannot be cared for by daughters when they grow old, even if they have no sons. Several sonless older women I encountered insisted that they would rather live alone, or even in an old age home in Calcutta, than with a married daughter. One woman, Pratima-masi (Auntie Pratima), a resident of a Calcutta old age home, explained her reasoning:

MASI: I have no sons, only three daughters. If I did have a son, I would have certainly lived with him. But we Bengalis hate very much to live with daughters.

SL: Why?

MASI: Because when we give our daughter's marriage she becomes other (*par*). I have given my daughter into an other's hand (*meye to parer hāte diechi*). My son-in-law is not my belly's issue (*peṭer santān nae*).

SL: But a daughter-in-law? She is not your belly's issue either, is she? [I was seeking to understand why elders felt so much more comfortable living with their sons' wives than with their married daughters.]

MASI: No, that's different. Even if my *boumā* (daughter-in-law) hit me with a cane, that would be all right. I could still live with her. Because she is my son's wife. But living with a *jāmāi* (daughter's husband), that's impossible. We Bengalis hate it. If there's a son, then the *baṃśa* (family line) remains, and the *boumā* becomes part of the *baṃśa*. But a daughter's *baṃśa* is different than ours. We don't hold a daughter's *baṃśa* (*meyer baṃśa āmrā to dhari na*).

So a *boumā,* who is not one's belly's issue but comes into one's own house and becomes part of one's own *baṃśa,* becomes closer in many ways than a daughter, who *is* a mother's own belly's issue but marries away to become part of an unrelated person's household and lineage.

Parents also incur a considerable loss of respect (*asammān*) if they live with or are cared for by a married daughter. Many I spoke with stressed that Bengalis believe that married daughters and sons-in-law should be given to and not taken from. Another woman in an old age home explained: "It's not right to live with daughters. Bengalis feel a disrespect (*asammān*) if they live with their daughters. They live with their sons. But I have no son. . . . I visit my daughter's house sometimes, but I never stay longer than two or three days. Even if they tell me to stay I don't. Because it's my daughter's and *jāmāi*'s house. And among Bengalis we must give to daughters and *jāmāi*s, but we can't take from them. In taking from them a disrespect happens."

The proper direction of the flow of gifts is from a woman's natal to her marital household (Fruzzetti 1982:60). The major gift that instigates this pattern is the father's offering of his daughter—*kanyādān,* or "gift of a virgin"—to his son-in-law (*jāmāi*) at marriage. Throughout the daughter's married lifetime, dowry and other gifts are expected to flow predominantly from her natal to her marital home. Thus in Mangaldihi, Purnima, a daughter-in-law, received money from her father's home to give to her father-in-law (though not, as we saw, without considerable resistance on her own and on her natal family's part because the demand was seen as excessive). Husbands and wife-takers are regarded as superior to wives and wife-givers; the proper flow of gifts upward reflects this hierarchical ordering. A married daughter's parents, then, incur a significant loss of respect if they cannot continue to make occasional gifts to their married daughter's household, or if they are required to ask their daughter's husband for monetary assistance or other goods. Presumably, this concern with "respect" (*sammān*) was even more important to some than having a family to live with, for many of the women in the Navanir old age home had daughters but no sons.

Finally, many sonless older women explained that if they went to live in their married daughters' homes, there would be a considerable amount of trouble, discomfort, and uneasiness, especially if the daughter's own parents-in-law were living there. Arguing and overcrowding would result. And the daughter's mother would have no power (*śakti*) or real place in the household. She would be simply "dependent" (*parādhīn*): that is, someone who is supported without giving anything in return. I rarely heard this term applied to a mother in her son's home, for a mother's earlier years of giving to the household and its junior members were taken into account, ensuring her rightful place when she no longer worked in the household.

Nonetheless, some sonless mothers who had no other options did end up seeking to live with their married daughters. Two elderly sonless women came to Mangaldihi while I was there. One was a Brahman woman whom most of the village's young women called Bukun's Didima (Bukun's maternal grandmother), after her daughter's daughter, Bukun. One winter day I noticed a thin and stooped woman dressed in a plain white widow's sari descend from the noon bus: this was Bukun's Didima. She made it to their home and announced that her health and eyesight had deteriorated so much that she could no longer live alone. She came with a few meager possessions and the considerable sum of six thousand rupees, all of her savings, which she bequeathed to her daughter's household to offset the expense of feeding and caring for her until she died.

Several months later, though, after she had returned from a visit to her other married daughter's home, Bukun's Didima requested that her first daughter return the six thousand rupees. She had decided that she could no longer tolerate living in her daughters' homes and wanted to try again to live alone in her own house. But by that point, her daughter's household was decidedly not eager to return the money. For the rest of the afternoon, Bukun's Didima argued and pleaded with them, especially with her three granddaughters. The granddaughters shouted at her, "How dare you come now to take away your money?! You came when you were sick, and we served you, fed you, rubbed oil on your body, and made you well. We said you could stay here with us for the rest of your life. But now that you're well, you want to take your money back and go. What kind of gratitude is that? That's not right! You're a small, low person (*choṭolok*)!" They called her all sorts of derogatory names (most of which I could not understand) and spitefully mimicked her when she cried, "I'm going to die, I'm going to die right here!" They said they would not feed her any rice until she changed her mind, and finally she left, wailing, to eat at a neighbor's house. Many people crowded around to watch. They said that this is what happens when an old woman goes to live in her daughter's home.

Several months later, Bukun's grandmother was still with her married daughter in Mangaldihi. One sultry summer afternoon, she spoke to me of her predicament in low tones: "This [my daughter's house] is an other's house (*parer ghar*). When I gave my daughter's marriage she became other (*par*). That's why I don't like it here. . . . But first I'm going to take my six thousand rupees and then only will I go. They've eaten up my six thousand rupees and they aren't giving it back. But I'm going to take it back." When I left Mangaldihi, Bukun's Didima was still there with her daughter. They argued continually, and the older woman preferred to spend most of her time in neighboring households.

Another woman, called by most villagers "Khudi Thakrun's daughter" (after her mother, whom she continued to visit frequently), was also compelled to live with her married daughter in her old age. She had been widowed much earlier in her life when she was nineteen and her only daughter was a toddler. Like Bukun's grandmother, Khudi Thakrun's daughter had felt obligated to give her married daughter and son-in-law her wealth in exchange for being cared for in old age. But she lamented that ever since she had transferred her property to them, they no longer cared for her as they once did. She came to my home one afternoon to tell me the tale of her suffering:

> I have given everything that I had to my daughter. Now I have nothing at all. I am now sitting dressed as a beggar (*bhikhāri*). I have nothing at all. I've given everything to my daughter and *jāmāi*. I had a house in my name, and even that I gave to them. Everything. . . . And now I live there [with my daughter] and eat there. I have no more power (*śakti*), no more strength (*kshamatā*), no more material wealth (*artha*), no more money. I have become old (*buṛo*); I can't do anything. So now I have to sit and be fed. But now they no longer look after me like they used to. . . . Three days later [after I gave them my property] and they no longer love me like they did. I gave everything to them and now they don't really care about what's left. I've become old, without strength; I can't do anything any longer, and can't give anything more. And they no longer look after me. This is my life of sadness.

Old women feel that they are expected to "pay" their daughters and *jāmāis,* who are "other" (*par*) rather than "own" (*nijer*) people, for care and service provided in old age. Such a property-based relationship is not one of ease, and it is apt to wither once the elder's property is gone.

Installing a *ghar jāmāi,* or "house son-in-law," is one final way that some parents of daughters plan to be cared for in their old age: they acquire an inmarrying son-in-law to settle with their daughter in their own home. The son-in-law and daughter both receive a kind of "payment" for doing this, for they stand to inherit the parents' home and most or all of their property when they die (and they are also able to live on the property until then). A *ghar jāmāi* is generally from a poor family, or a younger son in a family of several sons—someone who would have had difficulty supporting a wife and family on his own. He agrees to move into his wife's household in exchange for the property he will live on and inherit.

This arrangement was generally considered to be difficult for all concerned, and particularly embarrassing for the *jāmāi* (and, to a lesser extent, for the married daughter). Here the *jāmāi* becomes in some ways like a wife: he shifts from house to house and is contained in the house of another, rather than practicing the more prestigious male pattern of developing and refining himself in a continuous, straight line, in the home and on the land of his fathers' fathers (see also Sax 1991:82–83). Daughters were sometimes embarrassed to marry such a feminine-seeming man. They also expressed reluctance to miss the opportunity of being honored as a new bride in a new home, intimating that the new *bou* status, however difficult to endure, was valued as well. Many parents of only daughters therefore did not choose this arrangement. One mother of three daughters and no sons, Subra-di, told me firmly: "We don't want to place a *ghar jāmāi* in our house. Our daughters wouldn't like it, and neither would we. It would make us all feel uneasy (*aśānti*). We will just live alone."

Thus as daughters become "other" (*par*) to their parents when they are married, parents cannot count on them for care in old age. Yet a mother's bonds with sons and their wives are not as inescapable and enduring as those without sons might imagine. I heard many old mothers of sons say the same things about the "otherness" of their *bous,* their sons' wives, that mothers of daughters say of their married daughters. One woman explained why she did not wish to live with her son and his wife: "My son's wife is actually not my own child. She's a daughter of another house (*parer gharer meye*)." And another woman, a Calcutta old age home resident, told me regretfully that she had come to the home because she had only sons and no daughters: "I have no daughter who could look after me. Daughters are more 'loving' [she used the English word] than sons."

All old people, both those with sons and those with daughters, must grapple with depending on juniors—women—who are in many ways "other" to them. It is necessary to the family cycle and continuity that parents bring daughters-in-law into their homes for their sons and send their own daughters out to the homes of others. But in so doing they cause their sons and daughters to become enmeshed in bonds that will, to some degree, inevitably distance them from their peripheralized parents. Those I knew often blamed this distancing for the neglect and unreciprocated houseflows afflicting older people.

THE DEGENERATE WAYS OF MODERN SOCIETY

The kinds of conflicts and problems Bengalis perceived to be built into family relations cannot be understood without considering as well Bengali constructions of modernity. Dominant discourses in the 1980s and 1990s—in Mangaldihi and Calcutta, and in Indian newspapers, magazines, and gerontological texts—assert that social problems have burgeoned in modern times. In these discussions, images of a bad old age are often invoked as paradigmatic signs of a disintegrating "modern" (*ādhunik*) society. Lawrence Cohen (1998) offers a penetrating, detailed analysis of discourses of old age, senility, and modernity in Indian gerontological literature and among the urban middle class in Varanasi and other north Indian cities. After looking briefly at some of the same cosmopolitan discourses (encountered mainly during my many visits to Calcutta), I will relate these to Mangaldihi perspectives on modernity and the modern afflictions of old age.

Since the early 1980s, a profusion of literature on aging has appeared in Indian gerontological and sociological texts, journal articles, and popular magazines.[7] Most of it is organized around the strikingly uniform theme of a looming "problem of aging," framed as an increasing number of old people and a decreasing social desire to take care of them. The cover story of the 30 September 1991 issue of *India Today* exemplifies this trend. It is titled "The Greying of India," and its cover blurb reads: "With life expectancy going up, the number of people above 60 has risen past 50 million. Coupled with this, rapid urbanization is disrupting traditional relationships, leaving Indian society struggling to cope with a new dimension of alienation and despair" (M. Jain and Menon 1991).

Sarita Ravindranath's story "*Sans* Everything . . . But Not *Sans* Rights" (*Statesmen,* 1 February 1997) covers the recent passing of the Himachal

Pradesh Maintenance of Parents and Dependents Bill, which requires children in the state of Himachal Pradesh to provide for their aged parents. This bill was necessary, Ravindranath and local public officials contend, because of the sharp decline in family bonds in today's India. "[A]ged and infirm parents are now left beggared and destitute on the scrap heap of society. It has become necessary to provide compassionate and speedy remedy to alleviate their sufferings," the Himachal Pradesh minister, Vidya Dhar, states in the bill's preface (qtd. in Ravindranath 1997). But Chittatosh Mukherjee (retired chief justice and chairman of the state Human Rights Commission) comments that legislation can only do so much to remedy a family's and society's ills. "A man might get enough money to sustain himself, but where will he go for love and affection?" he asks. "As long as there were strong family bonds, there was no need for written law to dictate that you have to care for your parents." The article concludes:

> Whatever its merits or defects, it is unlikely that the joint family system, with its insistence on caring for the elderly, will make a comeback to Indian society. As more and more people leave home in search of a better life, the neglected ones are parents, who most often invest their life savings in their child's education and growth. And while it is impractical to tie children to their parents' strings for life, it is as important to ensure the rights of the elderly to lead a dignified life. . . . Only the law . . . can reach out and help bent, sad people stand up straight with pride.

One of the primary forces of change and modern affliction in these narratives is Westernization. The "joint family," a multigenerational household in which elders make up an intrinsic part, is often described as something "uniquely Indian" or "characteristic of Indian culture." For example, in his preface (1975:ii) to J. D. Pathak's *Inquiry into Disorders of the Old,* S. P. Jain professes: "The old were well looked after in the joint family system, so characteristic of the Indian Culture." Madhu Jain and Ramesh Menon (1991:26) declare that "Age was synonymous with wisdom, values and a host of things that made Indian society so unique." In contrast, the "West" is associated with old age homes, negative images of aging, independence (that is, small or nonexistent families), and individualism. In fact, the first old age homes in India were products of colonial penetration, constructed by Christian groups such as the Little Sisters of the Poor from the late nineteenth century onward and inhabited (until very recently) almost exclusively by Anglo-Indians. The cover story of the 7 January 1983 issue of *Femina*—"Old Age: Are We Heading the Way of the West?"—focuses on the rapid growth of India's old age homes, negative media images of the elderly, and modern youth's reluctance to care for the aged. British colonial rule, comments Ashis Nandy (1988:16–17), also played a decisive role in "delegitimizing" old age in India by importing Europe's "modern" ideology, which casts the adult male as the perfect, socially productive, physically fit human being and the elderly (as well as the effeminate) as relatively socially inconsequential.[8]

Urbanization also figures in urban middle-class narratives of the problems of aging in contemporary society. Indian gerontological literature blames what it calls the breakup of the joint family at least as much on the growth of India's cities, bolstered by an increasing stream of new inhabitants from the countryside, as on the forces of colonialism and Westernization. The argument goes that urban houses (and thus families) tend to be smaller than those in villages, and their walls more divisive and isolating; they are less likely to include old people, who are commonly left behind on village lands. The chaos and separations brought about with the emergence of the postcolonial order in South Asia, and the partition of India from Pakistan and Bangladesh, are featured in these modernity narratives as well. People I knew—especially those in the newer neighborhoods of southern Calcutta, which are replete with middle-class refugees from what was formerly East Pakistan, now Bangladesh—often spoke poignantly of postindependence and postpartition as *overly* independent (*svādhīn*) and maya-reduced times. People torn away from their ancestral lands and homes live now in compact urban apartments, making multigenerational family relationships ever harder to sustain.

People in Mangaldihi also talked continually about how things had gone awry in current times: families were breaking up, old people were being left alone, and (partly as a consequence, partly as a cause) the society (*samāj*) as a whole was deteriorating. Cohen finds that (unlike his urban middle-class informants) those living in the low-caste Nagwa slum of Varanasi where he did comparative fieldwork did not invoke the modern or the West to ground a rhetoric of the weaknesses of old age or the collapse of families. Rather, the afflictions of old age were blamed on poverty, the caste order, oldness itself, and frictions between brothers (which broke families into small units). Bad families were not spoken of as a recent or unusual phenomenon (1988:223–48). In Mangaldihi, however, there was a pervasive sense that the "modern" (*ādhunik*) was at the root of many social ills. This sentiment, though expressed across caste and class lines, was most pronounced in upper-caste neighborhoods.

The three main villains of modern affliction in Mangaldihi were Westernization, urbanization, and women. Many of the less literate in Mangaldihi were not quite certain where the "West" (or *bilāt*—England, America, foreign places) was located or just what it entailed. People asked, Was *bilāt*—or my country, America—near Darjeeling? Delhi? Was Hindi spoken there? Others were acutely interested in and informed about India's longtime engagement with the West via British colonialism, the increasing globalization of the media and the national economy, and the outmigration of Indians to places such as the United States. A good proportion of Mangaldihi's Brahman men commuted to nearby cities for work, read English language newspapers daily, and watched international television programs in their or their neighbors' homes. It was in these Brahman neighborhoods that people most often invoked the West, *bilāt,* or "foreign winds" as a key source of the travails of modernity. Gurusaday Mukherjee commented that popular American television programs and British-style education systems were in part responsible for the failure of young people to respect and fear their elders as they once had. Subal, an older Bagdi man, concurred. He said that the school education of his sons and grandsons had led to a new lack of respect and loss of authority for old people: "The old people's words are not mixing with the young people's any more. Now the young people's intelligence has become very [or 'too,' *beśi*] great." Some people in Mangaldihi had heard of old age homes in Europe and America, and compared them disparagingly to their ashrams or shelters for dying cows. And they noted with dismay that this system was penetrating their own society. Many Mangaldihi women were fascinated by the tape-recorded interviews I brought back from the two Navanir old age homes in Calcutta; they crowded around my tape recorder to listen to the residents' stories, then would often analyze these women's predicaments in terms of the Westernized modern era in which they all were finding themselves.

Some in Mangaldihi also linked the general decline in the quality of village life, and the increasing precariousness of the condition of old people within their families, to urban migration. Large numbers of residents have left the Mangaldihi region over the past several decades—especially the better educated and the higher castes, who can find salaried jobs in the cities. In 1990, about 14 percent (or 243 out of a total population of 1,700) of those whom Mangaldihians themselves considered to be Mangaldihi residents actually lived most of the time away from "home," returning from the city only periodically to attend major festivals, at harvest times to sell crops that had been cultivated by their sharecroppers, or to visit relatives remaining in the village. Although I knew of no families that abandoned their older members completely, in several cases sons left their parents alone for some years, usually until one spouse died.[9] When that happened, the sons and their families would return to Mangaldihi for the elaborate funeral rituals and, after the funeral was over, take away the surviving parent, often arranging to have him or her shift from house to house among the various sons living in different cities. Such urban migration not only left some old people alone for long intervals but also left houses disturbingly empty. Friends and I would walk down village lanes and see homes boarded up, to be vitalized only once or twice a year by voices and the warmth of cooking fires. People would say, "How great our village used to be! Crowded with people at all times . . . " They did not like passing by those lonely homes.

Although women do not play much of a role in the largely de-gendered gerontological texts focused on the urban middle class, they figure prominently as agents of change in the rural men's and women's narratives I heard. Modern-day daughters-in-law, I was told, are better educated; they go out and get jobs, they are interested in makeup and movies, they desire their independence, and they are not willing to serve their husbands' parents as daughters-in-law once did. The tellers of such stories are mainly old women (young women, of course, might applaud such changes), who are also portrayed as suffering the most from neglect by young women—and thus women become both the agents and victims of modernity. One middle-aged Mangaldihi woman, Bani, told me: "Our 'joint families' are becoming ruined (*naṣṭa*) and separate (*pṛthak*), because women have learned how to go out. They are irritated by all the household hassles." An elderly widowed Kayastha woman similarly spoke of the role young women play in the decline of traditional values: "Back then, *saṃsār* (family life) was very pure (*pabitra*). Daughters-in-law kept their saris pulled up over their heads [a sign of modesty and deference to elders], and the young were devoted to and served the old. . . . In this age," she went on, "daughters-in-law want their independence. They want to live separately (*pṛthak*)."

Susan Wadley finds that residents of the village of Karimpur, north India, express similar concerns about new household authority patterns and family separations in modern times, also blaming these in part on the daughter-in-law's new demands (1994:236). This song was sung by a group of Brahman girls at a wedding, presumably with a degree of irony (p. 238):

> Mother-in-law, gone, gone is your rule,
> The age of the daughter-in-law has come.
> The mother-in-law spreads a bed,
> The daughter-in-law lies down.
> "Mother-in-law, please massage my feet."
> The age of the daughter-in-law has come.

Patricia and Roger Jeffery (1996:161–62) hear similar voices: "Daughters-in-law used to be afraid of their mothers-in-law. We used to tremble with fear . . . These days, it's the mother-in-law who fears the daughter-in-law."

These contemporary rural critiques of modernity both recall and provide a revealing contrast with late-nineteenth- and early-twentieth-century Bengali anticolonial nationalist discourses, which were gendered in parallel ways.[10] In those earlier debates, Partha Chatterjee shows, women (and the home, family, religion) were represented as upholding a "traditional," Indian spiritual inner domain, distinct from an increasingly "Western" material outer world. Nationalists asserted that although European power had relied on superior material culture in subjugating non-European peoples, it could not colonize the inner, essential identity of the East, which must be preserved in the home. He observes: "In the world, imitation of and adaptation to Western norms was a necessity; at home, they were tantamount to annihilation of one's very identity" (1993:121). But a striking proportion of the literature on Bengali women in the nineteenth century concerned their threatened Westernization. Contemporary writers suggested that the "Westernized woman was fond of useless luxury and cared little for the well-being of the home" (p. 122). Even more damning, "A woman identified as Westernized . . . would invite the ascription of all that the 'normal' woman (mother/sister/wife/daughter) is not—brazen, avaricious, irreligious, sexually promiscuous" (p. 131). In Mangaldihi, remarkably similar discourses, though not as explicitly wrapped up with nationalist and countercolonial sentiments, still formed part of an overall narrative deploring recent changes and yearning for a more "traditional" Bengali past. In this past, women (*young* women)—as submissive and caring daughters-in-law, mothers, and wives—guaranteed close multigenerational families, the social-moral order, a good old age.

To be sure, we have little or no evidence that the past really was more perfect, harmonious, and filled with joint families, submissive young women, and venerated elders than the present is. In the abundant gerontological and sociological literature on the contemporary "problem" of aging in India, no baseline or longitudinal data have been presented to support the assertions of rampant joint-family decline (see Cohen 1992:132–35; L. Martin 1990:104–10; S. Vatuk 1991:263). In fact, one of the few longitudinal studies of family structure in India that we do have (Kolenda 1987b) shows that contrary to popular belief, the proportion of joint families in the village of Lonikand near Poona, at least, did not dwindle over the years but has increased from 29 percent in 1819 to 45.6 percent in 1967 (Reddy 1988:63). Data from another study of thirteen villages in Bihar (Biswas

1985:246) show that the proportion of men and women aged sixty and over living with sons remained relatively constant between 1960 and 1982, at about 80 percent (L. Martin 1990:107). As suggestive as they may be, neither of these small studies provides conclusive evidence about how the family in India either has or has not changed over time. It is therefore impossible to tell precisely if or how quickly the joint family is declining, or to what extent it ever did exist in the past as the "self-sufficient unit, . . . centre of universe for the whole family" (Gangrade 1988:27).

In addition, alarmist statements in the media about the increasing numbers of old people in India (and the subsequent inability of families and society to care for them) fail to take into account that most census studies show no dramatic change in the proportion of persons sixty and over in the Indian population, because fertility remains high (Cohen 1992:133; S. Vatuk 1991:264). Based on numbers alone, we cannot easily predict that there will be ever more old people in India with ever fewer young people available to care for them.

Yet despite their apparent lack of grounding in fact, such narratives of aging and modernity are pervasive and widely felt as persuasive. Arguably one must consider discourse about the degenerate ways of a modern society in the context of a general devolutionary outlook that permeates the thinking of many in West Bengal, and in India more widely. According to the well-known theory of the four *yugas* or ages, things get progressively worse rather than better as time passes. When this world first came into being many thousands of years ago, people lived in the Satya Yuga, the age of truth and goodness in which *dharma* or moral-religious order flourished. But ever since then, the social and material world has gradually deteriorated until, according to my informants, about five thousand years ago we entered the fourth and most degenerate of all ages, the Kali Yuga. In addition to stories about the worsening of family ties and the mistreatment of old people, I constantly heard tales of regret about other deteriorations: mangoes are not as large and sweet, cow's milk does not flow as abundantly, trees do not provide as much shade, villagers do not share the same fellow feeling, people are no longer trustworthy and honest.

Such narratives of modern decline must also be placed in the historical context of colonialism, nationalism, and postcolonialism in Bengal. Partha Chatterjee scrutinizes Bengali narratives of modern decline and likewise asks: "Why is it the case that for more than a hundred years the foremost proponents of our modernity have been so vocal about the signs of social decline rather than progress?" (1997:203). To answer, he suggests, we must look at the interpenetration of modernity with the history of colonialism. He points out (p. 194) that the word *ādhunik*, in its modern Bengali sense of "modern," was not in use in the nineteenth century. The term then employed was *nabya* (new)—the new that was explicitly linked to Western education and thought, the civilization inaugurated under English rule. Because of the way that the history of Bengali modernity has been intertwined with the history of colonialism, Chatterjee argues, Bengali attitudes toward modernity "cannot but be deeply ambiguous" (p. 204). He proposes that "At the opposite end from 'these days' marked by incompleteness and lack of fulfillment, we construct a picture of 'those days' when there was beauty, prosperity and a healthy sociability, and which was, above all, our own creation" (p. 210). These narratives of modernity impart a sense of a more true and beautiful, a morally superior, an "own" Indian or Bengali past, at the same time that they frame current social problems (some of which may also have existed long before today) as part of historically specific processes of change in a postcolonial and global era.

I will close this section with two narratives portraying visions of the deterioration of modern society, the changing constitution of persons and social relations, and the concomitant afflictions plaguing old people. The first is the story of a resident of one of the Navanir homes for the aged in Calcutta. This *māsimā* (or "maternal aunt," as the home's residents are called) was a woman who had never married, and whose numerous nephews and nieces born of her ten brothers and sisters refused to care for her. She said that people used to consider *pisis*, paternal aunts, close relatives but that they now treat *pisis* as *par*, "other," and send them to old age homes. She blamed much of the change in her society on the introduction of Western-style "family planning" or birth control policies, which have reduced the size of families and contributed to a general decline in "family love" (*saṃsārik bhālobāsā*):

> You in your country have "family planning" so there are only one or two children per family. But not us. Now, which system is better? I think our system is better. Because I heard that in your country old people become *asahāy* (helpless, solitary). But not so in our country, at least not before. The old people lived on their land in the villages. They would do *pūjās* (religious rituals), read the Gita, Mahabharata, and Ramayana. Their sons would serve them. But now with "family planning," disaster has come. There's no binding (*bandhan*) any more in the family. The sons become educated, get jobs, and take their wives with them to live. Who will look after the old people? That's why I

> came here. No one thinks of anyone else any more. I'm still embarrassed to say that I live in a "home." But what can I do? Who will look after me? . . . I'm saying that family planning is not good. Our hearts have become small. We used to feel a sense of duty toward our *kākās, jeṭhās, ṭhākurdās* (uncles and grandfathers). But we don't even know the names of our relatives any more. One person is building a big house and another is going to an [old age] home. Affection and compassion (*māyā-dayā*) no longer exist like they did.

This woman failed to note the irony in her account: though she had ten brothers and sisters, reflecting a family before "family planning," she still had no one to care for her in her old age. The culprits in her tale are not her family, however, but modernity and Westernization—penetrating into the inner sanctum of families through government-sponsored birth control programs.

My second example is a song that richly portrays a view of the manifold deteriorations of society in modern times, with particular attention to the disregard of elders and a general disintegration of family life. The song, titled "Modern Society" ("Ādhunik Samāj"), was composed in the 1980s by Ranjit Chitrakar, a *paṭuyā* singer and scroll painter of Medinipur District, West Bengal. Patuas were previously very popular in Bengal; they traveled from village to village singing narrative songs illustrated by their scrolls, called *paṭs*, and they sold these scrolls in the markets around Calcutta's famous Kali temple at Kalighat.[11] Their stories were traditionally drawn from Hindu mythology, but in the late nineteenth century they began also to provide critical and satirical commentary on features of contemporary society, like the newfangled English-educated *bābu*, or Bengali gentleman—or, as in this tale, the maltreatment of old people, the brazenness of women, and the misguided laws of the government in modern times. I heard and recorded this song in Calcutta in 1989; two of the *paṭ* illustrations that go with it appear below, on pages 98–99 (figures 5 and 6).

MODERN SOCIETY

Listen, listen everyone carefully.
Listen carefully to a song about Kali Yuga.
When Kali is spoken of, the head is filled with embarrassment.
It is only about people going to the cinema day and night.

When a groom goes to get married he looks for the best-looking bride.
If her color is dirty or if she has squinty eyes,
Snow-white powder is spread all over her dark body
And *kājal* (eyeliner) is painted on her eyes to make them long and wide.

In the Satya Yuga people got married when they were over thirty.
But in the dark Kali Yuga people are marrying before age sixteen.

And when brides go to their husbands, they go with their heads uncovered and smiling.[12]
They tell their husbands, "I want to go to the cinema with you."

A twelve-year-old girl runs away with a little boy and has two children,
And all the while the government is making laws about taking medicine [i.e., birth control pills].
And then there are old women of sixty years still wearing conch shell bracelets and vermilion,[13]
Who leave their old husbands to find themselves a young groom.

Seeing the events of Kali Yuga, everyone's head spins.
The people of Kali Yuga don't tell the truth, but only lies.
The age is afflicted with the sins of going to cinemas.
All of the practices of our land have become depraved.

. . . .

The daughter-in-law rubs so many kinds of oil on her hair.
But the old mother-in-law is left only to use the kerosene oil from the lamp.
The daughter-in-law's combed hair shines with oil in the mirror,
While the old lady's hair is tangled and bedraggled.
The daughter-in-law sleeps on a high bed with three pillows,
While the old lady lies on a board with a torn bedsheet.

. . . .

In the Satya Yuga there used to be wealth in the fields,
But in the dark Kali age the crops are ruined by sins.
Seeing all these events, Laksmi is leaving people's houses.[14]
In the Kali Yuga everyone is eating rice separately out of separate cooking pots.
And they steal from their fathers without feeding them rice.

There is a law from the government about abolishing low castes,
And there is nothing to eat except wheat and flour.[15]
As much as people sell and buy, that much prices are rising.
And taxes are increasing steadily in each house.

There came a law from the government that widows can remarry.
So now a mother of three or four sons says she must get married.
She says, "I won't live with my sons—what happiness do I have from them?"
She dresses up again, with snow-white powder, soap, and shoes, and says,
"I will go to my father's house to look for a new groom."
And if the new husband has a sister or mother, they are just thorns in the road.

. . . . . .

This song is over, but there is a lot more to say.
I will write more, older brother, if I live.

Figure 5. "Father and son's fight." *Paṭ illustration by Ranjit Chitrakar. A son and wife beat up his parents. Note how the senior couple is dressed in white. The daughter-in-law's eyeglasses are a sign of her "modernity."*

My name is Ranjit Chitrakar.
My address is Medinipur.

This song captures the sense that prevails among rural and urban middle-class Bengalis of the incoherence and degeneration of modern society and the postcolonial state. This degeneration is manifest most starkly in the separations and reversals in intergenerational family relationships: new brides go boldly to their husbands and in-laws with their heads immodestly uncovered; old married women leave their husbands to find new, younger grooms; daughters-in-law treat themselves to luxuries while abandoning their mothers-in-law to torn sheets and unkempt hair; sons steal from their fathers without feeding them rice; and old widows leave their own sons to remarry, while throwing their new mothers-in-law into the road. Here

Figure 6. "Get out of the road, sir! I'm going to the cinema." *Paṭ illustration by Ranjit Chitrakar. A "modern" daughter-in-law, wearing slacks, eyeglasses, and a watch, embarks brazenly on a motor scooter.*

again, women are painted as the primary agents, as well as the primary victims, of the present evils. The government is also held to account for fashioning laws that ostensibly aim to remedy social ills (abolishing caste, permitting widow remarriage) but that in fact result in increased poverty, chaos, and distress.

THREE LIVES

Though I have discussed consensus and contest in separate chapters, in the real exchanges of everyday life they do not exist in neat isolation. The very people who strove to sustain long-term relations across generations, and who stressed to me the "Bengali-ness" of their family ties (see chapter 2), also experienced distressing intergenerational conflicts and saw the modern postcolonial age as rife with such conflict. The following description of the ambiguities and nuances of the family lives of three elderly people in Mangaldihi provides a fitting conclusion for both aspects of my examination.

Khudi Thakrun

Khudi Thakrun was proud to be the oldest or most "increased" (*bṛiddha*) person in Mangaldihi. Nearing one hundred years old, her face was made of an intricate design of wrinkles, her white hair was cropped short in the style of old widows, and she roamed the village covered sparsely with a man's white dhoti, with her loose breasts hanging low.[16] She had one of the strongest, most willful characters in the village, which was perhaps intensified by her advanced age. She lived alternately in the separate homes of her three sons and *bous*, who cared for her attentively. She continued (unusually for someone of her age and sex) to maintain substantial control over her own money and land, and she still lent money and collected interest to increase her wealth, and to buy extra mangoes and sweets to satisfy her palate.

Khudi Thakrun was the only surviving and much-beloved child of her very wealthy Brahman father. Before she was born, her parents had had four sons and four daughters, all of whom died in infancy. So upon her birth, her mother had a Bagdi woman come to the birth room to buy her for a piece of broken puffed rice called *khud;* that is how she got her name Khudi ("little broken piece of puffed rice"). This act, she explains, enabled her to live.[17] As an only child, she was greatly adored, and abundant good food and expensive clothing were lavished on her throughout her girlhood.

When Khudi was just eleven and it was time for her to marry, she told her parents that she refused to move away from them by marrying into another village. So her parents married her to a seventeen-year-old boy from Mangaldihi. Mukherjee, to whom she referred by his last name, was also from one of the larger and wealthier families in Mangaldihi. After Khudi Thakrun's father died and she inherited all of his wealth (including acres of land, thirty ponds, a large house, and thousands of rupees), she became probably the wealthiest person in Mangaldihi, as well as a senior member of one of Mangaldihi's largest and oldest families.

She and her husband themselves had several children who died in infancy before her first son, Gurusaday, survived. When he was born, she promised Syamcand, the dominant Krishna deity in the village, that she would give him a pure gold belt if her son lived. Gurusaday did survive, and the icon of Syamcand still wears that gold belt today. She later bore two more sons and three daughters, who all survived past infancy. After Khudi Thakrun and her husband gave their youngest daughter's marriage when she was ten, Khudi

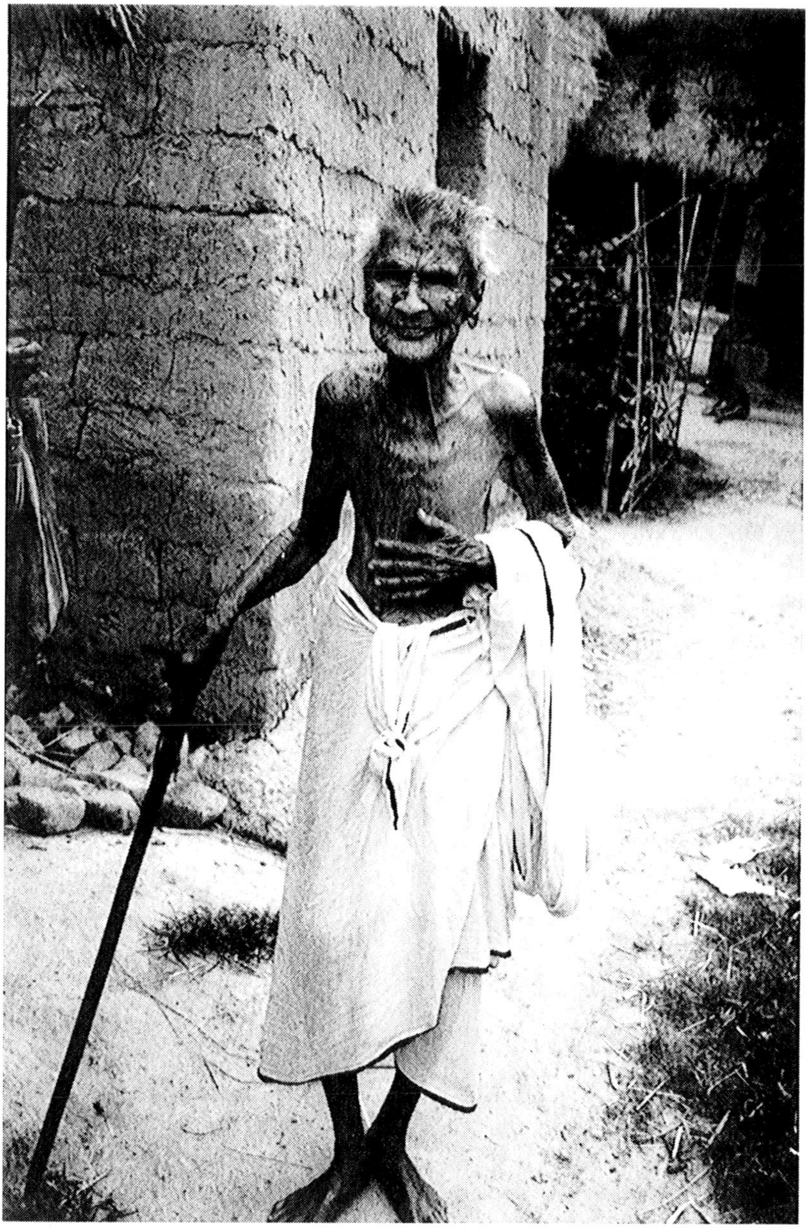

Khudi Thakrun.

Thakrun would not go near her husband or even speak to him out of fear that she would become pregnant again. But several years later she did become pregnant with another son; and when he was only ten days old, her husband died. Khudi Thakrun said that she herself was over fifty at the time.

When I met her over forty years later, she was being cared for by her three sons and their wives. Her daughters-in-law told me that she used to rule firmly over them, controlling every aspect of their household affairs. She would argue and even fight with them, and they were afraid of her. For several years after her husband died, she substantially controlled the family's property and financial affairs. This is unusual for a widow in Mangaldihi, but Khudi Thakrun had grown up in many ways as her father's son, and much of the family property was in her name. Her wealth to some extent transformed her gender.

But more recently she had lost a considerable amount of her power. Several years earlier, her three sons had become separate (*pṛthak*) and she transferred almost all of her property to them, keeping just a small bit of land in her name so that she could have some money to use for her own interests and thus maintain some independence. She still asked her sons about their financial matters—how the crops did every year, how many fish were in the ponds—but by and large she let them run things themselves. Her *bou*s explained to me that she could no longer dominate their household affairs. The middle *bou* remarked: "She used to have so much power (*śakti*). But now what can she do? Even if she shouts at us, we don't heed her too much. She can't tell what we're doing anyway, she has become so blind and deaf." After the sons became separate, they decided to divide up the care of their strong-willed mother, as none of them wanted to be solely responsible for her. So Khudi Thakrun began a regimen of moving from house to house, spending four months out of the year with each son. All three houses were within a stone's throw of each other.

I talked frequently with Khudi Thakrun, her sons, *bou*s, and neighbors about her and her relationships with her family members. Khudi Thakrun never complained about the treatment she received from her juniors. She said that all of her sons and *bou*s looked after and served her well, and she especially praised her middle *bou* for her excellent cooking and attentiveness, and her youngest grandson for his unusual devotion to her.

The juniors themselves, however, complained about her considerably. They seemed almost to dread the months that she would spend in their homes, for she was so demanding. She insisted on eating the best foods—particularly fruit, which is difficult to obtain and very expensive, and abundant quantities of milk. When she was at the house of her oldest son, Gurusaday, who was the poorest of the three brothers (the only one without a salaried job), her juniors complained that none of the other household members could have any milk, because she drank all that their two cows could supply. When she wanted something, such as tea, a snack, or mustard oil to put on her body, she demanded in her deep, raspy voice that it be brought instantly. Her middle *bou* threw up her hands in exasperation one day when I was visiting and exclaimed, "I can't stand it any more! She's so hard of hearing, she can't even hear me when I tell her, 'I'm coming, I'm coming!'" One aggravated *bou* told me once when Khudi Thakrun was staying at their house, "It's not necessary to live as long as Ma. It's past time for her to die." Her oldest son would chastise and criticize his mother as well. When she would see me at his house talking with him, she sometimes tried to come over to sit by me, but her son would jump up, wave his walking stick at her, and yell, "Get away! Get away! This is no place for you!" and then turn to me and say, "What a difficult person! My mother is such a difficult person!"

But they were all concerned with *dharma* and believed strongly that serving Khudi Thakrun was an integral part of living correctly and upholding the moral-religious order of the world. Gurusaday would lecture me for hours on end about the importance of giving service and respectful devotion to elders as a preeminent form of Hindu *dharma*. Her middle *bou* added quickly after one critical outburst: "But we still feed her and give her respect. Otherwise our great sin (*mahāpāp*) would happen. It is our *dharma* to care for her." The sons, wives, and grandchildren all did *praṇām* to her daily, demonstrating their respectful devotion and seeking her blessings.

It was perhaps their strong concern with fulfilling their duties to their elders, as well as their concern for the family reputation or "name" (*nām*), that caused Khudi Thakrun's sons and *bous* such great irritation at her habit of roaming the village almost daily to seek out fruit and sweets from other people's households. Whenever she got news that someone had come back from a trip or that some family's relatives had arrived from another village, she would immediately pick up her walking stick and walk over to see what kind of delicious fruit or sweets had arrived. When local fruit began to ripen, she made regular visits to anyone who had trees—such as mango, banana, and *kul* (sour plum)—in their yards. She would commission people who worked in or visited cities to bring back treats for her, either giving them some of her own money to do so or simply asking them to give the treats to her. No one felt comfortable refusing her: because of her age, such refusal would be an act of disrespect, an act of *adharma,* which might result in a curse or slander. I myself quickly became one of her most favored sources of bananas and mangoes.

All of these requests for food made her sons look bad. A neighboring woman said to me once, "Such an old woman with three capable sons is still going around pestering others for food! Chi! Chi! An old woman with three sons like that is not supposed to ask others for things; her sons are supposed to give them to her." The sons and their wives in fact did try to curtail her activities, but to little effect. When two of her grandsons and her middle daughter-in-law found out that she had asked me to bring her back a cotton bedsheet from Calcutta, they were furious at her. They called me over to find out if it was true and then scolded her: "Why are you asking some girl who has come here from a foreign country to give things to you? You have three sons. They can give things to you. You also have plenty of money of your own."

In this case, an old woman's sons and daughters-in-law strove sincerely to serve their aged mother attentively and to fulfill all her needs. They saw service to their mother as a moral and religious obligation, as well as important to maintaining their prestige in the community. But the mother herself had been very strong-willed and independent her whole life, and she was unwilling to become passive and peripheral, like most elders receiving care. Her wealth and determination both gave her a considerable amount of power over her children and allowed her to maintain independent ties with the world—neighbors, friends, debtors—that were not channeled through her kin, as people expected at her age and as her children would have liked. The family struggles over curtailing her transactions did not seem to bother her much, however; they primarily irritated and worried her sons and daughters-in-law.

Bhogi Bagdi

Bhogi Bagdi was an elderly Bagdi widow who had two sons but lived alone. The first time I met her, she was sitting at the edge of the path that ran in front of her small mud house, holding her head in her hands and moaning loudly. My companion Hena and I asked her what was wrong, and she answered plaintively, "My daughter died." Hena countered, "That happened several months ago. Why are you crying now?" Bhogi answered that her *bous* had just been arguing with her, that she had no one who would feed her or look after her, and that she might as well just die right there on the path.

I soon learned that the path in front of her house was one of Bhogi's favorite places to sit; I often found her there, moaning about her inconsiderate sons or chatting with and watching the various people go by. She was

Bhogi Bagdi.

a short, sturdy woman who had grown quite stooped over the years. She kept her thin, white hair pulled back in a loose knot, and she dressed in old, plain white saris. She had very large, deep eyes that seemed to spill over with self-pity.

Her two sons lived with their wives and children in houses a few yards away from hers. They had become separate (*pṛthak*) several years earlier when her husband died and his meager landholdings were divided among them. The house that she lived in was still hers, and in another village she owned a bit of land that she had inherited from her father. Her daughter's daughter looked after that land, and Bhogi was able to support herself—though just barely, she insisted—off its rice.

Bhogi's constant lament was that her sons and *bous* did not look after her. Sometimes she blamed this neglect on her own bad fate, saying that she must now be suffering the fruits of her bad karma from previous births. But at other times she blamed her sons. Once, when I asked her why her sons did not look after her, she replied, "They want to have sex all the time with their wives and other girls. If I'm there, it's inconvenient for them." She also said that although her older son gave her a cup of tea every once in a while, her younger son gave her nothing, not even a drop of tea or a few kind words. "He's even saying now that he's not from my stomach, that he came up from the earth or something," she added bitterly. She saw herself as someone who had no one. Tears would well in her eyes as she hung her head and said, "I have no one of my own." One day when I asked if I could take her photo, she answered sarcastically: "Why do you want to take my photo? My sons won't look at it. What would I do with it? Stuff it up my crotch?"

Bhogi's daughters-in-law had a different story to tell. They told me that they tried every day to care for her; that they brought her cooked food, tea, and even an occasional sari; but she would only slander them, curse at them, and say that the food was no good. They explained that their *śāśuṛī*, Bhogi, actually had a whole storehouse of rice, dal, tea, sugar, and salt that she had accumulated over the years from people's donations to her and from her land, but she did not like to draw on her supplies. (Bhogi had also told me about her store of goods, which she said she was saving for the future when she may need them even more.) But that was one reason, her younger *bou* explained, that many people did not want to help Bhogi out: they knew she had so much, even more than they did. Furthermore, hoarding food instead of giving it away was considered to be inappropriate, greedy behavior, particularly at Bhogi's age.

The *bous* claimed as well that Bhogi's unruly personality, and her tendency to swear and scold, made her a very unpleasant person to care for.

The younger *bou* said that sometimes her older sister-in-law chided her for continuing to try to feed their mother-in-law, saying, "You should just leave her alone. If she's acting like this, then she doesn't need us to care for her." "But what can I do?" the younger *bou* asked, "I still feed her. She is my *śāśuṛī*, after all."

Yet Bhogi seemed to find it important to deny that her sons and daughters-in-law wished to care for her. I once asked her if they ever brought her food and she admitted that sometimes they did, but added scornfully, "It's just because they're eyeing my house. They each have a greedy desire (*lobh*) for this house, and they think that if they feed me now, I'll give it to them." She insisted, though, that she would not leave the house to them: "I've already written that I will give it to my daughter's daughter. She's the only one who's good to me. She's the only one who loves me." Many people like Bhogi seemed to consider daughters and granddaughters more "loving" than sons and daughters-in-law, perhaps because daughters were not thought to be acting out of obligation—they had none, as we have seen—but out of affection. This pattern reveals intriguing reversals surrounding daughters and their attachments to natal families: sentiments like Bhogi's focused not on lineage (*baṃśa*) but on maya, affection.

On another occasion, Bhogi denied that her sons and *bous* tried to care for her at all. The following is an excerpt from our conversation:

BHOGI: Ever since my daughter died, my life has been full of suffering (*kaṣṭa*). Even after my husband died, it wasn't so bad, because I had my daughter to look after me. She fed me good things and loved me. But now I don't have anyone. Ask anyone, and they'll tell you that I have no one.

SL: What about your two sons and *bous*?

BHOGI: Oh, them. They don't look after me at all, not a bit. They don't even feed me a cup of tea.

SL: Your younger *bou* told me that she does feed you, that she wants to feed you.

BHOGI: No, they don't do anything at all.

SL: Where did you get this sari? [I continued to probe, noticing that she was wearing an unusually clean, new-looking sari that day.]

BHOGI: This? Well, my older son and *bou* gave it to me at *pūjā* (festival) time. But I didn't ask for it or anything. They just gave it—left it at my house. They didn't hand it to me, they just left it there. What will I do? They left it, so I'll wear it.

Just as villagers criticized Khudi Thakrun for asking other people for food when she had sons of her own, so neighbors would chastise Bhogi Bagdi for crying in front of others, trying to get their pity, when she had two sons. A neighboring Brahman woman, Bani, scolded her one day: "Don't whine so much in front of others! Why should they give you tea and *muṛi* (parched rice) when you have two sons and *bous* of your own to feed you?"

Bhogi Bagdi was a woman who had almost cut off all transactions with others. She did not easily accept what was offered to her by her sons, nor did she give out her store of goods to them. She had no real relations of exchange with either her kin or with others, and her self-isolation on the extreme peripheries of family and village life complicated her old age. Although she had two sons and *bous* who lived right next to her, in many ways she was, as she claimed, a person with no one of her own.

Sekh Abdul Gani

Sekh Abdul Gani was a senior Muslim man who lived with his wife, four sons, two daughters-in-law, and several grandchildren. He had become blind several years before I met him, and he spent most of his time simply sitting in a clearing in front of his house, near where children played or men threshed rice, or within the inner courtyard of his home with his wife, daughters-in-law, and grandchildren. He lived in the one large Muslim neighborhood of Mangaldihi, at the northern end of the village.

When I first came upon him, he was sitting in the morning winter sun, leaning against a haystack in the clearing in front of his home. He had the long gray beard typical of older Muslim men, and his blank eyes gazed upward and outward beyond all the passersby, the earthen homes, and the tall, golden haystacks. I went over to talk with him, and he began to tell me a tale of woe, of how his fate was bad, his body had deteriorated, and his sons did not care for him. He said that he lived with his wife and that she gave him a little bit of rice, but that without her he would surely die. He moaned and struck his forehead with his hand, saying: "My fate is very bad. I have four sons but they don't look after me. Neither do my *bous*. I can't see with my eyes, and I have such problems with my feet and arms that I can hardly walk. When I get up, I keep falling down. But my sons, they don't help me. They just say, '*Tu more jā!* (You die!).' And their kids don't help me either."

In this retelling of his sons' dismissal of him, he used the *tui* or *tu* form of "you." This form of the Bengali second-person pronoun is usually reserved for addressing inferiors such as young children or servants, or for addressing intimate childhood friends. It is gravely insulting to address a

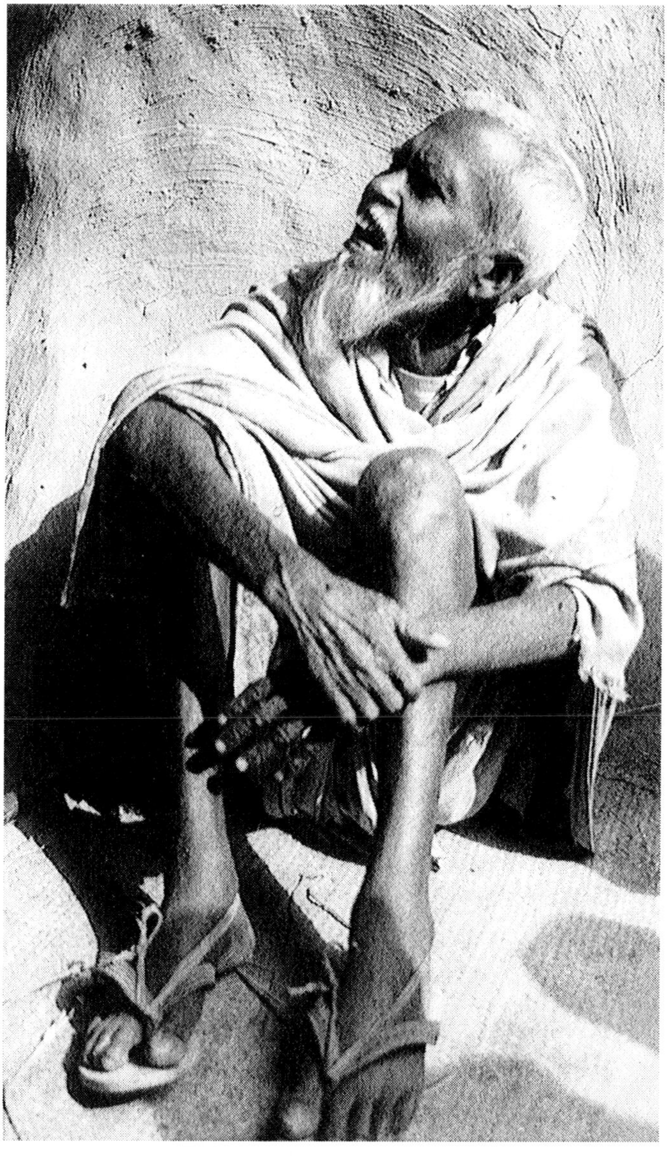

Sekh Abdul Gani.

parent, especially a father, as *tui.* Children usually call their fathers *tumi* (second-person equal) or occasionally, if their relationship is a formal one, *āpni* (second-person superior).

He then turned his head to face the small crowd of neighborhood children who had gathered behind me, and said, "You! You, Najrul's daughter! Speak up! I know you're there." One girl sheepishly and reluctantly replied. The old man said to her, "See, here you are and I'm sitting here dying in the sun and you won't even bring me a glass of water." She squirmed a bit but did not say anything. He turned to me and said, "That's my middle son's daughter. See, no one looks after me. Only my wife gives me a little bit of rice." He added that his sons argued with him all the time and did not listen to what he said. Such disrespect (*asammān*), he insisted, was possible only in these modern times. "I used to respect and be devoted to my parents so much," he said. "But these days sons no longer pay attention to who is their *guru* (superior, respected person). They don't have any respect for superiors. They don't fear their elders. They don't listen to their words. They used to listen. But not any more."

The next time I went back to visit I was expecting to hear more of the old man's complaints. But to my surprise, he seemed to be in an entirely different mood and portrayed his family relationships in an altogether new light. I asked him if his fate (*bhāgya*) was good or bad, and this time he answered: "Some good and some bad. From my second marriage [his first wife had left him without bearing any children], I had four sons and two daughters. This is my good luck. Now I am sick, but my sons are able to do the farming for me. If I didn't have sons, I would have had to sell everything and just sit here. My luck is very good that I have four sons. And because of the sons, my *baṃśa* (family line) will remain. There will be a lot of *baṃśa.* We are all of one *baṃśa,* and my sons will be four parts."

He proudly told me that his four sons all still lived and ate together with him and his wife, and that the responsibility for running the household was now in his oldest son's hands. The old man himself had willingly passed on the responsibility of being head of the household (*kartā*) to his son many years earlier. He explained: "All the responsibility has been in my oldest son's hands for about the past twenty to twenty-five years. That was after my son grew up and we gave his marriage. At that time my health wasn't good. I had [high blood] 'pressure' [he used the English word] and I would make all sorts of mistakes. From then on, I told my son to look after everything." When I asked him if his sons still argued with him a lot, he answered, "We both argue with each other, it's not just that they argue with me. Arguing doesn't happen alone. Just like clapping doesn't take place with just one hand." He seemed no longer to wish to blame his condition on his sons.

The old man alternated between complaining about and praising his juniors in this way for the rest of the time that I knew him. But during the few days before he died, he seemed pleased to have all of his needs attentively cared for by his juniors. I watched as his two daughters-in-law took turns by his side, massaging his feet and legs, changing his soiled bedsheets, and patiently spoon-feeding him water, tea, and small bits of cooked food. His wife, sons, and grandchildren stood and sat respectfully in the room around him. He told me the day before his death that he was happy to die surrounded by his family. He said, "Let my children be happy, and I will die."

The structure of Sekh Abdul Gani's family was exactly what most Bengalis believe families properly should be. He lived together with his sons, daughters-in-law, and grandchildren in the same household, eating the same food. He had already passed control over the household's financial affairs to his oldest son, so he could rest without worry in his old age while his son pursued his own aims and supported the family as a householder. The old man died surrounded by his younger relatives, who could both care for him in his death and carry on his family line.

But these relationships were also accompanied by ongoing struggles and dissatisfaction. The old man saw himself at times as extended and cared for by his sons, and at times as neglected by them. The four sons for their part often complained, neighbors told me, of their irritation in having to listen to their decrepit father. But they were saddened by the loss when he died; and they also had to face the separation from each other as four fatherless brothers moved into separate households.

Part Two

AGING AND DYING

4 White Saris and Sweet Mangoes, Partings and Ties

In the previous two chapters, aging and gender were considered from the perspective of persons who strive to maintain family relations in the face of such menaces as intergenerational conflicts and the changes brought by modernity. For both women and men in Mangaldihi, however, a central problem of aging was not how to maintain family ties that threatened to be too loose but how to loosen bonds—to kin, places, things, one's own body—that had become very tight. This is the problem I hinted at in the preface, in describing Mejo Ma's predicament—how could she die, when she was clinging so tightly to her world?—and in chapter 1, when I discussed the villagers' worries about the difficulties of my own departure from the village, after I had become so much a part of their net of maya. Bengalis believe they face a kind of tragedy in the life course. The ties making up persons—what they often call the bindings of maya—are in general likely to increase in number and intensity with the length of life; and yet it is also in later life when these ties must be loosened, as part of preparing for the myriad leave-takings of death. They perceive old age as a paradoxical time of life, when relations are the most fragile but the pulls of maya the strongest.

Men and women seemed equally affected by this aspect of aging. Unlike men, however, women also experienced the (often painful) unmaking and remaking of their personhoods, not only in aging and dying but also in marriage and widowhood. Before I turn to those subjects (in part 3), however, I wish to explore in part 2 the ways both women and men in Mangaldihi envisioned and confronted this complexly ambiguous dimension of the human condition: its irrevocable transience, on the one hand, yet its compelling intensity, on the other. I will also reflect briefly on how Bengali theories of aging speak to some of the trends in contemporary academic and popular thinking on aging in the United States.

THE PROBLEM OF MAYA

Maya is a multivalent concept found in all Indian languages. In its commonly glossed sense, "illusion," maya refers to the nature of the everyday, lived world of experience, known as *saṃsāra* in Sanskrit and in Bengali as *saṃsār*. As Wendy Doniger O'Flaherty (1984:116) notes, the world of *saṃsāra* has long been viewed by many Indians as unreal or illusory (that is, full of maya), either because other realities, such as God or *brahman*, are deemed to be more transcendent or true or because of its own ultimate impermanence. Margaret Trawick, too, takes maya as illusion and writes of it as the ambiguous, baffling, and deceptive nature of "the experience of life itself" (1990b:39, 104).

In rural West Bengal, although some more sophisticated and philosophically minded people speak of maya as "illusion," maya is more commonly equated with affects such as attachment (*āsakti*), affection (*sneha, mamatā*), compassion (*dayā*), or love (*bhālobāsā*). The term bears similar meanings in everyday Nepali.[1] A mother has maya for her son, and a son for his mother. Husbands and wives have maya for each other. People have maya for their houses, the trees that grow in their courtyards, and their belongings. People feel maya when they see a helpless person being hurt or a tiny calf bleating for its mother. Maya not only consists of what we would classify as emotional ties but involves substantial or bodily connections as well. Persons see themselves as substantially *part* of and *tied* to the people, belongings, land, and houses that make up their personhoods and lived-in worlds. These ties, for Bengalis, are all part of maya.[2]

Bengalis refer to maya as taking the form of "bindings" (*māyār bandhan*) or a "net" (*māyā jāl*) in which people, and all living beings, are enmeshed. Strands of this net can be experienced as "pulls" (*māyār ṭān*). The bindings of maya can also be loosened or "cut" (*māyā kāṭā jāe*) by acts such as moving away from a home or village, ceasing to give to and receive from others, or arguing; but we will see that "cutting" maya is something that most Bengalis believe to be extremely difficult to do.

Because maya means (at least in part) affection or attachment for others, it struck me, when I first began to hear Mangaldihi villagers speak of it, as a desirable quality, or at least one that many Americans would seek to cultivate. But people in Mangaldihi thought of maya (as both attachment and illusion) as problematic. Maya is, in fact, classified by Bengalis as one of six chief evils or "vices" (*ripus*) that plague human existence, along with anger (*krodh*), passion (*kām*), greed (*lobh*), pride (*ahaṃkār*), and jealousy (*hiṃsā*). One day I was talking to a young man, Babu, and my companion-assistant, Hena, about the meanings of maya. They explained that maya means "love" (*bhālobāsā*), "affection" (*sneha, mamatā*), and the "pull" (*ṭān*) persons feel for other people and things. Then Hena added: "Maya is a very bad thing." I was surprised and remarked, "We don't think of maya [translated in my mind here as 'affection' or 'love'] as a bad thing at all." They both replied straightaway, "Then you must not have much maya."

Hena, Babu, and others gradually led me to appreciate that maya is "bad" (*khārāp*) because it causes immense pain and suffering. Life is full of separations and losses, as sisters and daughters leave for their husbands' homes, grandparents and parents die, a favorite calf is sold, a beloved sari is torn; and the more maya people have for all of these things, the more they suffer the pain of separation. In fact, maya creates problems whenever there will be separations or conflicting attachments, which is ultimately the condition of all human relationships; according to those I knew, relationships are overwhelmingly intense but inherently ephemeral. The moment people feel the first tugs of maya, they immediately become sad thinking of the separation and loss to follow.[3] Those whose reasoning is more abstract fault maya for hindering one's perception of God (*bhagavān*) or "truth" (*satya*). Gurusaday Mukherjee explained to me that everything we have maya for is false or mistaken (*bhul*), because these things are not ultimately real or lasting. In this sense, maya means what Buddhists and Vedantists have called "illusion." God creates all the things we have maya for so that we will remain in the world; but as long as we have maya, we cannot find God or truth.

These understandings resonate with those conveyed in the Gopi Chand epic translated in Ann Gold's *Carnival of Parting* (1992). The epic, although Rajasthani, is said to have originated in Bengal. Maya here is presented as a complex intertwining of illusion, love for women, creative divine grace, delusive magicians' skills, and binding human attachments (see also Gold 1989, 1991). One telling refrain of the tale goes "Meeting is good, and parting is bad, and the noose of Maya's net is always very bad" (1992:331–33).

I ended up spending many hours talking with older people about maya. Gradually, I focused on some central questions: Does maya decrease with age—as Hindu texts stressing the values of renunciation in late life suggest *should* at least happen[4]—or does maya increase as people grow older? And if maya increases, then how do people manage their multiplying connections as they face the myriad leave-takings of death?

Long Lives and Increasing Maya

The responses to my questions about maya were complicated and varied, and they depended largely on people's personalities, family living situations, material wealth, physical health, and so on. Of those who had plenty—of kin and possessions—most argued that maya definitely increases with age. Of those who had almost nothing—such as beggars and dwellers in old age homes—many claimed that for them, maya had all but disappeared. In Mangaldihi, by far the majority of villagers I asked concurred that maya, for most people, increases with the length of life.

They provided several reasons for this conclusion. First, villagers argued quite logically that because kin such as children and grandchildren (and a spouse and affines) tend to increase in number as a person grows older, then maya necessarily increases as well. Here is how Billo's Ma, an older Bagdi woman, put it:

SL: Does maya decrease or increase with age? (*Bayaser sange māyā ki kame nā bāṛe jāe?*)

BILLO'S MA: It doesn't decrease. It increases. You have sons and daughters, and then your children have children. Won't maya increase then?

My companion, Hena, and her friend Babu expressed the same idea in a slightly different way:

BABU: For ordinary people who do *saṃsār* [i.e., have a family], maya increases day by day.

SL: Why?

HENA: When you are young you have maya and pull (*ṭān*) only for your mother, father, and older sister. But then when you marry, maya increases—for all of the people of your *śvaśur ghar* (father-in-law's house). And then you have kids, and then they have kids. You see, from all of this, maya is increasing. Look at Khudi Thakrun. Almost everyone in the village is her relative! She will never be able to abandon maya—never.

Choto Ma, an aged Brahman woman living with her two married sons, their wives, and two grandsons, similarly explained her increase in maya by pointing to her increasing attachment, especially for her daughters-in-law, or *bous*:

SL: Does maya increase or decrease with age?

CHOTO MA: With age? With age maya increases of course! As much

> as age happens, that much I feel, "Let my *bous* live well, let my *bous* live happily, let my *bous* wear good clothes"—and all that gives me much happiness. And if the village girls wear very nice clothes, that makes me very happy, too. That's all maya. Maya increases, of course! If my *bous* don't eat, then I think, "My *bous* haven't eaten yet," and I tell them, "Have some water, have some *muṛi* (parched rice), have some rice." I want to give them food when I eat. That's all maya.

Many villagers I spoke with used the same reasoning. This argument seems to require that a person highlight *junior* rather than senior kin, for older relatives would inevitably decrease as they merged into the collective body of deceased ancestors.[5] But given the large families that nearly everyone in Mangaldihi favored, people expected the numbers of their direct, collateral, and affinal descendants to increase. Thus people were generally thought to be made up of more and more ties with kin as they moved through life.

People also seemed to feel that maya is felt more intensely for junior rather than senior kin: like affection (*sneha*) and blessings, maya flows more powerfully downward than upward. One elderly Kayastha woman, Mita's Ma, expressed this view quite explicitly, as she explained that the mother's maya for her son is greater than the son's maya for his mother, and that the grandmother's maya for her grandchild is the greatest of all:

SL: Does maya increase with age or decrease?

MITA'S MA: Maya increases with age.

SL: Why does it increase?

MITA'S MA: At that time, with age (*bayaser sange*), strength is decreasing. [Old people] aren't able to work any more, and they aren't receiving money. They worry about how their children will get money and eat when they go away. At that time maya increases.
And, compared to her son's, a mother's maya is greater [i.e., a mother has more maya for her son than the son has for his mother]. And there is even greater maya for the son's child than for the son himself. [Just like] there is even greater maya for money's interest than for money itself. Let's say you gave a loan or put money in the bank. You want the interest to be brought to you quickly! [You say,] "Bring me the interest! Bring me the interest!" And in that way, after a person's child has a child, [the grandparent] doesn't feel that much maya

> for her own child, she feels the most maya for the grandchild.
>
> . . . [My mother] was dying on her bed, and even then she called to her granddaughter, my daughter, and said, "Eat. Here, have this milk." You see? She was dying on her bed, and even then she had maya.

Other people in Mangaldihi explained that not only does the number of kin increase, but also connections with all things—including possessions, money, houses, and village soil—accumulate and intensify over a long life. As Khudi Thakrun's middle-aged son, Gurusaday, put it: "For 'increased' people (*bṛiddha lok*), maya and desire (*kāmanā*) increase and increase (*bāṛe bāṛe*)! If they don't learn to abandon it at a young age, then this desire increases. At the time of death, however many possessions [a person] has, that much maya and *āsakti* (deep love or attachment) will he have—for all of those things." He went on to explain: "If you throw ghee in a fire, then the fire increases. In this way, desire and maya increase and increase as one gets old. People should think, 'I've received and done [things] all of my life. I won't do any more.' But instead they think, 'Let more happen, let more happen!' You see, it's like adding ghee to the fire. The more he gets, the more he wants!" He repeated this last phrase several times in English—"The more he gets, the more he wants! The more he gets, the more he wants!"—with a wide grin and enthusiastic voice, seemingly proud to have come up with such a wise proclamation in my tongue. And indeed this man's mother, Khudi Thakrun, was an excellent example of someone who in old age displayed this kind of passion for attachment.

Gurusaday Mukherjee explicated his statement further: the "fire" here refers to *bhog* (pleasure or enjoyment), and "maya is related to *bhog*." He said that the "ghee" thrown into the fire includes good food, money, sexual pleasure, nice clothes, sweet scents—the whole range of possessions, relationships, and pleasures. The more of these things a person encounters and acquires as the years go by, the stronger becomes his or her desire for them all—just as adding fuel to a fire makes it necessary to add even more fuel. So maya for the things and pleasures of the world increases over a long life, as a person's pleasurable experiences and possessions accumulate.

Some offered a third explanation of maya's increase in late life: as people grow closer to death, they become more and more aware that they will have to part from all of the people and things they have grown so close to, and this awareness of impending separation causes feelings of connection or maya to intensify. On another occasion when I asked Gurusaday if maya increases or decreases with age, he answered, as I related in the preface:

"Maya increases. . . . Why? Because [in old age a person] realizes that he will have to leave everything in this earth and go away." As he spoke, tears rose in his eyes, and he added: "When I die, then I will have to leave everyone and everything—my children and everything. Then all of the love (*bhālobāsā*) and all of the affection (*sneha*) that I will have—that is all maya. It will make tears come."

But a few people told me that maya *de*creases with age, or perhaps stays the same. Thus one aged Brahman man—Khudi Thakrun's youngest brother-in-law, Anil Mukherjee—answered my questions: "Maya? Before it increased. Now what will increase any more? It hasn't decreased, nor has it increased. It will stay until I die." Most if not all of those who believed that maya decreases were people who considered themselves to be already living "outside of *saṃsār*," such as wandering beggars, old age home dwellers, and childless widows, none of whom had real families of their own. They were distinctly in the minority, however, as most Mangaldihi villagers professed that the number of connections and the intensity of these connections—and thus maya—continue to grow with the length of one's life.

The Dangers of Maya in Late Life

If maya becomes increasingly strong over the life course, then the living of one's final years—facing losses, separations, and death—can be very painful indeed. Furthermore, people fear that those who have very strong attachments may hang on in painfully decrepit old age rather than die, or may turn into a lingering ghost (*bhūt*) after death. The older people of Mangaldihi spoke and worried about maya all the time—chiding their friends for having too much maya, claiming sometimes that their own maya had all but disappeared, or wondering how they would be able to cut their maya and leave.

Maya is most troubling to the old because it hampers the soul (*ātmā*) after death. Maya, according to Bengalis I knew, can result in a person (or the person's soul) being quite literally "bound" (*bandhan karā*) to his or her body, surroundings, and relationships, caught as in a "net" (*māyājāl*) and therefore unable to die, even if very ill and feeble, and unable to depart from his or her previous residence and relations after death. One frail aged woman, Ananda's Ma, worried about the binding nature of maya: "It's time for me to die now. But I'm not able to shed off maya. That's why I'm not dying. How will I leave all my kids and things and go? When I cut the maya, then I will go. But how will the maya be cut?" Choto Ma expressed her concerns about maya this way: "I worry about *saṃsār* (household life, this household). How will my kids and everything all live well [after I die]? How will I go and leave this all behind? The more age happens, the more my strength decreases, and it becomes difficult to live. My time for dying has come already. If I die, I will receive peace, relief (*khālās*). But there's maya. How will I cut the maya and go?"

In another conversation I had with Choto Ma and her longtime friend and sister-in-law, Mejo Ma, which also focused on the problems maya can cause to those facing death, Choto Ma interrupted to chide Mejo Ma for having too much maya.

MEJO MA: If I died now it would be good. I have no wish to continue living. Now I'm thinking—I'll go, I'll go. [pause] But there's maya.

SL: Maya for whom?

MEJO MA: For everyone.

SL: Will you try to reduce maya?

MEJO MA It doesn't happen. Even if you try to reduce maya, it doesn't happen. Your insides go *jigjigjigjig* [i.e., twinge or flutter], wanting to see everyone again. Maya can't be cut at all (*māyā kichutei kāṭā jāe nā*).

SL: Is it good to cut maya?

MEJO MA: It's good. [Slight pause.] I don't exactly know.

CHOTO MA: She gets scared when she's alone at night. She lies awake until twelve o'clock thinking, "I'm going to die. I'm going to die. If I die it will be good." But then when she thinks of Yamaraj [the god of death] coming, she thinks, "How will I go? I won't be able to go. I want to see my children, talk to them, and then go."

MEJO MA: Yes, I must see one of my grandchildren's weddings before I go.

CHOTO MA: See! That's maya! She's showing her maya! She won't be able to go until the maya is cut.

It was common for people, especially older women, to talk like this about who among them does or does not have much maya, scolding one another for having too much maya and lingering on past the proper time for dying. One day as I was walking through the village with a married Brahman woman, Bani, we came upon Bhogi Bagdi as she was sitting in the lane in front of her home, complaining (as usual) about her sufferings and the neglect of her sons. Bani said first to me, disapprovingly: "Bhogi is in her decrepit age (*jārā bayas*), but she is still 'lingering' [she used the English word]." She then turned to Bhogi: "You must have a lot of wishes (*icchā*) left. Otherwise you wouldn't keep on living like this." Bhogi protested: "No, no! The longer I live, the more pain (*kaṣṭa*) I suffer. If I die it will be good." But Bani insisted that Bhogi's wishes must be causing her to linger on, and warned that until she "cut [her] maya" she would not be able to die.

Not only can maya cause people to hang on into wasted old age, but it can also make the process of dying itself very slow and painful. I asked one elderly Kayastha woman, Mita's Ma, who was blind in one eye and lame in one leg, "Is it good to try to get rid of maya before death?" She answered: "At the time of death, maya does not go away. It does not go away easily. At the time of death, [the person] is lying in the bed, and all the people are around him. He cannot say anything, but if you look at his eyes, you will see that tears are coming out of them. He will cry. He can't say anything; he's unconscious; his eyes are closed. But you will see that water is coming out of his eyes. Then people will say, 'He is crying from maya; he is not able to go' (*māyāte kānnā kā̃dche; jete pārche nā*)."

After death, a person with too much maya may cling to his or her familiar places and relations in the form of a lingering ghost, or *bhūt*.[6] Gurusaday Mukherjee described this danger: "If someone dies with very much maya or love (*bhālobāsā*), then he will try to love after death. He will hang around his household in the form of his subtle body (*sūkṣma deha*) and bother people. Some people call this a ghost (*bhūt*)."

Mita's Ma, the old and partially blind Kayastha woman, worried about this possibility. She told me of the suffering of the ghost—how it becomes confused, hungry, and trapped, and painfully longs to be reunited with its former household:

MITA'S MA:	If there is a lot of maya, then one can become a ghost.
SL:	One can become a ghost?
MITA'S MA:	Yes, if there is a lot of maya, then [the *ātmā* or soul] stays caught [near] the house (*ghar*). The more the household people cry, the more the *ātmā* cannot leave. The *ātmā* tries to get inside the house, but it can't. It has become closed. Then the *ātmā* becomes hungry. But it doesn't know how to get in. No one can see it.[7]
MITA'S MA'S DAUGHTER:	[who had been listening] The *ātmā* becomes late [*deri*; perhaps "late for reaching where it is supposed to go after death"] because it wants to have some water. [Its] throat becomes such a way (*ki rakam*) for the sake of the house.

MITA'S MA: Yes, for the house, the house. The house is where his maya is. And for that reason, he cannot leave. He will take another birth within the same *baṃśa* (family line)—that is what I have heard.

SL: Is that a good thing? [To me, the idea of a longing person being reborn within the same family line sounded rather nice.]

MITA'S MA: No, the good thing is to go to heaven (*svarga*), to attain release (*mukti*).

In this scenario, the maya not only of the dying person but of the clinging and mourning survivors as well is a problem, keeping him bound to his former household as a ghost: "The more the household people cry," Mita's Ma reports, "the more the *ātmā* cannot leave." T. N. Madan (1987:125) observes that Hindus generally believe that excessive attachment and clinging on the part of surviving relatives can cause one's death to be lingering and painful.

Mangaldihi villagers most commonly defined the desired state of *mukti* or "release," named by Mita's Ma, as liberation from the particular binding ties of a lifetime; above all, it entails freedom from lingering ghosthood. *Mukti* also means the attainment of peace (*śānti* or *khālās*) and, perhaps, an opportunity to dwell temporarily in the realm of heaven, or *svarga*. Some villagers, much more rarely, spoke as well of *mukti* or *moksha* as the state of absolute freedom from all ties to the world of *saṃsār*, a permanent end to the cycle of rebirths and redeaths; but all agreed that this state was virtually impossible to achieve and not much worth striving for.[8] It is maya that can prevent both forms of *moksha*—as permanent freedom from all ties and as freedom from the ties of one particular life—from being achieved.

LOOSENING TIES, DISASSEMBLING PERSONS

Many in Mangaldihi experienced a conflict between the natural drive to maximize connections and the wish to minimize the complexities of life and pains of separation at death. To deal with this conflict, many older people tried various approaches to undo the growing ties of their maya. I suggest here that the everyday routines often practiced by older people that constituted *aging* worked also as techniques for loosening their ties of maya or disassembling their personhoods, at least a bit.

The set of practices associated with retirement to the "senior stage" (*buṛo bayas*) in Mangaldihi seemed to help in dissolving extensions of the person. Such practices included decentering and "cooling" the body and heart-mind (*mānas*), as well as giving up one's possessions and powers to others. Aging persons could decenter themselves by physically relocating either inside or outside the household. Pierre Bourdieu (1977:89–91) has suggested that in the plan and usage of a house, fundamental cultural principles are generated, experienced, and objectified. But most ethnographers (including Bourdieu) generally overlook the ways in which hierarchies and values associated with age may index (or be indexed by) uses of domestic space.

In Mangaldihi households, a primary dimension of the structuring of old age was a movement from center to periphery (see chapter 2). The hub of activity and commingling was usually the central courtyard or the main front veranda of a house. This was where people congregated and socialized, ate, prepared food, studied, negotiated business deals, and frequently slept—often together, in long lines of mats spread on the floor. Senior men and women, who had adult sons and resident daughters-in-law to succeed them, tended to move to the outskirts of the household, perhaps resting on a string cot at one end of the veranda, or tending a young child in a patch of warm winter sun, or cutting vegetables with a curved iron kitchen knife (while leaving the actual cooking to a daughter-in-law), or listening to and watching the activities of visitors and kin. Such moves toward the periphery indicated their freedom from former ties and duties, while also signaling surrender of the kinds of control over goods and people that are best exercised from centers. It is thus unsurprising that retirement to the edges of activity was experienced ambivalently by most senior women and men, and was often accompanied by serious intergenerational conflict: the peripheral elder may rise in the hierarchy of respect and gain freedom from encumbering ties and responsibilities, but he or she loses tangible political and economic powers.[9]

In addition, retirees displayed their greater detachment from family centers by moving beyond the confines of household space: they spent more of their days at others' houses chatting, playing cards, and drinking tea; resting on the cool platforms of temples; and loitering at shops or on roadsides, simply watching people come and go. These behaviors, appropriate for them, would have been criticized among younger persons, especially young women, as defections from duty. Most saw their seniority as presenting opportunities for leaving the village to visit married daughters or undertake pilgrimages to faraway holy places.

Senior people also tended to remove themselves increasingly from the "heat" of a household's major transactional flows. Thus elders were usually fed before and separately from others, a privilege that reflected their seniority and at the same time kept them from mixing their substance with others'. The principal married couple of a house whose sons were not yet married were felt to be at the warm, reproductive, and redistributive human "center" (*mājhkhāne*) of life in a Bengali household; they made decisions for and gave food, knowledge, and services to all the others around them, including retirees and the young children who were located on the household's peripheries. Couples who had passed that central reproductive and culinary stage commonly became celibate, conventionally saying, "It's the time of the young ones now; our time has passed," or feeling it "embarrassing" or "improper" for two generations simultaneously to engage in sexual relations (see also S. Vatuk 1990:74). These curtailments of household givings and receivings were desirable, a few villagers told me, because they reduced possible competition, as well as making the retired heads more "separate" (*pṛthak*) in anticipation of their moves toward ultimate separation. Nitai Mukherjee, my companion Hena's father, described his late-life strategies: "I don't give anything to anyone, and I don't take anything from anyone either. I have become absolutely separate (*pṛthak*), absolutely singular (*ekā*). Before I didn't understand things so well and I used to mix (*miśtām*) with people, but not any more."

Retirees who took peripheral places in Mangaldihi households spoke also of the bodily changes that accompanied this transition. Older people characterized their bodies as increasingly "cool" (*ṭhāṇḍā*) and "dry" (*śukna*).[10] According to local theories, cooling and drying constrict the channels through which an individual's substances flow and mix with those of others, thereby making the bodies of older people relatively self-contained. Although people viewed bodily cooling and drying as part of the physiology of aging, most also took steps to encourage these natural internal changes.

Thus some people, especially upper-caste widows and men who professed spiritual goals, began methodically excluding from their diets any "hot" (*garam*) foods (such as meat, fish, onions, and garlic), which they thought would excite their worldly passions and attachments (I discuss widows' dietary practices further in chapter 7). The celibacy commonly practiced by (and expected of) elders was also regarded as a "cooling" lifestyle, and many older women and men told me that because of the cooling and drying of their bodies, they would not be able to engage in sexual activity even if they had wanted to. By wearing clothing that was mainly white (a "cool" color), most older people advertised their celibacy or widowhood, their claims of sexual purity, and their general intention to renounce the world for the sake of their soul-selves. The transition to white was especially dramatic for women, who during their reproductive years generally favored red, a "hot" color signaling sexuality, fertility, and auspicious attachments.

Verbal techniques, too, could both reduce worldly connections and promote heavenly ones. Arguing and cursing were sometimes used, perhaps unwittingly, to promote alienation. This may be why the aged Bhogi Bagdi used to sit in the middle of the dusty lane in front of her mud house, loudly berating and effectively driving away any of her sons, sons' wives, or neighbors who might be within hearing. Younger people could practice similar methods to reduce their maya, when necessary. Over the weeks before Hena was to be married, she would sometimes plead with me to argue with her, and she would pick fights with me. She had been living in my home for about six or seven months and we had become very close. Once after we had quarreled she apologized and explained, "You see, if we fight with each other now, then I can cut the maya a little *before* I have to leave."

Some elders similarly attempted to loosen their bonds with their own bodies by denigrating their flesh, which they compared with old clothing that should be discarded, or with rice plants that have dropped their seeds and are about to wither away. Others spent hours every day and fell asleep at night chanting the names of deities so they might weaken their own earthly ties and accustom their souls to the discourses of the heavenly abodes they desired.

People diminished their ties of maya to things as well, freeing themselves of their favorite possessions in late life—giving away property, jewelry, favorite saris, keepsakes. Gurusaday Mukherjee explained, "Maya and attachment (*āsakti*) increase in proportion to the amount of possessions held. For this reason," he added, "wise people won't wear shoes or eyeglasses in old age." One Brahman widow, Petan Pisi, told me: "Last December I gave all my land to my daughter in writing. . . . [Now I am] completely possessionless (*nisva*)." To be possessionless (*nisva*) is also a way of saying that one is "without self" (from *ni*, "without," and *sva*, "self"), for possessions help make up a person or self. She went on to explain that property both is heavy (*bhārī*) in itself and also ties one to others who wish to share in it: "I didn't keep all of those heavy things. Wealth (*artha*) is a very heavy thing. Many people wanted it. One would say, 'Give me this,' and another would say, 'Give me that.' Yet another would say, 'Come stay with me, I'll look after you.' But I didn't give anything to anyone but my daughter. I said, 'When I have someone from my own belly, I'll give it to her.' . . . I have no need for money. It's a very heavy thing. What I need is Gavinda (God)."

Thakakrisna Thakur, at age ninety-six the second oldest person in Mangaldihi, described how he had abandoned his possessions, including the sacred thread or *paitā* that Brahman men wear, in an attempt to free himself from the bindings (*bandhan*) that seemed to be keeping him alive. He spoke in a pained voice, soft and raspy with age, as he lay on a straw mat at one edge of the family's veranda: "I tore off both the sacred thread (*paitā*) and *baiṣṇab mālā*,[11] because I felt that they were binding (*bandhan*). I thought that if I opened them then I would die. How many more days will I have to suffer like this? . . . I have abandoned all things. Before I never threw anything out, not even one piece of grain, but now I have given it all away." When I asked Satya Narayan Mukherjee, Hena's white-bearded uncle, "What more do you want to do in the rest of your life?" he answered: "If my daughters' weddings happen, then I would like to start an ashram. I will say God's name from the ashram for the rest of my life. . . . I want to live completely without attachments (*nirlipta bhābe*). I want to have no more responsibilities (*dāyitva*). This is my inner wish—to go on to this stage. . . . If wealth (*artha*) exists there is no peace (*śānti*). That's why people say, 'Happiness is at the cremation ground; peace is at the cremation ground.' . . . He who is happy is he who abandons (*tyāgī*)."

By moving from the center to the peripheries of household life, cooling the body, diminishing their substance by giving away possessions, and transcending the self and its ties by mingling with God, many Mangaldihi seniors strove to shrink those personal extensions that were known as maya. But we must recognize that those who spoke the most explicitly about the need to cut maya in late life were the well-off and upper castes. The most conspicuously favored with property and plentiful descendants were said to be in the most danger of becoming excessively bound by maya. Most of the lower-caste people in Mangaldihi, for instance, could not afford eyeglasses, so they would not have the luxury of rejecting them to draw back on themselves in old age. Although lower-caste people did sometimes voice concerns to me about maya, they were often much more worried about immediate economic needs, such as procuring the next meal, or a shawl to keep warm, than about how to achieve a peaceful old age, death, and afterlife. Some of the criticisms I heard in lower-caste neighborhoods against people like Khudi Thakrun—who maintained what some condemned as an unseemly hold over her wealth into her senior years—could thus be viewed as a (limited) form of attack by the weaker and poorer against superiors, one of their "weapons of the weak" (James Scott 1985): a circumscribed way of valorizing the "poor" or "small" person (*garib lok, choṭo lok*) over the "rich" and "big" (*boṛo*).

PILGRIMS, BEGGARS, AND OLD AGE HOME DWELLERS

Although dominant discourses in the Mangaldihi region, as throughout north India, proclaim that elderly people should live with their descendants within homes filled with extended family, I could not help noticing, as I traveled through train stations, cities, pilgrimage spots, and even Mangaldihi's lanes, that many did not follow the "appropriate" course. The majority of pilgrims in West Bengal, on spiritual bus tours or living permanently around temples at holy sites, are white-clad people old enough to be grandparents. Beggars in rural Bengal are also more often than not advanced in age, with white hair and garb and leaning on long walking sticks. Other people now are turning to old age homes in Calcutta (or other such major north Indian cities) to live out their final days. It may seem strange to group together these three classes of people—pilgrims, beggars, and old age home dwellers—but I gradually discovered profound similarities in their experiences. All were living, temporarily or permanently, outside of *saṃsār,* or household life. Most of the beggars and old age home residents I met (and some of the pilgrims, especially the permanent ones) had been forced to leave their households because they had no money, land, or sons on whom they could depend for support. In many ways, they were the poorest of the poor. Yet over time I was struck by a common refrain in many of their stories: "This life has been so painful," one old woman, widowed in childhood, told me from the courtyard of the temple where she resided, "but in one sense it's been good: I don't have all the bindings of maya."

Taking Pilgrimages in Late Life: Loosening Ties through Outer Wandering

Over the first year or so of my stay in Mangaldihi, I had heard many older people tell the stories of their pilgrimages to holy "crossing places" (*tīrtha-sthāns*),[12] such as Gaya, Hardwar, and Varanasi along the Ganges, and to Puri at the wondrous ocean in Orissa. They spoke, as Ann Gold (1988:263) notes of pilgrims in Rajasthan, of pilgrimage as an appropriate activity for the old. But although I had written in my various research proposals that I, too, would go on one of the popular *darśan* bus pilgrimages and investigate the meanings and aims of pilgrimage for older Bengalis, my sojourn in Mangaldihi had almost come to a close before I found a pilgrimage leaving from the region. One day early in my second spring, just when it was becoming almost too hot to consider taking such a journey, three older Mangaldihi women, all widows from the Kulu (a middle-caste) neighborhood, informed me that they had signed up to go to Puri. The bus would be leaving in three days, loaded with people from a number of surrounding villages.

I immediately sought out the leader of the bus tour at the local government ration store to reserve a place. But three days later, as I waited seven hours with my fellow Mangaldihi pilgrims by the side of a sparsely shaded road for a bus that, it seemed, would never come, I began to have misgivings: If the bus is seven hours late now, what will the rest of the trip be like? Summer is setting in—will I be able to bear the sweltering heat for a week on a crammed bus? And what if there are no older folk besides my Mangaldihi companions on this tour? After all, I had come to India to study aging, not pilgrimage per se. Would I have to suffer a week on a crowded bus pilgrimage without gaining anything tangible for my research?

The last of these worries, if not the others, was assuaged as the bus finally arrived. I wearily boarded and was pleased to see a sea of white saris and dhotis, the sure sign of a busload of people who consider themselves "senior" (*buṛo*). Indeed, about 70 percent of the people on this bus were quite advanced in age. There were forty-five pilgrims on the journey; thirty-one could be classified as old, with married children, graying hair, and predominantly white clothing. About two-thirds of these elders, or almost half of the total group, were widows. The five young men who acted as guides confirmed that the pilgrims on such bus tours usually were older people. (Although, they added, it would be easier for the *guides* if the pilgrims were younger. "Have you noticed how these people have to urinate and defecate all the time? Did you see how we had to carry that old grandfather down from the Sun temple outside of Puri?")

The pilgrims were from a variety of castes, high and low—including Brahmans (11), Kayasthas (9), Kulus (9), Chasas (7), Suris (3), Doms (4), and Borgis (2)—and they came from five different villages in the Mangaldihi region. About half of the pilgrims (most of the widows) were traveling alone; the others came with one or a few relatives, usually a spouse, son, or sibling. All were fairly well-to-do, for taking such a journey requires considerable funds—the initial bus fare of 150 rupees, plus the constant stream of money that pours out to temple gods, pilgrim priests, beggars, and tea stalls along the way. The weeklong trip culminated at the Jagannath temple and ocean at Puri, but the bus also stopped at numerous smaller temples and *tīrthasthāns*, including the old terra-cotta temples at Vishnupur in West Bengal and Bhubaneswar in Orissa. At night we slept either on the bus or on the ground next to it, with the exception of two relatively luxurious nights spent at a *dharmaśālā*, or pilgrim's shelter, in Puri. Most people's diets consisted largely of parched rice (*muṛi*) brought from home, though some of the wealthier pilgrims and those less finicky about purity sought out hot meals of rice and dal at small roadside restaurants known as "hotels."

In examining this bus journey, I focus only on how Bengalis view the relationship between pilgrimage and the self in old age.[13] The pilgrims on our weeklong bus tour, and older people from Mangaldihi who had gone on other pilgrimages, responded in several ways to my questions about why old age is considered an appropriate time for taking pilgrimages. First, some said, it is their last opportunity to go. After this, they will die, or their bodies will become too weak (*durbal*) and decrepit (*jārā*) to withstand such a journey. Most also stressed that with their children married, they are for the first time free to leave home. Younger people, several said, are "in the field of *saṃsār*"; they are too busy with household work to have the luxury of departing on such trips. But for those who have sons and daughters-in-law to take care of household responsibilities, old age offers a new opportunity to journey. Several older women also mentioned that they felt free to go on pilgrimages only after they had ceased to menstruate. It is a "great sin" (*mahāpāp*) to go on a pilgrimage—and especially to bow down before a temple god—while menstruating; so postmenopausal women are most fit to be pilgrims (see chapter 6 for more on menopause). Several younger women of Mangaldihi spoke to me longingly about going on the bus tour to Puri, and even toyed with the idea among themselves and with their husbands up until the very end. But in the end each decided that she could not go—either because of household responsibilities, the inability to attain a husband's permission, fear of menstruation, or lack of funds. People also told them, "Your time for pilgrimage has not come yet. You can go later."

For older pilgrims who have the freedom from *saṃsār* to embark on pilgrimages, journeying to distant temples and crossing places can be a particularly effective means of loosening all ties to household life. Several pilgrims mentioned explicitly that they saw the pilgrimage as an important point of transition from life in the household to a life of focus on God. Gold notes that some of the older pilgrims on her bus trip from Rajasthan to Puri also spoke of the trip "as a major break in their ways of living. After they returned they would devote themselves single-mindedly to praising God" (1988:263).

To be sure, older pilgrims on this and other journeys gave other reasons for going on pilgrimages as well. Though quite varied, these divided people into two major categories: those who went simply "to see" (*dekhte*) and those who went "to do *tīrtha*" (*tīrtha karte*, literally "to do crossing," or to go on a pilgrimage). Many claimed that their motivation for taking the journey was to do both. "Seeing" includes the pleasures of traveling, viewing distant places and sites, meeting new people, bringing back souvenirs, and having fun (*ānanda karā*). Most of the younger pilgrims on the bus tour emphasized these reasons, and many of the older people also included the joys of "seeing" in recounting the fruits of the journey.

"Doing *tīrtha*" is another matter altogether. To do *tīrtha* distinctly involves suffering and exertion (*kaṣṭa*). I learned this on the first morning of the trip, when—after we had all suffered through an entire day waiting impatiently for the bus to come, and then spent a restless night on a stalled bus only about three hours down the road from our village homes—many of the pilgrims began to complain loudly that they were hungry, tired, and needed a place to relieve themselves; that we hadn't gotten anywhere yet; and that something must be terribly wrong with our guides for getting us off to such an unpromising start. Several of the other pilgrims, however, chided the complainers (including me, who was one of the more vocal among them), saying, "To do *tīrtha* you must suffer." They added, "If you wanted to sleep and eat, you should have stayed at home. We've come to do *tīrtha*. Therefore we must suffer (*kaṣṭa karte hae*)." And: "If the journey is comfortable, then traveling (*beṛāno*) happens, but not *tīrtha*. To do *tīrtha*, you must have troubles (*kaṣṭa*) along the way." Doing *tīrtha* was also thought to involve taking *darśan* (auspicious sight) of gods, eating *prasād* (the leftovers of deities), and giving out money to deities, temple priests, and beggars; but it seemed to me that perhaps the most important ingredient was suffering (*kaṣṭa*).

The sufferings to be endured on a proper pilgrimage include, I came to learn, sleeping on the ground and on cramped bus seats, going barefoot, wearing crumpled clothing, becoming hungry and thin, giving out too much money into the insistent hands of pilgrim priests and beggars, being plagued by mosquitoes, getting dysentery from foreign waters, and simply being far away from the comforts and company of home life. These kinds of sufferings are useful in that they all entail giving up things, emptying oneself, and loosening attachments to the people, goods, and ways of home. As Gold writes: "Pilgrimage helps to loosen all kinds of bonds. . . . The effect is one of lightening: the returning pilgrim should be thinner and poorer" (1988: 263). Bengali pilgrims say that without lightening oneself and enduring hardships in this way, one cannot really reach God. And lightening the self through suffering can also be an effective technique of reducing the bindings of maya. It is specifically through *kaṣṭa*—by forsaking material comforts, the pleasures of home life, the company of loved ones, the tastes of plentiful food—that persons diminish their substance, become lighter and freer, cut the ties of maya. Effective pilgrimage must involve troubles because, Bengalis say, any time that maya is "cut," *kaṣṭa* must be endured.

Most on this pilgrimage remarked, however, that even while enduring the rigorous practice of pilgrimage, they cannot fully cut maya. One pilgrim, a well-educated older man of the Suri caste named Bhudeb Saha, told a few fellow pilgrims on the final day of our journey: "I came on this pilgrimage to do two works (*kāj*). One was to take *darśan* of the gods. The other was to give up all the things of *saṃsār* (household life). But," he added in a somber tone, full of emotion, while gesturing to his wife sitting next to him, "I left everything to come, but I couldn't leave her." A fellow pilgrim asked in a teasing tone, smiling, "What will happen when you die? Then you will *have* to cut your maya and leave her." The first pilgrim did not respond. Tears welled in his eyes and he sat silently for a moment. Then he wiped his eyes dry and changed the subject.

Other pilgrims complained that they had suffered *too* much on the journey, that they had become *too* empty. They did not see such a degree of self-diminishing to be necessary and were looking forward to returning to the familiar comforts and attachments of home. One elderly Brahman pilgrim, who had made the journey with his wife, stated decisively on the final day: "From now on I'm staying at home. I don't want to go on any more pilgrimages. All of these people want to take all of our money. They have taken everything out of my bag and left me completely empty (*khāli*). From now on I'm not going to leave home." Even when they sought to move away from household life on a pilgrimage, most said that it is impossible to cut the ties of maya altogether. In the end, people tend to cling to at least a few possessions or persons they hold most dear, such as a spouse, home, or money.

Wandering Beggars

Like pilgrims, most of the beggars in rural West Bengal are older people. Most villages in the Mangaldihi region support a few regular senior beggars. Mangaldihi had three. Although begging is not usually begun by choice, and although it entails even more suffering than the temporary rigors of pilgrimage, some beggars whom I encountered claimed that a life of begging produces many of the same fruits, and even more dramatically: an emptying and lightening of the self, a loosening of ties. By wandering continually from place to place, beggars loosen their attachments to particular homes, villages, and soils. By living essentially alone, they ease their attachments to kin, neighbors, and friends. By eating food prepared and offered by numerous others, beggars become partially mixed with many but thoroughly mixed with none. By living without possessions and dispersing money as soon as it is received, beggars forsake binding ties with belongings and material wealth. Beggars become some of the lightest, most unconnected, and peripheral people of all, similar to the *sannyāsīs*, or ascetics, that Hindu texts recommend as modeling the last life stage. Granted, none of the beggars who spoke to me of the advantages of begging had purposefully left behind a prosperous family of caring sons in order to cultivate an ascetic, wandering lifestyle. Each had been driven to begging out of poverty, and usually out of sonlessness as well. Yet several explicitly described how, after many days of begging, they had come to realize the maya-reducing benefits of such a reduced, yogic life.

The beggar who voiced this perspective most articulately was Prafulla Adhikari, known in Mangaldihi as "Cluber Dadu" or the Club's Grandfather, as he was initially found and brought to Mangaldihi by several youths of the Mangaldihi young men's "club" on one of their picnic outings to a nearby Kali temple and cremation ground. They had found the old beggar asleep lying face down on the ground, drunk, and when he woke up they persuaded him to return with them to Mangaldihi. This happened several months before I moved into the village. Cluber Dadu was a Brahman man who had never married and had spent most of his life moving from location to location doing temporary jobs—working in a supply office for the British, cooking for a medical college, running errands for a Calcutta bank, and the like. But after he had lost a job as a threshing machine operator several years earlier, he had not been able to find any more work. "Age had happened," he explained. "I didn't have the strength I used to. From then on [I have had] this profession, of begging."

It was not easy for him to begin begging. After he had exhausted his meager savings, he had spent several days sitting in a tea shop in a small town named Gargariya near Mangaldihi, consuming nothing but two or three cups of tea a day. One noon, the local schoolteacher invited him to his home to eat a meal, but that was just one meal. Finally, after four days had passed like this, another old beggar came to the shop and said, "Hey, you should come begging with me." "It was he who first taught me how to beg," Cluber Dadu told me. "I went with him for the first time to beg at a Muci [leatherworking caste] house. Then I couldn't really do it right. It used to bother me a lot. But now it's gotten all right. If [one's] headwriting [i.e., fate written on one's forehead] is bad, then my type of condition happens. Now I have only one identity—as a beggar (*bhikhāri*). I have no house. I live on the road."

In Mangaldihi, Cluber Dadu did end up gaining a house of sorts, though he continued to view himself as homeless. A prosperous Kulu man of the village donated a ten-foot square piece of land across from the village post office on which several young men built a tiny mud hut. There Cluber Dadu spent most of his nights. By day he would wander around the village begging. Some days people would offer him leftovers from a cooked meal or even invite him in to eat, and on other days he would simply boil up whatever rice he had collected in his begging bowl and eat that. Sometimes he would leave for a few days or even months, but over the eighteen months that I was there he continued to return to Mangaldihi as his most frequent abode.

This man described his life as one full of sadness (*dukha*), suffering (*kaṣṭa*), and silent hunger. But at the same time, he spoke of the advantages of his life as a drifting beggar, because it had made him free of the bindings of maya, giving him much greater peace (*śānti*) than could be enjoyed by those who pursue a household life. He narrated his life story one winter afternoon, from his cramped mud hut; some excerpts follow.

> Ever since then I began a life of begging. But this kind of life is happy. Because whether I eat or don't eat, there's no one to see it or worry about it. No hassles. On the days that I beg, I eat. If I don't beg, I don't eat. I have no wife or sons, none of the hassles of household life (*saṃsār*). I live outside of *saṃsār*. I can perceive *saṃsār*, but I don't have the bindings (*bandhan*) of maya. . . .

I asked then, "Is it good or bad to have the bindings of maya?" He continued:

> It is good if the bindings of maya do not exist. In this way the *ātmā* (soul) receives peace (*śānti*). Because the bindings of maya are passing [or "momentary," *samayik*]. It is good to attain release (*mukti*) from this passing binding. . . . I didn't use to understand this. But even then, without understanding, I didn't do *saṃsār* [i.e., make a family life]. Now I realize that this [absence of *saṃsār*] is right. Household people (*saṃsāri lok*) are very rarely happy. They worry. But I don't have any of that. As a result, I do suffer some, but I gain much more peace (*śānti*).

Of course, he did worry at times, if not about how to feed a wife and sons, then about who would perform his funeral rites after he died, or how long he would remain welcome in Mangaldihi. One day he came to tell me that he had decided to leave Mangaldihi, for he had begun to feel that people no longer greeted him warmly and gave to him openly as they once did. He sang me a song that he said he had composed about his life:

> Of those whose lives are filled only with tears,
> I am among that group.
> Not a garland of plums, but a necklace of thorns
> I have worn around my neck.
>
> This is not a song
> but the crying of my heart.
> The dew of all of life's sorrows
> is falling in the dark forest night.

Begging may bring peace and a freedom from the binding ties of maya, but it entails much suffering (*kaṣṭa*). The Dadu sings, "The dew of all of life's sorrows is falling in the dark forest night," that is, where there is no one even to watch it fall.

Old Age Home Dwellers

Old age homes are still a relatively new and rare phenomenon in India. As I noted in chapter 3, various Christian-run homes for the aged have existed in India for over a hundred years, and they are viewed by many as vestiges of a colonial era. Residents of such Christian homes for the aged are primarily Anglo-Indians and converted Christians; few are Hindus or Muslims. In 1978, however, the first non-Christian old age home in north India opened in south Calcutta. The home was called Navanir (New Nest) Home for the Aged and was founded by a nonprofit organization, the Women's Coordinating Council, primarily to house well-educated Calcutta women (mostly childless widows and never-married women) who had no place to go.[14] A second Navanir home was opened in 1982, and old age homes have sprung up in several other major Indian cities as well.

Old age homes were viewed by most people I spoke with as features of an overly Westernized and degenerate modern society, a society that is characterized by excessive independence and a lack of family love (see chapter 3). But they were also being reinterpreted, by some of the residents (or *māsīmās*, "maternal aunties") who live in them, as a kind of *Indian* institution—a place comparable perhaps to the "forest" that Hindu texts describe "forest dwellers" (*vānaprastha*) as living in during their third stage of life, as they leave the realm of the household. Several of the Navanir women I interviewed made just this comparison, saying that it was all right that they lived in such a home, for it was like entering the "forest-dwelling" stage of life. Several were also relieved that such an institution existed (regardless of its potential spiritual benefits), for they felt that their other options might have been limited to living on the streets. Many also spoke of living in an old age home as a process of cutting maya for kin, homes, and belongings—for they had had to leave all these persons and things behind.

Most of the Navanir women agreed that particularly for them, maya should be cut in old age, even if the tendency is for it to increase—because they are being forced to live apart from their loved ones and things. How painful it is to live in an old age home if you still have maya for your family and belongings! several told me. Several declared simply, It is time to die—what more need do I have of maya? One woman who had been a schoolteacher most of her life and had never married explained the problem of maya, particularly as it pertained to those living in old age homes:

> Maya increases [with age], I think. At least as far as I understand, as age increases, so does maya increase. But, at present, it is better not to make so much maya, not to have so much maya. . . . Why? Because we [in Navanir] have to live apart from everyone. I see everyone here [in this home]—there are those who have made families, those who have fit and worthy sons and grandchildren—who have everyone!—and still, even then, they have had to come here. So, what good does maya do? And it's time for us to go [i.e., die]. So what need is there for maya? But maya is such a thing—that it cannot be moved out from the heart.

After years of living in an old age home such as Navanir, though, many acknowledged that their maya had begun to abate. Since maya tends to increase with increased sharing and exchanging of food, words, beds, household spaces, and the like, maya wanes when people live apart from and cut off exchanges with each other. Incidentally, that is why Americans, several of these knowledgeable urban "aunts" said, do not have much maya for each other or for their elders: families in America are small and separated. Women in Navanir left behind not only kin but most of their possessions, coming to live in a dormitory-style setting with four residents to a room, each with a cot and a corner in which to place a few belongings. Several mentioned that they consciously strove to loosen their bonds to the world even more after entering the home, by turning their minds toward God, chanting God's name, and performing *pūjās* (religious rituals).

Still, even after making the radical and separative move to an old age home, most said that it takes a long time of immense sadness (*dukha*) and suffering (*kaṣṭa*) to cause maya to be cut. Just as maya intensifies slowly as people live together, so it takes a long time to fade away. Many of the old age home aunts wept in their interviews with me, thinking of sons, daughters, nephews, or nieces whom they no longer see. One woman, the widowed mother of an only daughter, admitted: "For me, maya hasn't completely left yet [she laughed a bit sheepishly, apologetically]. I've only been here for a short time—three years—and I was with them [my daughter and son-in-law] for so long. So that's why I still have it. But I'm trying to turn my mind toward God. Because what need have I for maya now? It's time for me to go. So what need is there for maya? I try to keep my mind strong. But maya does not go away easily."

THE JOYS AND PERILS OF REMAINING "HOT" AND CENTRAL, EVEN IN A RIPE OLD AGE

Not all the people I knew in and around Mangaldihi spent their old age practicing techniques of cooling and decentering. Khudi Thakrun, Mangaldihi village's oldest member (described more fully in chapter 3), was a notable example of a woman who remained "hot" and central, fully engrossed with family and village affairs, even at her ripe old age of ninety-seven. Granted, this Brahman widow did practice some of the cooling and decentering techniques cultivated by most older Bengalis: she wore entirely plain white clothing and ate a strict vegetarian diet; she ate most of her meals separate from others, before anyone else in her household; she slept in a room of her own; and, after arranging all of her children's marriages and becoming a widow, she had embarked on several pilgrimages.

However, she remained in many ways one of the more centrally involved figures of the village. She roamed the village daily—arranging marriages and spreading village news, giving loans and collecting interest to increase her wealth, and ever searching for mangoes and bananas to eat. Quite unlike most elderly people, especially women, Khudi Thakrun continued to hold a considerable amount of money and property in her own name. Indeed, she continued to work at increasing her wealth, loaning out money to desperate and impoverished, mostly lower-caste, people and charging them high interest rates—ten rupees a month for each one hundred rupees lent—until the entire sum was repaid. She had cultivated relations with virtually everyone in the village, either as a relative (she was the daughter of one and wife of another of the village's largest families), as a lender (almost every low-caste family had borrowed money from her at one time or another), or as a neighbor and visitor. She also persisted in attempting to control her three daughters-in-law with an iron will and a hot (*garam*) temper.

Khudi Thakrun enjoyed all of these involvements and showed little desire to have things any other way. She kept seeking out and accruing relationships and attachments, with no thought of dispersing them. She boasted about all the village people being related to her, as "her people," and about how much of the land and wealth of the village was hers as well: "The whole village is filled with *my* people (*āmār-i lok*). And all these ponds, four houses, and acres of land—it's all mine!" On another occasion she gloated about the huge funeral she would have: "There will be tons of people and a huge feast. . . . After all, the whole village is mine! Here is both my father's house and my husband's house. Huh! They are all my people."

Other villagers worried, though, about the dangers of such binding attachments and involvements, especially at Khudi Thakrun's age. People of all neighborhoods often spoke with disapproval about Khudi Thakrun's excessively involved ways. Sadan Bhattacharyya, a temple priest, told me: "[Khudi Thakrun] eats her mangoes and cottage cheese [both very expensive foods] by eating interest off all the poor people in the village.[15] At this age it would be better for her not to do that. Her age has happened (*bayas hayeche*). At this time, it would be better for her not to acquire so much sin (*pāp*), but to accrue merit (*puṇya*) instead." Another Brahman man was similarly critical:

> Eating interest in such a way is a great sin (*mahāpāp*) for anyone. But at her age—nearing and perhaps surpassing one hundred—the sin is especially bad! In old age, people should stop worrying about money and especially stop making money off others! Instead, they should know that their sons will feed and clothe them and will look after the house and business affairs, so they can turn toward *dharma* and God. They should think about how God will be taking me now.
>
> Also, in old age, people should desire to feed others if they come upon some good food. Most old people want to give food to their kids, grandkids, or servants. But instead [Khudi Thakrun] will eat in front of everyone else, and even *take* from them and eat! . . . All this is part of her nature as a great sinner (*mahāpāpi*).

A group of poor women from one of the Bagdi neighborhoods also condemned Khudi Thakrun's ways, especially her practice of loaning money to desperate people at high interest rates. They described how she comes right into their courtyards at the end of every month to collect her interest, shaking her cane at them and refusing to leave until she is paid. "She eats huge piles of good food—have you seen it? Cottage cheese, mangoes, sweets. And she does this by eating the interest off poor people like us," one woman griped. "Certainly her sin is piling up from all of these actions," another exclaimed. "Especially at her age!"

Even Khudi Thakrun's own daughters-in-law and grandchildren pondered the excesses of her attachments, particularly for food. I came upon them joking together one afternoon that she will certainly turn into a craving ghost when she dies and will go around pestering people for mangoes and other treats. When they saw me they added, laughing still, that Khudi Thakrun would certainly be visiting *me* in my dreams after her death, pleading for good food as she so often did at the end of her life.

Villagers both close to and more distant from Khudi Thakrun seemed to agree that there was something disturbing about her absorption in the pleasures of making money and eating good food. They could point to the tangible dangers of her being weighed down by heavy sin or stuck in the world as a pestering ghost. But they also simply felt strongly that there is something not quite right or appropriate about a person of Khudi Thakrun's age being so involved with worldly matters.[16] Other wealthy villagers loaned money at the same rate that Khudi Thakrun did (including my landlord, who criticized her for the practice), and other wealthy villagers ate delicious foods, such as mangoes, sweets, and cottage cheese. Their practices were not the target of disparaging comments. Yet there was general agreement (though not on the part of Khudi Thakrun herself) that in old age—even if the ideal cannot be perfectly achieved—it is best for people to begin to give things away, rather than to take them in; to loosen ties to the world, rather than to cultivate them: in short, to strive to reduce the bindings of maya. Khudi Thakrun demonstrated in her own life the ironies and dilemmas of wealth and family: she was blessed with having probably more wealth and more kin than any other person in the village; and it was those very blessings that, according to many, bound and burdened her.

THE VALUES OF ATTACHMENT AND RENUNCIATION

Another model of personhood, and the potentially conflicting values of attachment and renunciation in late life, is found in the well-known *āśrama dharma* theory of life stages described briefly in chapter 2. According to this schema, persons (specifically upper-caste males) move through four life stages: they are first celibate students, then become householders enmeshed in family and social ties, later move on to live as "forest dwellers" or hermits (*vānaprastha*), and ultimately become renouncers (*sannyāsī*). As a renouncer, a man strives to become free from all attachments to people, places, things, and even his own body, through taking leave of family members, abnegating caste identity, giving up all possessions, performing his own funeral rites, begging, and constantly moving from place to place so that no new attachments will develop. If a person is able to free himself from all binding attachments in this way, he may be able to attain ultimate "release" (*moksha*) from the cycle of rebirths, redeaths, and reattachments to worldly life, or *saṃsār*.

Scholars of Indian society and religions have given much attention to this model, suggesting that these life stages, with their accompanying values, goals, and practices, provide a key to understanding Hindu personhood, religion, and society.[17] Specifically, they have seen a fundamental opposition in Indian society and culture between the values of attachment or involvement in worldly life, on the one hand, and renunciation or detachment, on the other. According to these scholars, the classical theory of the *āśramas* is one brilliant attempt to reconcile these opposing values by assigning them to chronologically distinct phases of life: worldly values are pursued as an adult householder, and renunciation is pursued at the end of life as an ascetic or sannyasi.[18] In this way, asserts Louis Dumont, the value of renunciation is given a limited and lesser position in a hierarchy of Hindu values. Renunciation is dangerously "fatal to" more worldly values, because it is aimed toward a "negation of the world"; thus it is relegated to the latest possible life stage only, after all worldly obligations have been fulfilled (1980b [1960]:274).

But I did not find that such accounts of the tension between householding and renunciation in Hinduism matched the emotional complexity and ambiguous quality of everyday lived life in Mangaldihi. For most people I knew, techniques of renunciation were not practiced in old age to oppose or negate life in the world. Rather, they seemed to cultivate techniques of detachment as a means of dealing *with* the world and the intensity of affections and attachments that extended living in the world entails. For if, as we have seen, connections and affections—the bindings of maya—increase in number and intensity over a long life, then one's final years facing losses, separations, and death can be very painful and difficult indeed. Nor did the Mangaldihi villagers find values such as renunciation and attachment arranged in a coherent, single line of precedence or chronology, as Dumont and other scholars—relying largely on their studies of classical texts—have suggested. Instead, values were experienced and pursued by Mangaldihi villagers as fundamentally varied, as coexisting and creating quandaries. People did not single-mindedly work at loosening the ties that make up their selves as they grew old; they also wanted to see another grandchild's wedding, to be cared for in a crowded household, to travel with a long-loved spouse, to eat another sweet mango, to increase their family's wealth. Old age for Bengalis contains a dilemma: it is the time of life when connections are the most numerous and strongly felt, and also the time when relationships—with all the people, places, and things one has become a part of over a long life—are the most transient.

Ann Gold's exquisite examination of the story of King Gopi Chand (1989, 1992) resonates strikingly with these Bengali villagers' sentiments. Gopi Chand (whose tale has a place in popular folk traditions from Punjab to Bengal) was a king who left his family and palaces to be initiated as a renouncer and gain immortality. Unlike other more standard sagas of Indian renouncers, though, Gopi Chand's journey away from worldly life is not easy or total. He yearns again and again for the "things of his ruling condition"

(1989:772–73), especially his loved ones, his family. Gold reflects: "Gopi Chand's sorrowful partings are reminiscent of the ones that come to every human being when confronted by mortality and its inevitable severances. Thus they are emphatically shared by rapt audiences when the village bard narrates his tale" (p. 773). Villagers with whom Gold talked praised the scenes of parting as the "best" parts of the performance (p. 784), because they were felt to be the most poignant, the closest to their own everyday experiences. T. N. Madan (1987) similarly finds that in the daily lives of Kashmiri Brahmans, renunciation and householding are not neatly opposed. His Kashmiri informants held up detachment as a value to be pursued *in the midst of worldly involvements,* not in order to reject the world altogether but to resist being overly enmeshed in it.

The processes and concerns I have described, surrounding the loosening of ties in late life, are similar to some of those proposed by Claire Cumming and William Henry in their well-known and controversial "disengagement theory" of aging. Their theory postulates that as a person ages, a mutual withdrawal occurs on the part of the aging person and others in his or her social system. In this process of disengagement, awareness of approaching death plays an important role: "The apprehension of death as a not-so-distant goal may be a time of redefinition of the self as less bound to the surrounding network of interaction." By the end of a person's life, Cumming and Henry go on, "his bonds have been all but severed—disengagement is complete, he is free to die" (1961:226–27).[19]

This theory has been widely critiqued by American gerontologists and sociologists over the years since it was proposed, in part (and rightly so, I believe) for its overly universal, de-cultured claims (Hochschild 1975). Some may have objected because, as Cumming and Henry themselves report (1961:18–22), many Americans seem to be uncomfortable proposing that any significant changes occur at all in old age; instead, many wish to define "successful aging" as a process that entails, ideally, no new changes or characteristics at all. A radical process of "disengagement" would mean movement toward a new and different stage of life, and thus an undesired end to a "permanent" adulthood. This "successful [perhaps better called *non-*] aging," or—as I refer to it elsewhere (Lamb 1993:20–27)—"permanent persons" theory, is reflected nicely in current book titles in the contemporary United States, such as *The Ageless Self* (Kaufman 1986) and *Declining to Decline* (Gullette 1997).[20] It is also reflected in the proliferation of technologies for disciplining and reconstructing aging bodies so that they are no longer visibly marked as old. Age-calibrated exercise routines, hormone replacement therapy, special diets, hair dyes, antiaging skin creams, and cosmetic surgery work not so much to redefine the aging body but rather, as Kathleen Woodward (1991:161) also observes, "to virtually eliminate it—to make it indistinguishable from a young or middle-aged body."

Perhaps also playing a significant role in academic and popular reactions to the disengagement theory of aging is the sense shared by many Americans that they are *already,* even in their younger years, quite (or at least sufficiently) disengaged from others. When I have spoken to Americans, old and young, about the routines practiced by many Bengalis aimed at loosening ties in late life, a consistent response has been, "How depressing." The thought of their ties becoming even looser in old age than they already are makes them feel cold and lonely. Even in youth many in America and Europe tend to think of themselves, as I discussed in chapter 1, as separate "individuals";[21] they tend *not* to think of themselves as substantially—physically—interconnected with those whom they touch and with whom they live, eat, and transact. Many Americans live alone for significant portions of their lives, especially in old age, and value sleeping in separate rooms and certainly separate beds, unless they are joined by a spouse or lover.

But in the village of Mangaldihi, people tended to live their whole lives in households crowded with others; to sleep every night in large beds or on overlapping mats intertwined with siblings, parents, children, and neighbors; to think of and experience themselves as being substantially, as well as emotionally, *part* of others. And they thought, too, that such substantial-emotional interconnections tend naturally to increase over a long life rather than decrease. There it makes sense that the problem of how to loosen bonds in late life, and become separate enough to be able to depart in death, could be perceived as pressing.

5 Dealing with Mortality

An enormous amount has been written about Hindu funeral rituals by anthropologists and historians of religion,[1] and one might think that there is nothing new to be said. But almost all previous studies of death in India have focused on the funeral rites themselves and not on how people think about and plan for death in their everyday lives, particularly as they grow old.[2] Rituals of death themselves are important and fascinating, but they certainly do not exhaust the human encounter with death. How does the experience of death fit with daily life? what about bereavement? the sentiments of those facing their own deaths?

Anthropological studies of death in general, not just those concerned with South Asia, have concentrated on ritual rather than on everyday life, bereavement, or emotion. There are good reasons for this focus: rituals are usually public and easy to observe, and rituals pertaining to death usually aim largely at maintaining the social structure as a whole, repairing the torn social fabric—a major concern of anthropology, particularly in the modernist era.[3] Renato Rosaldo has commented, "Ethnographies written in accord with classic norms consider death under the rubric of ritual rather than bereavement. Ritual itself is defined by its formality and routine; under such descriptions, it more nearly resembles a recipe, a fixed program, or a book of etiquette than an open-ended human process." He adds: "Ethnographies that in this manner eliminate intense emotions not only distort their descriptions but also remove potentially key variables from their explanations" (1989:12).

Rosaldo (1989:12–13) goes on to examine a classic anthropological study, William Douglas's *Death in Murelaga* (1969), that succeeds in presenting death in a detached, formalized manner. Douglas provides a window into Basque social structure by focusing not only on mortuary rituals but also on an old woman dying after a full life. Douglas, and after him Rosaldo (though not without some irony), seems to take this case—an old person's death—as a natural example of an "easy death." Is this because they (we?) often assume that it is "appropriate" for old people to die, that they are "ready" for it? As we saw in the previous chapter, however, even in a community (like the one I knew in West Bengal) where death is something expected, planned for, and indeed in many ways looked forward to by older people, it is still not easy or simple to achieve. Furthermore, as Rosaldo himself notes, regardless of how "easy" or not the death may be for the old person him- or herself who is dying, the sentiments of the survivors must also be considered.

I focus on these subjects in the present chapter, exploring first the ways the Bengalis I knew thought about and experienced death—their own and others'—in their everyday lives. I will then take a new look at Hindu rituals of death and dying, interpreting them through the lens of maya. The many death rituals I observed in and around Mangaldihi seemed consistently to focus on the problem I began to explore in chapter 4: the ambiguities and complexities of maya, as fundamental to the nature of human relationships. Rituals of death enacted a necessary radical separation, a severing of maya; yet they were also ways by which people remade their connections, mixing again with the spirits of those with whom they once made their lives.

I do not concentrate here on gender differences, which are in many ways neutralized by death. However, I briefly explore men's and women's differing positions as ancestors, and in chapter 7 I look at the sharply contrasting ways that women and men face the death of a spouse.

"HOW AM I GOING TO DIE?"

Talking about and planning for death—figuring out *how,* emotionally and practically, to die—was an important part of later life for Mangaldihi villagers. People I knew showed a range of emotions and concerns. Many said that it was appropriate and desirable for older people to express an emotional and spiritual readiness for death, even to embrace and pray for death eagerly. People said that such attitudes helped make the leave-takings of death easier and smoother and deterred the elderly from prolonging life when they had reached the fitting time for passing away.

I first encountered these feelings in a conversation with Choto Ma, a white-haired and white-saried Brahman widow who lived (next to her sister-in-law, Mejo Ma) in a household crowded with descendants, neighbors, and the smoke from several cooking fires. Choto Ma's eighty-year-old eyes sparked with a lively wit and thoughtful intelligence, and she quickly became one of my most valuable informants and dearest friends in the village. Just a few weeks after I had moved into Mangaldihi, we were sitting with several others on the cool, polished floor of the Madan Gopal temple next to her home. She mentioned wistfully how hard it would be for them all to cut their maya for me when I left the village after a year and a half. I replied that I would probably be able to visit every five years or so, but Choto Ma said resolutely, "I won't be here anymore at that time." I quickly responded, "Oh, yes you will! You may live to be one hundred," in a manner consistent (I believed) with American etiquette, which mandates a protest when someone states that he or she is not much longer for this world. Choto Ma and the others sucked in their breath quickly and admonished, "Don't say that!" "Why?" I asked, confused. "Because," Choto Ma answered, "What if it happened [that I would live that long]? Now I can walk around, eat, see. If I go now, it will be good. At any time now, I will just go—"; and, with a smile, she stuck her tongue out, closed her eyes, and threw back her head in a gesture meant to indicate her coming death.

I was shocked by her gesture but soon found that expressing an open acceptance of and readiness for death was considered to be appropriate and desirable in the elderly and was a part of their everyday conversations. When I would greet an older person by casually asking how he or she was, a common response would be "I'm ready to go at any time now. I'm just waiting for God to take me away." I heard very different responses when I visited the Little Sisters of the Poor—a Christian, largely Anglo-Indian home for the aged in Calcutta. There, residents would usually answer the same question, "I just thank God that I'm still here," or "I thank God for each day," or "I can't complain. I'm very lucky still to be alive." Such contrasting expressions most likely in large part reflect the differing views of death in the Hindu and Christian religious traditions.

There were several elements to the widespread Mangaldihi stance of ready acceptance of death. First, people wanted to be able to die while their bodies were still in good working condition. They wished to avoid the decrepitude and prolonged suffering—for both themselves and their families, on whom they would depend—that living to too great an age often entails.[4] Choto Ma's sentiments—"Now I can walk around, eat, see. If I go now, it will be good"—were generally shared. The "Club's Grandfather," Prafulla Adhikari, also expressed his wish to die "while still moving" (*calte calte*), fearing particularly the need to depend on other people for care: "It would be good if I could go now while still moving and able to care for myself. That is my main worry. Now I am healthy and experiencing no troubles. It would be good if I went now before I suffered or caused anyone trouble. People's own sons and daughters often don't even look after them. Who then will look after me?" Mejo Ma had a similar answer when I asked her how long she wanted to live: "I can go any time now. I don't want to live anymore. If your body does not exist (*deha nā thākle*), then who wants to live? When you get old (*buṛo*), your hands and feet break, your eyesight weakens. I'm ready to go right now."

Older villagers also viewed readiness for death as a stage of their family's development. If a person's children were all married and had produced sons, and especially if grandchildren were married and reproducing as well, people would say that it was time to die. Their major life tasks in the family had been fulfilled: they had produced children and grandchildren to carry on the family line; they had guided their juniors through the sequence of life cycle rites, or *saṃskārs*; and by that point most had also performed the funeral rites for their parents. Khudi Thakrun frequently predicted her death to me: "I'll die in about a month," or, "You'll see my death and eat at my funeral feast before you leave." When I would ask her if this would be good or bad, she would smile and answer, "It would be fine. All my sons are taken care of now, so I can go." Later, when one of her grandson's weddings was approaching, she began to express the desire to see just that one wedding; but she always added that she would be ready to die at any time after that.

In addition, conceptions about the nature of death were crucial to older people's emotional and spiritual readiness to die. For Hindus, death is not an end to life but rather a change in form. Most Hindus believe that in death (*mṛtyu*) the spirit or soul (*ātmā*) leaves a body that has now grown useless and is ready to be discarded. A person is made up, more knowledgeable and well-read folk say, of a gross material body (*sthūla śarīr*) and a subtle body (*sūkṣma śarīr*) that houses the soul (*ātmā*). The material body is commonly imaged as being constituted of "five elements" (*pā̃cbhūt*)—ether, air, fire, water, and earth—which are dispersed and recycled after death. The body particles that a deceased person has shared with kin, land, houses, possessions, and so on live on in the bodies of the people and things left behind. The soul (*ātmā*) itself is changeless in life and in death; it simply takes on new forms. After death, the *ātmā* first becomes a departed spirit (*pret*) and then an ancestor (*pitṛ*). It also (unless it attains ultimate "release" from the cycle of births and deaths) is reborn within a new body, either here on earth or in "heaven" (*svarga*). Both body and soul therefore extend into past and future persons and things. A person is never wholly new when born, and never wholly gone when dead (see also Parry 1989:505).

When people spoke of their own deaths as well as of death in general, they took such extensions for granted. My landlord Dulal Mukherjee used the common metaphor of old clothes when explaining the discardability of the body in death: "Just like when your clothes get old, and you throw them out and put on new clothes, so the body (*deha*) is also discarded at death and the soul (*ātmā*) accepts a new body." Gurusaday Mukherjee defined death to me this way: "Death is a transformation of the body (*deha*), an abandoning of the body. The family (*saṃsār*) is transformed. But the soul (*ātmā*) does not change." People often spoke also about the kinds of lives and bodies they would assume after dying. One elderly and energetic Bagdi woman, Billo's Ma, responded when I asked her what will happen after she dies: "What God causes [me] to do I will do. . . . Another birth will happen. Does life have a death? Life has no death (*jībaner maraṇ nei*). Not ever. Some people say, 'When you die, you'll be a cow or a bug.' I'll be *something*, at least. There is never a death to life." Bhogi Bagdi answered the question similarly: "How can I know? Maybe I'll be a dog, or maybe a cat, or maybe a person (*mānuṣ*). Only God knows. What God does will happen."

Older people also anticipated with pleasure the way their sons would continue to nurture them as ancestors. These were visions held by older men more often than by women, because men held more important positions in the family line as ancestors (see below). One man spoke with a sense of pride and ease: "When I die, I will still be here with my sons. I will abandon my body, but my sons will feed me water and rice balls (*piṇḍas*)."

Preparing to Die: Praying, Talking of Funerals, and Dealing with Fears

Since, according to Mangaldihi villagers, there was no sense in clinging to an old body and completed life span, they saw cultivating an emotional and spiritual readiness for death as key to loosening the attachments that otherwise would keep people bound to their current bodies and lives. Villagers believed that if they were ready and willing to die, then they could die when the proper time arrives; but if they retained a desire to keep on living and were still attached to the things of their lives, then they would not die. Choto Ma told me that she anticipated her deceased husband calling her at her time of death, but she would only go with him if she were ready to relinquish her attachments to life:

> When I die, . . . [my husband] will come here and call me. He'll call me by saying, "Come, come!" At that time if I am able to see him, then he'll take me. If I am lying here easily when he comes and says, "Hey, after all this time, come!" then I will die. But if I say, "No, my time still

> hasn't come; I won't go yet. I still want to 'eat' [i.e., experience] my son's service (*āmi ekhano āmār cheler sevā khāi*)," then he won't take me. And if I say, "Yes, let's go. Take me away with you. I don't have any more desire (*icchā*) left to live," then [I will die].

One common technique to develop such a readiness for death was praying to God and chanting the names of deities. Mejo Ma told me that she spent hours every day chanting God's name, especially as she fell asleep at night: "I keep praying to God to take me now. I say God's name so that my death will happen now." One evening, as we stood at the Syamcand temple watching *ārati*, the circling of lights before the deities, Syam Thakur told me: "I think of God now, so that my sins will be wiped away, washed away, and I will be clean (*pariṣkār*) when I die. I don't want to live any more."

As families and neighbors gathered together in courtyards over late afternoon tea, conversations not infrequently turned toward the funeral plans of those who were becoming advanced in age. I spent several afternoons with elderly women in Mangaldihi listening to them talk about the kinds of funeral rituals and feasts that would be held for them. On one occasion Choto Ma and Mejo Ma discussed at length where they would like to be cremated and why. Mejo Ma spoke of being taken to Bakresbar, a pilgrimage site for Siva where many of Mangaldihi's wealthier people were cremated, to be with all her relatives who were taken there; she looked forward to traveling there on the truck with all of her surviving descendants, who would be singing *kīrtan* (hymns about Krishna) as they went. But her sister-in-law, Choto Ma, preferred to be cremated right in the village of Mangaldihi, because then she would be carried on the shoulders of local Brahmans and burned by the young Brahman men of the village. "I will be able to look down and see everyone," she said with anticipatory pleasure.

Then Mejo Ma spoke with delight of all the food her children would feed her as a departed spirit or ghost (discussed in more detail below): "When they feed me mango, sweets, and banana, I will gobble it all up (*gab-gab kare khābo*). [She laughed.] I'll take it all away on a plate as a ghost. I'll eat whatever they give me. [She laughed again.] Then on the tenth day, the day of shaving, they will cook *piṇḍa*s (rice balls). "What are the *piṇḍa*s for?" I asked. "I don't know," she answered without concern, "but they have to be given [to the dead person]. I'll also eat *piṇḍa*s! Everyone who dies has to eat them." Likewise, Khudi Thakrun envisioned the rituals following her death in detail: "My death will be a big deal!" she said with pride, because she was so senior and wealthy, and had so many relatives. "There will be over forty people going on the truck [to the cremation ground], a huge feast, and lots of *kīrtan* [singing for Krishna]! You'll get to see it all before you leave."[5]

At other times I heard older people express fear and reluctance to die, even though such statements seemed to be less publicly acceptable than professions of readiness for death. Some, though quite "increased" (*bṛiddha*) in years or in poor health, had children or grandchildren who remained unmarried or childless. Anil Mukherjee, Khudi Thakrun's youngest and only surviving brother-in-law, was one of the more senior men in the village, with a weak and ailing body, a voice raspy with age, and eyes that could barely see; but uncharacteristically for someone in his condition, he frequently expressed his desire to keep on living so that he could see all of his sons married. He laughed a little sheepishly when I asked if he still wished to live, responding: "I do still have a little bit of a wish to live (*bā̃cte ektuku cāi*). These sons—they've all grown up. If their marriages happen I will experience peace (*śānti*). If I could see that, I would receive peace and go. But what hand do I have in this?" he added sadly. "If it's in my fate, then it will happen. If not . . . ," his voice trailed off.

Others expressed fears about the process of dying itself. Will it be very painful at the moment the soul leaves the body? Will I die all alone or surrounded by people? Will I be able to face and accept death, or will I run from it, like someone fleeing from a poisonous snake? I taped a lengthy discussion of these questions by Mejo Ma, Choto Ma, and some of their family members, in the courtyard of Choto Ma's home, where family and neighbors often gathered in late mornings and afternoons to socialize and have tea. I included part of this conversation in chapter 4 and present more of it here, as it touches on these women's complex and ambiguous feelings about death—their eagerness to die, on the one hand, and yet their fears of death and lingering attachments to life, on the other.

SL: How are you liking life?

MEJO MA: If I died it would be good. I have no wish to continue living. Now I'm thinking—I'll go, I'll go. [Pause.] But there's maya. . . .

CHOTO MA: She gets scared when she's alone at night. She lies awake until twelve o'clock thinking, "I'm going to die. I'm going to die. If I die it will be good." But then when she thinks of Yamaraj [the god of death] coming, she thinks, "How will I go? I won't be able to go. I want to see my children, talk to them, and then go."

MEJO MA: Yes, I must see one of my grandchildren's weddings before I go.

CHOTO MA: That's maya! She's showing her maya! She won't be able to go until the maya is cut.

PULAK: [a neighborhood young man, a friend of Choto Ma's grandson]: Oh, Mejo Ma, tell us when you're going to die. Are you afraid of dying?

MEJO MA: No, I'm not afraid of dying. I tell God to let me receive a little water at the time of death. I don't ask for anything else.

PULAK: Do you still wish to live?

CHOTO MA: Yes, she wants to live very much!

MEJO MA: No I don't! I just want to see one grandchild's wedding and then go. Any grandchild will do. That's all.

At this point, the neighbors and kin present shouted at Mejo Ma that there were plenty of good grooms around—she should simply choose one for her eldest granddaughter. Mejo Ma protested that she and her family had not been able to find anyone suitable. The conversation went on:

PULAK: What do you want to happen before you die?

MEJO MA: If I could die while speaking that would be good. I become afraid when I lie alone at night. If my life goes out at that time then I won't even receive a drop of water at the time of death.

SL: Is it good to receive water at the time of death?

MEJO MA: Yes. When life is leaving there is extreme pain. If you take a thorn out [of the body] how much pain is there! So also when life is going out [of the body] there is pain and suffering.[6] If you receive water the suffering is eased a bit.

PULAK: Do you say God's name?

MEJO MA: Yes.

SL: Why?

MEJO MA: So that I can go well. So that my death happens well.

On another occasion Choto Ma spoke at length about her own thoughts, expectations, and fears surrounding her approaching death. Like Mejo Ma, she wishes for death at the same time that she resists it.

SL: Do you still have the wish to live?

CHOTO MA: No, I don't still have any wish to live. But what will I do? I am being compelled to live. When God takes me, then I will go. If I say now, "Let death happen, let death happen," then will it happen? No, it won't happen. . . .

SL: Do you still have any wishes (*icchā*) left in life?

CHOTO MA: There are no more wishes left. But I do have in my heart that I will see Dipu's and Rakhi's [her grandchildren's] weddings. When will they happen?

She paused a bit, worried, but went on with new enthusiasm:

> But if I don't see them, that's also good. To go would be even better. If I go away myself that's even better. So I don't have so many wishes. It's not that I *have* to see these weddings. It's in God's hands. I say sometimes, "Lord (*Ṭhākur*), take me away at this time." I feel that way. But what can I do? I am compelled to live. I don't have any more wishes. [I worry about] becoming dependent (*parādhīn*). What will happen? What won't happen? Will I be able to work or not? Baba, what condition will I die in? Who will continue to take care of me? Lord, please take me right away, so I won't have to suffer! Don't you agree? But what can I do? I am being compelled to live. But I don't have any wish to!

Then, after another short pause, she changed her stance:

> But there is always a fear of death. Let a snake come. If a snake comes, will I be able to say, "Bite me"? No, I won't. If a snake comes, will I be able to pick it up and stand with it right by my head? No, I'll run away. That's what life is like. I say, "No, no. I won't die! There's a snake, I'm going to run away!" That would happen, wouldn't it?

I asked her, "What will happen after you die?" and she replied:

> How will I know what happens after I die? I won't be able to know anything then. You will all know how I died, whether I suffered or not at death, or whether I died suddenly. Maybe if I die slowly over four or eight days, then I will know what happens. But if I die suddenly, then I won't know what happens to me. And if I get a fever for several days, then I will worry, "Oh, I've been lying here for four days, what will happen?" I will worry, don't you think?
>
> And then when I die, who will take me where to do what [i.e., perform the funeral rites]—all that I won't be able to understand. Do you think I will be able to see if they take me to Bakresbar [to be cremated], or just throw me in the water somewhere? I won't be able to perceive any of that.

Here, Choto Ma doubts that she will have any awareness of the events following her death, but moments later she tells with anticipation how she *will* be able to experience and enjoy the company of her relatives at her funeral rites. When I asked her, "Which would be better—taking you to Bakresbar or throwing you in some water?" she answered:

> Taking me to Bakresbar of course! Is it good to be simply thrown into a pond? And if they give me [to the flames] in the village, that's also good. I'll be able to go on Brahmans' shoulders. The Brahmans will light the fire. That's even better. If I am taken to Bakresbar, who knows who will carry me? Compared to that, it is better to be carried on the shoulders of village Brahmans, and burned at the hands of village Brahmans. But no one gives [cremation] in the village.[7] . . . People would say, "No, this is Candi's mother. A Brahman's mother. Why will they give [her cremation] in the village? Go give [her] at Bakresbar. Or go give [her] at the Ganges. A mother of two sons! When such great sons exist, does anyone give [their mother] in the village? No. Giving in the village will not do." Even if I tell them now, "Give me in the village. I will be able to see the village people, and go on the shoulders of Brahmans, be burned at the hands of Brahmans, that would be best," still they won't give me here. They will say, "No, father went to Bakresbar. *Jeṭhā* (father's brother) went to Bakresbar, so-and-so went there and so-and-so went there. We'll also give you at Bakresbar." And our mother's brother's house is in Bakresbar. We have a house of lineage (*goṣṭhī*) members there. And they won't give [my cremation] just in the middle of Bakresbar. They'll do it under the banyan tree, by the river.

Choto Ma desires to leave the entangling engagements and pains of this old life and body, to avoid becoming a burdensome dependent, and to move on—to her long-deceased husband, God, the loving family excursion to her cremation pyre, and future rebirths. However, just as it is difficult, perhaps impossible, to fully cut the ties of maya, so it is difficult to fully embrace death. In the end, Choto Ma says, won't she and others recoil from death, with an instinctive fear? Lingering bonds of maya or affection tug at the heart, and wishes to see a grandchild's wedding, to drink water from a loved one's hand, and to remain surrounded by known relatives rather than pass alone into a new world persist, never to be completely fulfilled.

RITUALS OF DEATH: MAKING AND REMAKING PERSONS AND FAMILIES

Quite a number of deaths took place over the period of my stay in Mangaldihi: nineteen in all. During the sticky month of Sraban (July–August) of my first year, there were five unrelated deaths in rapid succession, and my notebooks that month treated almost nothing else. These deaths occurred among people of different stages of life, castes, and classes, differences reflected in the reactions of the survivors and the elaborateness of funeral rites performed.

As one would expect, the sudden loss of a loved one in the prime of his or her life, leaving behind small children, a youthful spouse, or living parents, ignited the most heart-wrenching grief among the survivors. One young woman committed suicide soon after returning to her parents after a soured marriage; her mother was overcome for months with inconsolable anguish. To die amid the engrossing attachments and unfulfilled dreams of an incomplete life span was regarded as extremely painful, both for the deceased and for the survivors. The survivors find it impossible to let go suddenly of their affections for their dead one; and the deceased's spirit, people said, can also have difficulty quitting the relationships of its unfulfilled life. However, the majority of deaths during my stay were of older people in the final stages of their lives. These deaths evoked grief and mourning, but often mixed with the mourning was also a sense of fulfillment and even celebration—that a person had reached a ripe old age, left behind the sons of sons, and had moved on successfully to the realm of ancestors, to heaven, and to a new, perhaps better, rebirth.

The stage of life at which death occurred mandated the specific ritual performance. Very young children, especially those who had not yet gone through the first feeding of rice ceremony, usually received abbreviated funeral rites only, for these children had not yet been fully incorporated into the social world; their deaths accordingly did not require the full complexity of rituals to sever and rearrange family ties. Their bodies were most often buried discreetly in the open land beyond the village, and their deaths inflicted only minimal restrictions of death-separation impurity on the family. Those who died unexpectedly and tragically in the middle of their life (e.g., suicides and accident victims) required some of the most elaborate funeral rituals, as they were regarded as having the greatest potential of becoming ghosts, because their unfulfilled desires and attachments were so strong. Special rituals to "cut" the ties and cravings potentially trapping the spirit as a ghost had to be performed, preferably at a major "crossing place" (*tīrthasthān*) such as Gaya, which was said to be able to bring release (*mukti*) to even the most troubled and clinging of spirits. Those who died in old age who had mature, living, and preferably male progeny received the full and elaborate series of funeral rites, but their deaths (though often mourned earnestly on a personal level) usually posed no great worries for the family as ritual performers, other than the considerable cost involved.

I begin by describing the events leading up to and the immediate aftermath of the unexpected death of the Middle Barber Wife, whose passing was one of the first I witnessed in Mangaldihi. This description gives a flavor of the family ambience in the aftermath and mourning of a death. I then focus on the rituals performed to manage the transformations of death. Rather than presenting here every detail in the complex sequence of rites—a task too large for the present project and one accomplished by several before me[8]—I concentrate on those features of the rituals that are important to my central themes: those rituals aimed at cutting maya and separating ties, and others intended to reassemble and extend persons within continuing family structures.

The Death of the Middle Barber Wife: Mourning and Aftermath

In the middle of the afternoon on 2 August 1989, the middle wife of the Barber family died. She was known by most in the village as Napiter Mejo Bou, the "Barber [family]'s Middle Wife," or as Narayan's Ma, after her only son. She died of heart trouble, perhaps a heart attack, during what could be considered her middle age. Two of her four children were married, she had seen the births of several grandchildren, she had begun to wear the predominantly white saris of older women, and her hair was turning gray; but she still had two unmarried children, a son and a daughter, at home. Within minutes of her death, a young woman from her neighborhood, Pratima, arrived breathlessly at my door, "Come quickly! The Middle Barber Wife just died! You need to take some photos!" This was, incidentally, the way I was informed of most major village events. As I rushed to the Barber family's home with various cameras slung over my shoulders, the whole village was calling out to spread the news, "The Middle Barber Wife just died! Narayan's Ma has died!"

When I arrived, the body was laid out on the floor of the house's front veranda, which was crowded with extended family and neighbors who were hovering around, stroking the body, weeping and wailing. She had already been bathed, dressed in a fresh white sari with a red border, and adorned with a wide strip of red *sindūr* in the part of her hair and red *āltā* on her feet (as she had been lucky enough to die as a married woman),[9] with a garland of flowers around her neck. Her long, gray-black hair was spread out behind her. The family pulled me in and had me take several photos of her in this condition. They also busied themselves with making prints of her feet, as is the usual practice, by painting her feet red with *āltā* and pressing them against white sheets of paper. The footprints would be saved as objects for her descendants' *praṇāms*.

As news of her death spread around the neighborhood and village, people of all castes began to arrive to pay their last respects and express their condolences to the family. Two nephews were sent to inform the woman's married daughters of the death, and within several hours they arrived from their husbands' villages, wailing and throwing themselves on the body of their mother.

The grief of the youngest and still unmarried daughter, Mona, a young woman in her early twenties, was visibly the most acute. She took the lead in performing the songs of mourning for her mother, in the stylized way typical of local women grieving a death. Her wailing alternated between recounting her mother's last scenes and speaking to her mother directly, expressing both affection for her and feelings of hurt at having been left behind. I did not have my tape recorder with me at the time, but soon afterward I wrote Mona's plaintive words in my notebook; in part they went something like this, sung to a repetitive rising and falling melody:

> Oh Ma, *go,*[10] why did you go away? Why did my mother die? Why did my mother go away? Everyone else has a mother, why don't I? At such a young age, my mother died. Oh Ma, you were acting strange all day, speaking wrong words (*bhul kathā*) and irritating us. I didn't understand anything. If I had known you were going to die, I would have gotten angry at you and cussed you out (*gāl ditām*), saying that I would eat poison and die if you died. Oh Ma, you wanted to eat a chicken, but that desire (*sādh*) wasn't fulfilled, because there wasn't enough money. Ma, why didn't we give you a chicken to eat? I cleaned up the house all morning. Ma didn't defecate since noon. Then it came out after she died—I cleaned it up and that didn't disgust me at all. I changed her clothes that got soaked with pee. Oh Ma, we don't have anyone but you. I thought I would go get my older sister to see you, but then you died. Oh Ma, *go,* why did you go away?

Occasionally, one of Mona's older sisters would take over the loud mourning cries, or the wails would subside briefly to muted sounds of comforting, as neighborhood women would stroke the children's arms and say, "Can a mother live forever? She was suffering; it's better that she went now." Or, "Look at her, she's sleeping. Look how she's sleeping, she looks so pretty." Or, "Death always follows birth. No one can live forever."

There was also repeated talk of how the woman died, with the story of her last moments told over again each time a new visitor arrived. The Middle Barber Wife had been taking medicine for heart trouble for some time, but on the morning of her death, everyone noticed that something more serious was wrong. Later they said that she must have suffered a stroke. She was talking strangely with "false words" (*bhul kathā*) all morning and she refused to eat. One of her nephews made a hurried trip to town to get some more medicine for her, but even that did not help. She became unconscious at one point and her daughter began to weep loudly beside her. But then suddenly she regained consciousness and said, "Don't worry, stop crying, I haven't died." And then a few moments later she died.

Because no one, including the dying woman herself, had expected her to die at that moment, the rituals that usually assist a person in dying were not performed for the Middle Barber Wife. Neighbors soon began to worry that this ritual lapse would result in the Middle Barber Wife becoming a lingering ghost (*bhūt*). At one point when Mona cried out that she had not understood that her mother would die, a neighbor woman scolded her mildly, "Well, you should have. She was speaking funny all day long. She ate so much medicine, but still she didn't get well."

Plans for the cremation began right away. There was some talk of taking her to the "crossing place" of Bakresbar for her last rites. But the expenses of this journey are considerable and the Barber family was poor; the deceased woman's husband did not seem to think that such expenditures were necessary. It was decided that the cremation would be performed in Mangaldihi before dawn. For the rest of the evening and night, relatives remained near the body of the woman, wailing and stroking her. In the still of the night, several hours before dawn, the body was taken out of the house and prepared for cremation.

CUTTING MAYA, THE SEPARATING OF TIES

As we have seen, a person's emotional and material attachments for other people, places, and things were considered to be exceedingly strong, often particularly so at the end of a long life. Villagers feared that at death they would not be able to "cut" (*kāṭā*) their maya and leave, lingering on instead in painful decrepitude, or hovering around after death as a hungry, lonely, and disembodied ghost. I found that therefore one of the central aims of the rituals of death and dying was to effect just this: to cut maya, or to separate ties, so that both the spirit of the deceased person and the survivors might begin to restructure their relationships and move on to new unions and forms of being.

As people explained it in Mangaldihi, death entails a series of separations: the deceased person's soul (*ātmā*) or departed spirit (*pret*) has to be separated from its previous body, house, belongings, and family; the family survivors have to separate themselves first from the body, and then from the departed spirit (*pret*) or ghost (*bhūt*) of the deceased; and family members have often to separate from each other, especially if it is the head of an extended family who has died. The funeral rituals performed over the ten- to thirty-day transitional period following a death served largely to accomplish this threefold separation. I highlight here three major ritual phases in this separative process: rites of dying; cremation, which dissolves the body; and death-separation impurity, which separates the lingering spirit from the family. Although other scholars have analyzed these rituals, I focus on a little-considered yet fundamental dimension: the rigorous process of cutting the ties of maya.

Rites of Dying: Helping Along the Leave-Takings of Death

Separations should begin before a person dies. In Mangaldihi, the series of rites that were performed prior to death were concerned largely with helping life (*jīban*) or the soul (*ātmā*) leave the body and scenes of its passing existence. These premortem rites could only be performed if the dying person or family members were aware that death was impending, and villagers therefore found it far preferable for a person to have prior knowledge of his or her coming death. In that case, when it was clear that death was approaching, the family would first purify a spot of the ground in the open courtyard by smearing it with cow dung and spreading sacred grass (*kuśa*) or *tulsī* leaves there; they would then move the person to the ground to die. Instead of a pillow, a small ball of cow dung or *tulsī* leaves could be placed under the head. This is done, villagers said, because "it is difficult for life to leave [the body]" when a person is lying on a bed or a pillow. By moving the dying person to the ground, they enable death to come more quickly and easily. Furthermore, villagers explained, the ground is preferred as a site of death because it is "pure" (*śuddha*), whereas beds are "impure" (*aśuddha*).

These two forms of reasoning—that the ground (or *māṭi*) is an *easier* place to die and that it is *pure* (*śuddha*)—are, I believe, related. Many scholars have noted the earth's "purity" as a site of death but have been unable to explain exactly in what sense it is pure and why its purity makes it a particularly desirable place to die.[11] According to Mangaldihi villagers, the purity of the earth (in this and other contexts) derives largely from its capacity to remain unmarked and uncorrupted by the people and things that come into contact with it. The ground was said to be a "pure" (*śuddha*) container by villagers because instead of transmitting impure properties, it transforms them in positive ways.[12]

For instance, a person who was in an impure state, or one who wished to remain in a pure state (for ritual or other purposes), would avoid touching any household object with which other people were in simultaneous contact; such a person would strive instead to transact with others only through the neutral channel of the ground. If a person handed an object to another by first placing the object on the ground and letting the other pick it up from there, the two would have avoided "touching" (*chōyā*). But if two or more people touched the same household object at the same time, or if they stood or sat simultaneously on the same mat or bed, their bodily substance and properties were transferred from one to the other: they were considered to have touched. By mediating their contact through the ground, people could retain their respective different states of "purity" (*śuddhatā*) and remain relatively unmixed with each other.

In contrast, people described beds as being permeated with the substances of other people, probably because they are the sites of many excretions and exchanges—such as of saliva through drooling, sexual fluids, and what we consider to be "ordinary" touching as arms and legs are strewn over others sleeping close to one. This means that if a person dies in a bed, he or she is dying while continuing to mix intimately with the substances of other family members, rather than separating from them. Beds were also inappropriate places to die because they were considered to be relatively luxurious household possessions, thereby themselves representing an attachment. Movement from a bed to the open ground before death thus constituted a dramatic movement from a condition of intimate embeddedness at the center of household life to a state of peripheral insulation. This was especially true if the ground chosen was open to the air and sky; being outside of *saṃsār,* it offered a separative and freeing place in which to die.

Next, after the dying person was placed on the ground, he or she was given a few drops of Ganges water and pieces of sacred *tulsī* leaf (a plant embodying Lord Krishna) to ingest. These potent cleansing substances were likewise said to bring about a quick and easy death. People believed that the moment the soul, or *ātmā,* leaves the body is extremely painful (as Mejo Ma put it, it is like having a deeply embedded thorn pulled from the body), but that giving water, especially Ganges water, at this moment leads to the soul's "release" (*mukti*)—at least from the binding ties of this life and possibly, some said, from all future lives in the world of *saṃsār.*

Then a family member would chant the name of God ("Hari Nam, Hari Nam") or read passages from the Bhagavad Gita at the head of the dying person, to encourage him or her to concentrate on God at the moment of death. This helps lead to release from binding ties as well as bringing the dying person closer to God and thereby perhaps heaven (*svarga*) or at least a good rebirth. Persons were also advised to think of God themselves during their dying moments.

Finally, especially if the person appeared to be having difficulty dying, a Brahman priest could be called to perform a ceremony called *anga prāyascitta* (body expiation), a rite that was said to make the body pure (*śuddha*) and to "cut the sins" (*pāp kāṭāno*) that might be keeping the soul bound to its present body and life.

Many scholars of Indian society have described and analyzed these rites of dying commonly practiced by Hindus all over India. Several have suggested that the Hindu rites of dying work as a means of purifying the dying person and his or her family, by cleansing the dying person of moral imperfections or sins (*pāp*) (Madan 1987:134–35; Parry 1982:82),[13] or by dispersing the inauspiciousness created by death (D. Mines 1990:121; Raheja 1988:147–56). Others have stated that the Hindu rites of dying are aimed primarily at release (*mukti*) from reincarnation, or at least at a better rebirth (Gold 1988:81; Madan 1987:124). The way Mangaldihi villagers told it, however, the most salient and immediate aim of the rites of dying was to assist the deceased in the very difficult process of loosening his or her ties to the things of life. In so doing, people also sometimes aimed to receive a better rebirth, to go to heaven (*svarga*), or even possibly to attain ultimate "release" (*mukti*) from repeated lives in the world; but everyone realized that the necessary and very difficult first step to achieve any of these goals was the attainment of immediate release (also called *mukti*) from the binding ties of maya of this particular life.

Cremation: Dissolution of the Material Body

After such preparatory rites, the next major separative act to be performed was cremation. The purpose of cremation was to reduce and disperse the gross material body (or *sthūla śarīr*) as completely as possible. Ritual priests explained that through cremation, the body is dispersed into the five cosmic elements (*pāc̃bhūt*) from which it came, leaving behind no traces of the body as it once was. All that tangibly remains after the funeral fire are bones (*asthi*), and even these are later immersed in the Ganges or some other holy waters, and thus made to flow away.

Mangaldihians believed that dispersing the body in this way was an important part of freeing the *pret-ātmā*, or spirit-soul, from the scenes of its previous life. Villagers said that the *ātmā* had a tremendous maya or attachment for the body, which was its "house" (*ghar* or *bāṛi*) throughout life. If the body is not burned, the soul's maya for the body may also remain unbroken. Hindu villagers were decidedly uncomfortable thinking about the bodies of Americans (or local Muslims, for that matter) being buried intact under the ground; it gave them the feeling of being stifled and trapped.

The body is also the primary site of the material-emotional attachments a person has for the people and things of his or her life. The spirit-soul is attached to the body per se as its house; but in addition, particles of the body are the main source of a spirit-soul's attachments to other persons and things. A person's body comes to be made up of the shared substances of many other people's bodies, of possessions long held, of houses long lived-in, and land long lived-on. Thus, by dispersing the elements of the material body the deceased person's ties to the loved people and things of this passing life—and not merely to the body itself as "home"—could be loosened. Conversely, cremation was an important means by which surviving family members loosened their attachments for the deceased. The material body of the deceased represents tangibly and visibly the person as he or she once was. By participating in the fiery destruction of this body, the survivors strove to come to terms with their loved one's physical demise.

In Mangaldihi the cremation ground, or *śmaśān*, was located to the southeast of the main inhabited area of the village—across the paved road running along the village's edge, and next to outspread rice fields and a large pond. There were separate sites for Brahman and Sudra (lower-caste) cremations, and the tribal Santal cremation ground was in a different place altogether. Cremation had to be performed on the day of death, before the following dawn. Relatives bathed the corpse a final time, wrapped it in a clean shroud, garlanded it with flowers, and placed it, at the threshold of the house, on a bier made of bamboo. All members of the household circumambulated the body three times in the auspicious clockwise direction, with their right side toward the body, as a final means of honoring it before the great separation.[14] The women of the household then took leave of the body by standing at the feet of the corpse and pressing their palms together in a final respectful salutation of *praṇām*. Women in Mangaldihi generally did not accompany the men and corpse to the cremation ground.[15]

The bamboo bier was carried on the shoulders of four men, usually junior male relatives of the deceased. Other male relatives and friends joined the procession. Most essential was the man who would act as chief mourner or "mouth-fire" (*mukhagni*) person, the one to place the fire (*agni*) in the mouth (*mukh*) of the corpse. This was preferably the eldest son of the deceased; but if no sons were available, then another male of the same family line could perform the chief mourner's duties. The chief mourner usually carried a small clay pot with the fire in it that would light the funeral pyre. As the group walked, they would sing *kīrtan* (hymns to Krishna) and chant the name of God.

When the procession crossed the main inhabited area of the village just across the paved road, they placed the framework and body on the ground next to a large pond, with head toward the village. There the chief mourner prepared three rice balls, or *piṇḍas*, to nourish the deceased person's spirit, placing a bit of each rice ball into the corpse's mouth and leaving the remainders on the ground for any other disembodied and potentially hungry spirits.[16] Then all proceeded directly to the cremation ground, where an oxcart had previously deposited a supply of fuel: wood, coal, straw, kerosene, and ghee. The men set about constructing the pyre, smearing the ground with purifying cow dung and placing on it straw, coal, and wood crisscrossed in layers. Kerosene and a bit of ghee were sprinkled on top.

The central severing act of the ritual followed: The body was lifted and placed on the funeral pyre with head facing south. The chief mourner circumambulated the corpse and pyre three times in the counterclockwise direction, with his left side toward the body, as a means of separating himself from it. Then solemnly, often with open weeping, he used a small wooden pole to place ghee and fire into the mouth of the body three times, the act that finally severs him from it and initiates the body's burning. He and others then lit the pyre in different places with grass torches.

As the men stood to one side to watch the burning in which the spirit-soul (*pret-ātmā*) separates from the body, they dramatized their own separation from the corpse. At home, before cremation, family members treated the body with reverence, sadness, and longing: they threw themselves on the body, stroked it, and discussed it as if it were still the locus of their family member's spirit and identity. They offered tender comments, such as "Look how pretty she looks. She looks like she's sleeping." But as cremation proceeded, the men began to treat the body as simply a material conglomerate of elements that needed to be disassembled. They made objective observations: "It's only the body now; the *ātmā* (soul) has gone." At the Middle Barber Wife's cremation, their talk quickly turned to a very detached discussion of how bodies burn. One remarked that women burn differently than men, and another worried that the legs, with their red-painted feet, had not yet ignited, as they were still sticking out of the fire. When the head caught on fire, one young man rolled back his own head, bared his teeth, and said light-heartedly, "Pretty soon the teeth will be sticking out, like this." When the body was fully cremated, the group of men came forward to sprinkle drops of Ganges water on the smoldering pyre. This was done to cool the overheating of the disembodied spirit (*pret*) that the fire caused and to feed the thirsty spirit, thus helping it on its way. The men then pressed their palms together in a final respectful act of *praṇām* before they moved together to a pond to bathe and return home.

Three days later, the chief mourner returned to the cremation site with a Barber and Brahman priest to collect the last remnants of the material body—a few pieces of bone or *asthi*—to be placed into a clay urn and later scattered into the Ganges river or some other holy waters. This final dispersing act was preferably done within ten days of the cremation, but for some it was considerably longer before they were able to afford and find time for the journey. Those who were very poor could scatter the bones into the waters of one of the village ponds, for any body of water can be viewed as comparable to the Ganges, if necessary. The flowing waters of the Ganges were thought to be potently freeing: placing the bones in such waters was said to lead to the immediate release (*mukti*) of the soul from the world of *saṃsār*, or at least from the ties of this particular life. It also brings peace (*śānti*) and well-being (*mangal*) to the soul. As one Kulu woman, who had deposited her husband's bones in the waters of the Ganges at Gaya, explained: "If just one bone piece falls into the Ganges, then the soul (*ātmā*) receives release (*mukti*) and accepts a new birth. If the bones are not given [into the Ganges], then [the dead person] remains a ghost (*bhūt hae hae*), wandering around its previous house."[17]

It is because of the potently freeing powers of the holy waters at "crossing places" (*tīrthasthāns*) that many villagers also wished to perform cremations directly at these sites. For Mangaldihi villagers who could afford it, the Saivite pilgrimage site of Bakresbar was the preferred place of cremation, and I estimate that almost 50 percent of the village bodies were taken to be burned there. A few also made the longer journey to Udanpur on the Ganges river in West Bengal. Wealthier families rented trucks to carry the corpse and accompanying male relatives and friends to Bakresbar, and poorer families took the four- to five-hour walk through the dusty lanes of villages and over the raised walkways of rice fields, carrying the corpse on their shoulders and singing *kīrtan* as they went. Being cremated at a crossing place—where gods and humans meet, desires and attachments are dissipated, and the river of death can be easily forded—loosens bonds even more effectively than does ordinary village cremation.[18]

Rabilal Ruidas, Mangaldihi's old blind beggar of the Muci or leatherworker and musician caste, one day sang for me what he called "A Song of Death" (*marār gān*) about the poignant process of cutting maya for loved kin and possessions at the cremation ground. He told me that members of his caste give voice to songs like this as they stand around watching the cremation fire burn:

A SONG OF DEATH

That maya that is certainly about to be cut,
In that maya of yours you lie at the cremation ghat,
No matter how much you say, "This is mine, this is mine,"
Everything of yours is empty now. . . .

Wealth, property, no one, nothing will be your own any more. . . .
They take you on four shoulders singing, "Hari, Hari."
Even your own mother and aunt will be cut from you.
No one will be your own any more.

Love goes, love goes, you know.
Do not love me any more.
That maya that is certainly about to be cut.
When you are lying on the cremation ground, who will be your own?

Death-Separation Impurity: The Containing of Bodies, the Cutting of Maya

The ties of maya—here those between the living and the deceased—are not completely dissolved at the cremation ground. After cremation, for a transitional period of ten days (for Brahmans) to thirty days (for Sudras), the disembodied spirit or *pret* (literally, "departed") was said to linger on, near its previous body and home. Over this period, villagers said, the *pret* is perpetually hungry and thirsty for water, food, and attention, often just as reluctant to separate from its former family and surroundings as the family is to separate from it.

It was during this transitional period that surviving kin were thrown into a condition of death-separation impurity (called *aśauc,* literally "not pure").[19] This condition lasts anywhere from one day to the full ten- to thirty-day period of *pret*-hood, depending on caste, age, and closeness to the deceased. Juniors in the deceased's family line, or *baṃśa*—a wife, sons and their wives, unmarried daughters, grandsons, and unmarried granddaughters—suffered the most extensive death-separation impurity. Other kin, such as married daughters or those in a senior relation to the deceased (e.g., a parent, a husband), had more abbreviated periods of death-separation impurity.[20]

Those in the condition of death-separation impurity (whom I will call "survivors" or "mourners") practiced a cluster of activities to make their bodies—as well as the departed spirit or *pret*—relatively cool, dry, and self-contained. Together these practices constitute what McKim Marriott (1976) would term a "minimal transactional strategy." By cooling and containing their bodies, and thus transacting only minimally with others, survivors loosened their ties with the deceased and kept their own bodies—which were partly dead—temporarily separate from other living persons.

One of the principal ways that bodily-social transformations were effected during death-separation impurity was through a change in diet. Survivors avoided hot (*garam*), nonvegetarian (*āmiṣ*) foods, such as meat, fish, eggs, onions, garlic, betel nut, and a certain kind of "heating" dal (*musur ḍāl*), in order to help cool down the body to make it more self-contained. As I have discussed above, being cool (*ṭhāṇḍā*) was associated with detachment, asceticism, stasis, old age, widowhood, death, and the color white. Hot (*garam*) states, conversely, were associated with attachment, passion (*kām*), sexuality and fertility, marriage, anger, cooking, the mixing together of substances, and redness. Although death itself (*mṛtyu*) was often spoken of as a cool state, the *pret* and family during the transitional period seemed to be overly *hot* in certain ways. The *pret*, along with the survivors, had to be fed only cooling, vegetarian foods, such as milk, fruit, and water. Furthermore, the *pret* was said to take shelter over this period in a special plant called a *benā gāch* (verbena), which was particularly known for being able to withstand heat. A *pret* that became a troublesome ghost (*bhūt*) caused harm to the household primarily in "heating" ways—by pestering (*jālāno*, literally "causing to burn"), blowing hot winds into the home, igniting heating arguments and burning fevers, and in extreme cases even causing the house to burn down.

The overheated nature of the spirit and survivors over this transitional period may have been caused by the heat of the cremation fire. It may also have been connected to the intensity of attachments and desires (both often considered to be "hot") that persist after death. Even though death itself was often spoken of as a cold state, during the transitional period of *pret*-hood old attachments and desires remained strong and heating. By eating cooling, vegetarian diets the survivors and the *pret* could both begin to cool their natures, an important step in the process of attenuating their lingering attachments.

In addition to abstaining from hot foods, the survivors also strove to dry out their bodies (*śarīr ukiye rākhte*) by avoiding warm, salted, and wet foods such as ordinary boiled rice (*bhāt* made from *siddha cāl:* rice grains prepared by boiling) and by limiting intake of the drier sun-dried rice (*ātap cāl*) to only one meal a day (and even sun-dried rice could not be eaten on the first three days following death).[21] For boiled rice, death-impure persons substituted dry puffed or parched rice (*khai* or *muṛi*) in the evenings. This was eaten cold and separately from moist foods, such as vegetables or milk, so that it could retain its dry (*śukna*) state.

According to Bengalis, boiled rice (*bhāt*) is the most uniting of all foods. More than any other, it entails the sharing of substance among those who cook or serve it and those who mutually partake of it. Boiled rice, even if it has not been eaten yet, was considered to be *ẽṭo:* that is, food that is permeated with the substance of those who have cooked, handled, or eaten it. For this reason, boiled rice had the most restrictions on where, when, and with whom it could or could not be eaten. Many upper-caste villagers, even if they would take tea or fried foods in other people's homes, would never eat boiled rice in an unrelated person's house or a restaurant, especially if the cook or server was of a lower caste. Boiled rice was thus the primary food (along with nonvegetarian, *āmiṣ*, food) that was avoided by those aiming to cool or contain their bodies: those with fevers, those fasting for spiritual or ritual purposes, those who were widows (see chapter 7), those suffering birth-separation impurity, and those suffering death-separation impurity. By avoiding boiled rice and substituting other drier foods, villagers were said "to keep the body dry" (*śarīr śukiye rākhte*) and therefore, as I see it, relatively distanced from others. To be moist is to have a fluid and open body, capable of transacting with others; to be dry is to be relatively self-contained. The *pret,* too, could not be fed boiled rice over this period.

Other foods and spices that had to be avoided included ordinary salt (which is, some said, an *āmiṣ* and hot food and therefore unacceptable);[22] oil (a moisturizing substance that could neither be used in cooking nor applied to the body); green vegetables that are moisturizing, slimy, *lālā-jātīya* (saliva-like), like okra; and turmeric (a particularly auspicious substance). Some of these forbidden foods, such as oil and saliva-like greens, could be prescribed for old people whose bodies had become *too* dry; but they were to be avoided by death-impure people who had to cultivate a dry and cool bodily state.

In addition to changing their diets, the surviving kin had to avoid fire by refraining from using their cooking hearths on the day of the death. They had also to discard on the outskirts of the village any previously cooked food or used clay cooking pots. Clay pots were regarded as highly permeable, absorbing the substances both of the people who cooked with or ate from them and of the food, particularly cooked rice, that was cooked within them. Even if washed, these pots were considered *ẽṭo,* that is, permeated with saliva or cooked rice, two of the most connective household substances. The modern aluminum and stainless steel pots and dishes now common in most village households, however, were regarded as relatively impermeable, and could be cleansed and reused. By discarding the used clay pots, the family cleared away old connections with the dead person. They also made a break with the substances of the whole previous household—now devoid of a member—thereby making it possible to form new household relationships after the period of mourning.

Persons "impure" from a death had also to refrain from other activities considered to be uniting, heating, auspicious, or particularly luxurious, such as having sex, sharing food with others, combing or oiling the hair, using soap, shaving, applying red *sindūr* or *āltā* to their bodies, wearing shoes, using an umbrella, or wearing new clothing. The chief mourner, the man who placed the fire in the corpse's mouth (and thus the most dangerously "hot" of the survivors), was required in addition to wear only plain, pure white cotton clothing (called *khādi* or *mārkin*), sleep on the ground (on a straw mat or wool blanket), and carry around his own wool seat (*āsan*) to sit on. Ordinary cotton clothing, seats, and bedding were considered unfit because they were not uniquely pure (*pabitra*) and were easily contaminated or permeated by the substances of those who handled them. If of a Sudra caste, the chief mourner had also to wear a protective iron key around his neck to keep ghosts away. Heat opens the body to a ghost's invasion. The density of iron (*lohā*), one Brahman man explained, can counteract the attraction (*ākarṣaṇ*) that the ghost has for the chief mourner. It is perhaps because Brahmans were thought to be in general cooler (and thus more resistant to heating penetrations?) than non-Brahmans that they did not need to wear an iron key to keep ghosts away.

When I asked villagers why it is necessary for family members of a dead person to perform this rigorous set of *aśauc* practices, I received various responses. The most common was simply that the observances of death-separation impurity must be practiced—it is *dharma* (part of upholding the social-moral order) to do so, and *dharma* would be ruined if they were not practiced. Villagers also frequently suggested that *aśauc* is a way of expressing the family's grief (*śok*) at having lost a loved member, and in particular a way of demonstrating a kind of "fellow feeling" (or *sambedanā*) with the deceased, because the practices of *aśauc* actually bring the observant survivors to a condition similar to the dead person's: bereft of normal food, intimate company, household luxuries, good clothing, and bodily adornments.[23]

After observing several deaths in Mangaldihi, I was also inclining toward the belief that death-separation impurity had a lot to do with cutting maya, though no one gave me this reason directly. I was thus surprised when one day a local Brahman priest, Nimai Bhattcharj, after explaining first that *aśauc* had to do with expressing sympathy for the deceased, told me: "And there is another aim of the practices of *aśauc*—to become free from the bindings of maya."

This priest was in fact the only villager to state so explicitly that by practicing *aśauc,* both the survivors and the deceased person's spirit are able to loosen the bindings of maya they have for each other. But other villagers supported such reasoning; they frequently explained that if *aśauc* is not observed properly, the dead person's spirit may return to its former household as a disturbing ghost (*bhūt*); or the spirit may even enter the womb of a household wife, only to die as a fetus and thereby incite the household people to perform again the practices of *aśauc* more thoroughly and effectively. Indeed, while I was in Mangaldihi the fetus of one of the young wives in a Kulu household died in the womb, and the whole family decided to undergo an especially rigorous period of death-separation impurity. They believed that the fetus must have held the spirit of a recently deceased ancestor for whom the observances of *aśauc* had not been satisfactorily performed; and thus the spirit was still unable to depart from its former household. To perform *aśauc* properly means to cut maya, to allow the deceased to leave; not to perform *aśauc* means to keep the deceased's spirit near.

The practices of death impurity have been closely scrutinized by numerous scholars of Indian society.[24] Many, as Jonathan Parry observes, have not found it easy to specify "why death is supposed to cause it [impurity], or how the regime of mourning helps to get rid of it" (1994:217). Some have interpreted death impurity as a means of handling involvement with the severely polluting dead body (e.g., Dumont and Pocock 1959; Orenstein 1970; Pandey 1969:256–57). But more widely accepted is the view that it is a particular way of acknowledging the transitional condition between the severing of old relationships after a death and the establishing of new ones (Das 1982:126; D. Mines 1990:127; Nicholas 1988:174; Parry 1982:85). Veena Das interprets this time as one of "liminality"; the practices of death impurity serve to "symbolize" the liminal condition of the survivors, who are temporarily outside of the ordinary social world as they deal with the departed spirit or *preta* (1982:126). Diane Mines (1990) sees death impurity as part of a temporary state of ritual "incapacity" (her translation of the term *aśauca*) of the family body, caused by the loss of one of its vital members.

In Mangaldihi, at least, a primary aim of the practices of death-separation impurity was very practical: to separate and to loosen ties—between the family survivors and the spirit of the deceased, between the family body as it will be and the family body as it once was, and also (temporarily) between the family survivors and those community members unaffected by the death. These practices do not merely "symbolize," "express," or "point to" a state of separative liminality, as Das claims (1982:126–27). Rather, they work pragmatically to *effect* such a separative state—and if they are not properly performed, then the desired separative state will not be created. These practices have power not simply because of what they refer to or express but, more fundamentally, because of what they perform.

EXTENDING CONTINUITIES

I have been emphasizing up until now the separations that death entails; but death is only a relative separation. In Hindu mythology, cosmic destruction (or *pralaya*) is often a necessary prelude to creative regeneration; so in death, as Jonathan Parry (1982) and Diane Mines (1990:122) aptly observe, the destruction of the material body (and other social ties, I would add) is necessary to the regeneration of life. The separations of death, however painful and difficult to achieve, are only partial; ultimately, new unions are created out of the old, loosened ties. During the latter phase of the period of mourning, the survivors concentrate on such regenerative funeral rites. By ritually feeding, reproducing a new body for, transporting to the ancestor world, and remembering the spirit of the deceased, they work to re-form family relationships and extend the family line.

Feeding, Fostering, and Reproducing a Body for the Departed Spirit: Re-creating Channels of Relatedness

It was primarily through a series of ritual feedings that channels of relatedness between living and deceased kin were re-formed in Mangaldihi. Just as people strove to cut off social ties largely by refusing to share food with others (and by ingesting a cool and dry diet), so in sharing food with and feeding others they sought to create and sustain relationships. Over the ten- to thirty-day transitional period while the spirit of the deceased lingered near its former home as a *pret,* it had to be nourished with food and water just like a living person. The family provided this nourishment through a series of "faithful offerings," or *śrāddhas,* to the deceased.

The most characteristic offering in a *śrāddha* is a *piṇḍa,* a ball of food made from rice pasted together with other ingredients. *Piṇḍa* is a multivalent term, meaning at the same time "rice ball" and "body" (or "body particle"). Through feeding the spirit *piṇḍa*s and other foods, the family would accomplish several ends: they nourished the departed spirit, they produced a new body for the spirit, and they re-created and sustained a "shared body" (or "shared rice ball," *sapiṇḍa*) relationship with the spirit as an ancestor. In addition, through abundantly feeding the departed spirit, families could try to make up for any possible lapses in providing care while the person was still alive. People would tell me that many families (though no family would openly admit this of themselves) withhold sufficient quantities of food from very elderly and incontinent members, hoping to avoid cleaning up the elder's excessive bowel movements. So, several villagers explained, after death families can compensate for what they had earlier withheld without reservation, feeding the departed spirit plentiful quantities of all the foods that the person loved best.

As we have seen, the first rice balls were given to the spirit of the deceased even before cremation, just after the funeral procession carrying the corpse crosses the threshold of the main inhabited area of the village. Here the chief mourner, usually the eldest son of the deceased person, prepared three *piṇḍas* to nourish the departed spirit for the three days between cremation and the next feeding. Bits of each *piṇḍa*—formed from sun-dried rice, honey, black sesame seeds, *tulsī* leaf, ghee, and banana—were placed in the corpse's mouth.

The next series of food and water offerings to the departed spirit took place at the edge of a pond where a verbena plant (*benā gāch*) was placed by the chief mourner in the name of the deceased, to be used as the departed spirit's first temporary resting place or shelter (*āśraya*). This plant was set in the ground on the fourth day following cremation, and it was there that the family offered the departed spirit food and water. Brahman families made offerings to the *pret* at the *benā* plant every day between the fourth and tenth days following the death; Sudra families (who observed a longer period of death-separation impurity) fed the *pret* on the fourth, nineteenth, and thirtieth days.

On these days, the mourners would make their way to the *benā* plant just after noon in a bathed and purified condition, and there they offered the *pret* water and some of its favorite (all vegetarian) foods, such as milk, yogurt, sweets, and fruit. As I noted above, the foods given to the *pret* must be "cooling" ones because of the need to attenuate previous ties; but at the same time, the very act of feeding the *pret* sustains and keeps open channels of relatedness. The feedings were performed with love, respect, and tender concern for the deceased's well-being. There was often much discussion about what the person liked to eat while alive, and attempts were made to provide these favorite foods. The family survivors had a real sense of actually feeding the dead person, who was terribly hungry and thirsty in this state, and they were sure that he or she would receive the food and enjoy eating it. As earlier quotations from villagers show, old people themselves often looked forward to eating these treats from the hands of their descendants after they died.

On the tenth day after death for Brahmans and on the thirtieth day for Sudras, the family made the departed spirit an even more important set of food offerings, which provided the *pret* with a temporary body. They were placed at the *benā* plant by the ghat or pond's edge, as part of a series of other ritual acts collectively called *ghāṭ kāj*, or "ghat work." Just after noon, the family made its way to the ghat accompanied by the family priest. The family members bathed and then offered the *pret* water and food (sweets, milk, fruit, etc.) at the *benā* plant, as they had on earlier days.

Then came the central ritual offering of the day. The chief mourner, with the help of the priest, prepared ten *piṇḍa*s by kneading together in a clay pot sun-dried rice, barley, black sesame seeds, milk, ghee, honey, and banana. Brahman families prepared the ingredients by boiling them over a small oven near the *benā* plant, while Sudra families simply kneaded them together raw. The mixture was then formed into ten balls, which the chief mourner gave to the deceased one after another. These *piṇḍa*s were said both to nourish the *pret* as food and to constitute a temporary body for it. The ten rice balls given to the *pret* are analogous to the time of a pregnancy—ten lunar months—and they were also said each to constitute a different part of the *pret*'s new, subtle body. Through these rice ball offerings, a son quite literally produced a new body for his parent or elder, just as the parent once gave the child his own body at birth.[25]

The chief mourner would then uproot the *benā* plant and immerse it in the pond, for now that the *pret* had a temporary body, it no longer required the *benā* plant as a resting place. All of the close kin bathed and had their nails cut by a Barber, and the men additionally had their heads and armpits shaved. Hair and nails, existing as they do on the peripheries of the body, were often associated by villagers with interpersonal exchanges, and they were manipulated to transform social relationships. The act of touching someone with one's unbound hair (as a mother does a departing bride-daughter) formed relations of shared bodily "oneness"; cutting the hair and nails diminished social bonds.[26] These separative acts—the discarding of the *benā* plant, shaving, nail trimming, and bathing—put an end to the most severe period of death-separation impurity, the phase when the survivors and the *pret* are closest. But such destructive acts of separation were performed only after the family had nourished and produced a new body for the *pret,* as a means of helping it on its way to forming new unions as an ancestor (*pitṛ*) and as the life force (*prāṇ*) reborn within a new fetus.

The day of "ghat work" was followed in Mangaldihi by a day called the day of *śrāddha* (faithful offerings) or the day of *kāj* (work). Early in the morning, the family priest and a Barber arrived to help the household wives set up the ritual space and gather together all the necessary ingredients. The central *śrāddha* of the day was performed in the house's courtyard, as relatives and guests began to arrive, casually looking on as they came and went. In this *śrāddha,* the family gave the departed spirit as *dān* (gifts) all of the food and supplies it would need on its yearlong journey to the realm of the ancestors. Next to the ritual space was laid a symbolic year's supply of food, including twelve portions of uncooked rice, potatoes, lentils, salt, sugar, turmeric, and chili peppers. Off to the side were arranged all the nonfood supplies that the *pret* would need on its journey, including (if the family could afford it) a cot, mattress, bedsheet, pillow, mosquito net, shoes, umbrella, dhoti or sari, cotton towel, oil lamp, brass plate, bowl, and cup. A framed photograph of the deceased person adorned with a garland of flowers was also generally placed on the cot.

At the culminating moment of the ritual, after a series of prayers and smaller offerings of water, betel nut, flowers, and so on were given, the chief mourner would ritually hand over all of the supplies as gifts to the Brahman priest, who accepted them in the name of the deceased person. In a Brahman *śrāddha,* a special "lower" form of Brahman called an *agradānī* (the first, or "earlier," *agra,* receiver of "gifts," *dān*) had to be present to receive the nonfood supplies intended for the deceased, as the usual Brahman priest could not accept these items from a Brahman family.[27] Gifts of small Gita books, sacred threads (*paitā*), betel nuts, betel-nut tree (*supāri*) leaves, and one-rupee coins were also made to three Brahman men at this point, to ensure the peace of the *pret-ātmā* and in particular (several villagers told me) to remove any of the *pret-ātmā*'s sins (*pāp*). Like the *agradānī* Brahman, these Brahman men seemed to be important receptacles of negative residues.

The family thus would provide the departed spirit not only with food and a new body, but also with all of the other basic necessities of daily life, such as clothing, dishes, and a bed. These things fostered the spirit just as they would a living family member; the same items had been used by the spirit, as a onetime parent or elder, to foster the family. Once these gifts were received, the *pret* would finally be able to depart on the journey to the realm of ancestors (*pitṛlok*).

As the *pret* journeyed away from them, the restrictions of death-separation impurity were lifted for all but the closest survivors, the sons and

Four brothers practice the separations of *aśauc* following their father's death.

their wives. The family would dramatize the end to its period of separation by offering a grand funeral feast to what were sometimes scores of relatives from near and far, neighbors, and other villagers. The food for the feast was as abundant and lavish as the family could afford, and it was by no means limited to the vegetarian items that the family and *pret* had been subsisting on until then. Large quantities of fish were served, with sauces prepared with plenty of "hot" onions and garlic. The feast food was also served over steaming piles of boiled rice (*bhāt*), another food that the bereaved family had being avoiding until this moment. The change in diet to hotter and more connective foods put an end to the separative phase of cooling and containing, as the survivors once again began to transact with others, rebuilding their network of ties.

The *pret,* like the family and guests, would also get to eat the feast food. A large banana-leaf plate of rice, fish, dal, vegetables, yogurt, and sweets was made up for the *pret* and was left out next to where the *śrāddha* had been performed, with a stick of incense and glass of water. This was the first time that the *pret* was able to eat heating, moisturizing, and connective non-vegetarian food and rice since the death, and people commonly remarked on how much the *pret* must be enjoying the delicious meal. The *pret* was also fed by a special meal given to twelve Brahman men, who were fed at the funeral feast before any of the other guests. Each had to be given a one-rupee coin, small Gita book, and betel nut as a form of payment (*dakshiṇā*) for the service of eating the meal in the name of the deceased and perhaps, one Brahman man suggested to me, to compensate for the burden of ingesting the deceased person's sins (*pāp*).

Meanwhile, while the feast was taking place, the chief mourner would perform the final *śrāddha* of the day, called the *piṇḍa dān*, or the "gift of a body of food."[28] This *śrāddha* was performed in a cowshed (*goyāla*), which was said to be the most pure (*pabitra*) place in the household, comparable to the banks of the Ganges river. There the chief mourner, again with the assistance of the Brahman priest and Barber (and if a Brahman family, with an *agradānī* Brahman as well), prepared one or more rice balls to offer to the *pret*, just like those offered earlier. The *piṇḍas* offered were intended exclusively for the deceased person's benefit, to nourish it as it made the yearlong journey to the ancestors. This form of *śrāddha* was thus termed an *ekoddiṣṭa śrāddha*, a *śrāddha* "intended for one." Altogether, twelve rice balls were supposed to be offered to the *pret* over the course of its yearlong journey, one for every lunar month. Some families did perform twelve such *śrāddhas* over the year; but most families sped up the process of nourishing the *pret*, either by providing all twelve *piṇḍas* at once on the funeral feast day or by offering three or four *piṇḍas* together over an abbreviated "year" of a few months.

After the *piṇḍas* were offered to the *pret*, the chief mourner, if a non-Brahman, picked them up and deposited them in a pond. At a Brahman *piṇḍa dān*, the *agradānī* Brahman had himself to eat the *piṇḍas* in the name of the deceased, just as he accepted the bed, umbrella, shoes, and other supplies for the dead person. This was a task that the *agradānī* Brahman was quite embarrassed and reluctant to perform. Guests at Brahman *śrāddhas* frequently whispered to me to make sure I noticed the eating of the *piṇḍas*, but the man himself always attempted to turn furtively away from me and others while he did so. Villagers explained that it was embarrassing (*lajjā hae*) to eat *piṇḍas* in the cowshed, but the *agradānī*'s reluctance may also have to do with the ingesting of sins or inauspiciousness generated by the death. Once the *piṇḍas* were gone, the chief mourner, any of the deceased's other sons, and their wives would all bathe. The chief mourner could discard the iron key meant to keep the ghost-spirit away from him. Now all remaining kin had put an end to their most restrictive period of death-separation impurity.

The cycle of food offerings to the departed spirit culminated with the *sapiṇḍi-karāna*, or "making of a *sapiṇḍa*," ritual performed one year (or an abbreviated symbolic year) later on the first anniversary of the death. This ritual has received much attention from anthropologists and historians of religion because it so dramatically represents Hindu notions of death and family (or *sapiṇḍa*) relationships.[29] Through this ritual, the deceased person is concretely merged with the bodies of his ancestors, or *pitṛs* (literally, "fathers"), thereby ending the yearlong transitional stage as a departed spirit, or *pret*. In Mangaldihi, spirits of deceased women, too, were merged with ancestral "fathers" (*pitṛs*), though (as discussed in a moment) they never became full ancestors in their own right.

Like the earlier *piṇḍa-dān* rituals, this final rite was performed by the chief mourner in a cowshed with the assistance of a Brahman priest. The chief mourner prepared *piṇḍas* as before, but this time he made four distinct *piṇḍas*, one for the dead person (who was usually the mourner's father or mother) and one for each of three ascending ancestors (or *pitṛs*) in the male line: his father (or, if the dead person is a woman, her husband's father), father's father, and father's father's father. Thus, if the deceased was male, the three ancestor *piṇḍas* would be for the three ascending ancestors in the paternal line (together with their wives, whose names would not be mentioned separately). If female, the *piṇḍas* would be for the deceased woman's *husband's* paternal ancestors (and their wives).[30]

These *piṇḍas* were simultaneously representations of the deceased elders and food offerings to them. The *piṇḍa* for the deceased person was placed on one banana-leaf plate, and the *piṇḍas* for each of the three ancestors were placed together in a row on another adjacent plate. The chief mourner offered each of the *piṇḍas* a series of respectful offerings, including flowers, water, betel nuts, and *kuśa* grass. Then came the climax: the chief mourner would take the rice ball for his deceased parent, divide it into three portions, and merge it carefully with the *piṇḍas* of each of the three ancestors. As Ralph Nicholas (1988:376) writes, "The gesture is simple and dramatic: both representationally and effectively, the particles of the body of the preta are merged with the particles of the ancestral bodies."

By performing this ritual of feeding rice balls and merging ancestral bodies, the surviving descendants effectively removed the spirit of the deceased from the environs of its previous home, putting an end to its singular and threatening condition as a *pret*. In the process, bodily connections between the spirit of the dead, his or her forefathers, and living descendants were recreated and sustained. As an ancestor (*pitṛ*), the deceased person's spirit would now be able to continue to share *piṇḍas*—body particles and rice balls—with the ancestors who had died before and with the living descendants who would continue to prepare and offer the *piṇḍas*, ideally for generations to come. Thus death constituted only a relative separation in the bodies of living and dead family members. By continuing to feed and share food with the departed person—first as *pret* and then as *pitṛ*—the living maintained their shared body (*sapiṇḍa*) relationship with the deceased, albeit in different forms.

It is important to note that women as ancestors had a much more tenuous, amorphous identity than men. As already mentioned, the term for ancestor (*pitṛ*) literally means "father." When a man made a *śrāddha* offering to his ancestors at a funeral or other ritual occasion,[31] he would commonly call out the name or kin term of his father, father's father, and father's father's father, as well as his mother's father and mother's father's father—three generations of male ancestors traced through both his father's and mother's paternal family lines. Ritual priests emphasized, when I asked, that women do also receive food and water during such rites, for when male ancestors are fed, the women as wives and "half bodies" of these ancestors are automatically nourished as well.[32] However, when I asked the women milling around whether female ancestors were nourished and honored, too, most were perturbed and uncertain. But even if her long-term identity as an ancestor might be tenuous, a woman's departed spirit during the initial days and months following death was attentively cared for and processed, receiving the full elaborate set of rituals.

If one looks back to table 4 (in chapter 2), it becomes clear that the kinds of gifts of food, clothing, a body, and so on that survivors provided to departed spirits and ancestors were precisely the same kinds of gifts that these deceased persons once gave, as parents, to their descendants. Just as children could not exist without their parents giving them birth and sustenance, so parents could not exist after death without being fed, nurtured, and provided with a new body by their children. Through this reciprocal indebtedness and interdependence between generations—a relationship that ideally extended throughout life, into old age, and after death—people in Mangaldihi maintained personal and family continuities over time on a most profound level.

Remembering: Spatiotemporal Extensions of Family Lines

Another way of re-forming and extending connections with a deceased person was by remembering him or her, and particularly by establishing in the home durable signs of the person who had died, such as photographs, footprints, and names written in books. In recent years photos had become especially popular, and villagers expended much energy and funds attempting to acquire pictures of their elders before they died. They escorted older relatives to photo studios in nearby towns, or convinced any relative or friend known to have a camera (including especially the resident American) to take their elders' photos. People carefully framed and placed these on the family altar next to colorful images of deities and other photographs of earlier ancestors. Almost every household had such an altar. The residents went there to light incense, garland the photos and images with flowers, and do *praṇām* to ancestors and deities. Photos of elders had to have the feet showing, so that younger relatives could do *praṇām* to them and symbolically take the dust from their feet. In *Camera Indica: The Social Life of Indian Photographs,* Christopher Pinney explores "the different kinds of work that the 'face' and the 'body' are required to do within different photographic traditions" (1997:10). Pinney observes of the Indian practice of retaining photos of ancestors: "In Bhatisuda . . . , photography never seems to merely duplicate the everyday world, but is, rather, prized for its capacity to make traces of persons endure" (p. 149).

Families in Mangaldihi likewise obtained the footprints of deceased elders by painting the feet of the dead body with red *āltā* and pressing white sheets of paper against them. These prints were often framed and displayed on household walls to facilitate *praṇām*. Families who owned books and writing materials also recorded the names of their ancestors so that when future generations made *piṇḍa* offerings, they would be able to remember and cite the names of the recipients.

Such signs were particularly important because of their power to extend lineage continuity beyond the lives and transient memories of living family members. They provided one connection between living and deceased kin, and extended kinship both spatially and temporally into future generations. The spatial domains of the ancestor and household worlds were linked: for even while the deceased was being transported to the realm of ancestors (*pitṛlok*), his or her visual forms were retained in the household. The temporal worlds of living and deceased kin were also linked and extended: Here, memory had to do not so much with bringing the past into the present as with extending the past (and present) into the future. Durable signs of deceased kin were established so that future generations could honor, know, and remember them.

As I mentioned in chapter 3, *baṃśa* is a multivalent term that means both "family line" and "bamboo." A family line is like a bamboo plant, Gurusaday Mukherjee explained, because if any individual part or branch of the bamboo dies off, other branches of bamboo spread out from it. But when a bamboo plant flowers, it has come to the end of its reproductive life and will no longer continue to extend. Such a bamboo plant quickly becomes inauspicious, villagers said, and is promptly removed from any household land, so that its unproductiveness and impending extinction will not spread to the family line. Similarly, an "extinct" person is also removed via elaborate separative rituals, but at the same time survivors make strenuous efforts to nourish and sustain memories of them and thus continue the family line or *baṃśa.* By giving them new bodies as well as feeding, fostering, remembering, and honoring them, survivors nurtured their deceased loved ones and the *baṃśa* to which all belonged. In so doing, by extending themselves as parts of others, both the living and the deceased were able to transcend the flux and impermanence of everyday life.

Part Three

GENDERED TRANSFORMATIONS

6 Transformations of Gender and Gendered Transformations

I sobbed and sobbed after my wedding. I couldn't stand to be away from my father. I fled home whenever I could, and I would stay there for days and days on end, until someone from my father-in-law's house would come to get me. Then I would sob and sob again. But slowly you visit less, you cry less. And now, in old age, there is hardly any more connection with my father's house.

Choto Ma

After the blood stopped, my body dried out. Even if I wanted to [have sex], I wouldn't be able to. I had four kids, then my blood dried up, and then my body dried up. Now I have desire (*lobh*) only for food.

Bhogi Bagdi

The women I knew in Mangaldihi often spoke of their lives in terms of the profound changes that they had experienced in their bodies, and in the kinds of social ties making up their personhoods, over the life course. In this and the following chapter, I take a more focused look at issues I first raised in the book's introduction: how does aging affect definitions of gender, and gender affect experiences of aging? These questions speak not only to how we think about gender relations in South Asia but also to how the ways the category of "woman" has been constructed in gender theory more broadly. I will explore two important and interrelated themes: first, the ways in which women's bodies in Mangaldihi were perceived, controlled, and transformed over their lives; and, second, the ways in which women experienced their changing ties of maya.

GENDERED BODIES AND EVERYDAY PRACTICES

Gender was constructed in Mangaldihi as elsewhere largely through the unceasing work of everyday life, through daily social interactions and sexual relations, through the ways women and men dressed and adorned their bodies, and through people's movements within and beyond the home. As an anthropologist in Mangaldihi, I first encountered and experienced local constructions of gender at the level of daily practices involving the body, or what Carol Delaney (1991:29) has referred to as the "bodily training" that anthropologists (perhaps especially women anthropologists) must go through when learning to fit into a new sociocultural setting. As a young, recently married woman, I was taught to dress, bathe, interact with others, keep my home, comport my body, and so on as a young village woman and wife does (with some important differences and freedoms because of my anomalous position as a foreigner and researcher).

The specificity and pervasiveness of the everyday bodily requirements that I was expected to observe seemed to me quite unwieldy, unaccustomed as I was to these forms of discipline (though ready to comply quite unconsciously with many of the expectations of my own culture, such as the requirements that women keep their legs together while sitting or be thin). I had to learn to wear saris, to keep my shoulders and legs covered at all times (even when bathing in a public area, as was commonly done), to bathe and change my clothes after defecating or touching anything "impure" (*aśuddha*), to keep my hair bound in a braid or a knot, to wash my hands after eating, to adorn the part of my hair with the red vermilion of married women, to refrain from keeping the company of men in my home, and so forth. Often it seemed that I could do nothing quite right, and my body was scrutinized for its imperfections and quirks. My skin was becoming too dark: from the Indian sun? from wandering too much beyond the home? I was too thin: would I be infertile, or unattractive to my husband when he rejoined me? My occasional pimples were also causes for concern and comment: were they caused, perhaps, by excessive sexual heat erupting from my body, heat that could not be spent with my husband far away? The process was difficult and at times irritating; but my learning to fit as a woman into village life provided a valuable avenue toward understanding what it was to be a woman in Mangaldihi.

Michel Foucault has written masterfully about how forms of power operate upon the body in modern societies. He argues that distinctly modern forms of power do not emanate from some central source or sovereign figure, but circulate throughout the entire social body via the most minute and pervasive everyday "micropractices," such as those I have described here—in people's gestures, habits, bodies, movements, desires, and self-surveillance (1973, 1975, 1979, 1980b, 1980c). Such a notion of capillary power—widely dispersed and anonymous—is particularly useful for analyzing gender relations, for it is through the mundane practices of everyday life that much of the structuring and playing out of gender hierarchies takes place.

As Sandra Bartky (1997:131–32) convincingly argues, however, Foucault himself consistently treats the body as if it were one, as if the bodily experiences of men and women did not differ. But in fact, in many (or all?) societies—certainly in the American and Bengali societies I know—there are disciplines that operate specifically upon women's bodies to produce uniquely feminine modalities of embodiment (see Bordo 1993:17–19). These disciplines, moreover, often do not emanate primarily from the kinds of modern institutions that are Foucault's focus (prisons, schools, hospitals, armies, and the like), but rather from the everyday bodily requirements taught to girls and women within their families and local communities.

I soon discovered that most of my training in my first few months in the village had to do, in the dominant patrilineal discourse of Mangaldihi, with containing, controlling, and channeling women's sexuality toward a husband, marriage, and fertile reproduction within a patrilineage. These bodily regulations were justified and explained largely in terms of perceived differences in the biologies of the two sexes. Women's bodies were commonly described to me as more "open" (*kholā*) than men's, as well as more "hot" (*garam*). As a result, women could be viewed as particularly vulnerable to impurity (*aśuddhatā*) and to engaging in improper sexual liaisons.

As I learned how Mangaldihians managed impurity in their daily lives, I was initially struck by their attitudes surrounding the relative openness of women. It was common for both women and men in Mangaldihi to describe women as "impure" (*aśuddha*), a quality that seemed to be tied to their regarding women—postpubertal and married women, at least—as more open and exposed to mixing than were men. Although people seemed to view the bodies of *both* women and men as relatively open or permeable, they saw women as being even more so.

Scholars have long noted that Hindus commonly attribute lesser purity to women. While Lynn Bennett (1983:216) finds the cause in a vague sense of sin and impurity attached to menstruation, Catherine Thompson (1985) adds that childbirth, like menstruation, is linked to female pollution, and that women are viewed as particularly polluting when they are not strongly identified with men. I. Julia Leslie (1989:250–52) also mentions the impurity of menstruation, viewed in many Hindu texts as a mark of both a woman's sexual appetite and her "innate impurity." She notes, too, that women are often compared in Hindu texts to Sudras (the lowest of the four *varṇas*, or caste groups, and defiling to the touch), because like Sudras women have lost the right to *upanayana,* the initiation ritual that upper-caste Hindu men undergo to become "twice-born" (1989:38–40, 251; cf. F. Smith 1991:18). Frederique Marglin, along with noting the impurity of menstrual blood and the "once-born" Sudra-like status of women, offers a more general interpretation of impurity.[1] Impurity, she suggests, has to do with violations of the boundaries of the body, as in menstruation and childbirth (as well as elimination, sexual intercourse, and wounds), with which women are presumably more involved than men (1977:265–66; 1985a:44; 1985c:19–20, 63).

In Mangaldihi, I was first exposed to notions about the impurity of women when I was confronted with people's bathing practices, as well as their attempts to teach *me* to control my bodily impurities, influxes, and outflows through bathing. Women apparently became *aśuddha* very easily—after sleeping in a bed (where saliva or sexual fluids may have spilled), touching unwashed clothing, handling unwashed dishes (which are *ẽṭo,* permeated with saliva), engaging in sexual relations, giving birth, menstruating, or touching any other impure person or thing. "Impurity" seemed to be defined in such contexts as a condition stemming from inappropriate, unmatched, or undesired mixing, often of bodily substances. Although this definition is similar to that offered by Marglin, it emphasizes *inappropriate, unmatched, or undesired* body crossings (what I have called "mixing"); as Marglin herself notes (1985b:66), and as I have explored throughout this book, many bodily crossings or mixings—such as ingesting the leftovers of a deity, or sharing food with intimate friends or kin—are not considered impure at all. Furthermore, in locating impurity in "overflows which cross the boundaries of the body," Marglin assumes that the body is ordinarily a "bounded entity" (1985b:67; cf. Marglin 1977, 1985a:44, 1985c:90), becoming impure whenever its boundaries are "violated." This assumption does not match local conceptions of the body or person (both male and female) as *ordinarily* relatively open and permeable.

The women I knew reacted to the perceived impurity of their bodies in ways that varied considerably. Many women, especially lower-caste women and those who were very busy with work, showed little concern with how pure or impure they might be at any given moment. But in the Brahman neighborhood in which I lived, it seemed that women were continually bathing, and requiring *me* to bathe, sometimes up to five or six times a day: after I defecated (which unfortunately could occur more than daily, especially when I was suffering from mild dysentery), or visited a lower-caste neighborhood, or came in contact accidentally with some dog-doo, or touched the external panel of a truck carrying a dead body and its mourners to the cremation ground, or returned from a bus trip (where people of many castes and backgrounds mingle closely), and on and on.

I am chagrined to confess, however, that for my first several months in the village, I did not notice that women were much more vulnerable than men to such daily impurities, and thus more frequently subjected to these bathing rituals. Then one day Gurusaday Mukherjee mentioned, quite by chance, that men do not have to bathe after coming into cursory contact with impure things. Men *may* choose to bathe after defecating or touching unmade beds or lower-caste people, but they do not *have* to; if they do not, no harm or *doṣ* will occur (unless, that is, they are going to enter a temple or make offerings to a deity, when special purity is required). I was astounded, not only because I realized that a male anthropologist in Mangaldihi would not have had to spend so many seemingly futile hours bathing, but also because I could not believe that I had been so oblivious to this crucial difference in men's and women's daily practices. I spent the next several weeks asking everyone, men and women, why it is that women were more vulnerable to impurity than men.

Their answers led me to believe, as I have already suggested, that most Mangaldihians viewed women as anatomically more open (*kholā*) than men, and thus more exposed to mixing. Mangaldihians usually explained women's openness by describing their involvement in menstruation, sexuality, and childbirth—all processes that involve substances going into and out of a woman's body. For instance, a woman is especially open, and also impure (*aśuddha*), during her menstrual period.[2] A girl's first menstruation marks the beginnings of a state of openness, and thus her readiness for marriage, sexual relations, and pregnancy. Menstruation was viewed as a time when excess blood flowed from the body, and a woman had to be "open" for this to occur. In contrast, a pregnant woman is temporarily "closed" (*bandha*); women who have stopped menstruating after menopause are permanently closed in this respect.

Sexual intercourse also involves opening a woman, and virgins were sometimes described as *bandha.* Intercourse, said Mangaldihians, takes place within the woman and outside the man. Sexual fluids or semen (*śukra*) leave the man at the moment of ejaculation to enter and permeate the woman. Once she has slept with a man, a woman contains some of his substance within her permanently, although a man can sleep with a woman with no real lasting effect. The process of childbirth itself was said to make women impure and leave them dangerously open for a period of one month after they gave birth or experienced a late miscarriage or abortion. To remedy this condition—to close and "dry out" (*śukote*) her body and womb—a woman had to undergo a drying, self-containing, and separative period of birth impurity (*aśauc*), similar to that occurring after a death in the family.[3]

The village women I knew had clear ideas about the relative openness and impurity of women's bodies. Subradi, a married Brahman woman, told me, "Women are always impure (*apabitra*), because everything happens to them (*oder sab kichu hae*)—menstruation, childbirth. These don't happen to men. For this reason if men touch a Muslim[4] or defecate, no harm (*doṣ*) happens to them, and they don't have to wash their clothes or bathe. But harm happens to a woman." My companion Hena offered similar comments: "Men are always pure (*śuddha*). [Especially Brahman men, she explained quickly, but even Bagdi men are relatively pure compared to women.] They don't menstruate or give birth. Women menstruate, give birth—all that happens to them. Men only defecate, and nothing else." As Subradi and Hena both put it, things "happen" to women (*oder sab kichu hae*)—menstruation, childbirth, defecation, and so on. As passive receivers of action, women have a greater vulnerability to outside agents. They are also involved in more processes during which things (bodily substances, even babies) go *out* from their bodies.

Hena later explained the difference between men and women this way: "[Men] can even come right back from defecating and touch the water jug to drink water! Could we [women] do this? Never!" Another woman said with some sarcasm while discussing the subject with me and a group of other wives, "A Brahman man can even drink alcohol and sleep with a Muci woman [member of the leatherworking caste, the lowest Hindu *jāti* in Mangaldihi] and no harm (*doṣ*) happens. A woman never could! This is just the human [or male] system (*mānuṣer bidhān*)."[5] Another woman added, "For men, mixing is OK (*miśāmiśe cale*) with all castes. No harm or fault happens to them."

One common north Indian saying illustrates this notion of the openness or permeability of women particularly vividly: Women are like unglazed earthen water jugs, which are permeable and become easily contaminated to such depth that they cannot be purified. Men are like impermeable brass jugs, which are difficult to contaminate and easy to purify (cf. Dube 1975:163, 1988:16; Jacobson 1978:98). Some told me that only when a Hindu man engages in prolonged contact with lower-caste people or non-Hindus—by eating with them, visiting frequently in the same home, or engaging in a long-term sexual relationship—will lasting impurities accrue to the man's body.

Brahmans in Mangaldihi also often compared women to low-caste people (or Sudras), saying that both were "impure" (*aśuddha*). Their reasons included the fact that lower-caste people in Mangaldihi were generally not able (even if they had wished, which many did not) to maintain the levels of purity commonly sought by Brahmans. For instance, they lacked sufficient clothing to be able to change soiled clothes during the day. They also lacked the time required to bathe repeatedly, as their days were filled with labor. Furthermore, because many Bagdi men and women worked outside of the home as field laborers or domestic servants, they were required to mix more indiscriminately with a diversity of people and *jātis*, often even cleaning the dishes or unwashed clothing (impure from defecation or menstruation) of others. According to dominant Brahman discourses, then, women and Sudras were "open" and subject to impurities in some of the same ways. In addition, neither women nor Sudras could wear the sacred thread indicating the "twice-born" and pure status of an upper-caste male.

A final point made to me about women's relative openness emphasized not their receptivity but their diffusion. It is women, people told me, who nurse children, cook, fetch water, feed and care for household gods, and handle on a daily basis all sorts of household things. That is why women, rather than men, must take the most care in regulating their mixings with others, lest they exude impurity or unwanted substances onto the household things and members they feed and care for.

Such notions about the relative openness of women's bodies are not uncommon cross-culturally. Thus Carol Delaney (1991:38) finds that in Turkish society the male body is viewed as self-contained whereas the female body is relatively unbounded. Renne Hirschon (1978:76–80) writes about the ambiguous nature of female "openness" in Greek society, while Jean Comaroff (1985:81) notes the relative lack of closure of female bodies among the Tswana of South Africa. But we must remember that in this community of north India, even the male body was not usually considered to be wholly bound; it was only *relatively* bound compared to the greater openness of the female body.

Another distinctive characteristic of the female body, according to many I knew, was its "hot" (*garam*) nature. Heat was viewed in Mangaldihi as an element of all mixing and mutuality in social life, including sexuality, attachment, love, and maya, as well as anger and the messy mixings of daily impurities. When people spoke to me of the heat of women's bodies, they most often were referring to female sexuality.

Both men and women, people told me, produce heating (*garam*) sexual fluids—uterine or menstrual blood (*ārtab, rakta*) and semen or seed (*śukra*). Both male and female sexual fluids are highly distilled forms of blood derived from the cooking of food within the body. But women have more sexual heat than men, at least during their postpubertal and premenopausal years, as is demonstrated by menstruation, which results from an overabundance of hot blood periodically draining from the body.[6]

For this reason, people generally agreed that it was safe, even desirable, for women to have regular sexual relations within marriage, as a way to expend and regulate bodily heat. But men had to be more careful to engage in sexual intercourse with only moderate frequency. While complete abstinence for men could lead to excessive bodily heating, very frequent sexual activity, nocturnal emission, or masturbation could result in excessive cooling and an unhealthy depletion of male vitality, even premature graying or impotence.[7] Many women told me that their husbands thought it best to have intercourse only once a week, although some had engaged in sexual activity almost every night during their first year or two of marriage (thereby causing some husbands concern).

The real danger for women and their families of this greater sexual heat attributed to women seemed to be the possibility of sexual liaisons outside of marriage. Sexuality *within* marriage, if not unduly excessive, was auspicious and desirable, both for the sake of pleasure and, even more important, for creating children and carrying on the family line. Marglin (1985a, 1985c:89–113) makes the important point that although female sexuality in the Hindu world is impure, it is also inherently auspicious. Marglin's Oriya informants also note that the separation required of women during their menstrual periods is designed not merely to prevent women from contaminating others but also to express reverence for women's creative capacities and to allow them, respectfully, to rest (1996:161 and passim; Marglin and Mishra 1993; Marglin and Simon 1994). In Mangaldihi married women spent much of their daily lives enhancing their sexual and reproductive powers (as well as their attractiveness for their husbands)—by wearing red (a symbol of heat, sexuality, fertility, and menstrual blood): they applied red vermilion to the parting of their hair, wore red bangles and saris, and painted red *āltā* on their feet.[8] Brides-to-be and pregnant young wives were also often fed especially well in their households; they were given delicious heating and nonvegetarian foods in order to enhance their bodily heat, sexuality, and fertility.

But the qualities of sexuality and heat could be very dangerous outside the context of marriage and the patrilineal family line. According to both male and female informants, women were even more likely than men to be unable to resist a sexual urge and be thrown into promiscuity. This perception has long been common throughout India. For instance, Ved and Sylvia

Vatuk (1979:215) quote a version of the ballad of the "Lustful Stepmother" popular in Uttar Pradesh in the mid-1940s: "King, there are thousands of old books describing lust, and all agree that 17/20ths of lust belongs to women, 3/20ths to men. That is why you cannot trust her. She has so much power in her body!" Marglin (1985c:60) similarly finds that among the Brahman temple servants in Puri, "women are believed to have four times the sexual power of men. . . . They are thus four times more likely than men to be unable to resist a sexual urge." And indeed, many women I knew did speak in general terms about the potential of women to succumb to sexual urges; yet when speaking of their *own* experiences, almost all described the men in their lives as pursuing sex more fervently than they. Several of E. Valentine Daniel's male informants similarly commented that although women have more sexual desire than men, they are better able than men to control themselves (1984:171–72). Consensus on these matters is thus difficult to reach.

Most in Mangaldihi seemed to agree, however, that the consequences of women engaging in sexual relations outside of marriage could be grave. An unmarried girl who has sexual relations and whose pregnancy becomes known ruins her reputation and that of her natal family, seriously jeopardizing her own and any younger sisters' chances for marriage. Mangaldihians told me that in earlier times such young women were thrown out of their households or even killed in order to protect the family's reputation (though no one could supply a specific instance of such extreme action). Nowadays a pregnant girl's family will usually try to find out who made her pregnant; and if the man is unmarried and of the same caste, her family will pressure his family into taking the girl as a wife, or at least providing a sizable sum of money for her future dowry—attempts that are not always successful, as a boy's family can use various strategies to duck responsibility, including blaming the whole affair on the natural promiscuity and sexual voracity of the young woman (Lamb 1992). Brothers or a savvy mother may also intercede early on to get the girl an abortion or induce a miscarriage, sometimes successfully keeping the whole matter a family secret. But no family wants to bring a child into the world who could not grow up as part of a father's family line and who would be a perpetual reminder of his mother's indiscretion. In the one case I knew in which an unmarried girl did give birth to a near full-term baby, the baby was immediately killed and buried on the outskirts of the village. According to letters I still receive from the family, the young woman and her younger sisters, years later, remain unable to marry.

A married woman might find it easier to hide an extramarital liaison, because a resulting pregnancy *could* be her husband's. (One village woman's two children, for example, looked distinctly like one of the main temple priests, *not* her husband. A few furtively gossiped to me—had I noticed?—but publicly people seemed to look the other way.) From a traditional perspective of patrilineality, however, the consequences for such a woman and her household were equally serious. To understand why, we must look briefly at local theories of procreation. In Mangaldihi, as in West Bengal and Bangladesh generally, conception was said to come about through the mixing of the man's "seed" (*bīj*), contained in his semen (*śukra*), with the woman's uterine blood (*ārtab*) within the womb (*garbha*), which is often referred to as a "field" (*kshetra*).[9] The child produced from this union could be called the "fruit," or *phal.* It is the man who is responsible for planting the "seed" of the future child in the womb or "field" of the woman. The seed is generated from the father's blood, and so by passing his seed on to his child, the father passes on his blood (*rakta*). The woman also contributes blood to the fetus and child, for she nourishes it with first her uterine blood and then her breast milk, both of which were viewed as distilled forms of blood. But it is the father—both men and women in Mangaldihi agreed—who is the one actively responsible for generating the child through producing and planting the "seed."

By passing on his seed, the father also passes on his *baṃśa,* or family line, to his child. At the time of conception, if the parents are married the mother has the same *baṃśa* as the father, since a woman becomes part of her husband's *baṃśa* at marriage. Nonetheless, Bengalis say that it is fathers, not mothers, who provide a *baṃśa* for their children. The forefather (*ādipuruṣ*) of a *baṃśa* is the "root" (*mūl*) male, and the family line ascends upward from this root through a line of fathers and sons, like a very long-growing and many-branched bamboo.

If a married woman has sexual relations with a man other than her husband, his sexual fluids and bodily substance enter her permanently. Not only is she thus tainted by a stranger or an "other" (*parer*) man's substance, but she could pass his residues on to her whole family—when she nourishes her children in her womb and with breast milk, when she cooks for her husband and household members, and when she makes offerings to the ancestors. Several Brahman women told me, too, that ancestors will not accept food offered by an adulteress (cf. Marglin 1985c:53). And obviously, if a married woman becomes pregnant with another man's seed, she threatens the continuity of her husband's and his ancestors' family line, for the child born to the family will not be sprouted from the same male line of "seeds." So

Marglin (1985c:66–67) describes the views of those in neighboring Orissa: "A woman, like a field, must be well guarded, for one wants to reap what one has sown and not what another has sown."

For men in Mangaldihi, chastity was also regarded as a virtue. Men who openly engaged in extramarital affairs could be said to have a "bad character" (*caritra khārāp*) or a "bad nature" (*svabhāb khārāp*). But the merit or demerit resulting from a man's sexual behavior affected mostly himself, not his household, ancestors, or the continuity of his family line.

Countermeasures: Containing the Body

Because of the perceived potential dangers of a woman's openness and sexuality, women and girls in the Mangaldihi region were taught by their senior kin to discipline their bodies—to attempt selectively (in certain contexts, especially in public and around men) to close themselves; they relied on spatial seclusion, cloth coverings, binding the hair, special diets, and the like. These disciplining techniques seemed to aim primarily at controlling and channeling a woman's powers toward desired ends within a patrilineage. Dominant discourses indicated that a woman's body was in most need of control or containment between the onset of puberty and marriage, as well as during the early years of marriage, because a woman was most vulnerable to violations—sexual and otherwise—of her body and household during those times.

One way of controlling a woman's vulnerability was through physical isolation. Prepubertal girls and boys enjoyed a relative freedom of movement through all the spaces of the village—walking to the primary school on the village outskirts, running to various stores on errands, playing in dusty lanes and on the banks of ponds. By the time girls graduated from the village's primary school, however, their spheres of movement became increasingly constricted. Most upper-caste and some lower-caste girls did venture beyond the village to attend high school (except during the four days of their menstrual periods); but they were expected at other times to remain largely within their own neighborhoods; lower-caste girls might fish or work in the fields, but always accompanied by their mothers or other female kin. Within their neighborhoods, unmarried girls still spent time out of their own houses, as they sat in the courtyards or on the doorsteps of their neighbors' homes, talked, played with friends, and watched people come and go. Girls of this age also often went on brief errands for their elders—to pick up a little sugar or a few matches, or to bring water from the pond or hand pump (attached to a tube well). But gradually, except if working out of the home with other women, they were pressed to confine themselves more strictly to their own homes and neighborhoods.

After women married and moved to their *śvaśur bāṛi* (father-in-law's home), their spatial domains contracted even further. Especially when newly married, a wife would rarely go out of the house at all, save her journeys once or twice a day (accompanied by other household women) to the fields to defecate and to a pond to bathe. Gradually, the demands of daily work required that most married women venture out of the house—to fetch water, to wash dishes, or (if the woman was of lower caste) to work in the fields or in other people's homes. Married women also congregated frequently at village temples to perform *vrata* rituals for the well-being of their households. And in the late afternoons when their household tasks eased, married women occasionally made brief visits to a neighbor woman's home for tea, or sat on a front doorstep talking with other women and children. But other than such necessary or brief interludes, married women confined their movements largely to the interiors of their homes: cooking, cleaning, caring for children, and talking among household members and guests.

Men, in contrast, lived and moved relatively "outside" (*bāire*) throughout their lives. The young men of Mangaldihi, both married and unmarried, congregated together in groups in the village's most public and central places, as well as on the village's outer peripheries and beyond. Young men gathered for hours every day at the village tea shops, read the daily newspapers at the central library, hung out in front of the two new video halls, sat in groups in the central village green, played soccer on the playing field on the village outskirts, sat on the paved road by the bus stop watching people come and go, and had "picnics" in the village's outer fields. These were places where women rarely ventured, and I often longed to be able to join them there—their activities looked fun and free. Hena agreed; but she advised me not to go. Men also made frequent outings to towns and villages beyond Mangaldihi, whether commuting to work or buying and selling goods in larger markets.

Women were also contained by their clothing, which covered their bodies and neutralized their sexuality. Young village girls wore knee-length, light cotton "frocks," which were gradually replaced with full-length *salwar-kameez* (pantsuits) and then saris as the girls passed through puberty and reached marriageable age. It was improper for married women, and mature unmarried girls, to expose too much of their bodies, including their calves and shoulders. Some girls found the transition to these more modest and restrictive forms of clothing quite disturbing. Choto described how horrible she felt when her parents first began to make her wear a *salwar-kameez* and veil to cover her legs, shoulders, and chest whenever she left the neighborhood. She had begun to develop earlier than her friends and could not understand why she had to wear these new clothes, why her body had suddenly become a private and shameful thing. Married women also covered their heads with the ends of their saris (as a *ghomṭā,* or veil) whenever they were in the presence of senior men in their husbands' households and villages. This veiling, performed as an act of respect and avoidance, served a double function: it protected men from overexposure to women's power and it protected women from unwanted male advances (cf. Papanek and Minault 1982).[10] For their part, men had a wide range of clothing available to them. Many who could afford it and those who commuted to jobs in cities enjoyed wearing Western-style shirts and trousers. But when days were warm and when they were casually hanging out at home or in tea stalls, or when they went to work in fields, most men wore *lungis* (informal loin cloths) or dhotis: cloths wrapped around the waist, with chest and calves exposed.

As a measure to curtail excessive openness, women were also expected to bind their hair, keeping it in braids or tied up in a knot. Women ordinarily bound their hair whenever going out in public, and in fact in my early days in the village people would disapprovingly wonder why I kept my hair loose or "open" (*kholā*), until I gave in and began routinely to tie my hair up. It was particularly important to bind the hair during menstruation, presumably to counter the woman's excessive openness during this period.[11]

Some women also employed cooling diets (avoiding "hot" foods such as fish, garlic, and onions) to close their bodies and restrain their sexuality. This regime was followed after childbirth (when a woman's body is dangerously open), after becoming a widow (when a woman has no legitimate means of expending sexual energy), and sometimes after entering puberty (especially if a girl suffers from acne, a condition said to come about from excessive sexual heat erupting through the skin). The bathing practices described above were also intended to contain the body (controlling its influxes and outflows) by purifying it of unwanted intrusions and by preventing these substances from entering women's households.

These countermeasures, particularly spatial seclusion and veiling, are known in much of north and central India as "purdah," a word literally meaning "a curtain."[12] The term (*pardā* in Bengali) is not commonly used in the Mangaldihi region of West Bengal, but women's daily practices often did create a protective "curtain" around them. These practices functioned to contain a woman's most important and intimate interactions within her household, and to channel her sexual and reproductive powers toward her husband and toward extending his patrilineage. A gentle, middle-aged Brahman priest illuminated their significance when he told me, "Women have more power (*śakti*) than men, but their powers come from serving others, not from acting alone."

COMPETING PERSPECTIVES: EVERYDAY FORMS OF RESISTANCE

How did women in Mangaldihi feel about all these forms of bodily training? Until recently, many ethnographies of gender in South Asia left the impression that women silently and compliantly accept a monolithic set of cultural values about the polluting and dangerous dimensions of their bodies and sexuality.[13] More recent work, however, has sought to uncover the ways in which many women are able to critique, reinterpret, or resist such dominant ideologies, through their songs, stories, gestures, and everyday practices (e.g., Raheja and Gold 1994, Das 1988, Jeffery and Jeffery 1996). Gloria Raheja and Ann Gold (1994:10) incisively argue (also citing Das 1988): "[T]o assume that such characterizations [of the polluting and dangerous dimensions of women's bodies] define the limits of women's self-understandings and moral discourse is to ignore or silence meanings that are voiced in ritual songs and stories . . . and in gestures and metamessages in ordinary language throughout northern India." Submission and silence, furthermore, do not necessarily indicate an unequivocal, fully internalized compliance or modesty; they may at times be conscious and expedient strategies deployed by women.[14] In Mangaldihi, the women I knew presented alternative visions and practices of the female body, working around and subtly challenging (even as they often voiced and acquiesced to) the kinds of dominant ideologies I have been describing thus far.

At the same time that I was taught by many of the women in my neighborhood how to manage my body—by bathing, being cautious about what I touched, binding my hair, and so forth—I was also taught how to get around some of these restrictions in more subtle or private ways. Though many women appeared to be meticulous about matters of purity, others seemed to observe these strictures just enough to avoid criticism, without having fully internalized or accepted notions about the dangers of female impurity. For instance, on several occasions when I and a female companion were returning from visiting a low-caste or non-Hindu (Muslim or Santal) neighborhood, my companion would whisper to me as we approached our neighborhood, "Let's not tell anyone that we touched anyone there—then we won't have to bathe." I should note, however, that this happened most often if the woman accompanying me was unmarried—indeed, only once did a married woman propose such a plan. Apparently women felt increasingly obligated as wives to comply with expected standards as they took on more responsibilities of upholding the household, cooking, caring for deities, and so on.

On another occasion, a young woman friend suddenly had to defecate just as we were about to catch a bus to make a trip to town. Whereas most in the village relieved themselves in the fields, my landlord let me make use of their fancy outhouse; it was a small brick building with two chambers, one for urinating and one for defecating. My friend suggested that she would use that outhouse (since she was with me) and said that if anyone noticed her going in, she would say that she had just gone into the urinating chamber (an action that would not require her to bathe), because she did not want to have to stop to bathe and change her clothes before going to town. "Great idea!" I said, happy to know that some women played with the rules. (I had previously thought of that same trick with the outhouse myself.)

Another example of a woman who did not seem fully to accept public notions about the gravity of female pollution was provided by a pilgrim on the bus tour I took from Mangaldihi to Puri (see chapter 4). The dominant ideology in the region held that menstruating women were not fit pilgrims and should not enter temples. One morning, however, some used menstrual rags were found in a corner of the bathroom of the pilgrim's guest house where the group had stayed the night. Some older women began exclaiming, "Chi! Chi! What a great sin (*mahāpāp*) to go on a pilgrimage while menstruating!" but then the matter was dropped. I later happened to find out who the menstruating woman was. She admitted to me that she realized that her period might begin on the pilgrimage, but she had really wanted to go. She added that she believed that no harm (*doṣ*) would occur, because her devotion (*bhaktī*) was pure (*pabitra*). (I was a bit relieved to hear this, because my period had unfortunately begun on the journey as well.)[15] As far as I could tell, she successfully kept the matter a secret, and none of the other women made any real effort to discover who the source of the rags was.

Even those who maintained strict bodily purity sometimes acted for reasons more complex than a simple acquiescence to the official views about female bodies. For instance, there was one Brahman woman in our neighborhood who was known to be extremely "finicky" or "fastidious" (*khũtkhũte*) about matters of purity. She was continually washing her hands, bathing, changing her clothes, and scrubbing the house. She made her two daughters bathe and change their clothes each time they reentered the home from school or play. She resisted touching other people or things, even her own daughters, except when necessary. Other women told me, as a partial explanation, that her husband was having a long-term, public affair with a low-caste woman, whom he kept in a separate home on the borders of the village. Perhaps maintaining an extreme state of bodily purity was the only way available to this woman to gain some control over her own body, and to close herself to the intrusions the other woman and her husband were making into her life.

I also encountered a wide diversity of women's perspectives and practices surrounding female sexuality, some of which subverted dominant patrilineal ideologies. Sexuality was a common and welcome topic of conversation among women, especially when a new bride was present. This gave women the opportunity to crowd around and probe her about her new sexual experiences: How was she enjoying it? How many times had they done it? One new bride, with her husband's apparent approval, came to ask me for tips from my own culture or experiences on how a woman can increase her sexual pleasure.

Some women (married and unmarried) had sexual relations outside of marriage, and seemed to be able to manage them with no serious consequences. I met one such amorously involved woman, whom I will call Keya, on my first afternoon in Mangaldihi. Shortly after I had deposited my few household belongings in the small mud hut in which I was to reside, two married women whom I guessed to be in their early thirties came to pay me a visit. We chatted for a little while about this and that, and then Keya, to my surprise, asked me how to say the names of the male and female sexual organs in English. I told her. She smiled with pleasure, and then began to say the words loudly while laughing with her friend; she repeated them for the rest of the afternoon, as they returned to their household work. (I was only slightly comforted by the hope that no one else, other than we three, would be able to understand what she was saying.) I later found out that probably some of her eagerness to discuss sexual matters in this strangely public yet surreptitious way stemmed from her engagement in a clandestine love affair with another married young man of the village. Her own marriage had been arranged against her will to a man considerably older than she was; he had married her after his first wife, her own sister, had died while he had been attempting to give her an abortion (I never knew precisely how or why). Keya had never been particularly romantically inclined toward her husband—nor he toward her, from what I could gather. In large part, her role in the marriage consisted of caring for her husband's children by her sister. One way that she could gain *some* degree of pleasure and agency in her life was through taking a lover. (Once, when her husband was out of town for a few days, she borrowed one of my lace American bras.)

In the one case I encountered (mentioned above) in which an unmarried girl, "Mithu," did become pregnant with tragic consequences, it is important to note that criticisms of the village women focused not on the ruined chastity or sexual promiscuity of the young girl (accusations voiced by the young man's family, in an attempt to thrust all blame squarely on her) but rather on the unforgivable naïveté of a young woman and her mother who did nothing to terminate a pregnancy before it became public. Underlying the village women's discourse seemed to be the notion that the virtue of a woman is tied not only or even primarily to traditional notions of chastity but also to the strategic capacity (or lack thereof) of a woman to construct a virtuous public image or "name" (*nām*). These conversations led me to realize that many of the women I knew strove to maintain an appearance of self-containment, purity, or chastity not so much because they believed that they *were* more sexually dangerous or impure than men, but because they understood that maintaining such a public image was the only way for them to preserve both their own honor and that of the men and women in their families whom they cared about.

Their complex, multilayered perspectives seemed to resonate with those of Dadi, the mother-in-law of the evocative film *Dadi's Family.* Remembering her earlier years as a young wife, Dadi speaks in her resolute and thoughtful mode: "I piled on the yeses, but I did what I wanted to do." Resistance must often be subtle. I do not want to deny the felt oppressiveness of many of the ideologies and practices that did discipline and control local women's bodies, movements, and lives, or to exaggerate or romanticize their capacities to resist. At the same time, it would be wrong and misleading to overlook the ways that women in Mangaldihi did in many contexts reinterpret, play with, subvert, and critically evaluate the disciplining practices and ideologies that otherwise often served to control their bodies and lives.

THE CHANGES OF AGE

Older Women

If one of our aims, as scholars of gender in South Asia and elsewhere, is to complicate our understandings of the structuring of gender relations, then it is important not only to look at the multiple, competing ways that women imagine and interpret, resist, and criticize dominant ideologies of gender in their societies, but also to examine the ways that women's bodies, identities, and forms of power (or subordination) are perceived to change over the life course. Women's bodies and identities in north India do not stay the same throughout their lives. A few scholars have acknowledged the shifting roles that Indian women assume within their households and families, as daughters, sisters, wives, mothers, and mothers-in-law. But almost no work has been done on how women's *bodies* are perceived to change over a lifetime, and the concomitant social and political implications of these changes (an exception is S. Vatuk 1992). As a result, ethnographies of gender in South Asia (including the earlier pages of this chapter) have tended to give the impression that local definitions of female embodiment revolve centrally around sexuality, fertility, childbirth, and menstruation, and that categories of gender are tied to differences between women and men perceived to be fixed and dichotomous. In Mangaldihi, however, as I first mentioned in the introduction, women were believed to undergo significant changes in their somatic (and related social) identities as they aged, in ways suggesting that to analyze local definitions of gender by concentrating only on women during their married and reproductive years would lead to seriously flawed conclusions.

According to the villagers, women experienced a relative closing and cooling of the body as they entered into postreproductive phases of life. Thus the qualities of "heat" and "openness" that were often used to describe female bodies in fact pertained to women during their premenopausal (and postpubertal) years only. Such bodily cooling also meant that older women could freely give up most countermeasures of purdah, or "curtaining" and containment, that many had earlier practiced. Menopause in and of itself did not constitute a very highly marked or visible transition in women's lives in Mangaldihi.[16] It was important; but many of the changes that went along with menopause (namely, a cessation in sexual and reproductive activities) usually began earlier, as women married off their children and moved to the more detached, celibate peripheries of household life (see chapter 4). Menopause nonetheless added an important dimension to an aging woman's bodily and social transitions: a "closing" of the body and, with this, an increased purity and freedom of interaction.

The process of menopause, which was called a "stopping (or closing) of menstruation" (*māsik bandha hāoyā*), was perceived to entail a cooling, drying, and relative closing of the woman's body. As menstruation involves the release of excess sexual-reproductive heat, so the stopping of the menstrual flow marks a depletion and cooling of this heat, and thus a decrease in (hot) sexual desires and reproductive capacities. Women said that after menopause, their bodies had become cool and dry and they no longer felt the heat of sexual desire. Early on in my stay, I asked Choto Ma if old people were hot or cold. She teased me at first for asking such a silly question. "Of course the bodies of young people like *you* are hot," she said, and her knowing smile indicated that she was referring at least in part to sexual heat. Then she added seriously, "Old people are not hot like that." Her friend and sister-in-law, Mejo Ma, added: "When you get old, everything becomes closed or stopped (*bandha*). That which happens between husband and wife stops. Menstruation stops. And then when your husband dies, eating all hot food stops as well.[17] This is so that the body will dry out and not be hot (*jāte śarīr śukiye jābe, garam habe nā*)."

Bhogi Bagdi also spoke to me of the cooling and drying of her body after menopause. She enjoyed sitting in the narrow, dusty lane in front of her house talking about sex, using vulgar language, and teasing the young people who visited her about their sexual practices. So I asked her one day if *she* still had sexual desire. She answered quickly (as I reported in an epigraph to this chapter): "No, of course not! After the blood stopped, my body dried out (*rakta bandha hāoyār par, śarīr śukiye geche*). Even if I wanted to [have sex], I wouldn't be able to. I had four kids, then my blood dried up, and then my body dried up (*deha śukiye geche*). Now I have desire (*lobh*) only for food."

Although most women began to refrain from engaging in sexual and reproductive activity before menopause, menopause nonetheless signified for women a complete stopping of sexual-reproductive processes—not only of the activities themselves but of the capacities to engage in them. The nature of the body thus fundamentally changed.

This cooling of somatic heat in conjunction with the cessation of menstrual flow could, some said, be accompanied by an increase in the heat of anger (*rāg*). Several mentioned that although old women no longer feel the heat of sexual desire, they do become easily "hot" or angry in the head (*māthā garam hae jāe*). While these might appear to be references to what we label "hot flashes," these sensations did not seem to be a culturally recognized phenomenon for Mangaldihians. I asked quite a few women about feeling warm during menopause, and only two mentioned that they had experienced this: one described a feeling of "fire" (*āgun*) in the head, and the other spoke of having "hot ears" (*garam kān*). More told me instead that women can become easily angry (also a "hot-headed" state) in older age. This transfer of heat from sexuality to anger did not seem to be viewed as gender specific, however: it could happen to older men as well (cf. Cohen 1998).

For women, the significance of this transition lay in their change to a state of increased purity, coolness, and relative boundedness of the body. It was at this point, after a woman's menstrual periods had stopped and especially if she was widowed and upper caste, that a woman was considered to be "pure" (*śuddha* or *pabitra*), comparable to a deity (*ṭhākurer moto*), and in some ways "like a man." The perception that postmenopausal women are in significant ways "like men" can also be found elsewhere in India (e.g., Flint 1975) and in other societies, such as the Kel Ewey Tuareg of northeastern Niger (Rasmussen 1987) and the Bedouins of Egypt (Abu-Lughod 1986:131, 133). When I would ask *why*, village women would explain that old women no longer menstruate, no longer give birth, no longer have sex, and (especially if they are upper-caste widows) no longer eat hot, nonvegetarian (*āmiṣ*) foods. This makes them continually "pure" (*śuddha*) like men, who also do not menstruate or give birth; and it makes them similar to the dominant deities of Mangaldihi as well (Syamcand and Madan Gopal, forms of Krishna), for these gods were only served cooling, vegetarian foods and were, of course, kept in a state of purity.[18] Furthermore, it was particularly postmenopausal *widows* who were described as "pure" and manlike, presumably because they were categorically free from the hot and female activities of sexuality and wifehood.[19] A married older woman, even if not sexually active, was still a wife (*sadhobā*, "with husband"), after all; and she continued to be associated with sexuality, fertility, and marital relations as long as she adorned her body with auspicious red vermilion and wore red-bordered saris, as a proper wife should.

According to local opinion, the sexual heat and desire (*kām*) of men also wanes in old age. But as men never have as much sexual heat and desire as women in the first place, their transformation toward increasing asexuality is not as dramatic. E. Valentine Daniel (1984:165) describes a similar perspective offered by a resident of Tamil Nadu. According to this informant, the sexual fluids (*intiriam*) of a male remain qualitatively and quantitatively the same throughout life. A woman, in contrast, produces vastly more sexual fluids than a man throughout most of her life, but about ten to twelve years following menopause she begins to produce only the smaller amount that a man does.

Young and older women alike in Mangaldihi spoke of the process of stopping menstruation and becoming more like a man as a positive one. In the United States, menopause is popularly conceived as a largely negative experience that signifies an irreversible process of female aging, with its loss of youth, beauty, and sexuality, and is accompanied by painful "symptoms" such as hot flashes and diseases such as osteoporosis (e.g., Lock 1982, 1993; E. Martin 1987). When I asked women in Mangaldihi what they thought about the end of menstruation, however, they almost uniformly replied that it was a good thing (see also S. Vatuk 1992:163–64). Ceasing to menstruate meant being free from the hassles of monthly bleeding and impurity, being able to travel (without fear of causing an embarrassing mess on a bus or train), being able to go on longer pilgrimages (without fear of bringing menstrual impurities before the deities), and being able to cook for temple and household gods whenever one liked—all practices (village women noted) available to men throughout their lives.[20] By the beginning of this phase, most women also felt that they had had enough children (except those widowed at a young age and not remarried, who could not expect to bear children anyway); so loss of fertility was not experienced with regret. A few women who had not yet stopped menstruating even complained to me, "Why do my periods keep coming? My time for stopping has come."

As women experienced menopause and a relative closing and cooling, they also made changes in how they dressed and adorned their bodies. As I mentioned in chapter 4, men and women both tended to wear more white and dress more simply as they entered old age. But the transformation in modes of dress was most striking for women. From wearing mostly red and other bright colors and adorning their bodies with jewelry, hair ribbons, and perfume in their young and newly married years, women in Mangaldihi in their later years took to wearing mainly the cool color of white and relinquishing bodily adornments. Older nonwidowed women could still wear saris with red-colored borders, and they continued to wear marriage bangles and red vermilion in the parts of their hair; but as their children married, they also increasingly wore saris that were predominantly white, as a sign of their older and postreproductive status. Most also gave up other forms of adornment, claiming that it was no longer appropriate or necessary for them to highlight their physical attractiveness. They thus avoided wearing fancy silk, polyester, and newly starched saris in favor of worn, simple cotton ones, and they limited any jewelry to perhaps a simple everyday chain and small pair of earrings.

Women whose children were largely grown and who were past childbearing also frequently quit wearing blouses under their saris, except when going out of the neighborhood or village. Blouses were mandatory for younger women to cover their breasts and shoulders (and even the sleeveless blouses now popular in India's cities were considered improperly revealing in Mangaldihi); but older women would say to me that for them, wearing blouses was an unnecessary kind of "dressing up" (*sājāno*). Older women began to reveal their calves much more, hiking their saris up to their knees on hot days and leaving off their petticoats. Khudi Thakrun frequently wandered around the village with her breasts and calves entirely exposed,

Young sisters-in-law in colorful saris: (*from left*) Ranga, Chobi, and Savitri, Brahman women married to three brothers.

Mejo Ma, Choto Ma, and Boro Ma: three Brahman sisters-in-law and friends dressed in white and out for a walk.

her white sari simply tied around her waist (much as a man would wear a dhoti or loin cloth), and her breasts, wrinkled and long from nursing nine children, hanging down almost to her waist (see photograph 1 in chapter 3). Older Brahman widows commonly began even to wear men's white dhotis in place of saris. Furthermore, women could increasingly relax their veiling practices as they advanced in seniority, pulling saris over their heads only on more formal occasions when senior male kin (whose numbers were decreasing) were present (see also U. Sharma 1978:223).

Covering the body reduces warmth and is a barrier to interaction; decorating the body attracts and invites attention. Both actions were thought appropriate in younger, sexually active women but inappropriate (as well as unnecessary) in older, postreproductive women. Nakedness, too, was interpreted in two different ways, depending on the life stage of the woman: it was sexually provocative in the young, and a sign of asexuality in the old.

Sylvia Vatuk (1992:164–67) similarly describes how older women with married children in western Uttar Pradesh and Delhi wear white and light-colored clothing and avoid adorning their bodies. She finds these practices to be seemingly paradoxical social constraints imposed on the sexuality of older women: Why, if older (postmenopausal and postreproductive) women are thought to be asexual, should their sexuality be controlled or constrained by restrictions on dress and physical adornment? My interpretation here is somewhat different: the modes of dress of older Indian women do not constitute a kind of personal or social "constraint" on an older woman's sexuality as much as they express her relative *a*sexuality. Although the cool, white, simple clothing of an older woman plays a part in transforming her into an asexual person (and thereby controls any lingering sexuality that would be considered inappropriate at this stage of life), it also serves as an index of an asexuality that, in Mangaldihi at least, was regarded as occurring naturally.

As women entered postreproductive life phases, they also transformed their gender by altering their spatial movements. As already noted, women were fairly domestic with little outside wandering as postpubertal unmarried girls, and then became very domestic and largely confined to their houses as wives. But as their daughters-in-law began to take over domestic work, and especially as they became widowed, older women spent more and more time out of their homes. Dressed in white, they roamed through village lanes visiting each others' homes, playing cards, congregating on the cool floors of temples, and sitting on the roadsides or by storefronts watching people come and go. They also frequented public rituals, plays, and other events that younger wives were often too busy or confined to attend. They traveled beyond Mangaldihi, paying extended visits to married daughters' homes and going on pilgrimages to faraway holy places. These external wanderings were facilitated by the cooling, closing, and decreasing sexuality of older women's bodies (whether natural or imposed), for they and their families no longer found it necessary to control and constrain their bodies and interactions. In these ways, being older struck me as a very freeing, open, and pleasurable phase of life for women.

Older Men

Men in Mangaldihi did not undergo nearly as marked a transformation in their modes of dress and spatial movements over their lives; nor were their sexuality and bodily natures as dramatically transformed. Just as it was impossible to tell from his clothing whether a man was married or single (for men wore no outer signs of marriage, as women did), it was also impossible to tell whether a man was "senior" (*buṛo*). Around Mangaldihi, the traditional dress of men at any life stage was a white dhoti and *panjābī* (long shirt) for everyday or more formal wear, and a colored *lungi* for casual wear. This clothing could be worn by younger and older men alike. Fashionable and well-educated younger men often wore Western-style slacks and shirts, and it remains to be seen whether they will continue wearing the same kind of clothing when they become senior.

Men, moreover, were seen to be living and moving relatively "outside" (*bāire*) throughout their lives. Older men who had reduced their economic responsibilities and had more free time often congregated together in public places, as older women did. But these older men's groups differed little from those of younger men, who also used their free time (which for many was plentiful, especially during seasons of agricultural lull) to gather together in public places.

Nonetheless, there were subtle signs of distinction between older and younger men's dress and spatial domains. Older men tended to dress more simply, while younger men were more preoccupied with looking handsome and appearing in fashion. Mangaldihi's younger men tended to oil their hair more frequently, to get new haircuts that they kept nicely combed, and to wear shoes and newer clothing. It was not uncommon for a young man to ask me if he was looking good. Older men, like older women, usually wore more simple, well-worn cotton clothing, frequently went without shoes, and paid less obvious attention to their appearance.

Furthermore, as a senior village man became increasingly weak or infirm, he would spend more and more time in the household, sitting or resting on

An older Bagdi man cares for a neighbor's child.

a cot in a corner of the courtyard or on the veranda, watching the household activities, receiving occasional visitors, and sometimes looking after small children. Therefore, as women were transformed in older age to become more like men in their bodily natures, spatial movements, and outer wanderings, men in a way became more like women—increasingly domestic and confined to the home.

People in Mangaldihi clearly used the body to define gender, but they did not rely on a male/female distinction based on dichotomous and fixed physiological differences, as is presumed in much contemporary feminist theory, which takes female physiology, sexuality, and reproductivity to define "woman" as a category across time and space (cf. Moore 1994:8–27; Nicholson 1994; Ortner 1996:137). Rather, the interrelated somatic, social, and political identities of gender—expressed and experienced via bodily regulations, spatial movements, dress, and perceived physiological processes—changed in profound ways over the life course. These changes made women (especially by late life) in some ways "like men," and men in some (though less acknowledged) ways like women.

WOMEN, MAYA, AND AGING

As women's bodies underwent important changes as they aged, what about the ties of their maya? Did the relative openness of women throughout much of their lives mean, for instance, that women, compared to men, were more connected to others, more entwined in a net of maya? Not exactly. At least, no one offered me precisely this explanation, though women in Mangaldihi perhaps even more than men did value crowded togetherness, seeking to work together, bathe together, and eat together, as Margaret Trawick (1990b:73) also found among the women she knew in Tamil Nadu.[21] The main difference between women and men with regard to maya was that women's ties were unmade and remade at a greater number of critical junctures in their lives, not only through aging and dying, but also in marriage and widowhood. The most important connections of males were made only once and tended to endure throughout and beyond their lifetimes, while those of females were repeatedly altered—first made, then unmade and remade, then often unmade once more.

In the dominant patrilineal discourse of Mangaldihi, women were said to be capable of such changes because their bodies were naturally more open than men's. The same traits of openness and permeability that made young women vulnerable to impurity and sexual violations could also be viewed as making women well-suited to marital exchange. According to one piece of proverbial wisdom, a woman would fare best if she were malleable like clay, to be cast into a shape of his choice by the potter (her husband), discarding earlier loyalties, attributes, and ties to become absorbed into her husband's family (cf. Dube 1988:18).

The positions of boys and girls in their natal families were differentiated from infancy and childhood. Infants of both sexes were initially connected with their kin and village by a ceremony to mark the first feeding of rice (*annaprāśana*). But male children were distinguished by the greater scale and elaboration of that ceremony, and among the upper castes by several other subsequent life cycle ceremonies of "marking" or "refining" (*saṃskāra*) (Lamb 1993:348–63). Among Brahmans, marriage thus might be the eighth connection-making ceremony for a boy, but only the second for a girl. During each of the male child's *saṃskāras*, the family would perform a *nāndīmukh*, a ritual offering to the ancestors meant to introduce and formally connect the boy to his patrilineage.

While the boy was commonly identified as a growing node of the patrilineage (*baṃśa*), meant to extend the patriline into future generations, a girl was often spoken of as a mere temporary sojourner awaiting her departure in marriage. Thus, she would have no ancestor-connecting *nāndīmukh* performed for her in infancy or childhood; only at her marriage were the ancestors asked for their parting blessings. Sayings, nursery rhymes, and everyday conversations conveyed to a daughter the unmistakable message that her stay in her parental home was short. I heard Mangaldihi girls at times singing lightheartedly a popular Bengali lullaby that struck me as painfully affecting:

> Rock-a-bye baby, combs in your pretty hair
> The bridegroom will come soon and take you away
> The drums beat loudly,
> The shehnai is playing softly
> A stranger's son has come to fetch me
> Come my playmates, come with our toys
> Let us play, for I shall never play again
> When I go off to the stranger's house.[22]

A phrase I would often hear was "A daughter is nothing at all. You just raise them for a few days, and then to others you give them away." People spoke of daughters as "belonging not to us but to others." The young girl who worked for me, Beli, said to me once: "If you're going to have children, you shouldn't have a daughter. You have to give a daughter away to an other's house (*parer ghar*)." Expressions from other regions of India convey similar sentiments: "Bringing up a daughter is like watering a plant in another's courtyard," goes a Telugu saying (Dube 1988:12) heard also in Uttar Pradesh (Jeffery, Jeffery, and Lyon 1989:23). Girls in Kangra, northwest India, hear that a daughter is a bird "who after eating the seeds set out, will fly," or a "guest who will soon depart" (Narayan 1986:69). Such sentiments do not imply that girls were unloved or unwanted. In fact, parents in Mangaldihi *wanted* to keep their daughters; they just couldn't. They seemed to love and cherish their daughters with an added intensity and poignancy in anticipation of their pending departure.[23]

Men in Mangaldihi, in contrast, usually resided—save perhaps for brief periods of work in other cities—within the same community and on the same soil where they were born. This is why, some men said, it is so difficult for them to loosen their ties of maya at the end of a lifetime, for they have become so deeply embedded within a family, community, home, soil. Among the several families I knew who had settled in Calcutta apartments after fleeing East Pakistan (now Bangladesh) at the time of partition, men spoke of having been forced painfully to cut apart the ties of their maya prematurely, as a woman does in marriage; they viewed the years following independence and partition as very "separate," "independent," and maya-reducing times.

For girls in Mangaldihi, it was through marriage that they became most marked and that the ties of their personhood were substantially unmade and remade. Throughout the three-day wedding, the bride would be made to absorb substances originating from her husband's body and household. She rubbed her body with turmeric paste with which he had first been anointed, she ate leftover food from his plate, she absorbed his sexual fluids, she moved to his place of residence, and there she mingled with his kin and mixed with the substances of his soil. The bride's surname and patrilineal membership (*baṃśa*) would also be formally changed to those of her husband. In this way, her marriage was generally interpreted as obscuring and greatly reducing, although not obliterating, the connections she once enjoyed with her natal home. She would no longer refer to persons of her natal family as her "own people" (*nijer lok*) but rather as her husband did—as her "relatives by marriage" (*kuṭumb*); for she was said to have become by marriage the "half body" (*ardhānginī*) of her husband (see also Inden and Nicholas 1977:39–51; Sax 1991:77–83).

For a girl, then, preparing to marry was in some ways like a first confrontation with mortality. The young brides who spoke to me anticipated the pain of cutting so many ties with their natal families, homes, and friends with dread, not comprehending how they would ever survive such an ordeal. These conversations were similar to those I had with older people about the separations at death. During the months preceding her wedding, my companion Hena would say to me through tears, "Your father gives you away. He makes you other. He wipes out the relation." She would also purposefully pick quarrels with me in order, she said, "to cut the maya" a bit before her actual departure.

Many analyses of Hindu marriage have long stressed that a bride's transfer to her marital kin is a complete break.[24] More recently, however, anthropological studies of kinship and gender in India have pointed to evidence of a woman's continuing ties to natal kin. William Sax (1991:77–126) and Gloria Raheja and Ann Gold (1994:73–120), for instance, argue that many writing on Indian social structure have for too long overemphasized the view of marriage as a complete transformation of a woman (an argument often grounded largely in textual analyses), overlooking other perspectives that stress that a woman's ties with her natal kin and place can never be entirely effaced (see also Dube 1988:18; Jacobson 1977; Raheja 1995).

In Mangaldihi, too, women and men both agreed that however neglected, violated, or abused their earlier ties might be after marriage, a connection does remain forever between a married daughter and her natal kin. Just as maya cannot be suddenly and completely cut in aging and dying (see chapters 4 and 5), neither can the "pull" (*ṭān*) of maya, "of blood," or "of the womb" between a girl and her natal home be wiped out entirely through marriage. Some of the rituals of marriage even served to affirm a departing bride's natal ties. Marriage was the only time (save once again, four days after her parents died) when a girl's *nāndīmukh,* ritual offering to her maternal and paternal ancestors, was performed in her name. On the day before her wedding, too, a bride would eat rice that she had collected uncooked from twenty-five neighborhood houses, to affirm her mutual ties with other village women even as she prepared to depart.

A married woman's practices after the wedding were also crucial. According to Mangaldihians, the extent to which a married woman would be able to sustain valuable ties with the people of her father's home depended largely on the amount of contact she succeeded in maintaining with them, through visiting and gift giving. During the first few years of marriage, young brides would often spend weeks or even months at their fathers' homes, returning eagerly whenever natal kin came to call for them. Married women commonly returned to their natal homes for the birth of their first child and on special ritual occasions, when married daughters and sisters were summoned; these included the largest annual Bengali festival, Durga Puja (worship of the goddess Durga during *her* annual visit to her father's home); Jamai Sasthi (day for honoring a married daughter's or sister's husband); and Bhai Phota (day on which married and unmarried sisters honor their brothers). Most married women thus had two houses they could call home—their *bāper bāṛi* (father's house) and their *śvaśur bāṛi* (father-in-law's house).

Maintaining these ties depended on negotiation as well as luck (her natal family's interest in her, the supportiveness of her in-laws in allowing her to leave, the distance between the two homes, the financial resources required for travel and gift giving). A married woman could not decide to visit her natal family on her own; she had to wait for someone from her father's house to come call for her. Women, though, sometimes sent letters or messages to their father's homes, asking to be called for. Some secretly stowed away change or an extra petticoat to give to their mothers when visiting.

We see here that to understand women's positions within families we must take into account not only patrilineal lineage, or *baṃśa,* but also maya, affection. *Baṃśa* is one thing (unmarried girls are in their fathers' *baṃśa*s; married women in their husbands'); but maya can be something different—imaged in terms of "love," ties of the "womb" and of "milk," gifts given, and time spent. Maya here can even be thought of as offering an alternative discourse to that of patrilineal kinship.

A married woman's persisting connections of maya with her natal kin notwithstanding, Mangaldihi villagers still stressed the transience of a woman's relations with her natal home. Mothers and wives emphasized this fleetingness at least as much as fathers and husbands did. Most mothers had known such separations from personal experience, and at each visit after marriage (whether their own or others') they might relive their earlier feelings. Most said that they felt always the pain of having the ties of their girlhood and family belittled or ignored in their husbands' homes. They spoke of the early years of marriage as a very vulnerable time, when they felt unattached, alone, lonely, homesick, even afraid. Choto Ma told me, "I sobbed and sobbed after my wedding. I couldn't stand to be away from my father." The "woman's point of view" was not simply that the ties of a woman to her natal home could not be effaced, as Sax (1991:83) suggests, but rather that these ties were often gradually and painfully ignored and attenuated, even violated. Women even more than men were acutely aware of women's tenuous relation to families and places—because they were the ones who most directly experienced the pain of having their natal substance devalued.

But as a woman lived in her marital home for many years, bore and raised children there, brought in daughters-in-law for her sons, experienced the births of grandchildren, and made friends among the other village wives, her ties gradually came to be more and more like a man's, deeply embedded within one household and place. Most older women told me that even their lingering connections with their natal homes slowly faded, as they visited less and formed stronger ties in their marital homes (cf. Jacobson 1977:276–77). In telling her own life story, Choto Ma spoke of how a woman eventually "cuts the 'link'" with her parents. "First she'll cry a lot," she said, "as I did. I sobbed and sobbed after my wedding. . . . But slowly you visit less, you cry less. And now, in old age, there is hardly any more connection with my father's house." A woman's marital home would gradually become—in both her own eyes and those of others—no longer simply a *śvaśur bāṛi,* or "father-in-law's house," but *her* home. By old age, many women for the first time had gained a sense of an enduring emotional and substantial connectedness to one home, a sense of a rightful place there, and a concomitant degree of power and authority over others. In these ways—as in how the nature of their aging bodies was perceived—older women's experiences and identities became, in significant respects, like men's.

We have observed in this chapter how perceptions and experiences surrounding gender were complex, fluctuating, and multifaceted. Mangaldihi women's and men's experiences of gender over the life course make it clear that it would be highly misleading to think here of men and women, maleness and femaleness (and purity and pollution, power and powerlessness) as static and neatly opposing categories. This important point has been made by other recent feminist theorists. Sherry Ortner (1996:116–38) looks, for instance, at the intersections of *class* and gender in Sherpa society, arguing that "analysis focused through a polarized male/female distinction may produce distortions at least as problematic as those which ignore women and gender in the first place," by masking the kinds of structural disadvantages that certain *categories* of men share with many women (p. 132). Chandra Mohanty (1991) similarly examines the problems (inherent in much Western feminist discourse) in positing a universal category of "women" and assuming a generalized notion of their subordination. Such an analytical move problematically "limits the definition of the female subject to gender identity, completely bypassing social class and ethnic identities" and the specificities of history, nation, and context (p. 64).[25]

Looking at *age* can likewise give our analyses of gender a valuable multidimensionality and specificity. Mangaldihi women's experiences of their bodies and sexuality, of expected forms of discipline and control, and of their positioning within families all shifted in profound ways over their lifetimes. "Women" were thus constructed in a variety of social and political contexts that existed simultaneously, altered with time, and were overlaid on top of one another. Looking at age in these ways fruitfully trains our gaze on flux, multivocality, and contradiction and provides insight into the complexities, ambiguities, and many dimensions of what it is to be a woman, and a man.

7 A Widow's Bonds

It's better not to get married at all than to be a widow. It's better not to get married at all. If you never marry, then at least you have the people from your father's house.

Pramila Mukherjee, Nabadwip refuge for destitute widows

How many kinds of pain we suffer if our husband doesn't live in our house! Just one pain? No. Pain in all directions. Burning pain; agony. Clothes, food, mixing with others, laughter, all of that ends.

Kayera Bou, Mangaldihi

Widowhood was the last phase of life for most women in Mangaldihi. The older women whose lives I have described over the previous pages—Khudi Thakrun, Bhogi Bagdi, Choto Ma, Mejo Ma—were mostly in this stage. They had almost expected to spend part of their lives as widows, since girls were younger than their husbands at marriage, generally outlived them, and usually did not remarry.

Widowhood was also a dreaded time of life. Depending on her caste and age at widowhood, a woman could expect to face any number of hardships. Her economic condition might be precarious. She might be forced to grow old childless, with no one to care for her. She might experience the wrenching emotional pain of losing a loved spouse. She might be considered by others to be dangerously inauspicious. And, especially if a Brahman, she would be pressed by her kin to wear white clothing; avoid all "hot," nonvegetarian foods; eat rice only once a day (an amount that left her almost fasting); avoid bodily adornments; and live in lifelong celibacy. Until recently, many Brahman families also required their widows to shave their head (a practice some of the most senior Mangaldihi widows still observed) and to sleep on the ground. In contrast, a man who lost his wife was not expected to observe any special practices and was usually encouraged to remarry. If not already senior and retired, he generally did. Thus in Mangaldihi, in 1990 out of 335 households there were only thirteen unremarried widowed men, but sixty-nine unremarried widowed women.

I take a look, in this final substantive chapter, at widowhood—both as an important dimension of women's experiences of old age and as an illuminating means of continuing to explore local gender constructions. How were women defined, perceived, and controlled—by themselves, and by others—when they were left without a husband? What do these perceptions and practices of widowhood tell us, ultimately, about gender?

BECOMING A WIDOW

When a husband died in Mangaldihi, his wife was taken by other widows of her household or neighborhood to a pond where she would perform the ritual to make her into a widow or *bidhobā*, literally "without a husband." Married women and unmarried girls were forbidden to watch the highly inauspicious ceremony (lest it cause their own future widowhood), so I describe the ritual here based only on what several widows reported to me.[1] Many still shuddered, thinking of that horrible day.

First, the bereaved woman removed her marriage bangles of conch shell, iron, and red *palā*, broke them, and threw them into the pond. They were said to have "gone cold" (*ṭhāṇḍā*). A married woman whose bangles accidentally broke would replace them immediately, lest the broken and cold state of the bangles lead to her husband's misfortune or death. A married woman never left her wrists bare; a widow's arms remained empty. The widow then wiped the red vermilion or *sindūr* from her forehead and from the part in her hair. She had worn these marks as symbols of her married state since her husband had first placed them on her at their wedding. With vermilion the husband had symbolically activated his wife's sexual and reproductive capacities, and these capacities were supposed to be lost with her husband's death. If she was wearing red *āltā* on her feet, she washed it off.

The woman next entered the water for the "widow's bath" (*bidhobār snān*), wearing for the last time one of the bright-colored saris she had worn as a married woman. When she emerged from the water she removed the colored sari to don a new white or subdued one. This sari was, when possible, supplied by the widow's mother's brother or some other male from her natal home, as a reminder of her natal attachments. From then on, the widow would avoid wearing red, the color of auspiciousness, warmth, sexuality, fertility, and married women. Brahman widows' saris (and those of some lower-caste widows who chose to emulate Brahmans) were almost entirely white, thinly bordered with dark colors such as deep blue, black, or green. Widows could also wear men's white dhotis. As I have previously noted, white was regarded as a "cool" (*ṭhāṇḍā*) color, symbolic of infertility, asexuality, asceticism, old age, widowhood, and death.

A final act in the making of a widow used to be the shaving of the head. In the past, high-caste widows had their heads shaved not just once but biweekly for the rest of their lives.[2] It used to be said that if a widow's hair was allowed to grow and be tied up in a braid, it would bind the deceased husband's spirit to her and to the places of his previous life. Mangaldihians also viewed head shaving as an act of renunciation and of severing ties. Young widows now rarely follow this ritual, but there were several older Brahman widows of Mangaldihi, including Khudi Thakrun, who continued to shave the white hair from their heads every two weeks as a sign of their widowhood.[3]

After completing their widow-making rituals, Mangaldihi widows took several different paths depending on their caste and life stage. For Brahmans, widow remarriage was absolutely forbidden, even if the widow was a young child who had never lived with her husband.[4] For all the other caste groups of Mangaldihi, although a woman could ordinarily go through a true marriage ceremony (*biye*) but once, widows could be remated (usually to a widowed man) by a simpler ritual called "joining" (*sāṅgā karā*), which effectively made them husband and wife. However, it was generally only women widowed at quite a young age and who were still childless who chose to do so. Widows with children feared either that they would have to leave their children behind with their in-laws or that their children would not be treated well in their new husband's home (see also Chen and Dreze 1992:18–19).[5] Some also expressed a reluctance to relinquish any rights they might have to their deceased husband's property, felt that they had borne enough children or were no longer of a marriageable age, or had a sense that widow remarriage was improper or embarrassing not only for Brahmans but for their caste as well. Widow remarriage in Mangaldihi, among any caste, was thus relatively rare.[6]

Widow remarriage in India must also be put into historical context. Although the British implemented the Widow Remarriage Act in 1856, thereby officially legalizing the practice, this bill had the (presumably) unintended consequence of reducing widows' rights among the lower castes, which had always condoned widow remarriage. The new act brought with it legal restrictions regarding the disposal of the widow's property and children on her remarriage: these were to remain within her deceased husband's patrilineage. Many widowed women, now facing a choice between marrying again and keeping their children and property, refrained from remarriage. Thus the economic interest of the high castes in not allowing widows to remarry was firmly protected by the act, and even legally extended across caste lines.[7]

Those in Mangaldihi who remained widowed had several different options (sometimes none particularly desirable) as to where they could reside. Most widows, especially if they had children, remained in their former husbands' or in-laws' homes and continued to find useful work there—caring for children, performing household chores, working in the fields, and so on. If a widow had sons who were grown and married, her rightful place unquestionably continued to be with them even after her husband had passed away.[8] Childless widows, or widows with very young children, often returned to their natal homes. If not wanted or comfortable in either natal or marital home, then some widows set up a separate household, usually adjoining that of natal or marital kin. Others moved away; north Indian pilgrimage spots such as Nabadwip, Varanasi, and Brindaban, as well as Calcutta's old age homes, are crowded with widows who feel they have no real family ties.

In West Bengal, a widow (as long as she does not remarry) is legally entitled to inherit a proportion of her husband's property, to be divided among herself and her sons.[9] In practice, though, few widows—especially among the upper castes, who as a rule had the most property at stake—actually maintained land in their own names. They either formally or informally passed control of property to their sons, if the sons were grown, or left it in the hands of their fathers-in-law, if the widow and her children were young. A few widows who would have liked to have kept their land told me that although they knew they were legally entitled to it, who would go to the courts to fight? In lower-caste communities in Mangaldihi, where the general sense that women needed to be protected by men was less strong, some widows did manage to maintain control over property or a house. But often not much more than a tiny plot of land was at stake. Thus in Mangaldihi in 1990, there were no Brahman widowed heads of household, but a total of fifteen among several other middle and lower castes (Bagdi, Baisnab, Kora, Kulu, and Muci). Only two of these fifteen, however, were able to support themselves with income from their land; the others had to work as daily laborers.[10]

After being widowed, Brahman women had to begin performing the restrictive set of widow's observances (*bidhobār pālan*) listed above, which include avoiding "hot," nonvegetarian foods (meat, fish, eggs, onions, garlic, and certain kinds of *ḍāl*); eating rice only once a day (substituting at other times "dry," *śukna*, foods such as *muṛi*, parched rice, or *ruṭi*, flat bread); fasting on the eleventh day of the lunar month (*ekādaśī*); wearing white; and giving up jewelry. Because of these dietary restrictions, a Brahman widow's food had usually to be cooked separately from that of other household members. If vegetarian food so much as touched nonvegetarian food, the widow could not eat it. Therefore, Brahman widows often kept a separate cooking fire and set of utensils for preparing their own food. At feasts, Brahman widows would eat together off to the side or in a corner.

There was considerable variation among the non-Brahman castes in Mangaldihi as to how many, if any, of these restrictions their widows followed. Most all of the non-Brahmans said that their widows did not *have* to observe them, but several lower-caste (including Barui, Kulu, and Suri) widows I knew said that they *chose* to wear white and avoid meat, fish, and eggs because they felt it was "proper" for widows to do so, or because, after their husbands died, they had no more "taste," "need," or "desire" for meat and brightly colored clothing. After all, Brahmans were the dominant caste in the village, in terms of not only numbers, property, and wealth but also, in some respects, moral codes. One way that members of lower castes strove to raise the ranking of their caste as a whole (or their own personal or family status) was to emulate the practices of Brahmans, a strategy that some scholars have labeled "Sanskritization" (e.g., Srinivas 1952; Singer 1972).

Across caste lines in Mangaldihi, as throughout north India, widows were considered to be inauspicious and thus had to refrain from participating in auspicious life cycle rituals such as marriage. Widows could attend and watch such ceremonies, but they could not perform any of the rituals; nor could they touch the bride or groom, or cook and serve food. Contrary to what Lina Fruzzetti finds in the Vishnupur region of West Bengal (1982:106), widowed mothers in Mangaldihi could not even participate in their own daughters' weddings.

I witnessed several women become widows over my stay in Mangaldihi and collected the stories of many others who vividly remembered the experience. Entering widowhood is painful and traumatic for most women, who simultaneously lose their husbands and are transformed into other, alien beings. Before moving on to analyze these transformations, I will relate the bitter story of how one Brahman woman of Mangaldihi—Kayera Bou, or "the wife from Kayera"—became a widow many years ago.

Kayera Bou and her husband had been married for about fifteen years, ever since she was sixteen and her husband nineteen, but they had produced no children together. Her husband had been ill with diabetes ("sugar") for several years before he died, and she stayed by his side constantly nursing him. She told me that her head had become "hot" (*garam*), or mentally unstable, because of worry about her husband's health and her childlessness. So her father came one day to take her away for a while to a mental health sanatorium in Ranchi, several hours away by train. Her husband died while she was away. I quote lengthy excerpts from the story she told me to preserve the power of her own words in describing her traumatic transformation into a widow:

> And so I came home two months later [from Ranchi]. I came wearing *sindūr, āltā,* everything. I had asked for it all to be put on, and they all lovingly put it on me for the journey. I didn't then have any good bracelets for my arms, so I said to my brother who had come to get me, "My husband's harm (*akalyāṇ*) will happen. Bring me some bracelets." I put on the bracelets, without knowing that I would immediately have to take them off again and break them. Our bracelets break [when we become widows]. We can't wear bracelets any more. When you get married, you have iron bracelets put on you. And *sindūr* (vermilion in the part of the hair). These are our signs of marriage. Both of these go away. These are both the husband's things, and both of these go away. For life.
>
> So I came home [to my father's house].[11] It was night when I arrived. My father made me some *śarbat* (sugar water) to drink. But my mother didn't come, because she knew she would start to cry. I asked where she was, and my father said that she was coming. They were keeping her away because she was crying so hard. My father didn't want to let me know right away. He said, "Let her rest a bit." And I was wearing *sindūr* and *āltā!* And what a fair complexion I had gained in Ranchi! Then my mother showed up weeping. I didn't understand anything.
>
> And then what we have to do [the widow's ritual] was done. Our maidservant took me to the water—my mother couldn't go. Those whose husbands are still alive can't watch the *kholā-parā* (widow's ritual).[12] My mother wanted to take me, but no one would let her because my father was still alive. So our maidservant, who was a widow, took me to the water. I had to take off all of those things and be bathed. And when I understood what was happening, I began to sob. I beat my head and cried all night long. I had to be taken to the water, take off all of those things and throw them away, and be bathed. Then where was the *āltā?* And where were the ornaments? And good clothes? Where was anything? One after another they were all sunk in the water. Everything became surrounded with gloom (*kāli*). When he left, everything became gloom. Sadness.
>
> When you didn't get any letters from your husband for a long time [she said to me], I could understand how awful you must feel. A husband is such a thing. I abandoned everything else, and my eagerness was for one person only. I was coming back from Ranchi with such hope and expectation. I sobbed and sobbed thinking of all the hope I had come from Ranchi with, expecting that I would see him again. . . .
>
> And then they said I wouldn't be able to eat all that any more. At night they began to take out some *muṛi* (parched rice) to feed me. My mother was saying, "I won't be able to give her *muṛi.* How can I give her *muṛi* and eat rice myself?" But my father told her that she would

have to. My mother said, "No! I won't be able to. I'm going to feed her rice. Society (*samāj*)! Let society happen [i.e., let people talk]! She's my child. I'm going to feed her. Then later whatever happens will happen."

But out of embarrassment (*lajjāe*) in front of everyone, she wasn't able to feed me [rice]. People would have seen and said to her, "Oh, you're feeding her *rice?*" Perhaps my husband's sister [who was married into that village] would see and say, "You're feeding her *this?*" and then she would go around slandering us and telling everyone that my mother was feeding me. That's the fault (*doṣ*) of Bengalis, isn't it? They go around talking about who's feeding whom what. While at the same time my mother was saying, "She's never eaten *muṛi* in her whole life. I can't give her *muṛi* now to chew. She'll never be able to eat *muṛi.*"

Muṛi at night, and vegetarian rice (*nirāmiṣ bhāt*) in the day. How many kinds of pain we suffer if our husband doesn't live in our house! Just one pain? No. Pain in all directions. Burning pain; agony. Clothes, food, mixing with others, laughter, all of that ends. If I just laugh with someone? Then others say, "Look! She's laughing with him. And her husband is dead. Chi! Chi!" And they begin to talk. My husband's relatives would say all those kinds of things. They would reproach me. They would say, "None of that will happen in our house. You've come to our house. You won't talk to any man." I lived in fear of them all. I wouldn't talk to anyone. My health was still good at that time. They thought maybe I would turn my mind toward someone and become infatuated, through mixing. They would tell me not to look at anyone else. That there was no one like one's own husband. That even to look at another man was bad. Our women have to live carefully like that. Just like unmarried women live carefully, so must widows live carefully. An unmarried girl's parents must look after her carefully as long as she's unmarried, and so must a widow's mother-in-law look after the widow when her husband dies. A widow must live in fear of her mother-in-law.

Everything for us is forbidden. Our food goes, our clothing goes, everything. Decorations, powder, all that. But if I put on a little powder, what will happen? Let them say what they will. They can't reproach me. I didn't do anything unjust (*anyāe*). Then why can't I fulfill a little fancy like that? And what if I want to wear a good, colored sari? But I can't wear one; it won't happen.

I heard many other stories like this one during my time in Mangaldihi. One woman told of how she was married at age two—as used to be common earlier in the century—and widowed at age eight, passing the rest of her life as a widow. Why do widows perform this rigorous set of practices that set them apart from other married women and from their own former selves? What do these practices reveal about the ways in which women, as wives and then as widows, were constituted as persons in Mangaldihi? The remainder of this chapter is devoted to answering these questions.

SEXUALITY AND SLANDER, DEVOTION AND DESTRUCTION

Widows and their families in Mangaldihi presented various explanations of why widows may choose, and their families may press them, to observe these rigors of widowhood. Their reasoning spoke to notions about female sexuality, the importance of honor or a "name," and the complex bodily and moral relationship between a woman and her husband.

Controlling Sexuality

The most common rationale as to why widows were pressed to eat vegetarian diets and rice only once a day, to fast on the eleventh day of the lunar month, to wear white, and to forsake bodily adornments was that these were defensive measures aimed at controlling a widow's sexuality. The widow's diet was said (by men and women, widows and nonwidows) to "reduce sexual desire (*kām*)," to "decrease blood (*rakta*)," to make the body "cool (*ṭhāṇḍā*)," to make the widow "thin and ugly," to keep her from "wanting any man." Sadanda's Ma, a senior Brahman widow, explained articulately: "These eating rules were originally designed to prevent young widows' bodies from becoming hot (*garam*) and so ruining their character (*svabhāb*) and *dharma* (social-moral order). Fasting is not for either *pāp* (sin) or *puṇya* (merit). Doing it doesn't produce *puṇya,* nor does not doing it make *pāp.* It is simply to weaken the body." A group of Brahman co-wives (or sisters-in-law) expressed similar ideas, agreeing that a widow follows the observances "to make her thin and ugly, and to reduce her sexual desire (*kām*), since she cannot remarry." (Their senior widowed mother-in-law listening to us interjected: "It's very difficult. It's better to die than do all of that.") Bhogi Bagdi commented, "If a widow wears a good colored sari, everyone will come to make love to her."

Recall that dominant discourses within Mangaldihi presented women as having more sexual heat and desire than men. This sexual heat could be particularly problematic for a widow, because (as people put it) her sexuality had been activated and opened through marriage but was now no longer controlled by a husband. Widows also had no acceptable way of dissipating the heat of their pent-up sexual desire. Several villagers commented that women who are accustomed to having sexual relations and suddenly cease have the most sexual desire of all. Many therefore felt that young widows constantly threatened to become promiscuous, injuring their own honor and that of their families and contaminating their bodies and households with the sexual fluids of other men.

In fact, the local prostitutes while I was in Mangaldihi *were* widows: one Brahman woman (who had actually been expelled by her family from the village and worked in a nearby town), one Bagdi woman, and one Muci woman. They were sometimes called *rāṇḍī*, a slang term (found in many north Indian languages) translatable as "slut" and used to refer both to prostitutes and to widows.[13] The double meaning of this term speaks not only to the fact that widows were often considered dangerously promiscuous but also to their precarious economic position. Some young widows, who are supported by neither their natal nor marital families, feel compelled to become prostitutes to survive.[14]

The Bagdi and Muci widow-prostitutes were both young women who had returned to Mangaldihi to live with their mothers (both of whom were, incidentally, also widows). Prostitute widows fared better in their natal communities than in their marital villages. (In fact, I never heard of a prostitute working from her marital community.) Because a woman, once married, is no longer a real part of her natal family line, her actions do not affect her natal family as much as they would her husband's family. Her natal family may also be more loving and understanding of the problems she faces. The Muci woman had a small child; perhaps that is why she had not remarried. The Bagdi woman, Pratima, was childless and ordinarily would have remarried, but her only close natal kin were a landless widowed mother and a young brother, neither of whom seemed to have had the means to arrange a second marriage for her. The Brahman widow-prostitute, Chobi, was a childless daughter from one of the most prestigious families of Mangaldihi, but her family members had broken off all relations with her many years earlier and would not even mention her name to me when giving me their family's genealogical information. When I ended up meeting her, she told me that she preferred her life as a prostitute in town to the life she would have had in the village as a lifelong Brahman widow.

Villagers cited the perceived dangers of women formerly married but now not matched with men in explaining why widows must rigorously discipline their bodies. Eating a vegetarian diet free of all hot (*garam*) foods—eggs, fish, meat, onions, garlic, heating forms of *ḍāl*—counteracts a widow's pent-up sexual heat to help keep her free from illicit sexual liaisons. A diet of cool foods was likewise recommended for those men, such as *sannyāsīs* or *sādhus* (ascetics), who had chosen to be celibate. Similarly, people told me, a widow must only eat rice once a day so that her body will become increasingly dry (*śukna*) and weak (*durbal*), processes that further reduce her sexual energy, curb her capacities to transact with others, and make her thinner and less attractive to men. Dressed in a plain white sari, bare of ornaments, thin from continual fasting, and perhaps also disfigured by cropped hair, a widow was supposed to become an asexual and unattractive woman.

For younger widows, such cooling and desiccating of their bodies was tantamount to premature aging. Although no one volunteered this comparison to me, when I tried it out on them most seemed to find it persuasive. Widows, like older people, wore white, were expected to cease sexual activity, and experienced the cooling and drying of their bodies. The difference was that older people performed these practices more or less willingly, aiming to loosen their ties of maya and cool their bodies and selves in preparation for dying (see chapter 4). The practices were viewed as in keeping with the natural changes taking place within their bodies and families during the "senior" or "grown" life phase. For younger widows, though, the fetters of widowhood served to transform them socially, before the time naturally determined by physiology, into old women. Several commented to me that older, postmenopausal widows actually would not *have* to observe the widow's restrictive code if they did not wish to, because their bodies were naturally cool and dry due to age; but most senior Brahman widows, at least, observed these practices anyway, out of "habit" or aversion to being criticized by others.

Protecting a "Name"

Probably the second most common reason I was given as to why widows felt compelled to observe the widow's regulations was their wish to avoid slander and to protect the honor or "name" (*nām*) of themselves and their families. When discussing with me why widows do not remarry, a group of Brahman women chimed together, "Because a household has a reputation, a respect, does it not? People would say, 'These people's daughter or daughter-in-law got married twice?! Her husband has already died once, and she's getting married again?!'" The women added that widows *do* have affairs; although an affair is "even worse" than remarrying (from the perspective of *dharma*, or morality), it can take place privately. There is more slander (*nindā*) from a public remarriage, so that is why widows do not remarry.

When, as we saw above, Kayera Bou's mother made the painful decision to feed her own newly widowed daughter dried *muṛi* rather than boiled rice, it was fear of slander, not a conviction of the moral necessity of the practice, that drove her: "My mother was saying, 'I won't be able to give her *muṛi*. How can I give her *muṛi* and eat rice myself'? But my father told her that she would have to. My mother said, "No! I won't be able to. . . . Society!

Let society happen! She's my child. . . . But out of embarrassment in front of everyone, she wasn't able to feed me [rice]. People would have seen and said to her, 'Oh, you're feeding her *rice?*' . . . That's the fault of Bengalis, isn't it? They go around talking about who's feeding whom what."

I asked Thakurma, a senior Suri widow, "What would happen if you wore a red sari?" Thakurma and her neighbor Bandana answered together, "People would slander! (*Loke nindā korbe!*)." I continued, "No harm would happen to your husband?" Bandana laughed a little and replied, "No, nothing at all will happen to *him*." Thakurma agreed: "Where is my husband's harm? He's gone." Bandana went on: "Nothing at all would happen to him. He didn't even forbid her to wear colored saris after he died; he said nothing like that. It's just that in our country, if widows wear colored saris, they will be slandered (*nindā habe*), they will feel embarrassed (*lajjā habe*)."

Widows motivated by a concern for their own, and their families', reputations did not necessarily internalize the ideologies of a widow's dangerous sexuality when choosing to accept the terms of widowhood; they rather wished to avoid dishonoring themselves and their kin. Kayera Bou's words reflected just such a stance: "But if I put on a little powder, what will happen? Let them say what they will. They can't reproach me. I didn't do anything unjust. Then why can't I fulfill a little fancy like that? And what if I want to wear a good, colored sari? But I can't wear one; it won't happen." Widows in the region who reached old age after long lives of ascetic widowhood often earned a great deal of respect for their self-sacrifice and perseverance. Working for that social acceptance and respect, however arduous to achieve, seemed for most more attractive than having to endure slander, and even ostracism, by openly thwarting the codes of widowhood.

Powers of Devotion

A third reason some villagers gave for the widow's disciplined lifestyle was that widows were continuing to live devoted to their husbands. Girls in the region were in many ways raised to think of devotion to a husband as one of the highest and most appropriate aims of a woman's life. During her marriage ceremony, a bride would speak mantras and take vows that were to infuse in her a lifelong devotion (*bhaktī*) for her husband, who was to be to her like a god or lord. In fact, two of the common Bengali terms for "husband"—*svāmī* and *pati*—also mean "lord" (cf. Fruzzetti 1982:13). One image of the virtuous wife found throughout north India is that of a *pativrata*, literally "she who takes a vow (*vrat*) of devotion to her husband (*pati*)." Married women in Mangaldihi did expend a good deal of daily effort serving their husbands—cooking, feeding them, supplying water, and so forth. They applied vermilion to their hair, wore married women's bangles, and performed women's rituals (*meyeder vrata*)—all practices aimed toward protecting the longevity and well-being of their husbands.

Even after a husband's death, some told me, a widow is able to continue to live a life of devotion to him. Gurusaday Mukherjee lectured me on several occasions as to the meaning and purpose of the widow's regime (perhaps from quite an idealized and traditional perspective, since of course he himself was not a widow): "Even these days, even though many are telling widows that they can remarry and eat nonvegetarian foods, they will willingly, on their own accord, remain as traditional widows, because their minds are focused on their husbands." Several widows of my acquaintance expressed similar views. Debu's Ma, a senior high-caste (Kayastha) widow from the neighboring village of Batikar, spoke with a serene certainty about the importance of following the widow's regime. I asked, "What would happen if you didn't do these things?" "It's a matter of *dharma* (morality, order)," she replied, "*Dharma* would be ruined." "Would your husband be harmed?" "Husband?" Debu's Ma laughed at first a bit, as if to disagree. Then she went on: "A husband is master, lord (*pati*) and must be treated with devotion (*bhaktī*). There is only one husband/lord (*pati*) in the world. Even though he is dead, he is everything. The sons and wife must live thinking about him. They do this for his blessing (*āśīrbād*). They do *praṇām* to his photograph or footprints every day. . . . A husband is the woman's guru; he is the highest lord (*parampati*). If a wife worships and serves her husband, then no other *dharma* is necessary." Other widows declared that along with upholding *dharma*, they could bring merit (*puṇya*) and good karma to themselves, their sons, their households, and *perhaps* their deceased husbands, through faithfully observing the widow's code.

Several villagers also spoke with admiration of those who had chosen to become Satis in the past, burning themselves on their husbands' funeral pyres, and they compared the wifely devotion of today's ascetic widows to that of a Sati (which literally means a "good woman").[15] The popular myths told by villagers about Behula, a woman who floats down the river of death with the corpse of her husband in her lap, and about Savitri, who wins her dead husband back from Yamaraj, the god of death, portray women who gain incredible, auspicious powers by remaining devoted to their husbands even after death. Both of these illustrative tales are well worth retelling here. Married women and girls in Mangaldihi gathered once a year to perform the story of Savitri and pay homage to her on the fourteenth day after the full moon in the hot summer month of Jyaistha. In doing so they both promoted the well-being and long lives of husbands and gained edification in wifely devotion. On the occasion I attended, a Brahman wife recited the story to about twenty-five other women, reading frequently from the paperback pamphlet *Meyeder Vratakathā* (n.d., ed. G. Bhattacharjya:62–66). The following is an abbreviated translation of the tale:[16]

> There was a king named Asvapati who ruled a land called Madra. He had a daughter, born to him by the grace of the goddess Savitri, whom he named Savitri. When it was time for her to marry, the king searched in all directions for a worthy groom, but to no avail. Finally, Savitri decided to go out herself to search for a husband, taking several companions with her. They traveled to many places and eventually came upon an ashram in a forest where an old blind man named Dyumatsen lived with his son and blind wife. Dyumatsen had been king of a nearby kingdom, but had lost it to enemies. When Savitri saw this man's son, Satyaban, she vowed that only he would be her husband.
>
> Savitri returned to her father to tell him of her decision, and the king asked a great seer what he knew of Savitri's chosen spouse. The seer said ominously, "Savitri's marriage with Satyaban cannot happen. For within a year after he is married, Satyaban will die."
>
> The king Asvapati became very distraught and tried to dissuade his daughter from marrying Satyaban. But Savitri was unwavering in her resolve, saying, "Father, he whom I have accepted in my mind as my lord and husband I cannot forsake. I will not be able to marry anyone but him." And seeing her firm resolve, the king and the seer both agreed that the marriage should take place.
>
> So Savitri was married to Satyaban. Savitri went to live in the ashram of her father-in-law, and began immediately to serve her blind old parents-in-law with much devotion. Savitri soon became beloved to them all. But she herself was stung every night by the memory of the words the seer had told her about the future. She counted every day from the wedding until there were only three days left before the end of the year.
>
> On that day, Satyaban was planning to set out for the forest to bring back some wood and fruit. Savitri pleaded with her mother-in-law to let her accompany him, and after finally receiving permission, she departed into the woods with her husband. Soon Satyaban's head began to ache sharply and he lay down with his head on Savitri's lap. He became still with pain and then lost consciousness. As Savitri watched, his life slowly left his body. Evening was coming on, but Savitri was not afraid. She took her husband's body into her lap and sat there.
>
> Presently Yamaraj, the god of death, arrived and said to Savitri, "Your husband has died. I have come here to take away his spirit (*prāṇ*). Go now and return to your home to do his funeral rites for him

properly." Saying this, Yamaraj took Satyaban's spirit out from his body and began walking away.

But Savitri began to follow right after Yamaraj. Yamaraj turned to ask, "Dear, where are you going?" Savitri answered, "God, wherever you take my husband, there I will go," and she began to plead with him to give her husband's life back. Yamaraj was impressed with Savitri's Sati-like[17] devotion to her husband, and said to her, "Sati! Aside from the boon of granting Satyaban's life, I will give you any three boons that you desire."

So Savitri first asked that sight be restored to both of her parents-in-law. Next she asked that her father-in-law regain rule over his kingdom. And finally she asked that her own father, who was sonless, be given one hundred sons. Yamaraj granted each of these boons, but still Savitri did not give up following him. So finally Yamaraj turned to her and said, "I will give you one more boon, other than the life of your husband, and then you will absolutely have to leave."

This time Savitri asked that she herself, with Satyaban's semen, would be the mother of one hundred sons. Without thinking, Yamaraj assented, and told her now finally to go on her way. But Savitri responded, "God, how can I give birth to a hundred sons if you do not give my husband's life back to me?" Yamaraj realized that he had lost in the game of wits (*buddhir khelā*) with Savitri, and he was compelled to restore Satyaban's life.

In this way, Savitri, acting as a Sati, gave her parents-in-law back their sight, her father-in-law back his kingdom, her father a hundred sons, and her husband his life.

The Bengali myth of Behula in the *Manasa Mangal* similarly tells of how a wife's self-sacrificing devotion brings her husband back even from death. Mangaldihi villagers knew this story well and told it to illustrate the powers of wifely devotion, as well as the merits of worshiping Manasa, the goddess of snakes. The following is an abbreviated reconstruction of the Behula story as it was sung to me over several long sessions by Rabilal Ruidas, the blind senior beggar of Mangaldihi's leatherworker (Muci) caste, also known as the musician (Bayen) caste:[18]

There was a man named Cando who had six sons and six daughters-in-law, but because he would not worship the goddess Manasa, the goddess of snakes, she caused each of his sons to die by snakebite one by one. The daughters-in-law thus turned one by one into widows, and soon there was no longer any red *āltā* on the feet of the house's daughters-in-law, no jingling of ornaments, and no colorful saris. The house was full of mourning and gloom.

Then a seventh son, named Lakhai, was born to Cando. When

Lakhai reached the age for marriage, Cando sent out his servants to locate a suitable bride. The girl Behula was chosen. But the goddess Manasa, still angry, visited Lakhai before the marriage, dressed as an old Brahman woman, and cursed him, declaring that he would die on his wedding night. Lakhai's father Cando was afraid and ordered blacksmiths to build an iron chamber, so tightly fitted that not even an ant or a breath of wind could enter it. This is where Lakhai and Behula would sleep on their wedding night. Manasa became angry, and she frightened the blacksmith into leaving a crack so that a snake could enter the wall of the chamber.

So the wedding happened with much pomp, and on the wedding night Lakhai and Behula retired together to the iron chamber. Behula prepared to wait up all night long to guard her husband. But even as she sat awake, a snake crawled through the crack and fatally bit Lakhai on the heel. His body was placed on a raft to float down the river,[19] and although everyone pleaded with Behula to stay, she would not leave his side. She headed down the river toward the land of the gods. Along the way she encountered animals hungry for her husband's body and men hungry for sexual favors from her. But for six months Behula warded off all of these dangers and persisted in her journey.

Finally Behula, with her husband's corpse still beside her, reached the place where the river meets the land of the gods. She went to Siva and told him her story, imploring him to restore her husband to life. Siva sent for the goddess Manasa and they made an agreement. Manasa would restore Behula's husband's life, along with the lives of his six brothers. In exchange, Behula would promise that her father-in-law and the whole family would henceforth perform *pūjās* for Manasa.

In this way, Behula brought her husband back to life, gave her parents-in-law back their seven sons, and turned her six sisters-in-law once again into married women.

Behula is perhaps the best-known human figure in Bengali mythology and is considered an exemplar of wifely devotion. Hem Barua describes her feat: "a victory for Behula's pure devotion, conjugal purity and faith that moves mountains. As an ideal wife she is second neither to Sita nor Savitri. Before the pure chastity and deep devotion of Behula, even heavenly powers bend and break" (1965:16; qtd. in W. L. Smith 1980:117).

A husband's death would appear to put an end to a woman's wifely powers of devotion and to be evidence of a woman's failure (a point I will return to shortly). But there was also a sense, expressed in such popular myths as well as in everyday talk, that if a widow remained devoted to her husband then to some extent she could keep her auspicious, life-maintaining powers alive. Her status as a wife was radically altered, but not entirely effaced. By accepting the lifestyle of widowhood, a woman continued to define herself and present herself to others as a wife devoted to her husband—thereby partially circumventing the reality of her husband's death.

Powers of Destruction

A fourth factor crucial to understanding the position of widows in Mangaldihi is tied to perceptions of a widow's dangerous, destructive potential. If a virtuous, devoted wife possesses the power to nurture and sustain her husband, then something must have been wrong or deficient (local reasoning went) in the nurturance provided by any woman whose husband died.[20] Widows frequently told me that they felt it was their fault that their husbands had died—either because of their failings as a wife, or because of some horrendous wrong performed in a previous life, or simply because of their own personal ill fate (*kapāl, adṛṣṭa*). Gurusaday Mukherjee gave me a list of conditions that could be considered the fruit of sins (*pāper phal*), with widowhood at the top of the list, followed by barrenness, the destruction of a lineage (*baṃśa*), blindness, and being a cow that has to labor in the fields.

Sometimes widows were imaged as devouring creatures. Gurusaday Mukherjee told me that a widow who does not behave properly becomes a vulture (*śākun*) in her next life, preying on the dead flesh of cows and other large animals. A senior Kayastha widow, Mita's Ma, who had become blind in one eye told me with grief that she saw herself as a *rākshasī*, a mythological female creature who devours everything, including people. Her husband had died early and then her son-in-law, leaving both mother and daughter widows. She said mournfully that she had "eaten" these people, and was fearful that she would cause some such disaster again (cf. M. Bandyopadhyay 1990:150). Rumors were spread that Pratima, the young Bagdi widow who had become a prostitute, had poisoned her husband. Another widow, Rani (of the Kora caste), told of how her husband had died "from diarrhea" when they were both still very young. Soon after, in just one day, her two-year-old son sickened and also died. "After that," she said, "my parents-in-law began pestering me even more. They didn't want to see any more of me. They called me a poison bride (*biṣkanyā*). So my brothers came to get me," and she never went back. A widow can also be feared as a devouring witch, as in Tarashankar Bandyopadhyay's story "The Witch" (1990).

This destructive potential was the primary reason that widows were considered to be so exceedingly inauspicious (*amangal, aśubha*) and were peripheralized within the family, if not expelled. Conversely, a husband whose wife died was not viewed as culpable or dangerous. I asked Mejo Ma, who had years earlier been married to a man whose previous *two* wives had died, if she had been nervous about *his* inauspiciousness when marrying him. She stated matter-of-factly (after admitting that she had actually not been told about his previous wives' deaths before the wedding), "No one blames a man for his wife's death; they only blame widows." Women were thus presented as having an agency that must be carefully controlled. They could use their powers to support and sustain others, but also to destroy.

UNSEVERABLE BONDS

The villagers' reasoning summarized above points to important facets of women's experiences of widowhood in Mangaldihi and to local constructions of what it is to be a woman. But it does not yet entirely explain how a woman's personhood—or the ties making up her self—were altered through the death of her spouse, and why a woman's transformation into widowhood was so different from that of a man.

To understand these issues it is crucial to take into account the kinds of connections women shared with their husbands. It seemed to me that the bodily connections (*samparka*) and ties of maya between a woman and her husband were believed in significant respects to remain, even after his death. What necessarily endured was not so much the emotional dimensions of maya (some widows spoke of an ongoing emotional attachment to their husbands, and others did not) but people's *perceptions* of a woman after marriage: a woman would always be defined in terms of her relationship with her husband, as his "half body" (*ardhāṅginī*), even if he died. Thus the widow was in effect married to a corpse, herself half dead. A widow in this way remained perpetually in a state similar to the death impurity (or *aśauc*) that other surviving relatives experienced only temporarily.

This comparison between the condition of widows and those suffering death-separation impurity first occurred to me as I began to notice their many correspondences (table 8). Widows and older people share many practices, too, but the codes for conduct of widows and death-impure persons are even more similar. Like a widow, persons suffering death impurity were expected to remain celibate; avoid "hot," nonvegetarian foods; limit intake of boiled rice; restrict their sharing of food with others; and avoid participating in auspicious rituals. Males suffering from death impurity and older, more traditional widows also had their heads shaved.

As discussed in chapter 5, these practices all reduced the likelihood that personal properties would be transferred among people. During the transi-

Table 8. Practices of Widows and Older and Death-Impure Persons

Prescribed Practices	*Widows*	*Older People*	*Death-Impure Persons*
Remain celibate	X	X	X
Religious orientation	X	X	?
Wear white	X	X	X*
"Cool" the body	X	X	X
Avoid "hot" foods	X	—	X
Limit intake of boiled rice (*bhāt*)	X	—	X
Restrict sharing food	X	—	X
Keep out of auspicious rituals	X	—	X
Shave the head	X†	—	X**
Sleep on the ground	X†	—	X†

KEY: — = Absent. X = Present.
*Performed by chief mourner only (usually the eldest son of the deceased).
†Traditionally prescribed but not commonly performed now.
**Performed at the end of the period of death impurity and by males only.

tional phase of death impurity, the survivors limited their interactions, both in order to separate themselves from the deceased person and to avoid infecting others in the community with their condition. The aim was to cut the lingering bodily emotional connections between the survivors and the deceased, so that the departed spirit as well as the survivors could move on to form new relationships. For other survivors, the practices of death-impurity ended with the final funeral rites after ten to thirty days. But the incapacity and inauspicious (*aśubha*) condition of the widow was permanent, because her putatively indissoluble merger with him in marriage appears to have made her the "half body" and lifelong soul mate of her husband. When he was dead, her living bodily presence made her not merely a sexual hazard (if she was still young) but also a repulsive anomaly.

Others, such as Parvati Athavale (1930:46–50), Veena Das (1979:98), and Pandurang Kane (1968–75:2.592), have compared the Hindu widow's practices to those not of death-impure persons but of the ascetic or sannyasi. Some of my informants, too, suggested that a widow is in some ways like a female ascetic. However, this comparison fails to adequately account for the widow's unusual relationship to death. Manisha Roy (1992 [1972]:146) suggests in passing that Bengali widows are "polluted," but she does not specify in what way. Recall that those in Mangaldihi did *not* regard widows as "polluted" or "impure" in the sense of the everyday impurities (*a-śuddhatā*) that stem from menstruation, sexual intercourse, saliva, dog-doo, contact with lower castes, and the like (see chapter 6). Indeed, in this regard high-caste and older widows especially were thought to be uniquely *pure* (*śuddha*), because their lifestyles (celibacy, vegetarian diets, being post-menopausal, etc.) made their bodies contained, cool, pure, like those of gods (*ṭhākur*) and men. I. Julia Leslie's study of the eighteenth-century *Guide to the Religious Status and Duties of Women* (*Strīdharmapaddhati*) by Tryambaka seems to support my assertion, though, that the widow's condition is similar to that of *death* impurity (*aśauc*). Tryambaka writes: "Just as the body, bereft of life, in that moment becomes impure [*aśucitaṃ*], so the woman bereft of her husband is always impure [*aśuciḥ*],[21] even if she has bathed properly. Of all inauspicious things, the widow is the most inauspicious" (qtd. in Leslie 1989:303).

To grasp the peculiar relationship of the widow to her dead husband, we must examine once more the nature of the Bengali marital union. As already noted, in a Bengali marriage the bride is described as becoming the "half body" or *ardhānginī* of her husband. Both the husband and wife become "whole" through this complementary union, but it is effected by an asymmetrical merger in which the woman becomes part of the *man's* body and not vice versa (cf. Inden and Nicholas 1976:41–50; Fruzzetti 1982:103–4). During the marriage ritual the bride repeatedly absorbs substances originating from the groom's body and household, changes her last name and lineage affiliation to match her husband, and moves to his place of residence. These actions seemed to create an irreversible, indestructible entity made of the husband plus wife: the woman would be part of her husband's body for life.

The asymmetry generally thus assumed in the marital relation was extreme, for the husband was not considered to be the wife's half body and, unlike her, was not said to be diminished by his partner's death. If she died first, his person remained whole and free to remarry; the temporary incapacity of death impurity for him lasted no longer than that of other close survivors. There was, in fact, no commonly used term to describe a widowed man in Mangaldihi, suggesting that male widowhood was not a highly marked category.[22]

Consistent with this logic, several people told me that even if the woman dies first, her spirit remains bound to her husband and wanders around near him. This would mean, of course, that the surviving husband was not entirely free after all, because he might have to contend with her spirit. It was not uncommon for a man's second wife to keep a photo of his deceased first

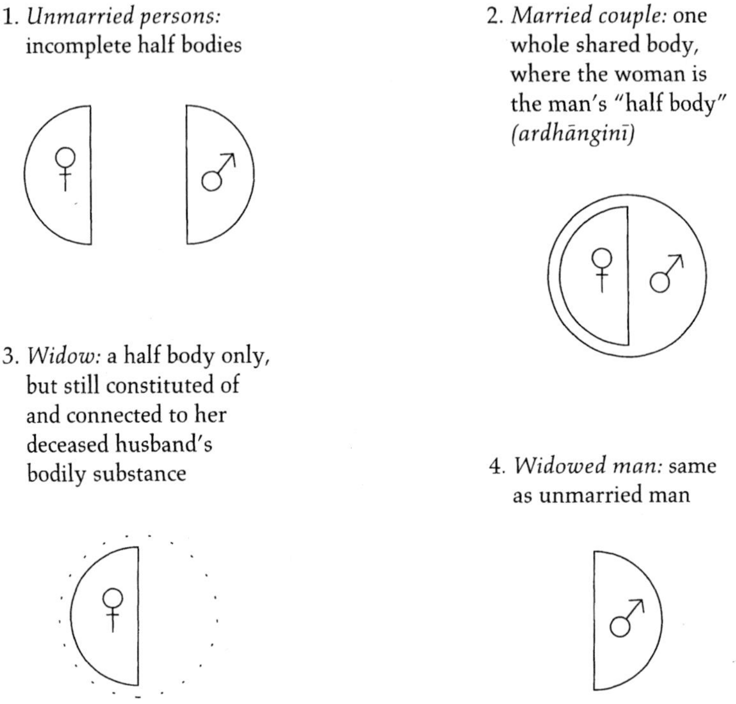
1. *Unmarried persons:* incomplete half bodies
2. *Married couple:* one whole shared body, where the woman is the man's "half body" *(ardhānginī)*
3. *Widow:* a half body only, but still constituted of and connected to her deceased husband's bodily substance
4. *Widowed man:* same as unmarried man

Figure 7. The widow and the widowed man.

wife in the family shrine, for instance, and to anoint it with vermilion every day. She thereby placated the first wife's spirit and aided the well-being (*mangal*) of her husband and household. In most respects, though, the widowed man seemed to be quite unhindered. One way to represent these enduring connections of a widow with her deceased husband—in contrast to the relative freedom of the widowed man—is sketched in figure 7.

If people in Mangaldihi viewed persons to be constituted of networks of relations, then women were in a peculiar position: their connections were made, remade, and unmade at several critical junctures over their lives, not only through aging and dying but also in marriage and widowhood. A daughter painfully attenuated her ties with her natal family and place, so that she could move on to form new ties within her husband's home. Their families' responses to the deaths of husbands often did even more than marriage to unmake women, mainly through once again curtailing their interpersonal connections with those in their families and communities. The only tie for a woman that seemed to be unambiguously unseverable, within the dominant patrilineal discourse of Mangaldihi, was the one she shared with her husband. That bond, which defined a woman's very bodily substance and identity, could not be cut by a married woman, even if her husband died. This logic underlay the solitary existence endured by most women in Mangaldihi as widows as the last phase of their lives.

Stories of Tagore: Widows Trapped between the Living and the Dead

I close this chapter by examining three short stories written by Rabindranath Tagore around the turn of the century that powerfully expose the oppressiveness of a system that constructs widows as trapped between life and death.[23] These stories were not told or mentioned to me by people in Mangaldihi. But as I sat reading them from the serene cottage I had rented and sometimes retreated to in nearby Santiniketan, the town where Tagore had lived and did much of his writing, I could not help being struck by the eloquence and vividness with which Tagore portrayed the condition of local widows that I had been struggling ethnographically to discern.

Tagore focused his short stories on the ongoing social changes and lives of ordinary people during the period of the Bengal renaissance and the rise of nationalism between the 1880s and 1920s. He often depicts the female condition, and the forces that oppress women, with particular sensitivity. For Tagore, as Kalpana Bardhan (1990:14) writes, "the oppressor is ultimately some aspect of the cultural ideology and the social situation in which both men and women find themselves trapped. . . . The tragedy lies in the distortions that their personalities and relationships suffer under the tyranny of social mores and beliefs." The three stories I look at treat the suffering of widows within such an ideological system, one that traps them between life and death, barring them from normal, fulfilling social relationships by making them into despised and inauspicious death-like creatures.

The first, "Mahamaya" (Tagore 1926:148–53), presents the awful, estranged life of a woman who becomes a widow the day after her wedding. The story opens with Mahamaya as a beautiful young woman whose parents, for whatever reasons, have not yet found a suitable groom for her. She is of a Kulin Brahman family, the highest rank of Brahmans. She falls in love with a young man of the village, Rajib, who is a Brahman, but not a Kulin Brahman. When Mahamaya's father finds out about their love, to protect the rank of the family he immediately arranges an alternative marriage for Mahamaya to a Kulin Brahman man.

This groom is already an old man; he has retired to a hut by the cremation ground where the Ganges flows, waiting to die. The wedding takes place in the hut, lit only by the dim glow of a cremation fire not far off, and the old man whispers the wedding mantras in a voice filled with the pain of his dying. Mahamaya becomes a widow the day after her wedding.

It is decided then that Mahamaya will become a *sahamṛtā*, one who dies with her husband. Her hands and feet are bound, and she is committed to the cremation pyre. The fire is lit and great flames leap out. But at that moment a huge storm comes upon them, releasing torrents of rain. All of the people gathered to watch take shelter in the hut, the fire goes out, and Mahamaya frees herself. She runs first to her father's home; finding no one there, she goes to Rajib. She and Rajib determine to leave together.

But Mahamaya never removes the veil, or *ghomṭā*, of her sari from her face, and she lives distant and estranged from Rajib: her face has been hideously scarred by the cremation fire. The thick veil of her sari does more than simply conceal her scars; it represents the shadow of death and the social attitudes that separate her from others as a widow.

> Mahamaya was now in Rajib's house, but there was no happiness in Rajib's life. Between them both was only the estrangement caused by Mahamaya's veil. That small veil was just as everlasting as death, and yet it caused even more pain than death. For the pain of separation in death gradually fades away, but behind this veil were living hopes that stabbed at one every moment of every day. Mahamaya lived behind her veil with a deep, silent sorrow. She was living as if overcast by death. Rajib himself began to feel withered and hindered by having to live next to this silent and deathlike creature in his household. He had lost the Mahamaya that he had once known and had gained instead this silent, veiled figure. (1926:152)

The widow is an inherently distressing figure because she is neither fully alive nor dead. Death is a more complete separation than widowhood; it can be handled and processed through funeral rites, and its pain slowly fades away. But the widow is uniquely disturbing because she stays within society, an ever-present reminder of what could have been. She lives in other people's households but is forever separated from them by the culturally imposed veil of her widowhood, thus existing permanently overshadowed by death.

The protagonist of a second story, "The Skeleton" (Tagore 1926:63–69), is a child widow who had died many years earlier. Her body had been donated to a school, which kept her skeleton for classroom study. One night a young student was sleeping in a room next to where the skeleton was kept when he heard something enter the room. It was the spirit of the person from whom the skeleton had come. She stayed throughout the night to tell the young man her story.

She had been married as a young child, and after only two months of marriage, her husband died and she became a widow. After looking at many signs, her father-in-law determined that she was, without a doubt, what they called a "poison bride" (*biṣkanyā*). Her parents-in-law expelled the ominous widow from their house and she returned quite happily to her parents' home, too young to understand what had happened to her.

There she grew up into a beautiful young woman. Men used to look at her and she at them, and she used to dress up secretly in colorful saris with bracelets on her arms, imagining men admiring and caressing her. Then a doctor moved into the first floor of their house, and she used to enjoy visiting him for carefree talk about medicines and about how to use poisons to help sick people die.

Then one day she heard that the doctor was getting married. On the evening of his wedding, the girl slipped some poison from his office into one of his drinks; soon thereafter, as flutes played, he left for the bride's house. She then dressed herself in a silk wedding sari, put a large streak of red vermilion in the part of her hair, and adorned herself with all of the jewelry from her chest. She took poison herself and lay down on her bed. She hoped that when people came to find her they would see her with a smile on her lips as a married woman.

"But where is that wedding night room? Where is that bride's dress?" she asks the listening man. "I woke up to a hollow rattling sound inside of me and noticed three young students using me to learn about bone science! In my chest where happiness and sadness used to throb and where petals of youth used to bloom every day, there was a master pointing with a rod about which bones have what names. And there was no sign of that last smile that I had placed on my lips" (Tagore 1926:68). The story ends here, when dawn arrives and the spirit of the skeleton/widow silently leaves the young man to himself.

The widow in this story is a "poison bride," causing the deaths of the men she unites with, and she is a lifeless skeleton, with passions and dreams but no means to fulfill them. This pattern—the woman as a poison bride causing her husband's death and then turning into a skeletal widow—is repeated twice. First the girl is a real bride who is perceived to have caused her husband's death by her nature as a poison bride, and next she is dressed as a bride who indeed does administer poison to a departing groom. At the end of each sequence, after causing her groom's death, she becomes a skeleton. Initially, it is her existence as a widow that is skeletal: she is a beautiful woman full of dreams and throbbing life, but she is forced to live without love, fulfillment, and the capacity to unite with others. By the story's end, the widow has literally become a hollow skeleton that possesses no signs of life or emotion.

A third story, "Living and Dead" (Tagore 1926:98–107), presents a young, childless widow, Kadambini, who is believed by others, and at first believes herself, to be dead, existing in the world only as a ghost. At the beginning of the story, she does appear to die suddenly, and her body is taken quickly to the cremation ground by men from her father-in-law's house. The men leave her to go off to gather fuel for the fire, and she awakens alone. She had not in fact died, but had only been temporarily unconscious. Seeing the cremation ground around her in the dead of the night, she believes that she *has* died and that she is now a ghost. She does not know where to go, but she feels that she belongs even less to her father-in-law's house than to her father's home, so she returns to her natal village to a childhood girlfriend who is now married. Eventually, when the girlfriend and her husband find out that Kadambini is supposed to have died, they chase her away screaming, calling her accursed and inauspicious. Kadambini then returns to her in-law's home and there finally realizes, when she holds her beloved nephew, that she is not a ghost. But the people of the household shriek when they see her, pleading with her not to bring misfortune upon their household and lineage, not to cause their only son to die. Kadambini finally drowns herself in a pond, and it is only by dying that she is able to prove to her tormentors that she had indeed been alive.

Here the widow's existence is compared to that of a departed spirit or ghost (*pret*). The widow is, as the title suggests, both living and dead, or perhaps neither living nor dead. She does not belong in the world of the living, and yet she is trapped there, as a lonely and inauspicious being. Kadambini ponders aloud about her condition—ostensibly that of a ghost—while at her childhood friend's house:

> Who am I to you? Am I of this world? You are all laughing, crying, loving, each of you engaged in your own business, and I am only watching like a shadow. I don't understand why God has left me in the midst of you and your worldly activities (*saṃsār*). You are afraid of my presence, lest I bring misfortune (*amangal*) into the joys of your daily lives. I, too, cannot understand what relation I have with any of you. But since God did not create another place for us to go, we must keep hovering about you, even after the vital links (*bandhan*) are severed. (Tagore 1926:104)

Widows, like ghosts, remain hovering around other people's households, even as in some ways their "vital links" have been severed by death. But like ghosts, widows cannot fully participate in household life; like ghosts, they are frightening and cause misfortune.

When Kadambini is referred to as a ghost, it is as a *pret,* a departed, disembodied spirit. A deceased person's spirit ordinarily becomes a *pret* before it moves on to rebirth and ancestorhood (see chapter 5). During this transitional stage, the *pret* maintains attachments to its previous life in the world, yearning for food and attention from former relatives and loved ones, until the sequence of funeral rites finally cuts these attachments. The widow similarly is in a transitional state between life and death, but for an indefinite, prolonged period. When Kadambini returns to her in-law's home, her brother-in-law beseeches her to cut all the "bindings of her maya" (*māyā-bandhan*) for the world. He pleads, "When you have taken leave of *saṃsār* (family, worldly life), then go ahead and tear open your bindings of maya. We'll perform all of the funeral rites" (Tagore 1926:107). Tagore suggests that widowhood presents a sobering contrast, for society had created no rituals that could release the widow from her liminal condition. So Kadambini finally kills herself, the only act that can free her from her terrible, equivocal condition as a ghostlike widow. Widows in these stories are caught between life and death by bonds that cannot be severed—tied both to their husbands who are dead and to a life now devoid of all pleasurable content.

We see here—in Tagore's stories, as in the discourses and practices of those I knew in Mangaldihi—a specific vision of a woman's personhood as being permanently and substantially joined to her husband's. A woman, once married to a man, was not easily perceived again as separate from him. In the dominant patrilineal discourse of Mangaldihi, women were transformed by marriage—in their emotions and substance—into the "half bodies" of their husbands; their lives were to be eternally devoted to their husbands' well-being and longevity, just as their bodies were constituted and defined in and through their husbands' bodily substances. A widow, especially if young, was disturbing not only in her possibly uncontained sexuality but in her liminality—someone who has forsaken her husband by remaining on earth, but who yet cannot ever be truly free from him to move on to form new or independent relationships and identities.

Of course, this was not the only discourse I heard from women (and men) in and around Mangaldihi. As I have stressed throughout these pages (as current postmodern sensibilities would hold), the "culture" of Mangaldihians was not univocal. Some women, and some men, rejected through their talk or practice such visions of the relationship of a woman to her husband, dead or alive, as necessarily all-encompassing. When Kayera Bou wore an occasional pair of small yet brilliant spring-green earrings, she was repudiating the ideologies dictating that a woman without a husband had no reason to dress up (though she *was* derided by neighborhood girls for doing so). When the young Brahman widow, Chobi, left Mangaldihi to take her own apartment and become a self-employed prostitute in town, she was choosing to reject a life defined in terms of her dead husband, asserting instead her own agency and independence (even if that meant forsaking all ties with former kin). Nonetheless, I cannot deny the force of local ideologies defining women and widows in terms of their husbands, evident in widows' everyday practices, movements, diets, dress, and self-perceptions. Hena's statement to me was telling: "If her husband dies, a woman's life has no more value (*dām*)."

Yet one of the themes that has been emerging throughout this book is that using *age* as a category of analysis can provide an alternative perspective. As has already become clear from the stories told and data presented about aging women's lives (see also chapters 3 and 6), the experiences of widowhood for those widowed at older and younger ages could be profoundly different (see also Lamb 1999). For women widowed at older ages, with grown sons to care for them, daughters-in-law to supervise, a rightful long-term place established in a home, and a body grown naturally asexual with age and thus free—as in the case of Khudi Thakrun, or Choto Ma, or Mejo Ma—widowhood did not generally have devastating social, economic, and emotional consequences. To be sure, these older widows would never be completely free from the inauspiciousness of widowhood, and they could continue for years to feel the emotional pain of losing and missing a husband. For them, widowhood also usually brought with it a transfer of a household's economic resources and property to the younger generation, and thus their further peripheralization into old age. But widowhood in late life could also be accompanied by increased freedoms and even respect—fewer obligations tying them to the home, an attribution (for Brahman widows especially) of increased "purity" and of "manlike" and "godlike" qualities—which many older widows seemed to end up enjoying. Thus suspended amid the countervailing currents of inauspiciousness and auspiciousness, restraint and freedom, authority and peripheralization, the greater portion of Mangaldihi women lived the last phases of their lives.

Afterword

Seventeen months into my stay in Mangaldihi I commented in my field-notes: "Almost everything about life here seems so ordinary to me now that it hardly seems worth describing." It was getting to be time to go. I went on: "Everyone talks to me constantly now about how I'll be leaving soon. They tell me that it will be sad for them when I go, that the village will cry for me, that its lanes will seem empty. But they tell me that it will be even harder for *me* to leave them: After having mixed with Mangaldihi's people for so many days, after having acquired a household full of things—a *janatā* stove, a kerosene lamp, a table and chair, a mosquito net, saris (some now worn and faded), a taste for *ālu posta,* potatoes with poppy seed paste—it will be painful for me to try to cut the maya and leave."

My last night was spent—with shutters thrown open to a luminous moon and the cooling relief of a night breeze—amid a clamor for all of my things. People came to carry away the accumulated pieces of my household. And then there were tears, especially among the younger neighborhood girls who had become my devoted companions. Is this what it is like to depart in the fullness of life? (Better, perhaps, to disperse things and ties earlier than at the moment of leaving.)

I began this book with several questions—intending to use aging as a lens to explore how social worlds were constituted and taken apart, and gender relations constructed and transformed, in a community of West Bengal, India. One question I opened with, but which I have still not fully resolved, concerns the power or authority of older women in India. The scattered comments that turn up on gender and aging in work on India have focused not on experiences of parting or the relinquishing of things, but on the apparent increasing power of women as they age. In anthropological and historical studies, if older women are discussed at all, they are generally presented as powerful matriarchs who have finally come into their own as senior mothers-in-law within joint families. Susan Wadley, for instance, proclaims: "The rural landowner's wife reaches her maximum potential as a matriarch of a joint household . . . , where she can exercise authority over sons, daughters-in-law, and grandchildren. . . . It is as senior female of a joint family that the Hindu woman attains her greatest power, authority, and autonomy" (1995:98). Prem Chowdhry goes further, suggesting that older women play a crucial role in upholding the patriarchal order in India that subordinates women: "[T]he older controlling woman who becomes herself a patriarch, imposes authority on behalf of men and perpetuates the patriarchal ideology, forms a class apart" (1994:18).

Do such claims ring true? Should we see the older South Asian woman as, finally, a figure of authority and power? What insights can we gain from focusing, as I have done here, on older women's—and men's—lives from the intertwined perspectives of family and kinship, the emotional experiences of aging and dying, changes in the body and sexuality, and the social and economic consequences of widowhood?

My data from West Bengal suggests that in important ways women do tend to gain more powers and freedoms as they age and become mothers-in-law. As female head of the household—after she gives her sons' marriages, witnesses her own mother-in-law gradually relinquishing authority (or dying), and separates from her husband's brothers' households—a woman can enjoy considerable authority and autonomy. She can make decisions about what to cook and how to spend and allocate money, and can direct the activities of daughters-in-law, her own daily movements, and the like.

Moreover, as I suggested at the end of chapter 6, older women in Mangaldihi tend to regard themselves, and to be regarded by others, increasingly as inherent, true parts of their marital patrilines and households. For this reason, it seems natural that older women often come to uphold and enforce some of the norms and values of kinship hierarchies (such as deference, purdah, etc.) that they might previously, as young wives, have challenged or critiqued. If the family or patriline is *theirs,* then ensuring the compliance of their daughters-in-law or granddaughters ensures their *own* honor, and that of the family that they have come to be invested in, to care about, to be a part of. In addition, prevalent notions about older women's bodies and sexuality enable older women to experience the tremendous freedom and relief that comes with having restrictions of purdah and domestic confinement lifted.

The matter is complex and nuanced, however. Significantly, aging for women does not stop with mother-in-law-hood. Wadley acknowledges this point, though she does not elaborate on it, stating that the woman "from ages forty to sixty" is often a significant authority figure in her household, "after which old age begins to take its toll and daughters-in-law gain power" (1995:99). In Mangaldihi, the women who were considered the most "senior" or "increased" (*buṛi*) were not the reigning mothers-in-law but those who had gradually relinquished their positions of authority in the household to move on to a new phase of life. These women ended up having little overt power in their households.

Yet such a shift was not experienced purely as a loss. Rather, a lessening of domestic powers often meant increased extradomestic opportunities. A woman cannot spend time outside of her home—hanging out all morning with friends playing cards or having tea, or going on pilgrimages and visits to faraway places—if she is the one responsible for managing the household. And Mangaldihi's most senior women often became much more lax about matters surrounding the control and propriety of junior women. Choto Ma, for instance, would gossip to me about the romantic escapades of her granddaughters and grandnieces, saying with a smile that these girls were not really "virgins" (*kumārīs*), but only "half virgins." When I asked her once if she was concerned about all that, she said, still with pleasure, "No. That's a matter for my *boumās* (daughters-in-law) now. They are the ones in charge of the household's women."

Furthermore, women's experiences of old age, and their degrees of power and agency, depended a great extent on—and varied greatly according to—their particular family and economic circumstances. The most important factor was whether or not a woman had sons willing to care for her (see chapters 2 and 3). Also important was a woman's marital status (see chapter 7) and economic circumstances. When listening to older women's own voices and stories about their lives, I was struck that they spoke much more frequently not of power and the reverence given to them by their sons and daughters-in-law, but of peripheralization and weakening, of pouring out love, wealth, and effort to raise their children and serve their families all of their lives and yet failing, in the end, to receive as much as they have given. Some older women, and men, who had markedly little emotional and economic support from their kin, acknowledged at times that at least their utter lack of kin and material comforts would mean that they could hope to face an easier passage into death and rebirth, that the ties of their maya would not be so binding (see chapter 4).

Thus, we see here that aging for women, as for men, is a highly polyvalent and complex phenomenon, charged with ambiguity. It is too simple to claim that the older Indian woman is a "powerful matriarch"; but it would be equally wrong to deny that aging brings most women certain important forms of power, agency, and freedom. This speaks to a more fundamental point, conveyed in different ways throughout the preceding chapters, concerning an underlying ambiguity or multivalence in the conceptual and practical worlds of the Bengalis I knew. Just as the implications of aging for older women and men were not one-dimensional, so too there was no simple definition of what makes a "man" or a "woman," or consistent set of life aims and values, or uniform conception of divinity. The everyday lived worlds of those in Mangaldihi (and, one suspects, of all people) were replete with conflicting features, counterstrivings, ambiguities, and paradoxes. As postmodernist critics of anthropological representations have for some time now insisted, ambiguity is not something to be gotten rid of, even in analytic accounts of human behavior. We as anthropologists must be prepared to entertain the probability, the inevitability even, of contradictions and multivocality in the conceptual and experiential worlds of those we seek to understand.

Margaret Trawick (1990b:37–43, 242–58) suggests that in Indian cultural worlds in particular, ambiguity is an especially salient and even cultivated quality. For Tamils, she writes, this ambiguity is what is known as maya. For Bengalis, too, maya can mean ambiguity, multivalence, or illusion. The most everyday, explicit meaning of maya for Bengalis is affection, attachment, or love; but as we have seen, this affection (for other people, for the body, for a home, for a deity) is fraught with ambivalence and ambiguity. Daughters and daughters-in-law are at once "one's own" and "other." Ties of maya grow in intensity over a long life, and yet it is in late life when they are the most ephemeral. Maya is something that is desired and cultivated; yet it is also one of the six human vices, that which causes pain and confusion. Maya means love and affection, and is something intensely felt; it also means illusion or ambiguity, that which cannot be known. The Bengalis I knew did not seem to view such ambiguities or multivalencies as problematic contradictions that must be resolved, but rather as an inherent part of everyday living in a complex, diverse, and never fully comprehended world. Like many other anthropologists of my generation, I have been concerned with how to reconstruct such views of "culture" that allow for and heed multivocality, ambiguity, contest, and process. Focusing on the divergent perspectives of age—as well as on gender, and on particular people's life experiences—has been one way for me to accomplish this.

At the same time, it is important to look for consensus, dominant forms within cultures, and meaningful generalizations. Jean and John Comaroff have argued that an analysis of the shared practices, symbols, and meanings that make up cultures and hegemonies is a necessary part of understanding even those situations in which the significance of signs and practices is contested (1991:21). On the one hand, they argue, we should take some of the lessons of critical postmodernism very seriously, in particular "the admonition to regard culture not as an *over*determining, closed system of signs but as a set of polyvalent practices, texts, and images that may, at any time, be contested." On the other hand, the Comaroffs insist that it will not do simply to abandon altogether any notion of cultural structure, for we must recognize that "[m]ost people live in a world in which many signs, and often the ones that count the most, look as though they are eternally fixed" (p. 17). Susan Bordo expresses similar concerns about the "taboo on generalization" and "the related contemporary panic over 'essentialism'" (1993:24). To focus *only* on multiple interpretations, "heterogeneity," and "difference" as principles for interpreting culture, history, and texts is to miss important effects of the everyday deployment of mass cultural representations, the ways that dominant forms within cultures and histories do exert force on people, shaping their lives and even their forms of resistance (pp. 24–30, 38–39).

Thus, although I have framed this project in large part as heeding older women's and men's voices to find alternative, even contestatory, perspectives on gender, kinship, and personhood in north India, I take issue with postmodernist positions (e.g., Abu-Lughod 1993)[1] that discard the very possibility of making any meaningful social analyses or generalizations. Not only are we (as anthropologists and scholars of the human condition) drawn to theorize about broader sociocultural forces, such as dominant ideologies, kinship and economic systems, structures of power, and forms of shared cultural identity; mapping these broader forces is also crucial to enabling us to understand *particular people's* lives. To focus exclusively on heterogeneity, difference, contest, and the like blinds us to the fact that there *are* dominant forms that people must contend with within cultures, and that people are fundamentally sociocultural beings.

I have therefore not just examined how, for instance, women at various stages of the life course may critique, resist, or offer divergent perspectives on more dominant kinship and gender ideologies. I have also scrutinized these dominant ideologies, signs, and practices themselves as important for understanding particular women's and men's lives, and the ways that their lives are to some extent shaped and constrained by the cultural circumstances in which they live.

Furthermore, I have wanted to explore and acknowledge the ways in which people often self-consciously represent *themselves* by referring to the shared values, identities, and practices of their "culture." Certainly many of the Bengalis I knew did so—for example, when speaking about the kinds of "Bengali" family moral systems that in many ways defined aging, gender, and kinship for them (see chapters 2 and 3), or about the meanings that maya has in their "Bengali" lives (see especially chapter 4). People seem to engage in such processes of self-representation particularly when confronted—via colonialism, the globalization of media and the economy, migration, the anthropological cross-cultural encounter—with the cultural and political-economic representations of others. Scholars such as Partha Chatterjee (1993, 1997), Pradip Bose (1995), and others have scrutinized the ways that the elite middle class, during Bengal's period of countercolonial nationalism, strove to fabricate and uphold what they envisioned to be their "own" cultural-moral order—lodged in the family, in women, in religion, in "tradition." The project of defining and negotiating a "Bengali" culture, for those living in rural villages such as Mangaldihi, may *perhaps* be more subtle than it was for late-nineteenth- and early-twentieth-century middle-class nationalists; but it is still going on. And that is just what we should expect, in a multiethnic, postcolonial, and increasingly globalized rural Bengal.

I have taken "culture" here, then, to be partially systematic yet also open-ended; to be coherent, and yet ambiguous; to be power-laden, and yet susceptible to resistance; to be made up of shared meanings, signs, and practices, and yet to be replete as well with divergent perspectives and contests.

Throughout these pages I have sought to use whenever possible the words, stories, categories, and comments of my friends in Mangaldihi, endeavoring to present their lives in a way congruent with their own perceptions. I know, however, that I cannot fully share nor replicate others' visions, and that the kinds of questions I am asking of the lives of Mangaldihi's residents were often strikingly different from the kinds of questions they were seeking to answer about themselves, about their own human lives in the world, and about me. Anthropological knowledge is always something produced in human interaction, a two-way process of constructing a particular vision of a certain set of cultural experiences and practices—a process that leaves both parties changed.

As Nancy Scheper-Hughes (1992:xii) observes, the anthropological "field" behind every ethnography is "a place both proximate and intimate (because we have lived some part of our lives there) as well as forever distant and unknowably 'other' (because our own destinies lie elsewhere)." Any act of "writing culture" is therefore necessarily partial, fragmentary, and biased. But at the same time, ethnography is a deeply felt account of real people's lives—based on seeing, listening, touching, recording, and sharing experience. And such an account is what I have attempted in these pages, striving to interpret as sensitively as possible a part of the lives of those with whom I lived for some eighteen (very vivid) months amid the dusty lanes and verdant rice fields of the village of Mangaldihi.

Notes

INTRODUCTION

1. The few studies of aging include Biswas (1987); Cohen (1992, 1995, 1998); Hiebert (1981); Roy (1992 [1972]:125–48); and S. Vatuk (1975, 1980, 1987, 1990, 1992, 1995).

2. See Abu-Lughod 1991, 1993; Brightman 1995; Clifford 1986, 1988; E. V. Daniel 1996; Knauft 1996; Raheja and Gold 1994:1–29; and R. Rosaldo 1989.

3. See George Stocking (1976) for an incisive look at the growing systematicity of the culture concept during the interwar period (1921–45). David Schneider (1968, 1976) provides a particularly vivid example of the systematicity and internal coherence of culture during a somewhat later period of American cultural anthropology, asserting, for instance: "A culture is a total system; it does not have loose ends and unintegrated pieces and parts that do not articulate with other parts. It holds together as a meaningful system" (1976:219).

4. Critics of modernist approaches include Abu-Lughod (1991, 1993:6–15) and Said (1978). Appadurai (1992:35–36) has characterized this traditional vision of culture as a "mode of thought" that "incarcerates" the native in a fixed "way of thinking that admits no fuzzy boundaries and is splendid in its internal consistency" (cf. Raheja and Gold 1994:2).

5. On the increasingly fluid boundaries of culture, see Appadurai 1996; Gupta and Ferguson 1997; Hannerz 1993, 1997; and Kearney 1995.

6. Postmodern analyses of women form a vast literature, but some important works include Haraway (1990), Minh-ha (1989), Mohanty (1991), Moore (1994), Ortner (1996), Riley (1988), Joan Scott (1988), and Spelman (1988).

7. Works critical of early feminist anthropology include Haraway (1990), hooks (1984), Mohanty (1991), Ortner (1996), Rich (1986), Joan Scott (1988), and Spelman (1988).

8. Notable exceptions to the lack of interest in older women include S. Vatuk (1975, 1987, 1992, 1995), Marriott (1998), Roy (1992 [1972]:125–148), and Wadley (1994:25–29, 1995:98–99). Menon and Shweder (1998) consider Oriya

Hindu women's "mature adulthood" (what we might term "middle age"), or *prauda.*

9. On purdah, sexuality, etc., see, e.g., Bennett 1983; Dube 1988; Fruzzetti 1982; Jeffery, Jeffery, and Lyon 1989; and Papanek and Minault 1982.

10. I am struck by how often media reports and popular discussions (in Calcutta, Mangaldihi, and the United States) on the recent intensification of dowry (or bride) burnings in India claim without evidence that the mother-in-law is primarily responsible for the murders. If true (and more research on the question is needed), it is hard to believe that she was acting alone. For more on dowry burnings, see Ghadially and Kumar 1988; Grover 1990; Kumari 1989; Nandy 1995; Stone and James 1997; and van Willigen and Channa 1991.

11. For edited volumes exploring aging, see Amoss and Harrell 1981; Fry 1980, 1981; Kerns and Brown 1992; Kertzer and Keith 1984; Myerhoff 1992; Myerhoff and Simic 1978; and Sokolovsky 1989. For book-length works, see Cohen 1998; Counts and Counts 1996; Hazan 1994; Kaufman 1986; Keith 1977; Lock 1993; Myerhoff 1979; Plath 1980; Rasmussen 1997; and Vesperi 1985. For reviews of much of this material, see Cohen 1994 and Keith 1980. For a related edited volume on *middle* age, see Shweder 1998.

12. Exceptions to the tendency to compartmentalize studies of the old are most common in research on societies where age stratification is a highly marked dimension of social organization. Anthropologists studying such societies in Africa and central Brazil have often brought analyses of age to a societal level (see, e.g., Maybury-Lewis 1979; La Fontaine 1978; Spencer 1976; T. Turner 1979; M. Wilson 1963). Hugh-Jones (1988) also attempts to integrate her analysis of the full life cycle with analyses of other domains of sociocultural life.

13. The arguments emphasizing the specifically female body are quite varied; see, e.g., Braidotti 1991; Cixous 1981; Gallop 1988; Kristeva 1980; Rich 1976; and Suleiman 1986. For discussions of this kind of argument, see Moore (1994, esp. pp. 17–21) and Nicholson (1994).

14. On the body as gendered, see, e.g., Butler 1990, 1993; Nicholson 1994; and Joan Scott 1988, 1993.

15. Henrietta Moore's observations (1994:33) are relevant here: "The idea of persons as divisible, partible and unbounded has now gained a certain acceptance in the discipline (see, for example, Marriott, 1976, and Strathern, 1988), but there is still considerable resistance to any suggestion that the body might not be the source of identity, or that experience (both of self and of the world) is not always possessed by or located in an interior self."

16. On our thinking on the relationship between body, sex, and gender, see Foucault 1980a, 1980b; Lacqueur 1990; and Nicholson 1994.

17. On gender identities over the course of one's life, see, e.g., Gutmann 1964, 1992; Hawkes, O'Connell, and Jones 1997; Kerns and Brown 1992; Poole 1981; Rasmussen 1987; and S. Vatuk 1975, 1987, 1992.

18. On negative changes in the female body, see, e.g., Beyene 1989:124; Boddy 1992; Chapkis 1986; Copper 1986; Healey 1986; and Kaufert and Lock 1992.

19. Some biological anthropologists have begun to attempt to incorporate

postmenopause into *evolutionary* theories. Thus recent work by Hawkes, O'Connell, and Jones (1989, 1997), based on a study of the Hadza hunters and gatherers of northern Tanzania, suggests that postmenopausal women are stronger and are able to work harder than almost all others in the community, as they gather food and wood and care for grandchildren. Hawkes, O'Connell, and Jones hypothesize that there may be an evolutionary advantage to menopause, which ensures that women live long enough to help their children bear and support children (cf. R. Alexander 1974; Gaulin 1980; Lancaster and King 1992; P. Mayer 1982). This perspective marks a break from that of other evolutionary theories, which have often presented menopause as a puzzling anomaly: why would women live beyond their reproductive years, when they have ostensibly completed their service to the species?

20. For a similar look at menopause and hormone replacement therapy in Australia, see Klein and Dumble 1994.

21. See Lamb 1993:34–53 for a more detailed account of Mangaldihi's history, political economy, and social structure.

22. In 1953, the West Bengal state government passed an estates acquisition act that aimed to abolish the *zamindari* system of large revenue-collecting landowners and to redistribute land to the landless (Basu and Bhattacharya 1963). The Bargadars Act of 1950, and more recent reforms in the late 1970s, also imparted rights to landless *bargādārs*, or sharecroppers who cultivate the land of others. Because of these reforms, Brahmans in Mangaldihi commonly state with some chagrin that the "age (*yuga*) of the Brahmans" has passed. Many of the village's lower-caste families do see themselves as better off than their forebears, although most have not come near to gaining the kind of economic security that upper-caste families in the region generally enjoy.

23. In fact, there were more households of Bagdis than Brahmans (table 1). But Brahman and other higher-caste families in Mangaldihi tended to maintain larger households (remaining more often "joint") than did lower-status and landless families. For these reasons, my census figures indicate that counted individually, Brahmans slightly outnumbered Bagdis. "Scheduled" is an official government classification of disadvantaged castes and tribes.

24. Teng (1996:143–44) makes this same point regarding the equation of "gender" with "women" in gender studies in the East Asian field.

CHAPTER 1. PERSONHOODS

1. Dipesh Chakrabarty (1996) has written an elegant essay examining Hindu-Bengali nostalgia for "the village," in the aftermath of the 1947 partition of West Bengal from East Bengal, when East Bengal became East Pakistan (in 1971, this same territory became Bangladesh).

2. On South Asian notions of person or self, see, e.g., E. V. Daniel 1984; Dumont 1980a; Ewing 1990, 1991; Lamb 1997b; Marriott 1976, 1990; Marriott and Inden 1977; McHugh 1989; M. Mines 1988, 1994; Ostor, Fruzzetti, and Barnett 1982; Parish 1994; Parry 1989; Roland 1988; and Shweder and Bourne 1984.

3. I write about "impurity" here at some length, partly because the topic has received so much attention in the anthropological literature on India and partly because it at first seemed to me so important to the local constitution of open persons and intersubstantial social relations. However, I gradually learned that social relations for Bengalis do not by any means center on avoiding impurity.

4. Spiro (1993) discusses these South Asianists particularly on pp. 115, 123–27, 132, where he concentrates on Shweder and Bourne's (1984) notion of a "sociocentric" self.

5. Spiro supports his argument on self-other differentiation by drawing on James (1981 [1890]) and Hallowell (1955).

6. On shared karma, see Wadley and Derr 1990 and S. Daniel 1983:28–35.

7. For a detailed examination of how diverse theories of karma are used simultaneously by Tamil villagers, see S. Daniel 1983.

8. On de-emphasizing individuality in South Asia, see, e.g., Marriott 1976, 1990; E. V. Daniel 1984; Dumont 1980a:185, 231–39, and passim; and Shweder and Bourne 1984. Note that "individuality" is a polysemous term whose implications differ among these scholars.

9. For examples emphasizing the South Asian "individual," see McHugh 1989; M. Mines 1988, 1994; M. Mines and Gourishankar 1990; and Parish 1994:127–29, 186–87. Marriott's position is also more complex, variable, and nuanced than simply holding Hindu persons to be "unbounded." Much of his work is devoted to what he sees as strenuous Hindu efforts toward closing boundaries (cooling oneself, minimizing interactions, "unmixing," etc.).

10. Much of the confusion surrounding the cross-cultural study of personhood stems from a lack of specificity about what is meant by terms such as "person" and "self." "Self" often implies what we might consider to be a psychological entity, such as an ego or a subjective experience of one's own being. I therefore prefer to use the broader, more open term "person." Beliefs about what it is to be a person in any cultural-historical setting might include notions and practices concerning some or all of the following: a subjective sense of self; a soul or spirit; the body; the mind; emotions; agency; gender or sex; race, ethnicity, or caste; relationships with other people, places, or things; a relationship with divinity; illness and well-being; power; karma or fate (perhaps ingrained in or written on the body or soul in some way); and the like. Our task as anthropologists studying personhood is to investigate what defines being a person, or being human, for the people we are striving to understand. For other discussions of what anthropologists mean by the terms "person" and "self," see Harris 1989; Lindholm 1997; Pollock 1996; and Whittaker 1992.

CHAPTER 2. FAMILY MORAL SYSTEMS

1. Susan Bordo (1993) also makes a strong argument against the "absolute heterogeneity of culture." She argues that a sole focus on heterogeneity blinds us to the fact that there *are* dominant, strongly "normalizing" forms people must contend with within cultures: "To struggle effectively against the coer-

civeness of those forms it is first necessary to recognize that they *have* dominance, and not to efface such recognition through a facile and abstract celebration of 'heterogeneity,' 'difference,' 'subversive reading,' and so forth" (pp. 29–30). E. V. Daniel (1996:361–62), too, discusses the interplay between consensus and contestation in cultural analysis. I explore these points a bit further in the afterword.

2. Both *buṛo* and *bṛiddha,* which are commonly translated into English as "senior" or "old," come from the same root: *bṛ,* meaning "to grow" or "to increase."

3. The significance of older women's white clothing will be discussed further in chapters 4, 6, and 7.

4. For accounts of the *āśrama dharma* schema in the *dharmaśāstras,* see Kane (1968–75:vol. 2) and Manu (1886, 1991).

5. In the *dharmaśāstra* texts, the *āśrama dharma* schema specifically applies only to an upper-caste man's life. Manu devotes little attention to defining the appropriate stages of a woman's life, which are determined by her relationships to the men on whom she depends for support and guidance—her father, her husband, and finally her sons (*The Laws of Manu* V.148, Manu 1886:195, 1991:115).

6. The category of debt has a complex genealogy in South Asian studies. Malamoud (1983) and Dumont (1983) examine the theology of debt in Hindu textual traditions, while Hardiman's analysis (1996) is part of his study of the quality of power that usurers have exercised over subaltern classes during the past several centuries in rural India. I look here at local understandings of debt as a means of binding family members across generations.

7. In chapter 6 I discuss reproductive processes in more detail. The man is said to provide the "seed" (*bīj* or *śukra*), which is the ultimate source of the body, but the woman as the "field" (*kshetra*) also contributes to the body by nourishing it with her uterine blood.

8. The Bengali term for "child" (*chele*) is also that for "son." Here, Gurusaday Mukherjee may have been expressing the duty of children in general to care for their aged parents, but it is also likely that he intended to foreground sons; for as this chapter goes on to show, it is primarily sons (and daughters-in-law) rather than daughters who are obligated to care for their parents in late life.

9. In fact, the obligation to beget children, particularly sons, is viewed in Hindu texts as one of the three "debts" (*ṛṇas*) that upper-caste or "twice-born" sons owe their parents, ancestors, and gods; the other two are studying the *veda,* or religious knowledge, and performing ritual sacrifices (e.g., see Dumont 1983). Only one person in Mangaldihi, however, a man who saw himself as a religious scholar, specifically spoke to me of these three debts.

10. As I discuss in chapter 6, a married daughter does in many ways become "other" (*par*) to her mother and natal kin. When a mother wipes her daughter's feet with hair, she simply lessens the severity of the cut between them.

11. Bengalis most commonly define *kuṭumb* as a class of relatives related by

marriage, although the category does not match that of American relatives "by marriage," or "in-laws." Persons who are classified as *kuṭumbs* include married daughters and sisters. Some people whom Americans would consider related by marriage, such as a husband and wife, or a married women and her husband's parents, are for Bengalis not *kuṭumbs* but rather *nijer lok* (own people). See Inden and Nicholas (1977:15–17) as well as chapter 6 for further discussion of such relationships.

12. Note here Saraswati's use of two different terms to refer to divinity. *Bhagavān* is usually translated as "God" and refers to deity in an unspecified, formless sense. *Ṭhākur* also means "lord" or "god," but usually refers to a specific manifestation of a deity within a visible form or *mūrti,* such as the visible images established within temples. Senior people are most often referred to as *ṭhākurs,* visible gods, rather than as *bhagavān,* a formless God.

13. These days, however, in keeping with growing sensitivities about class and caste hierarchies in West Bengal (which are due partly to the strong influence of the Communist Party), people rarely speak of "serving" their employers; instead, they "work for" them. Likewise, the common terms for "servant" (*jhi* for a female and *cākar* for a male) are used only rarely now; they are generally replaced with the more neutral "work person," *kājer lok.*

CHAPTER 3. CONFLICTING GENERATIONS

1. Davis (1983:129–30) explores this relationship as *sasuri-bou ma jhogra:* that is, rivalry (*jhogra*) between mother-in-law and daughter-in-law.

2. A more literal translation of "*Pāye paṛa uṭh putu!*" would be "Falling at your feet [I implore you], get up little boy!"

3. This story is also told and discussed in Lamb 1997a:60–72.

4. See also Lamb 1999 for a discussion of widows, caste, and property in Mangaldihi.

5. Cohen's Varanasi and Vatuk's New Delhi informants also tie money to good treatment in old age (Cohen 1998:241; S. Vatuk 1990:78–80).

6. Inden and Nicholas (1977:5) note that a *baṃśa* in its purest form *excludes* inmarrying wives and outmarrying daughters. In Mangaldihi, however, people explicitly stated that a wife comes to share her husband's and father-in-law's *baṃśa* through marriage, and that a daughter is part of her father's *baṃśa* until she is married.

7. For magazine and newspaper articles on aging, see M. Jain and Menon, "The Greying of India" (1991); Ravindranath, "*Sans* Everything . . . But Not *Sans* Rights" (1997); Satish, "The Old People . . . a Headache?" (1990); and the 7 January 1983 issue of *Femina,* which declared its theme: "Old Age: Are We Heading the Way of the West?" Gerontological books include Bhatia (1983); Biswas (1987); A. Bose and Gangrade (1988); Desai (1982); de Souza (1981); de Souza and Fernandes (1982); Pathak (1975); Pati and Jena (1989); M. Sharma and Dak (1987); and Soodan (1975). S. Vatuk (1991) and Cohen (1992, 1998) review and discuss much of this work.

8. See Mrinalini Sinha's *Colonial Masculinity: The "Manly Englishman" and the "Effeminate Bengali" in the Late Nineteenth Century* (1995) for a related discussion of "modern" Western masculinity and colonial domination.

9. Note that even when elderly parents were left behind in the village while junior family members moved off to a city to work, the family members involved often considered themselves to be part of one household, because they pooled many of their resources and made many important decisions jointly. Epstein (1973:207) has labeled this kind of family arrangement a "share family," and she suggests that it emerges particularly when families combine urban wage earning with rural farming.

10. On the gendering of anticolonial nationalist discourse, see in particular P. Chatterjee 1989, 1990, 1993.

11. See Banerjee 1989 for a more detailed discussion of Bengali *paṭ* scrolls and narratives during the nineteenth and early twentieth centuries.

12. New brides are generally expected to go to their husbands' homes with a *ghomṭā,* or part of the sari, pulled over their heads, to demonstrate modesty and deference.

13. Conch shell bracelets and vermilion worn in the part of the hair are the signs of a married woman whose husband is alive.

14. Laksmi is the goddess of wealth and prosperity.

15. That is, people are being forced to eat wheat instead of rice, the preferred Bengali staple.

16. In chapter 6, I discuss the implications of older women's dress, and the significance of the acceptability of their publicly exposing much of their bodies, including their breasts.

17. Such "purchases" are still performed today. If parents have lost one or several previous children, they often have a low-caste woman "buy" their new infant from them with something almost worthless, like a broken piece of puffed rice, or a three-cent coin. By calling attention to the child's purported worthlessness, the transaction helps divert the evil eye (*najar*) or jealousy (*hiṃsā*) that can bring harm to the child. (For studies of the evil eye in rural South Asia, see Maloney 1976 and Pocock 1981.)

CHAPTER 4. WHITE SARIS AND SWEET MANGOES, PARTINGS AND TIES

1. On the meanings of maya in Nepali, see Bennett 1983:39 and Parish 1994:156–64.

2. Anthropologists might find such a theory of maya as emotional-cum-bodily ties useful in addressing their growing number of questions on emotions and the relationship between emotions and the body (see, e.g., Desjarlais 1992; Lynch 1990a, 1990b:13–19; Lutz 1988).

3. Trawick (1990a:47) writes similarly of *pacam,* affection, within her Tamil family: "*Pacam,* the bond of affection, was cruel . . . because when the bond was broken, as always it had to be, the newly unbound person suffered pain. When

you become habituated to something, it becomes part of you, and, when you lose it, part of yourself is severed."

4. On the value of renunciation in late life, see, e.g., Kane 1968–75:vol. 2; Manu VI (1886:198–216, 1991:117–27); Dumont 1980b [1960]; and Tilak 1989:41–40.

5. Initially I assumed that senior relatives necessarily decrease. But such an interpretation may not be accurate, for maya can be felt quite strongly for deceased kin (see chapter 5).

6. Gold (1988:63–79) examines such lingering spirits of the dead in Rajasthan; many are said to be clinging to their previous habitations.

7. Other people sometimes referred to the body as the *ātmā*'s or soul's "house" (*ghar*), saying that the *ātmā* has a lot of maya for the body and does not want to leave it. In this conversation, Mita's Ma and her daughter seem to be speaking literally of the deceased person's house (*ghar*), as something the *ātmā* wishes, but does not know how, to reenter.

8. Gold (1988:234) similarly finds that villagers in Rajasthan most commonly define *moksha* not as absolute release from all births and deaths but rather as "liberation from the state of hovering, malevolent, and disembodied ghosthood," or as "departure from the scenes of one's previous life to dwell in 'heaven' (*svarg*)," in the process of moving on eventually to take a new, preferably human, birth.

9. See also chapter 2; Lamb 1997a; and S. Vatuk 1990:78–81.

10. Their discourse parallels the physiology of aging as described in the classical medical texts of Ayurveda, in which young adulthood is characterized by a surfeit of the humor *pitta* (hot bile), with an increase of the humor *vāta* (cool, dry wind) as one's years increase (Purohit 1955:191; Ray, Gupta, and Roy 1980:16, 44; Tilak 1989:71).

11. A *baiṣṇab mālā* is a necklace made of wooden *tulsī* beads that some devotees of Krishna wear.

12. I follow Eck (1981:344) and Gold (1989:4) in translating *tīrtha* as "crossing place": places where branches of rivers, the land and the sea, and gods and humans converge or cross over into each other. *Tīrtha* can also be translated as "pilgrimage."

13. A more detailed account of a Hindu bus pilgrimage can be found in Gold (1988:262–98). Although she describes a pilgrimage from Rajasthan to Puri, I found many similar features in the shorter pilgrimage I took from West Bengal to Puri.

14. I address in chapter 3 why women so overwhelmingly outnumber men in old age homes. Cohen (1998:116–20) also discusses the Navanir homes for the aged.

15. Earning interest from a loan is commonly called "eating" interest (*śodh khāoyāno*).

16. Sylvia Vatuk also notes that in the community she studied outside of Delhi, old people risk criticism or ridicule if they display undue concern over

the food offered to them, "because this suggests lingering attachment to another sensual enjoyment" (1990:75).

17. For scholarly analyses of the four life stages, see, e.g., Das 1979:101–2, 1982; Dumont 1980b [1960]; Heesterman 1985:26–44, 1988; and Tilak 1989. For discussions of the various ways Indians think about the *āśrama dharma* theory of life stages in relation to the course of their own lives, see also Hiebert 1981; Kakar 1979; and S. Vatuk 1980, 1990, 1992.

18. See Das 1979:101–2; Doniger O'Flaherty 1973:78; Dumont 1980b [1960]:274; Heesterman 1988:251–52; and Tilak 1989.

19. For fuller treatment of the disengagement theory of aging, see also Cumming 1964; Havighurst, Neugarten, and Tobin 1968; and Maddox 1964. S. Vatuk (1980) and Tilak (1989:3, 160) provide interesting discussions of this "American" hypothesis in the context of Indian cultural traditions.

20. Kaufman proposes that it is "old" people themselves in America who refuse to define themselves as old (hence her title, *The Ageless Self*), arguing that "Contrary to popular conceptions of old age, which tend to define it as a distinct period of life, old people themselves emphasize the continuity of the ageless self amid changes across the life span" (1986:13). Gullette (1997), too, rejects the American master narrative of *decline* in middle age, but *not* in order to hold up what I see as the alternative dominant American narrative of adulthood—permanence, agelessness. Instead, Gullette is advocating a set of wide-open possibilities for envisioning and practicing our later lives, possibilities that *could* but need not entail either decline or permanence.

21. On the "individualism" of Americans, see, e.g., Dumont 1985; Geertz 1983:59; MacFarlane 1978; and Tocqueville 1945 [1835].

CHAPTER 5. DEALING WITH MORTALITY

1. On Hindu funeral rituals, see, e.g., Das 1982:120–31, 1986; Gold 1988: 59–132; Inden and Nicholas 1977:62–66; Kane 1968–75; Kaushik 1976; Knipe 1977; Madan 1987:118–41; D. Mines 1990; Nicholas 1988; Orenstein 1970; Parry 1980, 1982, 1985, 1988, 1989, 1994; Raheja 1988:147–62; Stevenson 1971 [1920]; and Stone 1988.

2. Several exceptions to this generalization have taken a broader view of death: S. Vatuk (1990:83) briefly examines the attitudes toward death of older Indians in the suburbs of Delhi. Justice (1997) explores experiences of dying, among pilgrims and their families, at the holy city of Varanasi. Cohen (1998), in his discussions of the "dying space," Gold (1988), and Madan (1987) also consider how Indians think about and plan for their own or others' deaths. Das (1990) presents a moving analysis of experiences of bereavement in the aftermath of the riots that followed the 1984 assassination of Indira Gandhi in Delhi.

3. For a few examples of anthropological studies that approach death through mortuary rituals, see Bloch and Parry's *Death and the Regeneration of Life* (1982), an edited volume "focus[ing] on the significance of symbols of fertility

and rebirth in funeral rituals" (p. 1); Douglas's *Death in Murelaga: Funerary Ritual in a Spanish Basque Village* (1969); Huntington and Metcalf's *Celebrations of Death: The Anthropology of Mortuary Ritual* (1979); Metcalf's *Borneo Journey into Death: Berawan Eschatology from Its Rituals* (1982); and Parry's *Death in Banaras* (1994). On anthropological studies of death published in the 1960s, see Fabian (1973:178), who remarks that most studies "dealt only with the purely ceremonial aspects of death" (cited in R. Rosaldo 1989:227–28 n. 21).

4. S. Vatuk (1990:67,83) describes similar sentiments.

5. Despite Khudi Thakrun's frequent predictions of her death, she was still alive when I left Mangaldihi. In June 1991 I received a letter from her eldest son, Gurusaday, reporting that his mother had died a quiet and easy death at the age of ninety-eight, just a few days after the assassination of Rajiv Gandhi.

6. Although I heard this specific analogy of life as a thorn in the body only once, I think the image well conveys the common sentiment that life, or the soul, is deeply embedded in the body due to maya, and that it cannot depart without significant pain or difficulty.

7. That is, upper-caste and wealthier families in Mangaldihi did not usually perform cremations in the village. Those with sufficient means preferred to take their deceased to holy crossing places (*tīrthasthāns*) like Bakresbar, a site for Siva worship near Mangaldihi, or to Udanpur on the shores of the Ganges river.

8. For general descriptions of Hindu funeral rites, see, e.g., Das 1986; Gold 1988:79–99; Kaushik 1976; Parry 1980, 1982, 1985, 1988, 1989, 1994:151–225; Srinivas 1952; and Stevenson 1971 [1920].

9. See chapters 6 and 7 for more on the significance of the auspicious red *sindūr* and *āltā* worn by married women and forbidden to widows.

10. *Go* is an untranslatable term of affection used in addressing a person close to one, such as a mother or wife.

11. On the earth as pure, see Gold 1988:81; Kane 1968–75:4.182; Kaushik 1976:270; and Stevenson 1971 [1920]:142.

12. Perhaps villagers see the ground as transformative because of the earth's capacity to process and revitalize dead, decaying, and polluting matter, as Marriott suggested in a personal communication to Gold (Gold 1988:81 n. 23).

13. Parry (1982, 1994:158) further compares the dying person to a "sacrifier," who offers his or her own self or person to the gods. In this respect, the dying must make him- or herself a worthy sacrificial object free of impurities and work to *voluntarily* relinquish life.

14. Das (1982:121–22) and Parry (1994:179) discuss the corpse before cremation as pure and auspicious, thus requiring circumambulation in the auspicious clockwise direction. After the body has been laid on the cremation pyre, it becomes inauspicious and is circumambulated in a counterclockwise and separative direction.

15. No one seemed to mind, however, that I went along to observe several cremations. In fact, on several occasions the group of male mourners asked me to accompany them. They explained, "There's no reason why women *can't* go

to the cremation ground; it's just that they don't go." Parry's informants gave the reason that women do not accompany corpses to the cremation ground as their being "too faint hearted" (1994:152).

16. See also Kaushik (1976:271) and Das (1982:122), who write of offering *piṇḍas* on the way to the cremation ground as a means of feeding and appeasing ghosts or disembodied spirits. Raheja (1988:148) sees leaving these *piṇḍas* outside the village boundaries as a means of transferring the inauspiciousness created by death to the space outside the village and to the animals who may eat them there.

17. Gold (1988) provides an elaborate account of ways that Rajasthani villagers gather and sink bones (euphemistically called "flowers," or *phūl*) in holy waters after cremation.

18. Justice (1997:172) and Parry (1994:21, 26–30; 1988) describe the powers of India's greatest crossing place, Varanasi or Kashi, to bring release to anyone who dies or is cremated there.

19. *Aśauc* is commonly glossed by Indologists as "impure." But this form of impurity, incurred by related persons at both death and birth, is distinct from the everyday "impurities" (such as that incurred by touching leftover food, defecating, menstruating, etc.) most commonly referred to as *aśuddha* (also "not pure"). To avoid confusing these two forms of impurity, I have chosen to gloss *aśauc* as "death-separation impurity." D. Mines (1990) alternatively calls *aśauc* "incapacity," noting that it makes the survivors temporarily incapable of transacting with other persons.

20. On variations in periods of death impurity, see D. Mines 1990; Nicholas 1988; Orenstein 1970; and Parry 1994:218–22.

21. Bengalis have no single term "wetness" to refer to the category into which certain foods seem to fall. Instead, they were classified as those to be avoided if a *dry* (*śukna*) bodily state was to be created. It is these "nondry" foods (the most important of which is boiled rice, *bhāt*) that I refer to here as "wet."

22. McKim Marriott (personal communication, April 1992) suggests possible reasons for avoiding salt: it stimulates wetness, saliva; it is classified as a bile (*pitta*)-stimulating "hot" flavor in Ayurveda; and it is essential to a basic diet—and the food that makes up such a diet is used to seal alliances. In one of his three-dimensional diagrams, "Flavors (*rasas*) of the Ayurvedic year," Marriott puts salt in the same "high," "hot," "central" corner where the head of the house sits (1994:facing p. 6). Mangaldihians said that sea salt or *sindhuk nun* may be substituted for ordinary salt, for it is considered to be a pure (*śuddha*) and not an *āmiṣ* food, perhaps because it does not require human processing. Parry notes: "No salt should be added to the food which [the chief mourner] eats for the *pret*. To accept someone's salt is to accept that one is bound to them" (1994:218).

23. Some of Parry's informants similarly describe the purpose of death impurity as "a demonstration of sorrow" (1994:218).

24. On death impurity, see, e.g., Das 1982:120–31; Dumont and Pocock 1959; Kaushik 1976; D. Mines 1990; Nicholas 1988; Orenstein 1970; Parry 1982, 1994:181–84, 215–22; and Srinivas 1952.

25. On making a body for the departed via *piṇḍas*, see also Knipe 1977:114–15; Nicholas 1988:377–78; and Parry 1982:84–86.

26. Das (1982:127) also analyzes, somewhat differently, the symbolism of hair and nails in rituals of death.

27. The *agradānī* Brahman stands in a rather unenviable relationship to the deceased, as a kind of living receptacle of gifts intended for the dead person. That is why, my informants explained, the *agradānī* is thought to be a "lower" and rather embarrassing form of Brahman. The need for a special *agradānī* Brahman may also have something to do with his ingesting of sins (Parry 1980) and his receipt of the inauspiciousness (Raheja 1988:154–62) generated by a death.

28. Inden and Nicholas (1977:63–64) also describe the *piṇḍa dān*.

29. On the *sapiṇḍi-karāna*, see, e.g., Das 1982:122; Doniger O'Flaherty 1980; Gold 1988:90–94; Inden and Nicholas 1977:64; Knipe 1977; Nicholas 1988:375–76; and Parry 1982:84–85, 1994:204–6.

30. If a son were to predecease his father, his *piṇḍa* would be merged with his paternal grandfather (if deceased) and paternal great-grandfather only. In the case of an unmarried girl, no *sapiṇḍi-karāna* ritual would be performed. Parry's informants note that the spirit of an unmarried girl, who has no descent line, simply "disappears into the air" (1994:205).

31. Rites honoring ancestors were performed not only at funerals but on auspicious occasions such as weddings, as well as during other life cycle rites. A *śrāddha* performed on an auspicious occasion was called a *nāndīmukh*.

32. In chapter 6, I discuss further the representation, common throughout north India, of a wife as the "half body" (*ardhānginī*) of her husband.

CHAPTER 6. TRANSFORMATIONS OF GENDER AND GENDERED TRANSFORMATIONS

1. Marglin (1996) also demonstrates that the significance of menstruation does not lie solely in its impurity (see also Marglin and Mishra 1993; Marglin and Simon 1994). See further discussion later in this chapter.

2. For more detailed discussions of practices surrounding menstruation in South Asia, see Bennett 1983:215–18; Leslie 1989:283–84; Marglin 1985c:63, 1996:159–73; Marglin and Mishra 1993; Marglin and Simon 1994; and Thompson 1985:702–4.

3. As I explained in chapter 5 (and as D. Mines 1990 discusses), *aśuddha* and *aśauc* are recognized by Bengalis and other Indians as distinct conditions, although both terms are conventionally glossed by Indologists as "impure." *Aśuddha* refers to the kinds of everyday impurities focused on in this chapter, stemming from contact with feces, unwashed clothing, slept-in beds, low-caste people, non-Hindus, menstrual blood, afterbirth, corpses, etc.—mostly having to do with excessive, messy, or inappropriate mixings. *Aśauc* refers instead to a specific ritual period of what I have termed "separation impurity" that family members experience after a birth or death (see chapter 5). For more on the struc-

tural similarity of death and birth impurity, see Das 1982:128; Inden and Nicholas 1977:102–7; D. Mines 1990; and Nicholas 1988.

4. Hindus in Mangaldihi commonly use the example of "touching a Muslim" to describe how people become impure (*aśuddha*). Although Mangaldihi is a predominantly Hindu village, it is surrounded by smaller Muslim villages, and the Hindus there are especially concerned with preserving their separateness.

5. As in English, the Bengali term for "man" (*mānuṣ*) can refer either to males in particular or to humankind in general.

6. For other accounts of female (compared to male) sexuality in South Asia, see Jeffery, Jeffery, and Lyon 1989:24–25; Marglin 1985c:58, McGilvray 1982:31; and S. Vatuk 1992:160.

7. For similar perspectives on male sexuality, see Bottero 1991; Carstairs 1967; Jeffery, Jeffery, and Lyon 1989:24; Maloney, Aziz, and Sarker 1981:134–40; and McGilvray 1982.

8. Samanta (1992) provides a rich, in-depth discussion of the auspiciousness of sexuality, fertility, and the color red for Bengali married women (*sumaṅgalī*).

9. For views of the "seed" and "land" theory of procreation, and its implications for adultery, see E. V. Daniel 1984:163–70; Doniger [O'Flaherty] 1994; Fruzzetti 1982:121; Fruzzetti and Ostor 1984; Inden and Nicholas 1977:52; and Maloney, Aziz, and Sarker 1981.

10. For a nuanced interpretation of the use of veils in Rajasthan, see Raheja and Gold's discussion (1994:47–52) of the imagery of wraps in local women's songs, where they enhance and subtly reveal a woman's charms, rather than simply cutting off male gazes.

11. In some parts of Bengal, women must keep their hair *un*bound (*kholā*) during menstruation (Ralph Nicholas, personal letter, 29 August 1989). This practice, like binding the hair, may also reflect the open nature of menstruating women; but it appears to signify that state rather than bind or control it.

12. On purdah, see Jacobson 1982; Mehta 1981; Papanek and Minault 1982; and Raheja and Gold 1994:47–52, 168–81.

13. For examples of scholarship portraying acceptance of the dangerousness of female sexuality, see Bennett 1983; Jeffery, Jeffery, and Lyon 1989; and Kakar 1990:17–20. For critiques of these kinds of ethnographic representations, see Raheja and Gold 1994:9–14 and passim.

14. On strategic submission, see also Bourdieu 1977:164–65, and Raheja and Gold 1994:11, xxiii, xxix.

15. Of course, my primary reasons for going on the pilgrimage were not spiritual, so her reasoning might not absolve me. But, I told myself, I was not allowed into the inner part of most of the temples in any case, because of my non-Hindu status. So I also had my own ways of rationalizing my menstruating presence.

16. For recent work on the significance of menopause in various cultures, see Beyene 1989; Lock 1982, 1986a, 1986b, 1993; and E. Martin 1987:27–53, 166–78. For other work on menopause and South Asian women, see Cohen 1998:208–9; du Toit 1990; Flint 1975; George 1988; and V. Sharma and Saxena 1981.

17. Upper-caste widows in this region, like Mejo Ma herself, avoided eating "hot" (*garam*), nonvegetarian (*āmiṣ*) foods (see chapter 7).

18. In Mangaldihi, the dominant deities—forms of Krishna—were vegetarian. Some of the other favorite deities in Mangaldihi and the surrounding region, however, such as the goddesses Kali and Durga, were not; they were periodically served sacrificial goat meat.

19. See chapter 7 and Lamb 1999 for more on the ambiguities of "purity" for Bengali widows. Although many Bengalis seem to consider widows to be suffering from a perpetual state of *death* impurity (*aśauc*), this condition is quite distinct from that of being vulnerable to the kinds of *everyday* impurities (*śuddha*)—stemming from menstruation, defecation, sexual fluids, saliva, etc.—that plague many other women's lives. Older high-caste widows may, then, be distinctly *śuddha* (one sense of purity), at the same time that they suffer from *aśauc* (specifically death impurity). The confusion stems from Indologists' tendencies to use the same English term, "impurity," to refer to both conditions.

20. Freeman (1980) also explores how postmenopausal married women are more fit and able ritual performers than premenopausal women in Puri (eastern India), because of their increased purity and freedom from household responsibilities. Marglin (1985c:54, 59–60) notes that postmenopausal *widows* are the only female temple attendants she has seen in Puri.

21. Feminist theorists such as Nancy Chodorow (1978) and Carol Gilligan (1982) have challenged the adequacy of models of the autonomous individual to explain women's experiences (in the United States, at least), arguing that American women's self-conceptions tend to focus more on connectedness to others than do men's. But such a contrast does not hold for Bengalis. As we have seen, *both* men and women in Mangaldihi defined themselves strongly in terms of their relations with others. Gold, who explores compelling human attachments and illusions of maya through the tales of a Rajasthani bard, similarly observes: "Women loom large in Madhu Nath's stories as embodiments of illusion, or love, or intimacy, or bondage. But if women are in certain ways paradigmatic embodiments of illusion's net, they do not have exclusive dominion over attachment" (1992:323).

22. This translation comes from Dube (1988:13). A shehnai (*sānāi*) is a kind of wooden wind instrument.

23. See my discussion in chapter 2 of the daughter's departing ritual of giving her mother mouse's earth.

24. For examples of those arguing for a complete split at marriage, see Gough 1956:841–42; Inden and Nicholas 1977; A. Mayer 1960:161; Orenstein 1970:1366; and Trautmann 1981:291.

25. See also Alma Gottlieb's critique of the classic dualistic analogy—male : female :: pure : polluting; she argues that "a given society may contain a more multilayered understanding of gender relations than a single model would allow" (1989:66).

CHAPTER 7. A WIDOW'S BONDS

1. For a similar account of the widow's ritual in a different region of Bengal, see Fruzzetti 1982:105–6.

2. On head shaving, see Altekar 1962:160; Fuller 1900:58; Kane 1968–75:2.585; Karve 1963:66; and Subramanyam 1909.

3. It is perhaps significant that head shaving also gives widows a manlike appearance, though no one in Mangaldihi directly made this observation to me.

4. Child marriage (at least of girls under about fourteen) is not commonly practiced now, but earlier in the century many girls were married and then widowed while still children.

5. This problem of children in a new household could potentially be solved through levirate, the marriage of a widow to one of her husband's brothers. However, although levirate is practiced elsewhere in India (Kolenda 1982, 1987a), it is not common in this region of West Bengal (cf. Fruzzetti 1982:103).

6. See Wadley 1995 for an illuminating discussion of factors (such as caste, property, age, family types) affecting widow remarriage in Karimpur, north India.

7. On the effects of the Widow Remarriage Act, see Carrol 1983; Chattopadhyaya 1983:54; Chowdhry 1989:321, 1994:101–2; and Sangari and Vaid 1989:16–17.

8. Carol Vlassoff (1990) provides an interesting study of widows' perceptions of the value of sons in a village of Maharashtra. Although many of the widows in her study did not gain significant economic security from their sons, those living with sons evaluated their situations as happy.

9. See Agarwal 1994 and Chowdhry 1995 for discussions of Hindu widows' inheritance rights in historical context.

10. Lamb (1999) offers more detail about widows' sources of support (access to property, heading households, etc.) across caste, class, and age lines in Mangaldihi. Wadley (1995) provides an enlightening discussion of age, property, and widowhood in Karimpur, north India.

11. Kayera Bou first went to her father's home for several days, but she soon returned to her *śvaśur bāṛi* in Mangaldihi, where she still lives with her mother-in-law, her husband's sister's son, his wife, and their three children.

12. *Kholā-parā,* which literally means "taking off and putting on," is one name for the ritual of becoming a widow; it refers to the act of removing married woman's garb and putting on the widow's dress.

13. On "widow-prostitutes," see also Das 1979:97–98; Harlan 1995:218; and Minturn 1993:235–36.

14. Mahasweta Devi's "Dhowli" (1990:185–205) offers a powerful fictional portrayal of a beautiful, low-caste young widow who is forced, with tragic consequences, to become a prostitute after her Brahman lover deserts and turns against her.

15. For more on the historical practice of sati and British colonial reactions to it, see P. Chatterjee 1989, 1990; Hawley 1994; Mani 1990, 1992, 1998; Nandy

1990a; Narasimhan 1990; and Ward 1820. For discussions of the more recent incidence of sati in 1987, that of Rup Kanwar in Rajasthan, see Das 1995:107–17; Grover 1990:40–47; Harlan 1992:13; Nandy 1995; Narasimhan 1990; Oldenburg 1994; and Weisman 1987.

16. The *Mahābhārata* offers a similar archetype (see, e.g., Van Buitenen 1975:760–78).

17. Yamaraj calls Savitri a "good woman"; "Sati" is also the name given to women who follow their husbands in death by burning with them on the cremation pyre.

18. My research assistant Dipu helped me transcribe and edit the story. This version is included not as a richly textured example of an oral performance but rather for its thematic content. Dimock (1963:195–294), Sen (1923), and W. L. Smith (1980) provide other versions of the story.

19. According to W. L. Smith (1980:116), Bengalis commonly used to set the dead bodies of snakebite victims adrift down a river on a raft made of banana stalks, in the hope that they would be found by an *ojhā*, or healer, who would be able to revive them.

20. This form of reasoning is common throughout India (e.g., Chakravarti 1995:2250; Marglin 1985c:53–55; Samanta 1992:73).

21. The Sanskrit terms *aśucitaṃ* and *aśuciḥ* used here are related to the Bengali *aśauc*, meaning literally "impure," from *a* (negative prefix) and *śuci* (pure). Remember that in Bengali, *aśauc* refers specifically to the impurity stemming from death and childbirth only, and *not* to everyday impurity, *aśuddhatā*.

22. There is a Bengali word for widower, *bipatnīk* (without a wife); but this learned term was not in common usage in the Mangaldihi region, and in fact most whom I asked professed no knowledge of it.

23. These three stories ("Mahāmāyā," "Kangkāl," and "Jībita O Mṛita") appear in Bengali in Tagore's collection of stories titled *Galpaguccha* (1926). "Jībita O Mṛita" has also been translated into English by Kalpana Bardhan (1990:51–61) as "The Living and the Dead."

AFTERWORD

1. I admire Abu-Lughod's book (1993), particularly its vivid stories and even her provocative opening comments about the pitfalls of anthropological generalizations. However, I believe that Abu-Lughod takes her critiques too far and thus misses an opportunity to explore fundamental dimensions of what makes up the lives of the particular people with whom she is concerned. Generalizations are necessary even if one's primary aim is to understand particular lives, because generalized forces shape and constrain those lives.

Glossary

āltā	Red dye used by women to color the sides of their feet.
āmiṣ	Nonvegetarian food or diet (including meat, fish, eggs, onions, and garlic).
ā̃ṣ	Nonvegetarian diet (variant of *āmiṣ*).
aśauc	Impure; a period of separation impurity incurred by relatives following a birth or death.
āśrama	Stage of life; shelter. One of the four stages of life described in the Hindu *dharmaśāstra* texts, including student (*brahmacarya*), householder (*gṛhastha*), forest dweller (*vānaprastha*), and renouncer (*sannyāsī*).
aśuddha	Impure, in the everyday sense, as in having come into contact with substances such as menstrual blood, feces, unwashed clothing, lower-caste people, or non-Hindus.
ātmā	Soul; self.
baṃśa	Family line; specifically, a line of male descendants, including inmarrying wives and unmarried daughters. Bamboo.
bāper ghar	(A girl's or woman's) father's house, natal home. Also called *bāper bāṛi*.
bayas	Age, phase of life, life span; also vigor, prime of life. The phrase *bayas hayeche*, "age has happened," implies that much of a person's life span has occurred or passed, and perhaps that the phase of "vigor" has already happened and passed by as well.
bayaska	Of a particular (usually senior) age or life phase; aged.
bhagavān	God; divinity in the unspecified, formless sense.
bhaktī	Devotion; devotional, respectful love.
bhālobāsā	Love; egalitarian, mutual love.

bhāt	Boiled rice.
bhūt	Ghost.
bidhobā	Widow; literally, "without" (*bi*) a man or husband (*dhobā*).
boṛo	Big; (of people) rich, wealthy, or senior. Opposite of *choṭo* (little), used to refer to young ones, poor, or lower-caste people.
bou	Wife or daughter-in-law, used to refer to either one's own wife or the wife of someone junior in the household.
boumā	Daughter-in-law (literally, "wife-mother").
bṛiddha	Increased, grown; old, aged. From the root *bṛ*, meaning "to grow" or "to increase."
buṛi	Old (or senior, increased, grown) woman.
buṛo	Senior, increased, old (also from the root *bṛ*, "to grow" or "to increase"). Used most often to refer to a senior or elderly man (or woman), or sometimes to overly ripe produce (such as a wrinkled and soft eggplant).
dādu	Grandfather; an old man.
darśan	Auspicious sight of a powerful icon or living being; conveys a sense of power and blessings flowing in through the eyes (as well as devotion and prayers flowing out).
deha	Body.
dharma	Moral-religious order; right way of living; coherence.
dhoti	*Dhuti.* A long, usually plain white, cloth that men wear wrapped around as a lower garment (and that some older widowed women wear in place of a sari).
didimā	Maternal grandmother (literally, "older sister–mother").
durbal	Week, feeble, without strength.
ẽṭo	Leftover (after eating); that which has come into contact with the leavings of a meal or with cooked rice; permeated with saliva.
ghar jāmāi	House son-in-law, a man who comes to live in his father-in-law's home.
ghat	*Ghāṭ.* The bank of a pond or river.
gurujan	Respected persons; elders.
jāmāi	Son-in-law (or sister's husband), the husband of one's daughter or sister.
jārā	Decrepitude; state of being worn out or decayed or digested. Used to refer to a condition of decrepitude that some experience in advanced age.

jāti — Birth group; commonly translated as caste.

karma — Based on the root *kar,* "to do," the theory that fate comes in the form of the fruits of previous actions, performed in a past life or in this one.

kaṣṭa — Suffering, pain, hard effort, sorrow; the suffering or hardship that occurs when a person toils laboriously to achieve something, such as raise a child or go on a pilgrimage.

kuśa — A kind of holy grass used in many rituals, distinguished by its sharp points. The related term *kuśāgra* means "shrewd," "keen," or sharp as the tip of a blade of *kuśa* grass.

kuṭumb — A relative, especially as related by marriage. A married woman's *kuṭumbs* include her natal kin, while her husband and his natal kin become her *nijer lok* (own people).

lok — A person, people; a world, a sphere.

māsīmā — Mother's sister; auntie; a respectfully affectionate term often used in addressing older women.

māyā — Attachment, affection, compassion, bodily-emotional ties; illusion; the nature of the everyday, lived world of experience.

moksha — Release, specifically from the bonds of a particular life, or in the more ultimate sense of release from the cycle of rebirths, redeaths, and reattachments that make up *saṃsār.*

mukti — Release (variant of *moksha*).

muṛi — Parched (or puffed) rice.

nirāmiṣ — Vegetarian food or diet.

pāp — Sin, in the sense of major transgressions.

piṇḍa — Rice ball used in offerings made to spirits of recently deceased persons and to ancestors; the body; body particle.

pitṛ — Father, ancestor.

praṇām — A respectful gesture in which a junior bows down before a senior person or deity and symbolically or physically removes the dust from the senior's feet.

pret — Departed one; disembodied human spirit, during the transitional phase following death and before transformation into a *pitṛ,* or ancestor.

pūjā — Worship; devotion; ritual offerings given to deities; a religious celebration.

ṛṇ — Debt.

saṃsār — Family, family cycle, household life; the entire world of living beings; the endless cycle of rebirths and redeaths that are the nature of all existence this side of release. (Liter-

	ally, that which "flows together," from the roots *saṃ*, "together, with," and *sṛ*, "to flow, move.")
saṃskār	Life cycle ritual; refining, reshaping, polishing, marking.
sannyāsī	Renouncer; the final stage of life (*āśrama*), during which a man leaves behind all ties to family, caste, place, and possessions, focusing solely on God and release.
sapiṇḍa	Of the same body; relatives in a male line who offer *piṇḍas* to the same ancestors or who share body particles.
sari	*Sāṛi.* Woman's dress, a long cloth worn around the lower body with one end pulled over the shoulder, shoulders, or head.
śarīr	Body; literally, "that which decays" or "that which passes away." Often thought to consist of two complementary parts: a gross, material body (*sthūla śarīr*) and a subtle body (*sūkṣma śarīr*).
śāśuṛī	Mother-in-law (marital mother).
Scheduled Caste	A Government of India classification of disadvantaged castes and tribes (in part, a replacement for the derogatory term "untouchable").
sevā	Service, caring, filial respect; caring service performed respectfully for a senior person or deity.
sindūr	Vermilion, worn by married women in the part of their hair.
sneha	Affection, affectionate love; the love that flows down from a senior to a junior.
śrāddha	Offerings made with faith to spirits of dead kin and ancestors.
śuddha	Pure, as in the state of being unmixed with substances thought to be impure (*aśuddha*).
Sudra	The lowest of four major categories of caste (*varṇas*), consisting of Brahmans (priests), Kshatriyas (warriors, rulers), Vaisyas (merchants), and Sudras (laborers).
śvaśur	Father-in-law (marital father).
śvaśur ghar	Father-in-law's house; a woman's marital home. Also called *śvaśur bāṛi.*
ṭhākur	Lord, God; usually used to refer to a specific god, often as manifest in a visible form, such as the images of deities established within temples.
ṭhākurdādā	Paternal grandfather, literally "god–older brother."
ṭhākurmā	Paternal grandmother, literally "god-mother."
tīrtha	Pilgrimage center; crossing place, ford.

tulsī — A plant (related to basil) embodying Lord Krishna and used in many rituals as a purifying and freeing agent.

vānaprastha — Forest dweller; the third stage of life (*āśrama*), during which a man (with or without his wife) leaves behind his married children and possessions to dwell in relative solitude in the forest.

References

Abu-Lughod, Lila. 1986. *Veiled sentiments: Honor and poetry in a Bedouin society.* Berkeley: University of California Press.

———. 1991. Writing against culture. In *Recapturing anthropology,* edited by Richard Fox, 137–62. Santa Fe, N.M.: School of American Research Press.

———. 1993. *Writing women's worlds: Bedouin stories.* Berkeley: University of California Press.

Agarwal, Bina. 1994. *A field of one's own: Gender and land rights in South Asia.* Cambridge: Cambridge University Press.

Alexander, Jo, Debi Berrow, Lisa Domitrovich, Margarita Donnelly, and Cheryl McLean, eds. 1986. *Women and aging: An anthology by women.* Corvallis, Ore.: Calyx Books.

Alexander, Richard D. 1974. The evolution of social behavior. *Annual Review of Ecology and Systematics* 5:325–83.

Altekar, A. S. 1962. *The position of women in Hindu civilization.* Delhi: Motilal Banarsidass.

Amoss, Pamela T., and Stevan Harrell, eds. 1981. *Other ways of growing old: Anthropological perspectives.* Stanford: Stanford University Press.

Appadurai, Arjun. 1986. Is homo hierarchicus? *American Ethnologist* 13:745–61.

———. 1992. Putting hierarchy in its place. In *Rereading cultural anthropology,* edited by George E. Marcus, 34–47. Durham, N.C.: Duke University Press.

———. 1996. *Modernity at large: Cultural dimensions of globalization.* Minneapolis: University of Minnesota Press.

Athavale, Parvati. 1930. *My story: The autobiography of a Hindu widow.* Translated by Justin E. Abbott. New York: Putnam.

Bandyopadhyay, Bibhutibhushan. 1968. *Pather panchali: Song of the road.* Translated by T. W. Clark and Tarapada Mukherji. London: George Allen and Unwin.

Bandyopadhyay, Manik. 1990. The old woman. In *Of women, outcastes, peas-*

ants, and rebels: A selection of Bengali short stories, edited and translated by Kalpana Bardhan, 148–51. Berkeley: University of California Press.

Bandyopadhyay, Tarashankar. 1990. The witch. In *Of women, outcastes, peasants, and rebels: A selection of Bengali short stories,* edited and translated by Kalpana Bardhan, 110–27. Berkeley: University of California Press.

Banerjee, Sumanta. 1989. *The parlour and the streets: Elite and popular culture in nineteenth century Calcutta.* Calcutta: Seagull Books.

Bardhan, Kalpana, ed. and trans. 1990. *Of women, outcastes, peasants, and rebels: A selection of Bengali short stories.* Berkeley: University of California Press.

Barnett, Steve A. 1976. Coconuts and gold: Relational identity in a South Indian caste. *Contributions to Indian Sociology,* n.s., 10:133–56.

Bartky, Sandra. 1997. Foucault, femininity, and the modernization of patriarchal power. In *Writing on the body: Female embodiment and feminist theory,* edited by Katie Conboy, Nadia Medina, and Sarah Stanbury, 129–54. New York: Columbia University Press.

Barua, Hem. 1965. *Assamese literature.* New Delhi: National Book Trust.

Basu, S.-K., and S. K. Bhattacharya. 1963. *Land reforms in Bengal.* New Delhi: Oxford Book Company.

Behar, Ruth, and Deborah A. Gordon, eds. 1995. *Women writing culture.* Berkeley: University of California Press.

Bennett, Lynn. 1983. *Dangerous wives and sacred sisters: Social and symbolic roles of high-caste women in Nepal.* New York: Columbia University Press.

Berreman, Gerald. 1972. Behind many masks: Ethnography and impression management. In *Hindus of the Himalayas,* xvii–lvii. Berkeley: University of California Press.

Beyene, Yewoubdar. 1989. *From menarche to menopause: Reproductive lives of peasant women in two cultures.* Albany: State University of New York Press.

Bhatia, H. S. 1983. *Aging and society: A sociological study of retired public servants.* Udaipur: Arya's Book Centre Publishers.

Biswas, Suhas K. 1985. Dependency and family care of the aged in village India: A case study. *Journal of the Indian Anthropological Society* 20:238–57.

———, ed. 1987. *Aging in contemporary India.* Indian Anthropological Society Occasional Papers 8. Calcutta: Indian Anthropological Society.

Bloch, Maurice, and Jonathan Parry, eds. 1982. *Death and the regeneration of life.* Cambridge: Cambridge University Press.

Boddy, Janice. 1992. Bucking the agnatic system: Status and strategies in rural northern Sudan. In *In her prime: New views of middle-aged women,* edited by Virginia Kerns and Judith K. Brown, 141–54. Urbana: University of Illinois Press.

Bordo, Susan. 1990. Feminism, postmodernism, and gender-skepticism. In *Feminism/postmodernism,* edited by Linda J. Nicholson, 133–56. New York: Routledge.

———. 1993. *Unbearable weight: Feminism, Western culture, and the body.* Berkeley: University of California Press.

Bose, A. B., and K. D. Gangrade, eds. 1988. *The aging in India: Problems and potentialities.* New Delhi: Abhinav Publications.
Bose, Pradip Kumar. 1995. Sons of the nation: Child rearing in the new family. In *Texts of power: Emerging disciplines in colonial Bengal,* edited by Partha Chatterjee, 118–44. Minneapolis: University of Minnesota Press.
Bottèro, Alain. 1991. Consumption by semen loss in India and elsewhere. *Culture, Medicine, and Psychiatry* 15:303–20.
Bourdieu, Pierre. 1977. *Outline of a theory of practice.* Translated by Richard Nice. Cambridge: Cambridge University Press.
———. 1990. *The logic of practice.* Translated by Richard Nice. Stanford: Stanford University Press.
Braidotti, Rosi. 1991. *Patterns of dissonance.* Cambridge: Polity Press.
Brightman, Robert. 1995. Forget culture: Replacement, transcendence, relexification. *Cultural Anthropology* 10:509–46.
Brown, Judith. 1982. Cross-cultural perspectives on middle-aged women. *Current Anthropology* 23:143–56.
———. 1992. Lives of middle-aged women. In *In her prime: New views of middle-aged women,* edited by Virginia Kerns and Judith K. Brown, 17–32. Urbana: University of Illinois Press.
Butler, Judith. 1990. *Gender trouble: Feminism and the subversion of identity.* New York: Routledge.
———. 1993. *Bodies that matter.* New York: Routledge.
Caraka. 1981. *Caraka-Saṃhitā.* Edited and translated by Priyavrat Sharma. Vol. 1. Varanasi: Chaukhambha Orientalia.
Carrol, Lucy. 1983. Law, custom, and statutory social reform: The Hindu Women's Remarriage Act of 1856. *Indian Economic and Social History Review* 20:363–89.
Carstairs, G. Morris. 1967. *The twice born.* Bloomington: Indiana University Press.
Carter, Anthony T. 1982. Hierarchy and the concept of the person in western India. In *Concepts of person: Kinship, caste, and marriage in India,* edited by Akos Ostor, Lina Fruzzetti, and Steve Barnett, 118–42. Cambridge, Mass.: Harvard University Press.
Chakrabarty, Dipesh. 1996. Remembered villages: Representation of Hindu-Bengali memories in the aftermath of the partition. *Economic and Political Weekly,* 10 August, 2143–51.
Chakravarti, Uma. 1995. Gender, caste, and labour: Ideological and material structure of widowhood. *Economic and Political Weekly,* 9 September, 2248–56.
Chapkis, Wendy. 1986. *Beauty secrets: Women and the politics of appearance.* Boston: South End Press.
Chatterjee, Heramba Nath. 1965. *Studies in some aspects of Hindu samskaras in ancient India.* Calcutta: Sanskrit Pustak Bhandar.
Chatterjee, Partha. 1989. Colonialism, nationalism, and colonialized women: The contest in India. *American Ethnologist* 16:622–33.
———. 1990. The nationalist resolution of the women's question. In *Recast-*

ing women: Essays in Indian colonial history, edited by Kumkum Sangari and Sudesh Vaid, 233–53. New Brunswick, N.J.: Rutgers University Press.

———. 1993. *The nation and its fragments: Colonial and postcolonial histories.* Princeton: Princeton University Press.

———. 1997. *The present history of West Bengal: Essays in political criticism.* Delhi: Oxford University Press.

Chattopadhyaya, Kamaladevi. 1983. *Indian women's battle for freedom.* Delhi: Abhinav.

Chen, Marty, and Jean Dreze. 1992. *Widows and well-being in rural North India.* London: Development Economics Research Programme, London School of Economics.

Chodorow, Nancy. 1978. *The Reproduction of mothering: Psychoanalysis and the sociology of gender.* Berkeley: University of California Press.

Chowdhry, Prem. 1989. Customs in a peasant economy: Women in colonial Haryana. In *Recasting women: Essays in Indian colonial history,* edited by Kumkum Sangari and Sudesh Vaid, 302–36. New Brunswick, N.J.: Rutgers University Press.

———. 1994. *The veiled women: Shifting gender equations in rural Haryana, 1880–1990.* Delhi: Oxford University Press.

———. 1995. Contesting claims and counter-claims: Questions of the inheritance and sexuality of widows in a colonial state. *Contributions to Indian Sociology,* n.s., 29:65–82.

Cixous, Hélène. 1981. The laugh of the Medusa. Translated by Keith Cohen and Paula Cohen. In *New French feminisms: An anthology,* edited by Elaine Marks and Isabelle de Courtivron, 245–64. London: Harvester Press.

Clark, Margaret. 1972. Cultural values and dependency in later life. In *Aging and modernization,* edited by Donald O. Cowgill and Lowell D. Holmes, 263–74. New York: Appleton Century Crofts.

Clark, Margaret, and Barbara Anderson. 1967. *Culture and aging.* Springfield, Ill.: C. C. Thomas.

Clifford, James. 1986. Introduction: Partial truths. In *Writing culture: The poetics and politics of ethnography,* edited by James Clifford and George Marcus, 1–26. Berkeley: University of California Press.

———. 1988. *The predicament of culture: Twentieth-century ethnography, literature, and art.* Cambridge, Mass.: Harvard University Press.

Clifford, James, and George Marcus, eds. 1986. *Writing culture: The poetics and politics of ethnography.* Berkeley: University of California Press.

Cohen, Lawrence. 1992. No aging in India: The uses of gerontology. *Culture, Medicine, and Psychiatry* 16:123–61.

———. 1994. Old age: Cultural and critical perspectives. *Annual Review of Anthropology* 23:137–58.

———. 1995. Toward an anthropology of senility: Anger, weakness, and Alzheimer's in Banaras, India. *Medical Anthropology Quarterly* 9:314–34.

———. 1998. *No aging in India: Alzheimer's, the bad family, and other modern things.* Berkeley: University of California Press.

Comaroff, Jean. 1985. *Body of power, spirit of resistance: The culture and history of a South African people.* Chicago: University of Chicago Press.

Comaroff, Jean, and John Comaroff. 1991. *Of revelation and revolution.* Vol. 1, *Christianity, colonialism, and consciousness in South Africa.* Chicago: University of Chicago Press.

Comaroff, John, and Jean Comaroff. 1992. *Ethnography and the historical imagination.* Boulder, Colo.: Westview Press.

Copper, Baba. 1986. Voices: On becoming old women. In *Women and aging: An anthology by women,* edited by Jo Alexander et al., 47–57. Corvallis, Ore.: Calyx Books.

Counts, Dorothy Ayers. 1992. *Tamparonga:* "The big women" of Kaliai (Papua New Guinea). In *In her prime: New views of middle-aged women,* edited by Virginia Kerns and Judith K. Brown, 61–74. Urbana: University of Illinois Press.

Counts, Dorothy Ayers, and David R. Counts. 1996. *Over the next hill: An ethnography of RVing seniors in North America.* Orchard Park, N.Y.: Broadview Press.

Cumming, Elaine. 1964. New thoughts on the theory of disengagement. In *New thoughts on old age,* edited by Robert Kastenbaum, 3–18. New York: Springer-Verlag.

Cumming, Elaine, and William E. Henry. 1961. *Growing old: The process of disengagement.* New York: Basic Books.

Dadi's Family. 1988. By James MacDonald, Rina Gill, and Michael Camerini. Prod. Michael Ambrosino. Odyssey Series. Washington, D.C.: Public Broadcasting Association.

Daniel, E. Valentine. 1984. *Fluid signs: Being a person the Tamil way.* Berkeley: University of California Press.

———. 1996. Crushed glass, or, Is there a counterpoint to culture? In *Culture/contexture: Explorations in anthropology and literary studies,* edited by E. Valentine Daniel and Jeffrey M. Peck, 357–75. Berkeley: University of California Press.

Daniel, Sheryl B. 1983. The tool box approach of the Tamil to the issues of moral responsibility and human destiny. In *Karma: An anthropological inquiry,* edited by Charles F. Keyes and E. Valentine Daniel, 27–62. Berkeley: University of California Press.

Das, Veena. 1979. Reflections on the social construction of adulthood. In *Identity and adulthood,* edited by Sudhir Kakar, 89–104. Delhi: Oxford University Press.

———. 1982. *Structure and cognition: Aspects of Hindu caste and ritual.* 2d ed. Delhi: Oxford University Press.

———. 1986. The work of mourning: Death in a Punjabi family. In *The cultural transition: Human experience and social transformation in the Third World and Japan,* edited by Merry I. White and Susan Pollock, 179–210. Boston: Routledge and Kegan Paul.

———. 1988. Femininity and the orientation to the body. In *Socialisation, ed-*

ucation, and women: Explorations in gender identity, edited by Karuna Chanana, 193–207. New Delhi: Orient Longman.

———. 1990. Our work to cry, your work to listen. In *Mirrors of violence: Communities, riots, and survivors in South Asia,* edited by Veena Das, 345–98. Delhi: Oxford University Press.

———. 1995. *Critical events: An anthropological perspective on contemporary India.* Delhi: Oxford University Press.

Davis, Marvin. 1983. *Rank and rivalry: The politics of inequality in rural West Bengal.* Cambridge: Cambridge University Press.

Delaney, Carol. 1991. *The seed and the soil: Gender and sosmology in Turkish village society.* Berkeley: University of California Press.

Desai, K. G., ed. 1982. *Aging in India.* Bombay: Tata Institute of Social Sciences.

Desjarlais, Robert R. 1992. *Body and emotion: The aesthetics of illness and healing in the Nepal Himalayas.* Philadelphia: University of Pennsylvania Press.

de Souza, Alfred. 1981. *The social organisation of aging among the urban poor.* New Delhi: Indian Social Institute.

de Souza, Alfred, and Walter Fernandes, eds. 1982. *Aging in South Asia.* New Delhi: Indian Social Institute.

Deutsch, Helene. 1945. *The psychology of women: A psychoanalytic interpretation.* Vol. 2. New York: Grune and Stratton.

Devi, Mahasweta. 1988. Breast-giver, translated by Gayatri Chakravorty Spivak. In *In other worlds: Essays in cultural politics,* by Gayatri Chakravorty Spivak, 222–40. New York: Routledge.

———. 1990. Dhowli. In *Of women, outcastes, peasants, and rebels: A selection of Bengali short stories,* edited and translated by Kalpana Bardhan, 185–205. Berkeley: University of California Press.

di Leonardo, Micaela. 1991. Introduction: Gender, culture and political economy: Feminist anthropology in historical perspective. In *Gender at the crossroads of knowledge: Feminist anthropology in the postmodern era,* edited by Micaela di Leonardo, 1–48. Berkeley: University of California Press.

Dimock, Edward C. 1963. *The thief of love: Bengali tales from court and village.* Chicago: University of Chicago Press.

Doniger O'Flaherty, Wendy. 1973. *Siva: The erotic ascetic.* Oxford: Oxford University Press.

———. 1976. *The origins of evil in Hindu mythology.* Berkeley: University of California Press.

———. 1980. Karma and rebirth in the Vedas and Puranas. In *Karma and rebirth in classical Indian traditions,* edited by Wendy Doniger O'Flaherty, 3–37. Berkeley: University of California Press.

———. 1984. *Dreams, illusion, and other realities.* Chicago: University of Chicago Press.

———. 1994. Playing the field: Adultery as claim jumping. In *The sense of adharma,* edited by Ariel Glucklich, 169–88. Oxford: Oxford University Press.

Douglas, Mary. 1966. *Purity and danger.* London: Routledge and Kegan Paul.

———. 1970. *Natural symbols.* New York: Vintage Books.

Douglas, William. 1969. *Death in Murelaga: Funerary ritual in a Spanish Basque village.* Seattle: University of Washington Press.
Downs, Laura Lee. 1993. If "woman" is just an empty category, then why am I afraid to walk alone at night? Identity politics meets the postmodern subject. *Comparative Studies in Society and History* 35(2):414–51.
Dube, Leela. 1975. Woman's worlds—Three encounters. In *Encounter and experience: Personal accounts of fieldwork,* edited by A. Beteille and T. N. Madan, 157–77. Delhi: Vikas.
———. 1988. On the construction of gender: Hindu girls in patrilineal India. *Economic and Political Weekly,* 30 April, 11–19.
Dumont, Louis. 1980a. *Homo hierarchicus: The caste system and its implications.* Rev. ed. Translated by Mark Sainsbury, Louis Dumont, and Basia Gulati. Chicago: University of Chicago Press.
———. 1980b [1960]. World renunciation in Indian religions. Appendix B of *Homo hierarchicus,* 267–86. Chicago: University of Chicago Press.
———. 1983. The debt to ancestors and the category of sapinda. In *Debts and debtors,* edited by Charles Malamoud, 1–20. New Delhi: Vikas.
———. 1985. A modified view of our origins: The Christian beginnings of modern individualism. In *The category of the person: Anthropology, philosophy, history,* edited by Michael Carrithers, Steven Collins, and Steven Lukes, 93–122. Cambridge: Cambridge University Press.
Dumont, Louis, and David Pocock. 1959. Pure and impure. *Contributions to Indian Sociology* 3:9–39.
du Toit, Brian M. 1990. *Aging and menopause among Indian South African women.* Albany: State University of New York Press.
Eck, Diana. 1981. India's *tīrthas:* "Crossings" in sacred geography. *History of Religions* 20:323–44.
Epstein, T. Scarlett. 1973. *South India: Yesterday, today and tomorrow: Mysore villages revisited.* New York: Holmes and Meyer.
Ewing, Katherine P. 1990. The illusion of wholeness: Culture, self, and the experience of inconsistency. *Ethos* 18:251–78.
———. 1991. Can psychoanalytic theories explain the Pakistani woman? Intrapsychic autonomy and interpersonal engagement in the extended family. *Ethos* 19:131–60.
Fabian, Johannes. 1973. How others die—Reflections on the anthropology of death. In *Death in American experience,* edited by Arien Mack, 177–201. New York: Schocken.
Feher, Michel, ed., with Ramona Naddaff and Nadia Tazi. 1989. *Fragments for a history of the human body.* 3 vols. New York: Zone.
Flint, Marcha. 1975. The menopause: Reward or punishment? *Psychosomatics* 16:161–63.
Foucault, Michel. 1973. *Madness and civilization: A history of insanity in the age of reason.* Translated by Richard Howard. New York: Vintage.
———. 1975. *The birth of the clinic: An archeology of medical perception.* Translated by A. M. Sheridan Smith. New York: Vintage.

———. 1979. *Discipline and punish: The birth of the prison.* Translated by Alan Sheridan. New York: Vintage.

———. 1980a. *Herculine Barbin: Being the recently discovered memoirs of a nineteenth-century French hermaphrodite.* Introduced by Michel Foucault. Translated by Richard McDougall. New York: Pantheon.

———. 1980b. *The history of sexuality.* Vol. 1, *An Introduction.* Translated by Robert Hurley. New York: Vintage.

———. 1980c. *Power/knowledge: Selected interviews and other writings.* Edited by Colin Gordon. Translated by Colin Gordon et al. New York: Pantheon.

Freeman, James M. 1980. The ladies of Lord Krishna: Rituals of middle-aged women in Eastern India. In *Unspoken worlds: Women's religious lives in non-Western cultures,* edited by Nancy A. Falk and Rita M. Gross, 110–26. San Francisco: Harper and Row.

Fruzzetti, Lina M. 1982. *The gift of a virgin: Women, marriage, and ritual in a Bengali society.* New Brunswick, N.J.: Rutgers University Press.

Fruzzetti, Lina, and Akos Ostor. 1984. Seed and earth: A cultural analysis of a Bengali town. In *Kinship and ritual in Bengal: Anthropological essays,* 79–124. New Delhi: South Asian Publishers.

Fruzzetti, Lina, Akos Ostor, and Steve Barnett. 1982. The cultural construction of the person in Bengal and Tamilnadu. In *Concepts of person: Kinship, caste, and marriage in India,* edited by Akos Ostor, Lina Fruzzetti, and Steve Barnett, 8–30. Cambridge, Mass.: Harvard University Press.

Fry, Christine L., ed. 1980. *Aging in culture and society: Comparative viewpoints and strategies.* New York: Praeger.

Fry, Christine L., and contributors. 1981. *Dimensions: Aging, culture, and health.* New York: Praeger.

Fuller, Mrs. Marcus B. 1900. *The wrongs of Indian womanhood.* New York: Fleming H. Revell.

Gallop, Jane. 1988. *Thinking through the body.* New York: Columbia University Press.

Gangrade, K. D. 1988. Crisis of values: A sociological study of the old and the young. In *The aging in India: Problems and potentialities,* edited by A. B. Bose and K. D. Gangrade, 24–35. New Delhi: Abhinav Publications.

Gaulin, S. J. C. 1980. Sexual dimorphism in the human post-reproductive lifespan: Possible causes. *Journal of Human Evolution* 9:227–32.

Geertz, Clifford. 1973. *The interpretation of cultures.* New York: Basic Books.

———. 1983. "From the native's point of view": On the nature of anthropological understanding. In *Local knowledge: Further essays in interpretive anthropology,* 55–70. New York: Basic Books.

Gennep, Arnold van. 1960 [1908]. *The rites of passage.* Chicago: University of Chicago Press.

George, T. 1988. Menopause: Some interpretations of the results of a study among a non-Western group. *Maturitas* 10:109–16.

Ghadially, Rehanna, and Promod Kumar. 1988. Bride-burning: The psycho-social dynamics of dowry deaths. In *Women in Indian society,* edited by Rehana Ghadially, 167–77. New Delhi: Sage Publications.

Gilligan, Carol. 1982. *In a different voice: Psychological theory and women's development.* Cambridge, Mass.: Harvard University Press.

Gold, Ann Grodzins. 1988. *Fruitful journeys: The ways of Rajasthani pilgrims.* Berkeley: University of California Press.

———. 1989. The once and future yogi: Sentiments and signs in the tale of a renouncer-king. *Journal of Asian Studies* 48:770–86.

———. 1991. Gender and illusion in a Rajasthani yogic tradition. In *Gender, genre, and power in South Asian expressive traditions,* edited by Arjun Appadurai, Frank Korom, and Margaret Mills, 102–35. Philadelphia: University of Pennsylvania Press.

———. 1992. *A carnival of parting: The tales of King Bharthari and King Gopi Chand as sung and told by Madhu Natisar Nath of Ghatiyali, Rajasthan.* Berkeley: University of California Press.

———. 1999. Maya. In *Encyclopedia of women and world religion,* edited by Serinity Young, 2:635–36. New York: Macmillan.

Gottlieb, Alma. 1989. Rethinking female pollution: The Beng of Côte d'Ivoire. *Dialectical Anthropology* 14:65–79.

Gough, E. Kathleen. 1956. Brahman kinship in a Tamil village. *American Anthropologist* 58:826–53.

Gramsci, Antonio. 1971. *Selections from the prison notebooks.* Edited by Quintin Hoare and Geoffrey Nowell Smith. New York: International Publishers.

Grogan, Sarah. 1999. *Body image: Understanding body dissatisfaction in men, women, and children.* New York: Routledge.

Grover, Kanta. 1990. *Burning flesh.* New Delhi: Vikas Publishing.

Gullette, Margaret Morganroth. 1997. *Declining to decline: Cultural combat and the politics of the midlife.* Charlottesville: University Press of Virginia.

Gupta, Akhil and James Ferguson, eds. 1997. *Culture, power, place: Explorations in critical anthropology.* Durham, N.C.: Duke University Press.

Gutmann, David. 1964. An exploration of ego configurations in middle and later life. In *Personality in middle and later life,* edited by B. L. Neugarten and Associates, 114–48. New York: Atherton.

———. 1992. Beyond nurture: Developmental perspectives on the vital older woman. In *In her prime: New views of middle-aged women,* 221–33. Urbana: University of Illinois Press.

Hallowell, James. 1955. *Culture and experience.* Philadelphia: University of Pennsylvania Press.

Hannerz, Ulf. 1993. When culture is everywhere: Reflections on a favorite concept. *Ethnos* 58:95–111.

———. 1997. *Transnational connections: Culture, people, places.* New York: Routledge.

Haraway, Donna. 1990. *Simians, cyborgs, and women: The reinvention of nature.* London: Free Association Books.

Hardiman, David. 1996. *Feeding the Baniya: Peasants and usurers in western India.* Delhi: Oxford University Press.

Harlan, Lindsey. 1992. *Religion and Rajput women: The ethic of protection in contemporary narratives.* Berkeley: University of California Press.

———. 1995. Abandoning shame: *Mīrā* and the margins of marriage. In *From the margins of Hindu marriage: Essays on gender, religion, and culture,* edited by Lindsey Harlan and Paul R. Courtright, 204–27. New York: Oxford University Press.

Harlan, Lindsey, and Paul R. Courtright, eds. 1995. *From the margins of Hindu marriage: Essays on gender, religion, and culture.* New York: Oxford University Press.

Harris, Grace Dredys. 1989. Concepts of individual, self, and person in description and analysis. *American Anthropologist* 91:599–612.

Harvey, David. 1989. *The condition of postmodernity: An enquiry into the origins of cultural change.* Oxford: Basil Blackwell.

Havighurst, Robert J., Bernice L. Neugarten, and Sheldon S. Tobin. 1968. Disengagement and patterns of aging. In *Middle age and aging: A reader in social psychology,* edited by Bernice L. Neugarten, 161–72. Chicago: University of Chicago Press.

Hawkes, Kristen, James F. O'Connell, and Nicholas G. Blurton Jones. 1989. Hardworking Hadza grandmothers. In *Comparative socioecology: The behavioural ecology of humans and other mammals,* edited by V. Standen and R. A. Foley, 341–66. Oxford: Basil Blackwell.

———. 1997. Hadza women's time allocation, offspring provisioning, and the evolution of long postmenopausal life spans. *Current Anthropology* 38:551–77.

Hawley, John Stratton, ed. 1994. *Sati, the blessing and the curse: The burning of wives in India.* New York: Oxford University Press.

Hazan, Haim. 1994. *Old age: Constructions and deconstructions.* Cambridge: Cambridge University Press.

Healey, Shevy. 1986. Growing to be an old woman: Aging and ageism. In *Women and aging: An anthology by women,* edited by Jo Alexander et al., 58–62. Corvallis, Ore.: Calyx Books.

Heesterman, J. C. 1985. *The inner conflict of tradition: Essays in Indian ritual, kingship, and society.* Chicago: University of Chicago Press.

———. 1988. Householder and wanderer. In *Way of life: King, householder, renouncer,* edited by T. N. Madan, 251–71. New ed. Delhi: Motilal Banarsidass.

Hiebert, Paul G. 1981. Old age in a South Indian village. In *Other ways of growing old: Anthropological perspectives,* edited by Pamela T. Amoss and Stevan Harrell, 211–26. Stanford: Stanford University Press.

Hirschon, Renee. 1978. Open body/closed space: The transformation of female sexuality. In *Defining females: The nature of women in society,* edited by Shirley Ardener, 66–88. London: St. Martin's Press.

Hochschild, Arlie. 1975. Disengagement theory: A critique and proposal. *American Sociological Review* 40:553–69.

Hockings, Paul. 1980. *Sex and disease in a mountain community.* New Delhi: Vikas Publishing House.
hooks, bell. 1984. *Feminist theory from margin to center.* Boston: South End Press.
Hugh-Jones, Christine. 1988. *From the milk river: Spatial and temporal processes in Northwest Amazonia.* Cambridge: Cambridge University Press.
Huntington, Richard, and Peter Metcalf. 1979. *Celebrations of death: The anthropology of mortuary ritual.* Cambridge: Cambridge University Press.
Inden, Ronald B. 1976. *Marriage and rank in Bengali culture: A history of caste and class in middle period Bengal.* Berkeley: University of California Press.
Inden, Ronald B., and Ralph Nicholas. 1977. *Kinship in Bengali culture.* Chicago: University of Chicago Press.
Jackson, Michael. 1989. *Paths toward a clearing: Radical empiricism and ethnographic inquiry.* Bloomington: Indiana University Press.
Jacobson, Doranne. 1977. Flexibility in Central Indian kinship and residence. In *The new wind: Changing identities in South Asia,* edited by Kenneth David, 263–83. The Hague: Mouton Publishers.
———. 1978. The chaste wife: Cultural norm and individual experience. In *American studies in the anthropology of India,* edited by Sylvia Vatuk, 95–138. New Delhi: Manohar.
———. 1982. Purdah and the Hindu family in Central India. In *Separate worlds: Studies of purdah in South Asia,* edited by Hanna Papanek and Gail Minault, 81–109. Delhi: Chanakya.
Jaggar, Alison M., and Susan R. Bordo, eds. 1989. *Gender/body/knowledge: Feminist reconstructions of being and knowing.* New Brunswick, N.J.: Rutgers University Press.
Jain, Madhu, and Ramesh Menon. 1991. The greying of India. *India Today,* 30 September 1991, 24–33.
Jain, S. P. 1975. Preface to *Inquiry into disorders of the old,* by J. D. Pathak, i–vi. Bombay: Medical Research Centre, Bombay Hospital Trust.
James, William. 1981 [1890]. *The principles of psychology.* Cambridge, Mass.: Harvard University Press.
Jeffery, Patricia, and Roger Jeffery. 1996. *Don't marry me to a plowman! Women's everyday lives in rural north India.* Boulder, Colo.: Westview Press.
Jeffery, Patricia, Roger Jeffery, and Andrew Lyon. 1989. *Labour pains and labour power: Women and childbearing in India.* London: Zed Books.
Johnson, Mark. 1987. *The body in the mind: The bodily basis of meaning, imagination, and reason.* Chicago: University of Chicago Press.
Justice, Christopher. 1997. *Dying the good death: The pilgrimage to die in India's holy city.* Albany: State University of New York Press.
Kakar, Sudhir. 1979. Setting the stage: The traditional Hindu view and the psychology of Erik H. Erikson. In *Identity and adulthood,* edited by Sudhir Kakar, 3–12. Delhi: Oxford University Press.
———. 1982. *Shamans, mystics, and doctors: A psychological inquiry into India and its healing traditions.* New York: Alfred A. Knopf.

———. 1990. *Intimate relations: Exploring Indian sexuality.* Chicago: University of Chicago Press.

Kane, Pandurang Vaman. 1968–75. *History of Dharmasastra.* 2d ed. 5 vols. Poona: Bhandarkar Oriental Research Institute.

Karve, D. D., ed. and trans. 1963. *The new Brahmans: Five Maharashtrian families.* Berkeley: University of California Press.

Kaufert, Patricia A., and Margaret Lock. 1992. "What are women for?": Cultural constructions of menopausal women in Japan and Canada. In *In her prime: New views of middle-aged women,* edited by Virginia Kerns and Judith K. Brown, 201–20. Urbana: University of Illinois Press.

Kaufman, Sharon R. 1986. *The ageless self: Sources of meaning in late life.* Madison: University of Wisconsin Press.

Kaushik, Meena. 1976. The symbolic representation of death. *Contributions to Indian Sociology,* n.s., 10:265–92.

Kearney, Michael. 1995. The local and the global: The anthropology of globalization and transnationalism. *Annual Review of Anthropology* 24: 547–65.

Keith, Jennie. 1977. *Old people, new lives: Community creation in a retirement residence.* Chicago: University of Chicago Press.

———. 1980. The best is yet to be: Toward an anthropology of age. *Annual Review of Anthropology* 9:339–64.

Keith, Jennie, and David I. Kertzer. 1984. Introduction to *Age and anthropological theory,* edited by David I. Kertzer and Jennie Keith, 19–61. Ithaca: Cornell University Press.

Kerns, Virginia. 1992. Female control of sexuality: Garifuna women at middle age. In *In her prime: New views of middle-aged women,* 95–112. 2d ed. Urbana: University of Illinois Press.

Kerns, Virginia, and Judith K. Brown, eds. 1992. *In her prime: New views of middle-aged women.* 2d ed. Urbana: University of Illinois Press.

Kertzer, David I., and Jennie Keith, eds. 1984. *Age and anthropological theory.* Ithaca: Cornell University Press.

Keyes, Charles, and E. Valentine Daniel, eds. 1983. *Karma: An anthropological inquiry.* Berkeley: University of California Press.

Khare, R. S. 1976. *Hindu hearth and home.* Delhi: Vikas.

Klein, Renate, and Lynette J. Dumble. 1994. Disempowering midlife women: The science and politics of hormone replacement therapy (HRT). *Women's Studies International Forum* 17:327–43.

Knauft, Bruce M. 1996. *Genealogies for the present in cultural anthropology.* New York: Routledge.

Knipe, David. 1977. *Sapindikarana:* The Hindu rite of entry into heaven. In *Religious encounters with death: Insights from the history and anthropology of religions,* edited by Frank E. Reynolds and Earle H. Waugh, 111–24. University Park: Pennsylvania State University Press.

Kolenda, Pauline. 1982. Widowhood among "untouchable" Chuhras. In *Concepts of person: Kinship, caste, and marriage in India,* edited by Akos Ostor,

Lina Fruzzetti, and Steve Barnett, 172–220. Cambridge, Mass.: Harvard University Press.
———. 1987a. Living the levirate: The mating of an untouchable Chuhra widow. In *Dimensions of social life: Essays in honor of David G. Mandelbaum*, edited by Paul Hockings, 45–67. Berlin: Mouton de Gruyter.
———. 1987b. *Regional differences in family structure in India.* Jaipur: Rawat Publications.
Kristeva, Julia. 1980. *Desire in language.* Edited by Leon S. Roudiez. Translated by Thomas Gora, Alice Jardine, and Leon S. Roudiez. New York: Columbia University Press.
Kroker, Arthur, and Marilouise Kroker, eds. 1988. *Body invaders: Sexuality and the postmodern condition.* Basingstoke: Macmillan Education.
Kumari, Rajana. 1989. *Brides are not for burning: Dowry victims in India.* London: Sangam Books.
Kurin, Richard. 1981. Person, family, and kin in two Pakistani communities. Ph.D. diss., University of Chicago.
Kurtz, Stanley N. 1992. *All the mothers are one: Hindu India and the cultural reshaping of psychoanalysis.* New York: Columbia University Press.
Lacqueur, Thomas. 1990. *Making sex: Body and gender from the Greeks to Freud.* Cambridge, Mass.: Harvard University Press.
La Fontaine, J. S., ed. 1978. *Sex and age as principles of social differentiation.* New York: Academic Press.
———. 1985. Person and individual. In *The category of the person: Anthropology, philosophy, history,* edited by Michael Carrithers, Steven Collins, and Steven Lukes, 123–40. Cambridge: Cambridge University Press.
Lamb, Sarah. 1992. Sexuality, politics, and contested notions of women: Notes on an abortion in West Bengal. Paper presented at the American Anthropological Association annual meeting, December 1992, San Francisco.
———. 1993. Growing in the net of maya: Persons, gender, and life processes in a Bengali society. Ph.D. diss., University of Chicago.
———. 1997a. The beggared mother: Older women's narratives in West Bengal. *Oral Tradition* 12:54–75.
———. 1997b. The making and unmaking of persons: Notes on aging and gender in north India. *Ethos* 25:279–302.
———. 1999. Aging, gender, and widowhood: Perspectives from rural West Bengal. *Contributions to Indian Sociology,* n.s., 33:000–00.
Lambek, Michael, and Andrew Strathern, eds. 1998. *Bodies and persons: Comparative perspectives from Africa and Melanesia.* Cambridge: Cambridge University Press.
Lancaster, Jane B., and Barbara J. King. 1992. An evolutionary perspective on menopause. In *In her prime: New views of middle-aged women,* edited by Virginia Kerns and Judith K. Brown, 7–15. Urbana: University of Illinois Press.
Laxmi, Vijay. 1982. Keeping wrinkles at bay. *Femina,* 23 November–7 December 1982.
Lee, Richard B. 1992. Work, sexuality, and aging among !Kung women. In *In*

her prime: New views of middle-aged women, edited by Virginia Kerns and Judith K. Brown, 35–48. Urbana: University of Illinois Press.

Leslie, I. Julia. 1989. *The perfect wife: The orthodox Hindu woman according to the "Strīdharmapaddhati" of Tryambakayajvan.* Oxford: Oxford University Press.

Lindholm, Charles. 1997. Does the sociocentric self exist? Reflections on Markus and Kitayama's "Culture and the Self." *Journal of Anthropological Research* 53:405–22.

Linger, Daniel T. 1994. Has culture theory lost its minds? *Ethos* 22:284–315.

Lock, Margaret. 1982. Models and practice in medicine: Menopause as a syndrome or life transition? *Culture, Medicine, and Psychiatry* 6:261–80.

———. 1984. Licorice in Leviathan: The medicalization of care for the Japanese elderly. *Culture, Medicine, and Psychiatry* 8:121–39.

———. 1986a. Ambiguities of aging: Japanese experience and perceptions of menopause. *Culture, Medicine, and Psychiatry* 10:23–46.

———. 1986b. Introduction. *Culture, Medicine, and Psychiatry* 10:1–5.

———. 1993. *Encounters with aging: Mythologies of menopause in Japan and North America.* Berkeley: University of California Press.

Lock, Margaret, and Nancy Scheper-Hughes. 1987. The mindful body. *Medical Anthropology Quarterly* 1:6–41.

Lutz, Catherine A. 1988. *Unnatural emotions: Everyday sentiments on a Micronesian atoll and their challenge to Western theory.* Chicago: University of Chicago Press.

Lutz, Catherine A., and Lila Abu-Lughod, eds. 1990. *Language and the politics of emotion.* Cambridge: Cambridge University Press.

Lykes, M. Brinton. 1985. Gender and individualistic vs. collectivist bases for notions about the self. *Journal of Personality* 53:356–83.

Lynch, Owen M., ed. 1990a. *Divine passions: The social construction of emotion in India.* Berkeley: University of California Press.

———. 1990b. The social construction of emotions in India. In *Divine passions: The social construction of emotion in India,* edited by Owen M. Lynch, 3–34. Berkeley: University of California Press.

MacDonald, Barbara. 1986. Outside the sisterhood: Ageism in women's studies. In *Women and aging: An anthology by women,* edited by Jo Alexander et al., 20–25. Corvallis, Ore.: Calyx Books.

MacFarlane, Alan. 1978. *The origins of English individualism.* Oxford: Basil Blackwell.

Madan, T. N. 1987. *Non-renunciation: Themes and interpretations of Hindu culture.* Delhi: Oxford University Press.

———, ed. 1988. *Way of life: King, householder, renouncer.* New ed. Delhi: Motilal Banarsidass.

Maddox, G. L. 1964. Disengagement theory: A critical evaluation. *Gerontologist* 4(2, part 1):80–84.

Mahābhārata. 1975. Translated and edited by J. A. B. Van Buitenen. Vol. 2. Chicago: University of Chicago Press.

Majumdar, Durgadas. 1975. *West Bengal district gazetteers: Birbhum.* Calcutta: Government of West Bengal.

Malamoud, Charles. 1983. The theology of debt in Brahmanism. In *Debts and debtors,* edited by Charles Malamoud, 24–29. New Delhi: Vikas.

Malinowski, Bronislaw. 1926. *Crime and custom in savage society.* New York: Harcourt and Brace.

Maloney, Clarence. 1976. Don't say "pretty baby" lest you zap it with your eye: The evil eye in South Asia. In *The Evil Eye,* edited by Clarence Maloney, 102–48. New York: Columbia University Press.

Maloney, Clarence, K. M. Ashraful Aziz, and Profulla C. Sarker. 1981. *Beliefs and fertility in Bangladesh.* Dacca: Asiatic Press.

Manganaro, Marc. 1990. Textual play, power, and cultural critique: An orientation to modernist anthropology. In *Modernist anthropology: From fieldwork to text,* edited by Marc Manganaro, 3–47. Princeton: Princeton University Press.

Mani, Lata. 1990. Contentious traditions: The debate on *sati* in colonial India. In *Recasting women: Essays in Indian colonial history,* edited by Kumkum Sangari and Sudesh Vaid, 88–126. New Brunswick, N.J.: Rutgers University Press.

———. 1992. Cultural theory, colonial texts: Reading eye-witness accounts of widow burning. In *Cultural studies,* edited by Lawrence Grossberg, Cary Nelson, and Paula Treichler, 392–408. New York: Routledge.

———. 1998. *Contentious traditions: The debate on "sati" in colonial India.* Berkeley: University of California Press.

Manu. 1886. *The laws of Manu.* Translated by G. Buhler. Vol. 25, *Sacred books of the East.* Oxford: Clarendon Press.

———. 1991. *The laws of Manu.* Translated by Wendy Doniger, with Brian K. Smith. New York: Penguin.

Marglin, Frederique Apffel. 1977. Power, purity, and pollution: Aspects of the caste system reconsidered. *Contributions to Indian Sociology,* n.s., 11:245–70.

———. 1985a. Female sexuality in the Hindu world. In *Immaculate and Powerful: The Female in Sacred Image and Social Reality.,* edited by Clarissa W. Atkinson, C. H. Buchanan, and M. R. Miles, 39–60. Boston: Beacon Press.

———. 1985b. Types of opposition in Hindu culture. In *Purity and auspiciousness in Indian society,* edited by John B. Carman and Frederique Apffel Marglin, 65–83. Leiden: E. J. Brill.

———. 1985c. *Wives of the God-King: The rituals of the devadasis of Puri.* London: Oxford University Press.

———. 1996. Rationality, the body, and the world: From production to regeneration. In *Decolonizing knowledge: From development to dialogue,* edited by Frederique Apffel Marglin and Stephen A. Marglin, 142–81. Oxford: Clarendon Press.

Marglin, Frederique, and Purna Chandra Mishra. 1993. Sacred groves: Regenerating the body, the land, the community. In *Global ecology: A new arena of political conflict,* edited by Wolfgang Sachs, 197–207. London: Zed Books.

Marglin, Frederique, and Suzanne L. Simon. 1994. Feminist Orientalism and development. In *Feminist perspectives on sustainable development,* edited by Wendy Harcourt, 26–45. London: Zed Books.

Markus, Hazel Rose, and Shinobu Kitayama. 1991. Culture and the self: Implications for cognition, emotion, and motivation. *Psychological Review* 98:224–53.

Marriott, McKim. 1968. Caste ranking and food transactions: A matrix analysis. In *Structure and change in Indian society,* edited by Milton Singer and Bernard S. Cohn, 133–71. Chicago: Aldine.

———. 1976. Hindu transactions: Diversity without dualism. In *Transaction and meaning: Directions in the anthropology of exchange and symbolic behavior,* edited by Bruce Kapferer, 109–42. Philadelphia: Institute for the Study of Human Issues.

———. 1990. Constructing an Indian ethnosociology. In *India through Hindu categories,* edited by McKim Marriott, 1–39. New Delhi: Sage Publications.

———. 1994. *Caraka-Saṃhitā:* Selections from Hindu biology. Photocopy, Social Sciences Division, University of Chicago.

———. 1998. The female family core explored ethnosociologically. *Contributions to Indian Sociology,* n.s., 32:279–304.

Marriott, McKim, and Ronald Inden. 1974. Caste systems. In *Encyclopaedia Britannica.* 15th ed. 3:982–91.

———. 1977. Toward an ethnosociology of South Asian caste systems. In *The new wind: Changing identities in South Asia,* edited by Kenneth David, 227–38. The Hague: Mouton Publishers.

Marshall, Helen. 1996. Our bodies ourselves: Why we should add old fashioned empirical phenomenology to the new theories of the body. *Women's Studies International Forum* 19:253–65.

Martin, Emily. 1987. *The woman in the body: A cultural analysis of reproduction.* Boston: Beacon Press.

———. 1992. The end of the body? *American Ethnologist* 19:121–40.

Martin, Linda G. 1990. The status of South Asia's growing elderly population. *Journal of Cross-Cultural Gerontology* 5:93–117.

Mauss, Marcel. 1967 [1925]. *The gift: Forms and functions of exchange in archaic societies.* Translated by Ian Cunnison. New York: W. W. Norton.

———. 1979 [1935]. Body techniques. In *Sociology and psychology: Essays,* 97–123. Translated by Ben Brewster. London: Routledge and Kegan Paul.

———. 1985 [1938]. A category of the human mind: The notion of person, the notion of self. In *The category of the person: Anthropology, philosophy, history,* edited by Michael Carrithers, Steven Collins, and Steven Lukes, 1–25. Cambridge: Cambridge University Press.

Maybury-Lewis, David. 1979. Cultural categories of the central Ge. In *Dialectical societies: The Ge and Bororo of central Brazil,* edited by David Maybury-Lewis, 218–48. Cambridge, Mass.: Harvard University Press.

Mayer, Adrian C. 1960. *Caste and kinship in central India.* London: Routledge and Kegan Paul.

Mayer, Peter J. 1982. Evolutionary advantage of the menopause. *Human Ecology* 10:477–94.

McGilvray, D. B. 1982. Sexual power and fertility in Sri Lanka: Batticaloa Tamils and Moors. In *Ethnography of fertility and birth,* edited by C. P. MacCormack, 25–73. London: Academic Press.

McHugh, Ernestine L. 1989. Concepts of the person among the Gurungs of Nepal. *American Ethnologist* 16:75–86.

McKinlay, Sonja M., and Margot Jefferys. 1974. The menopausal syndrome. *British Journal of Preventive Social Medicine* 28:108–15.

Mehta, Anu, and Blossom Kochhar. 1982. Smoothening those furrows. *Femina,* 23 November–7 December 1982.

Mehta, Rama. 1981. *Inside the Haveli.* New Delhi: Arnold-Heinemann.

Mencher, Joan P. 1974. The caste system upside down. *Current Anthropology* 15:469–92.

Menon, Usha, and Richard A. Shweder. 1998. The return of the "white man's burden": The moral discourse of anthropology and the domestic life of Hindu women. In *Welcome to middle age! (and other cultural fictions),* edited by Richard Shweder, 139–88. Chicago: University of Chicago Press.

Merleau-Ponty, Maurice. 1962. *Phenomenology of perception.* Translated by Colin Smith. New York: Humanities Press.

Metcalf, Peter. 1982. *A Borneo journey into death: Berawan eschatology from its rituals.* Philadelphia: University of Pennsylvania Press.

Meyeder Vratakatha. N.d. Edited by Gopalcandra Bhattacharjya. Calcutta: Nirmal Book Agency.

Meyeder Vratakatha. N.d. Edited by Hiranmay Bhattacharjya. Calcutta: Rajendra Library.

Mines, Diane Paull. 1990. Hindu periods of death "impurity." In *India through Hindu categories,* edited by McKim Marriott, 103–30. New Delhi: Sage Publications.

Mines, Mattison. 1981. Indian transitions: A comparative analysis of adult stages of development. *Ethos* 9:95–121.

———. 1988. Conceptualizing the person: Hierarchical society and individual autonomy in India. *American Anthropologist* 71:1166–75.

———. 1994. *Public faces, private voices: Community and individuality in South India.* Berkeley: University of California Press.

Mines, Mattison, and Vijayalakshmi Gourishankar. 1990. Leadership and individuality in South Asia: The case of the south Indian big-man. *Journal of Asian Studies* 49:761–86.

Minh-ha, Trinh T. 1989. *Woman, native, other: Writing postcoloniality and feminism.* Bloomington: Indiana University Press.

Minturn, Leigh. 1993. *Sita's daughters: Coming out of purdah.* New York: Oxford University Press.

Mohanty, Chandra Talpade. 1991. Under Western eyes: Feminist scholarship and colonial discourses. In *Third World women and the politics of feminism,* edited by Chandra Mohanty, Ann Russo, and Lourdes Torres, 51–80. Bloomington: Indiana University Press.

Moksha (Salvation). 1993. Dir. Pankaj Butalia. Jane Balfour Films, London.

Moore, Henrietta L. 1994. *A passion for difference: Essays in anthropology and gender.* Bloomington: Indiana University Press.

Mukharji, T. N. 1890. *The sisters of Phulmani (or the child wives of India).* Calcutta: Perserverance Printing Works.

Munn, Nancy D. 1986. *The fame of Gawa: A symbolic study of value transformation in a Massim (Papua New Guinea) society.* Cambridge: Cambridge University Press.

Murray, D. W. 1993. What is the Western concept of the self? On forgetting David Hume. *Ethos* 21:3–23.

Myerhoff, Barbara. 1979. *Number our days.* New York: E. P. Dutton.

———. 1984. Rites and signs of ripening: The intertwining of ritual, time, and growing older. In *Age and anthropological theory,* edited by David I. Kertzer and Jennie Keith, 305–30. Ithaca: Cornell University Press.

———, ed. 1992. *Remembered lives: The work of ritual, storytelling, and growing older.* Ann Arbor: University of Michigan Press.

Myerhoff, Barbara, and Andrei Simic, eds. 1978. *Life's career—aging: Cultural variations on growing old.* Beverly Hills, Calif.: Sage.

Nandy, Ashis. 1988. *The intimate enemy: Loss and recovery of self under colonialism.* Delhi: Oxford University Press.

———. 1990a. Sati: A nineteenth century tale of women, violence, and protest. In *At the edge of psychology: Essays in politics and culture,* 1–31. New Delhi: Oxford University Press.

———. 1990b. Woman versus womanliness in India: An essay in cultural and political psychology. In *At the edge of psychology: Essays in politics and culture,* 32–46. New Delhi: Oxford University Press.

———. 1995. Sati in *Kali Yuga:* The public debate on Roop Kanwar's death. In *The savage Freud and other essays on possible and retrievable selves,* 32–52. Princeton: Princeton University Press.

Narasimhan, Sakuntala. 1990. *Sati: Widow burning in India.* New York: Doubleday.

Narayan, Kirin. 1986. Birds on a branch: Girlfriends and wedding songs in Kangra. *Ethos* 14:47–75.

Nemeroff, Carol, and Paul Rozin. 1994. The contagion concept in adult thinking in the United States: Transmission of germs and of interpersonal influence. *Ethos* 22:158–86.

Nicholas, Ralph. 1988. *Śrāddha,* impurity, and relations between the living and the dead. In *Way of life: King, householder, renouncer,* edited by T. N. Madan, 369–79. New ed. Delhi: Mogilal Banarsidass.

Nicholson, Linda J., ed. 1990. *Feminism/postmodernism.* New York: Routledge.

———. 1994. Interpreting gender. *Signs* 20:79–105.

O'Flaherty, Wendy Doniger: *see* Doniger O'Flaherty, Wendy.

Oldenburg, Veena Talway. 1994. The Roop Kanwar case: Feminist responses. In

Sati, the blessing and the curse: The burning of wives in India, edited by John S. Hawley, 101–30. New York: Oxford University Press.

O'Neill, John. 1985. *Five bodies: The human shape of modern society.* Ithaca: Cornell University Press.

Orenstein, Henry. 1970. Death and kinship in Hinduism: Structural and functional interpretations. *American Anthropologist* 72:1357–77.

Ortner, Sherry B. 1974. Is female to male as nature is to culture? In *Woman, culture, and society,* edited by Michelle Zimbalist Rosaldo and Louise Lamphere, 67–87. Stanford: Stanford University Press.

———. 1978. *Sherpas through their rituals.* New York: Cambridge University Press.

———. 1984. Theory in anthropology since the sixties. *Comparative Studies in Society and History* 26:126–66.

———. 1996. *Making gender: The politics and erotics of culture.* Boston: Beacon Press.

Ostor, Akos, Lina Fruzzetti, and Steve Barnett, eds. 1982. *Concepts of person: Kinship, caste, and marriage in India.* Cambridge, Mass.: Harvard University Press.

Pandey, Raj Bali. 1969. *Hindu Saṁskāras: Socio-religious study of the Hindu sacraments.* 2d ed. Delhi: Motilal Banarsidass.

Papanek, Hanna, and Gail Minault, eds. 1982. *Separate worlds: Studies of purdah in South Asia.* Delhi: Chanakya.

Parish, Steven M. 1994. *Moral knowing in a Hindu sacred city: An exploration of mind, emotion, and self.* New York: Columbia University Press.

Parry, Jonathan P. 1980. Ghosts, greed, and sin: The occupational identity of the Benares funeral priests. *Man,* n.s., 15:88–111.

———. 1982. Sacrificial death and the necrophagous ascetic. In *Death and the regeneration of life,* edited by Maurice Bloch and Jonathan Parry, 74–110. Cambridge: Cambridge University Press.

———. 1985. Death and digestion: The symbolism of food and eating in north Indian mortuary rites. *Man,* n.s., 20:612–30.

———. 1988. Death and cosmogony in Kashi. In *Way of life: King, householder, renouncer,* edited by T. N. Madan, 337–65. New ed. Delhi: Mogilal Banarsidass.

———. 1989. The end of the body. In *Fragments for a history of the human body,* edited by Michel Feher, with Ramona Naddaff and Nadia Tazi, 2:490–517. New York: Zone.

———. 1994. *Death in Banaras.* Cambridge: Cambridge University Press.

Pathak, J. D. 1975. *Inquiry into disorders of the old.* Bombay: Medical Research Centre, Bombay Hospital Trust.

Pati, R. N., and B. Jena, eds. 1989. *Aged in India.* New Delhi: Ashish.

Paul, Robert A. 1982. *The Sherpas of Nepal in the Tibetan cultural context.* Chicago: University of Chicago Press.

Pinney, Christopher. 1997. *Camera indica: The social life of Indian photographs.* Chicago: University of Chicago Press.

Plath, David W. 1980. *Long engagements: Maturity in modern Japan.* Stanford: Stanford University Press.

Pocock, D. F. 1981. The evil eye: Envy and greed among the Patidars of central Gujarat. In *The evil eye: A folklore casebook,* edited by Alan Dundes, 201–19. New York: Garland Publishing.

Pollock, David. 1996. Personhood and illness among the Kulina. *Medical Anthropology Quarterly* 10:319–41.

Poole, Fitz John Porter. 1981. Transforming "natural" woman: Female ritual leaders and gender ideology among Bimin-Kuskusmin. In *Sexual meanings: The cultural construction of gender and sexuality,* edited by Sherry B. Ortner and Harriet Whitehead, 116–65. Cambridge: Cambridge University Press.

Purohit, G. V. 1955. *Ayurvediyam Sariram.* Bombay: Board of Research in Ayurveda.

Rabinow, Paul. 1977. *Reflections on fieldwork in Morocco.* Berkeley: University of California Press.

Raheja, Gloria Goodwin. 1988. *The poison in the gift: Ritual, prestation, and the dominant caste in a North Indian village.* Chicago: University of Chicago Press.

———. 1995. "Crying when she's born, and crying when she goes away": Marriage and the idiom of the gift in Pahansu song performance. In *From the margins of Hindu marriage: Essays on gender, religion, and culture,* edited by Lindsey Harlan and Paul R. Courtright, 19–59. New York: Oxford University Press.

Raheja, Gloria Goodwin, and Ann Grodzins Gold. 1994. *Listen to the heron's words: Reimagining gender and kinship in north India.* Berkeley: University of California Press.

Rao, A. Venkoba. 1989. *Psychiatry of old age in India.* Madras: Macmillan India Press.

Rasmussen, Susan J. 1987. Interpreting androgynous woman: Female aging and personhood among the Kel Ewey Tuareg. *Ethnology* 26:17–30.

———. 1997. *The poetics and politics of Tuareg aging: Life course and personal destiny in Niger.* DeKalb: Northern Illinois University Press.

Ravindranath, Sarita. 1997. *Sans* everything . . . but not *sans* rights. *Statesman,* 1 February.

Ray, Priyadaranjan, Hirendranath Gupta, and Mira Roy. 1980. *Susruta Samhita: A scientific synopsis.* New Delhi: Indian National Science Academy.

Reddy, N. Subba. 1988. How much do we know about the Indian family? *South Asian Social Scientist* 4(1):63–70.

Rich, Adrienne. 1976. *Of Woman Born.* New York: W. W. Norton.

———. 1986. Compulsory heterosexuality and lesbian existence. In *Blood, bread, and poetry: Selected prose, 1979–1985,* 23–75. New York: Norton.

Riley, Denise. 1988. *"Am I that name?": Feminism and the category of "women" in history.* London: Macmillan.

Roland, Alan. 1988. *In search of self in India and Japan: Toward a cross-cultural psychology.* Princeton: Princeton University Press.

Rosaldo, Michelle Z. 1974. Woman, culture, and society: A theoretical overview. In *Women, Culture, and Society,* edited by Michelle Zimbalist Rosaldo and Louise Lamphere, 17–42. Stanford: Stanford University Press.

———. 1980. The use and abuse of anthropology: Reflections on cross-cultural understanding. *Signs* 5:389–417.

———. 1984. Toward an anthropology of self and feeling. In *Culture theory: Essays on mind, self, and emotion,* edited by Richard A. Shweder and Robert A. LeVine, 137–57. Cambridge: Cambridge University Press.

Rosaldo, Renato. 1989. *Culture and truth: The remaking of social analysis.* Boston: Beacon Press.

Roy, Manisha. 1992 [1972]. *Bengali women.* Chicago: University of Chicago Press.

Sacks, Karen Brodkin. 1992. Introduction: New views of middle-aged women. In *In her prime: New views of middle-aged women,* edited by Virginia Kerns and Judith K. Brown, 1–6. 2d ed. Urbana: University of Illinois Press.

Said, Edward E. 1978. *Orientalism.* New York: Pantheon.

Samanta, Suchitra. 1992. *Maṅgalmayīmā, Sumaṅgalī, Maṅgal:* Bengali perceptions of the divine feminine, motherhood, and "auspiciousness." *Contributions to Indian Sociology,* n.s., 26:51–75.

Samsad Bengali-English Dictionary. 1989. Edited by Sailendra Biswas, Birendramohan Dasgupta, and Subodhchandra Sengupta. Calcutta: Shishu Sahitya Samsad.

Sangari, Kumkum, and Sudesh Vaid. 1989. Recasting women: An introduction. In *Recasting women: Essays in Indian colonial history,* edited by Kumkum Sangari and Sudesh Vaid, 1–26. New Brunswick, N.J.: Rutgers University Press.

Sapir, Edward. 1949. *Selected writings of Edward Sapir in language, culture, and personality.* Edited by David G. Mandelbaum. Berkeley: University of California Press.

Saraswati, Baidyanath. 1977. *Brahmanic ritual traditions in the crucible of time.* New Delhi: Indian Institute of Advanced Study.

Satish, Veena. 1990. The old people . . . a headache? *Woman's Era,* 1 May, 70–71.

Sax, William S. 1991. *Mountain goddess: Gender and politics in a Himalayan pilgrimage.* Oxford: Oxford University Press.

Scheper-Hughes, Nancy. 1992. *Death without weeping: The violence of everyday life in Brazil.* Berkeley: University of California Press.

Scheper-Hughes, Nancy, and Margaret M. Lock. 1987. The mindful body: A prolegomenon to future work in medical anthropology. *Medical Anthropology Quarterly,* n.s., 1:6–41.

Schneider, David. 1968. *American kinship: A cultural account.* Englewood Cliffs, N.J.: Prentice-Hall.

———. 1976. Notes toward a theory of culture. In *Meaning in anthropology,* edited by Keith H. Basso and Henry A. Selby, 197–220. Albuquerque: University of New Mexico Press.

Schwartz, Theodore, Geoffrey M. White, and Catherine A. Lutz, eds. 1992. *New directions in psychological anthropology.* Cambridge: Cambridge University Press.

Scott, James C. 1985. *Weapons of the weak: Everyday forms of peasant resistance.* New Haven: Yale University Press.

Scott, Joan. 1988. *Gender and the politics of history.* New York: Columbia University Press.

———. 1993. The tip of the volcano. *Comparative Studies in Society and History* 35:438–51.

Sen, D. C., trans. 1923. *Behula.* London: Luzac.

Sharma, M. L., and T. M. Dak, eds. 1987. *Aging in India: Challenge for the society.* Delhi: Ajanta Publications.

Sharma, Ursula M. 1978. Women and their affines: The veil as a symbol of separation. *Man,* n.s., 13:218–33.

Sharma, V. K., and M. S. L. Saxena. 1981. Climacteric symptoms: A study in the Indian context. *Maturitas* 3:11–20.

Shostak, Marjorie. 1981. *Nisa: The life and words of a !Kung woman.* New York: Random House.

Shulman, David Dean. 1980. *Tamil temple myths: Sacrifice and divine marriage in the south Indian Saiva tradition.* Princeton: Princeton University Press.

Shweder, Richard A., ed. 1998. *Welcome to middle age! (and other cultural fictions).* Chicago: University of Chicago Press.

Shweder, Richard A., and Edmund J. Bourne. 1984. Does the concept of the person vary cross-culturally? In *Culture theory: Essays on mind, self, and emotion,* edited by Richard A. Shweder and Robert A. LeVine, 158–99. Cambridge: Cambridge University Press.

Shweder, Richard A. and Robert A. LeVine, eds. 1984. *Culture theory: Essays on mind, self, and emotion.* Cambridge: Cambridge University Press.

Singer, Milton. 1972. *When a great tradition modernizes: An anthropological approach to Indian civilization.* Chicago: University of Chicago Press.

Sinha, Mrinalini. 1995. *Colonial masculinity: The "manly Englishman" and the "effeminate Bengali" in the late nineteenth century.* Manchester: Manchester University Press.

Skultans, Vieda. 1970. The symbolic significance of menstruation and the menopause. *Man* 5:639–51.

Smith, Frederick M. 1991. Indra's curse, Varuṇa's noose, and the suppression of the woman in the Vedic *śrauta* ritual. In *Roles and rituals for Hindu women,* edited by Julia Leslie, 17–46. Cranbury, N.J.: Associated University Presses.

Smith, W. L. 1980. *The one-eyed goddess: A study of the Manasa Mangal.* Stockholm: Almqvist and Wiksell International.

Sokolovsky, Jay, ed. 1989. *The cultural context of aging: Worldwide perspectives.* Grandy, Mass.: Bergin and Garvey.

Soodan, Kirpal Singh. 1975. *Aging in India.* Calcutta: Minerva.

Spelman, Elizabeth V. 1988. *Inessential woman: Problems of exclusion in feminist thought.* Boston: Beacon Press.

Spencer, Paul. 1976. Opposing streams of the gerontocratic ladder: Two models of age organization in East Africa. *Man* 11:153–75.
Spiro, Melford E. 1982. *Buddhism and society: A great tradition and its Burmese vicissitudes.* Berkeley: University of California Press.
———. 1993. Is the Western conception of the self "peculiar" within the context of the world cultures? *Ethos* 21:107–53.
Spivak, Gayatri Chakravorty. 1988. A literary representation of the subaltern: A woman's text from the Third World. In *In other worlds: Essays in cultural politics,* 241–68. New York: Routledge.
Srinivas, Mysore N. 1952. *Religion and society among the Coorgs of south India.* Oxford: Clarendon Press.
Stevenson, Margaret Sinclair. 1971 [1920]. *The rites of the twice born.* London: Oxford University Press.
Stocking, George W., Jr. 1976. Ideas and institutions in American anthropology: Toward a history of the interwar period. In *Selected papers from the "American Anthropologist," 1921–1945,* edited by George W. Stocking, Jr., 1–53. Washington, D.C.: American Anthropological Association.
Stone, Linda. 1988. *Illness beliefs and feeding the dead in Hindu Nepal.* Lewiston, N.Y.: Edwin Mellen Press.
Stone, Linda, and Caroline James. 1997. Dowry, bride-burning, and female power in India. In *Gender in cross-cultural perspective,* edited by Caroline B. Brettell and Carolyn F. Sargent, 270–79. 2d ed. Upple Saddle River, N.J.: Prentice Hall.
Strathern, Marilyn. 1988. *The gender of the gift: Problems with women and problems with society in Melanesia.* Berkeley: University of California Press.
Subramanyam, M. 1909. *The tonsure of Hindu widows.* Madras: G. A. Nateson.
Suleiman, Susan. 1986. (Re)writing the body: The politics and poetics of female eroticism. In *The female body in Western culture,* edited by Susan Suleiman, 7–29. Cambridge, Mass.: Harvard University Press.
Sushruta Samhita [*Suśruta Saṃhitā*]. 1981 [1911]. Translated by Kunja Lal Bhishagratna. 3d ed. Varanasi: Chowkhamba Sanskrit Series Office.
Tagore [Thakur], Rabindranath. 1926. *Galpaguccha* (Collected stories). Calcutta: Visva-Bharati Granthayan Bibhag.
———. 1960. *Wings of death: The last poems of Rabindranath Tagore.* Translated by Aurobindo Bose. New York: Grove Press.
Teng, Jinhua Emma. 1996. The construction of the "traditional Chinese woman" in the Western academy: A critical review. *Signs* 22:115–51.
Thompson, Catherine. 1985. The power to pollute and the power to preserve: Perceptions of female power in a Hindu village. *Social Science and Medicine* 21:701–11.
Tilak, Shrinivas. 1989. *Religion and aging in the Indian tradition.* Albany: State University of New York Press.
Tocqueville, Alexis de. 1945 [1835]. *Democracy in America.* Vol. 2. New York: Vintage.

Trautmann, Thomas. 1981. *Dravidian kinship.* Berkeley: University of California Press.

Trawick, Margaret. 1990a. The ideology of love in a Tamil family. In *Divine passions: The social construction of emotion in India,* edited by Owen Lynch, 37–63. Berkeley: University of California Press.

———. 1990b. *Notes on love in a Tamil family.* Berkeley: University of California Press.

Trawick Egnor, Margaret. 1978. The sacred spell and other conceptions of life in Tamil culture. Ph.D. diss., University of Chicago.

Turner, Bryan. 1984. *The body and society: Explorations in social theory.* Oxford: Basil Blackwell.

Turner, Terence. 1979. Kinship, household, and community structure among the Kayapo. In *Dialectical societies: The Ge and Bororo of central Brazil,* edited by David Maybury-Lewis, 147–78. Cambridge, Mass.: Harvard University Press.

———. 1995. Social body and embodied subject: Bodiliness, subjectivity, and sociality among the Kayapo. *Cultural Anthropology* 10:143–70.

Turner, Victor. 1967. *The forest of symbols: Aspects of Ndembu ritual.* Ithaca: Cornell University Press.

Van Buitenen, J. A. B., trans. and ed. 1975. *The Mahabharata.* Vol. 2. Chicago: University of Chicago Press.

van der Veer, Peter. 1989. The power of detachment: Disciplines of body and mind in the Ramanandi order. *American Ethnologist* 16:458–70.

van Willigen, John, and V. C. Channa. 1991. Law, custom, and crimes against women: The problem of dowry death in India. *Human Organization* 50:369–76.

Vatuk, Sylvia. 1975. The aging woman in India: Self-perceptions and changing roles. In *Women in Contemporary India and South Asia,* edited by Alfred de Souza, 142–63. New Delhi: Manohar Publications.

———. 1980. Withdrawal and disengagement as a cultural response to aging in India. In *Aging in culture and society,* edited by Christine Fry, 126–48. New York: Praeger.

———. 1987. Authority, power, and autonomy in the life cycle of north Indian women. In *Dimensions of social life: Essays in honor of David G. Mandelbaum,* edited by Paul Hockings, 23–44. Berlin: Mouton de Gruyter.

———. 1990. "To be a burden on others": Dependency anxiety among the elderly in India. In *Divine passions: The social construction of emotion in India,* edited by Owen Lynch, 64–88. Berkeley: University of California Press.

———. 1991. Gerontology in India: The state of the art [Book review essay]. *Journal of Cross-Cultural Gerontology* 6:259–71.

———. 1992. Sexuality and the middle-aged woman in South Asia. In *In her prime: New views of middle-aged women,* edited by Virginia Kerns and Judith K. Brown, 155–72. 2d ed. Urbana: University of Illinois Press.

———. 1995. The Indian woman in later life: Some social and cultural considerations. In *Women's health in India: Risk and vulnerability,* edited by Monica Das Gupta, Lincoln C. Chen, and T. N. Krishnan, 289–306. Bombay: Oxford University Press.

Vatuk, Ved Prakash, and Sylvia Jane Vatuk. 1979. The lustful stepmother in the folklore of north-western India. In *Studies in Indian folk traditions,* edited by Ved Prakash Vatuk, 190–221. New Delhi: Manohar.

Vesperi, Maria D. 1985. *City of green benches: Growing old in a new downtown.* Ithaca: Cornell University Press.

Vidyasagar, Ishwar Chandra. 1855. *The remarriage of Hindu widows.* Calcutta: National Library.

Vlassoff, Carol. 1990. The value of sons in an Indian village: How widows see it. *Population Studies* 44:5–20.

Wadley, Susan Snow. 1980. *The powers of Tamil women.* South Asia Series 6. Syracuse, N.Y.: Maxwell School of Citizenship and Public Affairs, Syracuse University.

———. 1994. *Struggling with destiny in Karimpur, 1925–1984.* California: University of California Press.

———. 1995. No longer a wife: widows in rural north India. In *From the margins of Hindu marriage: Essays on gender, religion, and culture,* edited by Lindsey Harlan and Paul B. Courtright, 92–118. New York: Oxford University Press.

Wadley, Susan S., and Bruce W. Derr. 1990. Eating sins in Karimpur. In *India through Hindu categories,* edited by McKim Marriott, 131–48. New Delhi: Sage Publications.

Ward, William. 1820. *Letter to the Right Honorable J. C. Villiers on the education of the natives of India to which are added accounts of Hindoo widows recently burnt alive in Bengal.* Calcutta: National Library.

Weisman, Steven R. 1987. Indian widow's death at pyre creates shrine. *New York Times,* 19 September 1987.

White, Geoffrey M., and John Kirkpatrick, eds. 1985. *Person, self, and experience: Exploring Pacific ethnopsychologies.* Berkeley: University of California Press.

Whittaker, Elvi. 1992. The birth of the anthropological self and its career. *Ethos* 20:191–219.

Wilson, Monica. 1963. *Good company: A study of Nyakyusa age-villages.* London: Oxford University Press.

Wilson, Robert A., and Thelma A. Wilson. 1963. The fate of the nontreated postmenopausal woman: A plea for the maintenance of adequate estrogen from puberty to the grave. *Journal of the American Geriatrics Society* 11:347–62.

Wiser, Charlotte V. 1978. *Four families of Karimpur.* Syracuse, N.Y.: Syracuse University Press.

Woodward, Kathleen. 1991. *Aging and its discontents: Freud and other fictions.* Bloomington: Indiana University Press.

Zimmermann, Francis. 1979. Remarks on the body in Ayurvedic medicine. *South Asian Digest of Regional Writing* 18:10–26.

———. 1980. *Ṛtū-sātmya:* The seasonal cycle and the principle of appropri-

ateness. Translated by McKim Marriott and John Leavitt. *Social Science and Medicine* 14B:99–106.
———. 1987. *The jungle and the aroma of meats: An ecological theme in Hindu medicine.* Berkeley: University of California Press.
Zita, Jacquelyn N. 1998. *Body talk: Philosophical reflections on sex and gender.* New York: Columbia University Press.
Zola, Irving. 1972. The concept of trouble and sources of medical assistance. *Social Science and Medicine* 6:673–79.

Index

Text: 10/13 Aldus
Display: Aldus
Composition: Integrated Composition Systems